DATE DUE

AG 5 04			
JY 20 05			

DEMCO 38-296

ANALYSING
MUSICAL MULTIMEDIA

R

ANALYSING

MUSICAL

MULTIMEDIA

NICHOLAS COOK

CLARENDON PRESS · OXFORD
1998

ndon Street, Oxford OX2 6DP
v York
Bogota Buenos Aires
nnai Dar es Salaam
g Istanbul Karachi
lbourne Mexico City
ão Paolo Singapore
Taipei Tokyo Toronto Warsaw
and associated companies in
Berlin Ibadan

and associated companies in
Berlin Ibadan

Oxford is a trade mark of Oxford University Press

Published in the United States
by Oxford University Press Inc., New York

British Library Cataloguing in Publication Data
Data available

Library of Congress Cataloging in Publication Data
Cook, Nicholas, 1950–   .
Analysing musical multimedia / Nicholas Cook.
p.   cm.
Includes bibliographical references and index.
1. Mixed media (Music)—History and criticism.
2. Music—Philosophy and aesthetics.   I. Title.
ML3849.C73   1998   791—dc21   97–2414
ISBN 0–19–816589–7

1 3 5 7 9 10 8 6 4 2

Typeset by Hope Services (Abingdon) Ltd.
Printed in Great Britain
on acid-free paper by
Biddles Ltd
Guildford and King's Lynn

Preface

Analysing musical multimedia? What does that mean? Music videos, films, television commercials, CD-ROMs? Yes, all these things: but also songs, operas, ballet. But then why this book? Haven't people been analysing songs, operas, and ballets (well, songs and operas) for years?

Of course, they have. But they have been analysing them in substantial isolation from one another: there has been little cross-fertilization between the analysis of song and that of opera, and neither offers much of a model for analysing music videos or film. In other words, there exists virtually nothing in the way of a general theory of multimedia, such as one might expect to provide the explanatory backdrop, the terminological regulation, for analyses of its various—and diverse—genres. Somehow or other, it seems, analysts of genres like song and opera have got along without a proper theoretical framework for what they do. And of course the fact is that they *have* got along, and pretty successfully too, thanks largely to rich contextualization and thick description. I am not suggesting, then, that analysts of song and opera have been blundering round in the dark all these years, and that they will suddenly see the light when they get theory. At the same time, if it is true that (as Roger Parker says) existing analyses of opera 'prove dispiritingly dull, encouraging us again and again to search across repertories, revealing the same generic jewels, the same kinds of skillful adaptation between words and music, music and words',[1] then part of the reason may lie in the absence of a generalized theoretical framework for the analysis of multimedia. Theory, in music at least, is an intriguing blend of intellectual rigour and reckless risk-taking; its role is not so much tell it how it is, but rather to provide grit, to set up unyielding points of reference against which over-familiar observations may be measured, and so guard against the kind of easy, 'with-the-grain' interpretations that Parker condemns. The point of theory isn't to make analysis easier, more mechanical. It is to make analysis harder, to force it to interrogate its assumptions.

Analysing, then, implies generalization, and it also implies an oppositional relationship to sedimented but unquestioned habits of thought. What about *musical multimedia*? At one level, this formulation is a simple defence mechanism: originally I thought of calling this book 'Analysing multimedia' (and indeed gave a postgraduate seminar of

---

[1] Roger Parker, 'On Reading Nineteenth-Century Opera: Verdi through the Looking-Glass', in Arthur Groos and Roger Parker (eds.), *Reading Opera* (Princeton, 1988), 288–305: 305; see below, p. 133.

that name at Yale University, during which the idea of this book came into being[2]); but then I realized that this would set up expectations, both of scope and of methodology, which I, as a musicologist and/or music theorist, could not possibly satisfy. But the invocation of 'musical multimedia' is not just a pragmatic narrowing of the field. It is also the declaration of a methodological orientation. This book essentially sets out a music-to-other-media approach; it seeks to extend the boundaries of music theory to encompass—or at least map the frontier with—words and moving images (and bodily gestures, too, though I say less about them). This is not because I maintain that all multimedia genres are intrinsically musical (though many are), but because I think there is a need to swim against the tide of film-critical and other narrative-based approaches which reduce the role of music to that of a mere supplement—when, that is, it is mentioned at all. To be sure, films like Hitchcock's 'Psycho' are not 'musical multimedia' in the sense that the words and pictures are there to express a primarily musical perception; but an approach that reverses the customary assumption that Hollywood film music is simply stuck on as an afterthought, like a kind of sonorous sticking plaster, can go a long way to redress a balance that has swung too far away from music.

And then there are multimedia genres which really *are* 'musical': that is to say, in which music plays a constitutive role that has been conspicuously neglected in the critical literature. The most obvious example (as Andrew Goodwin has been saying for some time) is the music video, around which a plethora of post-modernist writing has developed—from most of which you could not tell that there was such a thing as music in music videos. Another is a genre which does not even have a name: what in this book I call 'music film'. (I do so by analogy with music video; it is a bonus, though, that the term 'music film' neatly inverts 'film music'). One of the aims of this book, then, is to put the *music* into the critical evaluation of these genres—to claim them for music theory, in other words, or at any rate to give music theory a stake in them. And another aim is, in a way, to do the same thing for traditional multimedia genres like song and opera—to claim them, that is to say, for an approach that theorizes them *as multimedia*, and so helps the transference of insights from these particular generic fields to the understanding of musical multimedia as a whole.

But in order to stop this sounding like an exercise in music-theoretical imperialism, I need to go on quickly to my third aim: to contribute to the current reformulation of music theory in a manner that loosens the grip on it of the ideology of musical autonomy—the compulsory

---

[2] My thanks, then, to Robert P. Morgan for setting up the seminar, and to its members for providing a sounding board for my ideas, and for sharing a lot of ideas of their own with me.

(and compulsive) cult of what Peter Kivy calls 'music alone'. To put it another way, I think that to locate the analysis of music in the broader context of the analysis of musical multimedia is a good way of helping to prise open a discipline which has been too inclined to look for answers at the expense of asking questions, and which has been too ready to generate its own disciplinary limits from within, as it were, rather than negotiating them with the world outside. According to Pieter van den Toorn, 'in modern times . . . music has succeeded as musical structure (i.e. as "music") or it has barely succeeded at all.'[3] Certainly *analysis* has succeeded as structure or not at all—indeed, the two terms have become more or less synonomous. But is the same really true of *music*? What about music in film? What about popular music (a multimedia performance art if ever there was one) and music videos? Isn't van den Toorn talking just about those repertories that are defined by music alone—abstract concert music—and in that case isn't his observation just a truism? Again, one might respond to him by asking: what price success? Perhaps, you could argue unpleasantly, it is the incarceration of modern music in the modern concert-hall—a sort of low-grade anechoic chamber—that has resulted in its current state of artistic asphyxiation and effective demise, at least in so far as such things can be evaluated in quantitative terms. (It has become hard to defend modern concert music without taking up a nakedly élitist stance.)

The truth is that music is booming; but it is booming outside music theory. Multimedia (a field which crosses effortlessly from the 'high' arts to the popular ones, and back again) confronts one with this fact, and leads one to ask what kind of conceptualization might underlie the contented closure, so to speak, of music theory. This is not just because of the range of genres that analysing musical multimedia requires one to take on board. It is also because thinking about the relationship between sounds and words in musical genres like song makes one think about the relationship between sounds and words in *musicology* ('music-word', as the etymology has it). In particular, if different media relate—as they often do—through mutual contrast rather than congruence, then may that not apply also to the relationship between musicological or music-theoretical discourse and the music it deals with? Is the purpose of our words to duplicate what is already in the music, or to say what the music does not (perhaps because it cannot) say? And why do we use words of music at all, if we believe that the defining feature of music—of music alone, 'pure' music—is its self-containedness, its aloof independence of other media? In fact, can we

---

[3] Pieter van den Toorn, *Stravinsky and* The Rite of Spring (Oxford, 1987), 17, 18.

sensibly speak of 'music alone', when it ceases to be alone the instant we speak of it? What begins as an analysis of musical multimedia, then, turns ineluctably into an analysis of analysis.

The book is divided into two parts, the first of which sets up a general theoretical framework, while the second consists of sustained analytical case-studies. Each part has its own introduction, though that of the first half can be read as an introduction to the book as a whole, for it presents the entire topic in miniature. Indeed, it was written originally as a free-standing piece,[4] and the book developed out of it. Although it is a drawback that the reader is unlikely to be able to gain access to the commercials in the original, the television commercial forms the ideal starting-point for analysing musical multimedia, because it presents the musical mediation of meaning in such a tangible manner: we *know* what the advertiser is trying to communicate, in a way that is rarely, if ever, the case of the more aesthetically free-ranging productions with which analysts and critics are more usually concerned. But it is also obvious, I think, that the account I offer is constrained by the vocabulary available for describing cross-media relationships—or rather, by the lack of a developed theoretical framework to underpin such a vocabulary. So this forms a natural jumping-off point for the three chapters that follow.

Chapter 1 begins with synaesthesia, because that is where thinking on multimedia began historically, and this enables me to provide a historical backdrop by examining a few well-known early experiments in what we now call multimedia (there was no word for it at the time). But synaesthesia—which might roughly be described as a kind of short-circuiting between different sensory modes—is all about sameness, whereas I argue that multimedia is predicated on difference: it has to be if, as I assume in this book, it is the *interaction* of different media that defines multimedia. Chapter 2, then, focuses on what might be called the basic semiotic mechanism of multimedia, which I describe by analogy with the literary metaphor; one of the benefits of this analogy is that it emphasizes the role of the listening and viewing subject in the construction of multimedia, and more particularly in the construction of a meaning that does not inhere in one medium or another, but emerges from the interaction between media and subject. (It is worth pointing out that the emerging CD-ROM technology exemplified by, for instance, the Rolling Stones's 'Voodoo Lounge'—which appeared as this book was nearing completion—makes explicit the interactive quality

---

[4] It began as an inaugural lecture at the University of Southampton, passed through a number of intermediate stages (culminating in a presentation at the Annual Meeting of the Society for Music Theory in Montreal in 1994), and ended up being published, in a slightly different form, as 'Music and Meaning in the Commercials', *Popular Music*, 13 (1994), 27–40.

that is merely implicit in more traditional multimedia genres.[5]) Then, in Chapter 3, I develop this into a theoretical framework that encompasses three basic models of multimedia, which I call conformance, complementation, and contest. Finally I test these models, and their associated terminology, against a broad range of writing on multimedia (with a particular emphasis on opera), which also provides an opportunity to locate the present book in the context of the broader literature on the subject.

There is one specific issue that I should address at this point. Terms like 'conformance' and 'contest' are arguably rather stilted; so why have I chosen them in preference to more straightforward words such as 'congruence', 'contrast', or 'conflict'? The answer is that I have done so precisely because they *are* stilted, or at any rate, not run-of-the-mill terms. And this is because I use them as reserved words, rather like function names in programming; once I have defined 'conformance' and 'contest', I deploy them in what is now a technical sense (one closely related, to be sure, to their ordinary meaning), and only in that sense. There is nothing worse than a theoretical vocabulary that tries to take possession of indispensably ordinary English words, and the result of my choices is that terms like 'congruence', 'contrast', and 'conflict' remain available for informal, everyday use. The words I use in a reserved sense are printed in bold on their first appearance in Chapter 3, and are also shown in Figure 3.1.

The second part of the book moves from theory to analytical application, in so far as these can be distinguished, and the transition is marked by a short introduction to some specific techniques and topics in multimedia analysis. What I put forward here is not a protocol to be followed rigidly and inexorably, but rather, a check-list of issues and ways in which these issues might be approached. The chapters that follow do not illustrate the analytical approach in any literal way, but

[5] Virgin 7243 8 41100 0 0. It is disappointing to record, however, that as *musical* multimedia 'Voodoo Lounge' is anything but interactive. The CD-ROM begins at the gates of an old Louisiana plantation mansion supposedly used by the Stones as a home from home, and you navigate your way through the various rooms of the mansion in a kind of low-grade virtual reality environment; on the way you meet the Stones themselves, together with a large number of other characters (most of them hot-panted girls whose only purpose in life appears to be to flaunt themselves in front of any available man). There is different music in different areas, generally continuous Stones numbers (which can be selected by visiting the 'mixer desk'), but occasionally repeating loops or environmental sounds. There are also video screens showing clips from concerts and interviews by the Stones, and a kind of audio-visual jukebox (the 'VoodooRaver') where you can select and control graphic displays that move in time with the music. The one thing you cannot do, however, is to control the music other than by deciding what piece is to play where, and by moving from one area to another. Even the jukebox only allows you to choose the song; it does not allow you to modify the music in any way. Nor do the musical transitions that result from moving around the mansion seem to have been designed for any intrinsic interest or effect. From a musical point of view, in short, the interactivity of 'Voodoo Lounge' is completely incidental; the CD-ROM is about as progressive as musical multimedia as it is in terms of the representation of women.

rather attempt to embed its results within the context of broader critical readings. Having said that, Chapter 4 (which is about Madonna's video 'Material Girl') offers the most systematic approach, in that it analyses each medium—music, words, pictures—against each of the others; in this way it attempts to reinstate the role of music within a video that bulks large in the critical literature, but whose music has been more or less completely ignored. Chapter 5 is the longest in the book, for it not only offers a close analytical reading of the *Rite of Spring* sequence from 'Fantasia', but attempts to set it in the context of the original Stravinsky/Nijinsky choreography. (It is here that I put forward the genre of 'music film'.) And finally, in Chapter 6, I offer a reading of Godard's sequence from the collaborative film 'Aria'—a sequence which is based on Lully's opera *Armide*, and which represents a kind of collision both between Lully's music and Godard's visualization and between the values of music film and those of film music.

Each of these chapters focuses on video or film—in other words on the association of music and moving pictures (although, in Chapters 5 and 6, this is set in the context of dance and opera respectively). That might be considered a rather restrictive construction of 'multimedia'. Originally I intended to begin with what seemed the simplest instance of multimedia: the juxtaposition of music and still images exemplified on record sleeves. But I came to the conclusion that everything that could be said about the relationship between these media could be said more pointedly and interestingly in the context of music's alignment with moving images. (The article on record sleeves which was to have formed part of this book is accordingly being published separately, though a few remnants of it are to be found in Chapter 2.[6]) As for the choice of case-studies in Chapters 4–6, this was guided largely by considerations of availability: each is based on materials that are available in any reasonably good video store at the time of writing, and that should have a good chance of staying that way. One reason why I particularly wanted to do this was in order to avoid having to rely on stills; it seems to me that stills are simply not useful in trying to analyse relationships between two media, or arts, whose essential quality lies in motion. Where I have included stills (in the Introduction to Part I), this is because access to the original materials is likely to prove impossible.

Of course, it is not necessary to have access to the original materials in order to catch the general drift of the book, to gain an overall impression of the kind of ground it covers and the conceptual apparatus it deploys. But if the argument of Chapters 4–6 is to be followed in detail,

---

[6] See Nicholas Cook, 'The Domestic *Gesamtkunstwerk*, or Record Sleeves and Reception', in Wyndham Thomas (ed.), *Composition-Performance-Reception* (Aldershot, forthcoming).

there is no alternative to obtaining the original materials under discussion.[7] In the case of Chapters 5 and 6 it will also be helpful to have a score of the music to hand, since I generally use this as a means of identifying the specific passages under discussion.

[7] These are: 'Madonna: The Immaculate Collection', Warner Music Vision 7599 38214-3 (PAL), 38195-3 (NTSC); 'Fantasia', Disney D211322 (PAL) and 1132 (NTSC); 'Aria', Vision Video VVD 546 (PAL), Lightyear Entertainment/Virgin Vision 54058-3 (NTSC).

Acknowledgements

I am indebted to Cambridge University Press for permission to reproduce sections of the Introduction to Part I from my article 'Music and Meaning in the Commercials' (published in *Popular Music* 13 (1994), 27–40); to California University Press, Professor Annabel Cohen, and Professor Sandra Marshall for permission to reproduce Fig. 2.2 from *Music Perception* 6 (1988), 109 (Fig. 8b); to Harcourt Brace and Company for permission to reproduce as Fig. 2.1 part of the endpaper from Sergei Eisenstein's *The Film Sense*; and to International Music Publications Limited and relevant copyright holders for permission to reproduce lyrics and a simplified musical transcription (Ex. 4.1) from 'Material Girl' by Peter Brown and Robert Rans. I would like to thank the following companies and advertising agencies for permission to include stills and, where relevant, musical transcriptions from their commercials in the Introduction to Part I: Citroen UK and EURO RSCG WNEK GOSPER; Prudential UK; Walkers Snack Foods Ltd and Hiller Nolton; Volvo Car UK Ltd and Abbott, Mead, Vickers. Thanks are also due to Warner (Erato) Recordings (translation of excerpts from *Armide*); Chandos Records (recording of Tchaikovsky's Second Symphony); and Sony Music Entertainment (recordings of Stravinsky's *Pulcinella*). I am grateful to Nicholas Dodd for allowing me to reproduce transcriptions of his music for the Prudential commercial 'Performance' (Ex. I.5–6). Finally I am indebted to Mr Ric Wadsworth for permission to reproduce the stills from the same commercial in which he appears (Figs. I.11–14).

Contents

PART I

Introduction: Music and Meaning in the Commercials 3
Fantasy and Reality 9
Structure and Process 16
Multimedia and Meaning: A Preliminary Sketch 20

1 Synaesthesia and Similarity 24
The Colour Hearing of Olivier Messiaen 29
Skriabin's Colour Hearing and *Prometheus* 34
Schoenberg's *Die glückliche Hand* 41
Eisenstein's Critique 49

2 Multimedia as Metaphor 57
Eisler's Error 57
The Metaphor Model 66
Similarity and Difference 75
Emergence 82
Multimedia and Meaning 86

3 Models of Multimedia 98
Three Basic Models 98
Primacy and Expression Theory 107
The Seeds of Conflict 116
Multimedia and Autonomy 126

PART II

Introduction: Steps towards Analysis 133
Some Approaches to Media Pairing 135
Media Identities 143

4 Credit Where It's Due: Madonna's 'Material Girl' 147
A Musicology of the Image? 147
Words and Music 151
Music and Pictures 158
Pictures, Words, and Performance 167
In Place of Closure 171

5 Disney's Dream: The *Rite of Spring* Sequence from 'Fantasia' 174
A Close Reading 177
The Rite in Context 196

6 Reading Film and Rereading opera: From *Armide* to 'Aria' 215
    'Ah! Si la liberté me doit être ravie' 220
    'Enfin, il est en ma puissance' 229
    Rereading Godard 243

Conclusion: The Lonely Muse 261

Index 273

PART I

Introduction: Music and Meaning in the Commercials

What does music mean, if anything? The question is one of the hardy perennials of musical aesthetics, and there is no shortage of answers to it. Indeed, there is a plethora of seemingly unrelated answers. We can talk about music's internal structure, about its symmetries and directional motions, about patterns of implication and their realization or lack of realization; moving from 'the music itself' to listeners' responses, approaches like this offer a psychological approach to meaning (and the work of Leonard Meyer and Eugene Narmour provide the best-known examples). Or we can approach the music from the opposite direction, talking about the context of its creation, the context of its performance, and the context of its reception; here the assumption is that music acquires meaning through its mediation of society. Or again, we can oscillate between these two viewpoints, on the assumption that meaning arises from the mutual mediation of music and society. That is the central assumption of musical hermeneutics, whether we are applying this term to the work of Hermann Kretzschmar in the 1890s or Lawrence Kramer in the 1990s.

The hermeneutic programme might be described as one of wrenching meaning out of music; as Kramer puts it, 'The text . . . does not give itself to understanding; it must be made to yield to understanding.'[1] (He goes on to provide what is in effect a protocol for achieving this.) The coerciveness of Kramer's vocabulary says something important about musical meaning. In itself, in the relatively autonomous environment of the concert-hall or the home, music rarely poses clearly articulated questions of meaning. Such questions arise not so much from the music as from the interpretive approaches that are brought to bear upon it. And this explains the plethora of answers to questions of musical meaning to which I referred: each answer is to a different question; or, more precisely, each answer follows as the consequence of posing the question of musical meaning in a different manner.

But if there is one thing that underlies this cacophony of divergent answers, it is the lack of consensus as to what kind of communication music is; or, indeed, whether it can properly be called communication at all. It is helpful at this point to contrast the concept of meaning with that of effect. Nobody could reasonably deny that music has effects, and in principle it is perfectly possible to discover what those effects are.

---

[1] Lawrence Kramer, *Music as Cultural Practice, 1800–1900* (Berkeley, 1990), 6.

With meaning, however, it is quite different; not only are there widely divergent explanations of musical meaning, but whole systems of musical aesthetics have been built on the premiss that music simply does not have meaning. Now what distinguishes the concept of meaning from that of effect is that the former is predicated on communication, on human agency, whereas the latter is not (that is why we talk about the effects of sunlight, not its meaning). It follows that any analysis of musical meaning needs to begin with a clear grasp of the communicative context within which this meaning is realized. But musical meaning is all too often discussed in the abstract, rather than in terms of specific contexts, as if it were somehow inherent in 'the music itself' regardless of the context of its production and reception. My purpose in this introductory chapter is to prise open the issue of musical meaning by examining the role that music plays within a contemporary multimedia context whose overall communicative function is rather well defined: the television commercial. In this way the analysis can proceed from communicative function—from meaning—to the part played by music in the realization of that meaning.

Example I.1 shows the opening of Mozart's Overture to *The Marriage of Figaro*. What does the music mean? Of course it's possible to find answers along the lines I mentioned above. But, to borrow Kramer's words, the music has to be *made* to yield them; in fact, the very question seems curiously unmotivated. The situation is very different, however, with the music from a recent commercial[2] for the Citroen ZX 16v, a compact hatchback with sporting pretensions; this time, answers to the question 'What does the music mean?' leap out as if of their own accord, and there is no longer any temptation to ask if it means anything at all. Yet the music is the same; Citroen's advertisers have based the commercial round the opening of Mozart's overture. In musical terms, the only changes are that the dynamic range of the music has been compressed in order to adapt it to the domestic circumstances of television viewing, and that pauses of about three seconds each have been inserted between bars 1 and 2, and again between bars 3 and 4, detaching the initial motifs from one another.

The commercial begins with a long shot of a spectacular French landscape, with the camera slowly zooming in on a picturesque rock formation crowned with ruined fortifications (Fig. I.1). There is silence, broken only by the twittering of birds and the tolling of a church bell in the distance. These sounds continue as the camera cuts to a Sunday artist; he is painting the picturesque rock formation (we can see the painting), and as he lifts a glass to his lips (Fig. I.2), the camera follows

---

[2] All four commercials discussed in this Introduction were broadcast on British television in late December 1992.

Ex. I.1 Mozart, Overture to Marriage of Figaro, opening

Fig. I.1   Fig. I.2

his motion, panning up and to the right. Suddenly there is a cut to a close-up of a red ZX 16v racing along a country lane; the beginning and ending of the shot are exactly synchronized with the first motif (bar 1) of Mozart's music. But this is nothing more than a brief interpolation, returning to the previous scene with the bird-song and bells; the camera continues its diagonal motion, following the line of the rising ground and passing over two more Sunday artists. Again there is a sudden cut to the ZX 16v, and again the shot is synchronized with Mozart's music (bars 2–3), though this time the music continues for a second or two after the scene returns to the landscape.

Up to this point the commercial's strategy is clear enough: it is establishing an opposition between the serenity of the countryside and the Sunday painters, on the one hand, and the technological dynamism and verve of the Citroen ZX 16v, on the other. Through its association with the car, the music communicates the liveliness of its engine, the precision of its road-holding. That is, the attributes of the music are transferred to the car; the liveliness and precision of Mozart's score (and these are two of its outstanding qualities) become the liveliness and precision of the ZX 16v. But this is only one of the roles that the music plays. At a more basic level, its very presence or absence sharpens the contrast of car and countryside. And here we come to an apparent paradox. The commercial associates the countryside with painting, with artistic and human values. Yet it aligns Mozart's music, one of the most enduring and universal symbols of high art, with technology rather than with artistic and human values. What is the explanation for this unexpected inversion of values?

The remainder of the commercial provides the answer; its overall message is that the ZX 16v represents an ideal synthesis of art and technology, and the music plays an essential role in articulating this dialectic. After the car's second brief appearance, the camera continues its diagonal motion, passing another painter, and yet again there is a cut to a shot of the ZX 16v hurtling along the lane, to the accompaniment of Mozart's music (bar 4). But this time the music continues as the camera cuts back to the landscape scene, panning over another painter—a woman (Fig. I.3.)—before coming to rest on a man. He is painting, too, but unlike all the other painters he does not have his back to the camera; in fact he is looking straight at it (Fig. I.4). He is not painting the picturesque rock. What, then, *is* he painting? At the exact moment of the *tutti* entry in the music (bar 8), the camera cuts to a new angle and the answer is revealed: the Citroen ZX 16v, silhouetted against the sky (Fig. I.5).

Fig. I.3

Fig. I.4

Fig. I.5

Everything that happens subsequently in the commercial is designed to reinforce this association of art and technology. We see the '16v' badge on the car, followed by the decisive gesture of the artist as he paints it (Figs I.6, I.7). Then we see the whole car, followed by its portrait. As the artist packs the painting and his easel into the car, a voice-over announces that 'The new Citroen ZX 16v turns heads even when it's standing still'; the woman, now seen in close-up, looks on indulgently. As the artist drives off, we are told that 'On the road, the new ZX will show you a new perspective on performance.' (The word 'perspective' is synchronized with a final shot of the painting, in case

Fig. I.6   Fig. I.7

anyone should miss the connection.) And as the Citroen logo and product name appear on the screen, the voice-over concludes: 'The new
Citroen ZX 16 valve: everything about it says quality.'

The final slogan is an accurate summary of what the commercial, as
a whole, is saying. It also summarizes what Mozart's music is being
used to say. Heard continuously through to the end of the commercial
(it fades out at bar 38), the music quickly reestablishes its natural association with the artistic and human values represented by the painters;
in this way it mediates the linkage of those values and the car with
which it was associated at the beginning of the commercial. At the
same time, the music imbues the product with the prestige that
attaches to classical music in general and (for people who recognize it)
to opera in particular. That, in short, is what the music *means*. Or
rather, it is what the music means *here*; after all, nobody would claim
that it means the same thing in its original role as the Overture to *The
Marriage of Figaro*.

Talking about 'what the music means here' is an improvement on
simply asking 'what the music means', because it makes allowance for
the context in which musical meaning emerges. But, as my use of the
word 'emerges' may suggest, even asking what the music means here
is problematic. Consider the grammar of the sentence: 'means' is a tran-
sitive verb, with 'what' as its object. To pose the question this way is
to suggest that meaning is something that music *has*. But that is not
what the Citroen commercial seems to show. To be sure, the music in
the commercial—Mozart's music—brings various attributes or qualities
with it, attributes or qualities that enter into the discursive structure of
the commercial and become associated with the product. But the particular significance of these attributes or qualities—their meaning in
terms of the commercial—emerges from their interaction with the
story-line, the voice-over, and the pictures. If the music gives meaning
to the images, then equally the images give meaning to the music.

Another way of putting this, to which I shall return, is that meaning is constructed or negotiated within the context of the commercial. In which case, instead of talking about meaning as something that the music *has*, we should be talking about it as something that the music *does* (and has done to it) within a given context. And as one of the most highly compressed (not to mention highly resourced) forms of multimedia production, television commercials constitute an exceptionally fertile arena for investigating the negotiation of musical meaning.

Fantasy and Reality

Apart from a little editing, Citroen's advertisers have simply taken Mozart's music as it comes, inserting their message within its existing framework. The music makes sense when heard by itself; operatic overtures have to, as indeed does all concert music. But music for commercials need not. Music that is custom-written for a commercial frequently makes little or no sense when heard by itself, away from the context of words and pictures. Typically it is far too fragmentary to make sense in its own terms. Its logic is not the logic of concert music.

A good example of this is a commercial for Walkers crisps,[3] with a story-line that falls into three parts. It begins in a school playground; a group of boys are eating crisps and looking at a magazine (Fig. I.8). 'It's all about what type of job you want when you leave school,' says one. 'I haven't got a clue,' says another. 'Nor have I,' says a third. 'I have,' says the remaining boy. Waving a crisp to emphasize his words (Fig. I.9), he announces: 'I *know* what I want to do.' And as he continues, a fantasy sequence begins; it is a parody of corporate soap opera, full of glass skyscrapers, stretch limousines, and nubile personal assistants (Fig. I.10). 'I want a job', he says, 'where you face a fresh challenge every day—where only the best is good enough. . . . A job where, when it comes to the crunch [!], I won't be found wanting.' The other boys clap facetiously, and the scene returns to the school playground. The final

Fig. I.8

Fig. I.9

[3] In Britain, 'crisps' means what are called 'chips' in other English-speaking countries.

Fig. I.10

section consists of the other boys trying to guess what the mystery job is. 'What's it, then,' they ask, 'brain surgeon? Prime Minister? Archbishop of Canterbury?' 'No', replies our hero, 'chief taster for Walkers crisps.' And as the other boys elbow him mockingly, a voice-over asks: 'Why *do* Walkers crisps taste so good?'

The music falls into three discrete sections separated by silences, and these sections are fully aligned with the story-line. The fantasy sequence is set throughout to up-tempo music with a driving rock beat; it sounds like American television theme music, and its assertive quality is heightened by a constant insistence on the tonic, D♭ (Ex. I.2).[4] The two playground sequences have music that is quite different from this. It is in D major—in effect, an unrelated key. The tempo is slower, and the instrumentation is classical in style, using acoustic instruments. The first time we hear it, at the beginning of the first playground

Ex. I.2–4

---

[4] All transcriptions are the author's.

sequence, it consists of a single melodic phrase that rises and then falls back; it goes nowhere (Ex. I.3). Moreover, it is too brief and too soft to make any real impact, and the lack of any bass-line gives it a quality of remoteness. In itself, then, the music of the first playground sequence does not really make sense; you might suspect the composer, or at any rate the sound engineers, of incompetence.

But it *does* make sense in relation to the music of the final playground sequence, which begins at the end of the dialogue (Ex. I.4). This is essentially the same music, except that it cadences much more conclusively on the upper fifth (in the first section it cadenced an octave lower). But there are important changes that are not shown. For one thing, the music in the final sequence is introduced by a harp glissando, synchronized with the words 'Walkers crisps'; decades of Hollywood film scores established the harp glissando as a symbol of changing consciousness, of the transition from reality to fantasy or (as in this case) back again. Again, it is played louder than before, with a prominent backing in high strings (the same backing is in fact there in the music for the first playground sequence, but is practically inaudible). Perhaps most importantly, a rhythmic bass-line is added, and this gives the music a fullness of sound, a presence, that it altogether lacked the first time round. In all these ways, the music of the first and last sequences draw meaning from one another: each can be defined in terms of what the other is not.

But that is not all. The music of the fantasy sequence has the same fullness and presence as the music of the final playground sequence. And this means that the final music represents a synthesis of what was previously opposed: it combines the classical style and melody of the opening music with the sonorous qualities of the fantasy music. Just as in the case of the Citroen commercial, then, the music contributes to a dialectical process whose goal is the establishment of the advertiser's message. But the alignment of music and story-line is rather different this time. The Walkers commercial takes the form of a quest narrative: it poses a problem (what do I want to be?) and eventually reveals the solution (chief taster for Walkers crisps). The principal function of the music is to heighten the narrative structure by creating a sense of denouement. Both the cadential quality of the final music and its synthesis of previously opposed elements contribute to this. It provides a coherence, a sense of meaningful progression, that is absent from the story-line considered by itself. In fact, it is hardly exaggerating to say that, in this commercial, purely musical relationships are being used to assert a message that only has to be expressed in words for its absurdity to be obvious: *eating Walkers crisps enables you to be what you want to be.*

My interpretation of this commercial may seem rather heavy-handed. But that reflects the fact that, like many British commercials, it is deliberately overblown. It incorporates elements of self-parody and hyperbole; the advertisers do not *really* expect you to believe that eating Walkers crisps will enable you to be what you want to be. But the strategies they employ are also to be found in any number of commercials whose messages *are* intended to be believed. A commercial for Prudential pension plans[5] provides an excellent illustration of this, because it has a message that is very close to the Walkers crisps one, and makes use of the same opposition of fantasy and reality to create it. The commercial opens with a young man slouched in a chair, listening to music on headphones (Fig. I.11); we can see him moving to its rhythm—it is evidently pop music of some kind—but we cannot hear it. We hear his voice (but it is in his mind, not out loud): 'I want to be . . . a musician.' The commercial is based on the young man's dreams. As we see him cutting grass in the local park, we hear him say, 'I want to cut my first album'; as he packs cereals in the supermarket, we hear him say, 'I want to be packing them in at Wembley'. Thereafter there is an extended visual sequence showing him playing with his band (Fig. I.12), while a voice-over (a different voice) explains that 'You'll probably work your way through more than one job before you can be what you want to be. That's why Prudential pension plans are designed to change from job to job with you.' As the voice-over finishes, the visuals return to reality: the young man is playing in a shopping mall, and an old woman asks him, 'Do you know "I want to be Bobby's girl"?' (Fig. I.13). As he mutters, 'Oh, no', the Prudential logo appears, and the voice-over concludes: 'Whatever you want to be you'll need the flexibility of a new Prudential pension.'

In the Walkers commercial, the opposition between fantasy and reality is expressed diachronically: reality is followed by fantasy, and fan-

Fig. I.11   Fig. I.12

[5] This commercial is one of a long-running series; a comprehensive account of its meaning would need to take account of this intertextual dimension—its longitudinal axis, so to speak.

Fig. I.13

tasy by reality. This also applies to the Prudential commercial, particularly in the transition from the fantasy of the band sequence (which is emphasized by its bluish monochrome) to the full-colour reality of the shopping mall. But the opposition between fantasy and reality is also realized synchronically through the oppositional alignment of different media. This happens in a number of ways. Words are sometimes opposed to images; thus, as I said, when the would-be pop star speaks of cutting his first album, we see him cutting grass—he is wearing ear defenders instead of the headphones he would like to be wearing—and when he dreams of 'packing them in at Wembley', we see him packing cereals in a supermarket. (The puns on 'cut' and 'pack' serve to heighten the opposition between word and image, fantasy and reality.) What is most striking about this commercial, however, is the consistent use of music in opposition to both words and images.

Apart from a few notes on the harmonica at the very end (of which more below), the music consists of a single slow melody in four balancing phrases; each except the last has an arch-shaped contour (Ex. I.5). There is no co-ordination between the beginnings and endings of the musical phrases and the pictures, except that the final note coincides with the Prudential logo. The phrases group themselves in pairs, with a half cadence in bar 4 being answered by the full cadence at the end. The melody is supported by a strong, functional bass-line, and the harmony is wholly diatonic (only chords I, II, V, and VI are used). Both melody and bass are played by strings, with an off-beat arpeggio pattern in the clarinets, resulting in a warm, reassuring sonority (Ex. I.6). The music, in short, is in a simplified classical style. But the story-line is all about pop music. The disjunction between what we see and what we hear starts right at the beginning, where we see the protagonist grooving to his Walkman in a rhythm that is totally unrelated to the sound-track. It reaches a climax when we see the rock band performing, but continue to hear classical music. And this throws great weight on to the one place in the commercial where there is what in the

language of film criticism is called 'diegetic' music (that is, music which is present within the represented scene). This is the final shot, a kind of coda following the Prudential logo, in which we see the young man straightening his tie (he is looking into the camera as if it were a wall mirror); then he plays a few notes on a harmonica (Fig. I.14), spins it in the air, catches it, and walks briskly away. This is a complex moment in terms of the construction of meaning, and it warrants close analysis.

The final shot refers back to another that came much earlier in the commercial, after the young man's initial words ('I want to be . . . a musician'). In this earlier shot it is his father who is straightening his

Fig. I.14

tie, again treating the camera as a mirror; we hear him say, 'You want to be earning your keep, my son.' This response to his son's aspirations, turning on the different senses of the word 'want', establishes an archetypal opposition of youth and age, freedom and authority, idealism and pragmatism. And the opposition of (unheard) pop music and (heard) classical music is aligned with these values in the most obvious, not to say cliché-ridden, manner. For the would-be pop star, the music his father cannot hear is a symbol of personal integrity and fulfilment, everything that his father denigrates. This becomes explicit in the later wall-mirror shot, where at first sight it might have seemed as if the young man has sold out after all. For now he is smartly dressed, with short hair, and we hear his voice saying 'I want to be in the office at eight on the dot'. But the diegetic harmonica at this point, which adds a bluesy flattened seventh to the final cadence and is the only music in a recognizably popular style to be heard during the entire commercial, gives us the real picture: the young man may have cut his hair, he may be in the office at eight on the dot, but he remains true to his own values. (His enigmatic smile, and the baffled look on his father's face, confirm the impression.) And this is central to the message which the commercial is designed to communicate to its audience. Pension plans that can be transferred from one job to another are relevant to people at the beginning, not the end, of their career; the commercial uses popular music to target a youthful audience. But then it has to hold that audience while communicating a message (you already need to be planning for your old age) that is profoundly antipathetic to youth culture. The commercial, in effect, needs to have it both ways. And that is what the diegetic harminica enables it to do.

The result is an unusually sophisticated commercial exploitation of musical values. Although popular music is being used as a symbol of youth, freedom, and idealism, it would not be correct to say that classical music is being used to symbolize age, authority, and pragmatism. Because it is remote from the action—because it is non-diegetic—the classical music of the sound-track is not directly associated with the father at all. Rather, it is associated with the voice-over, which is projected as a kind of authorial persona transcending the characters in the commercial. Prudential, it says, enables you to 'be what you want to be'; unlike the authoritarian father of the story-line, Prudential combines authority with understanding. In fact, the commercial seems to annex to Prudential the paternal qualities that the flesh-and-blood father conspicuously lacks. And the music contributes emphatically to this message. Rising above the petty squabbles of the story-line, its classical but at the same time warm style brings with it a sense of genuinely concerned understanding, the authority of experience, and so aligns itself *with* Prudential rather than (as might easily have been the case) *against* the would-be pop star.

We might call this oppositional structure a discourse of genre. And it is allied to a discourse of process. From around the point where the woman asks 'Do you know "I want to be Bobby's girl"?' (the first instance of diegetic speech in the commercial), there is a massive cadential process, a massive targeting of the final point of musical resolution. The tempo gets slower and slower; the harmony outlines a classic $II-V^7-I$ progression, while the melody rises towards the upper tonic, cadencing an octave higher than it began (a feature, incidentally, that is highly characteristic of commercials, reflecting—and contributing to—their generally end-oriented morphology). As I mentioned, the final phrase is the only one that is not arch-shaped, and its ascent to the upper tonic coincides with the appearance of the Prudential logo on the screen. In this way, a purely musical process is being used not just to highlight the product name, but also to assert what is really the fundamental message of the commercial—a message that is not spoken (and indeed cannot quite be spoken), but to which everything in the commercial seems to lead with the force of inevitability: *Prudential is the [re]solution of all your problems.*

That message, of course, could hardly get past the Advertising Standards Authority. But then the Advertising Standards Authority is not concerned with musical messages. It is concerned with verbal messages, and at the verbal level the Prudential commercial is making a perfectly verifiable factual statement: Prudential pension plans can be transferred from one job to another. The verbal message, however, is effectively subordinated to a series of far more comprehensive attitudinal messages that are communicated by means of music.

Structure and Process

Traditionally, musicians compose with notes, rhythms, and (sometimes) timbres. Only with post-modernism has the idea of 'composing with styles' or 'composing with genres' emerged, at least as a consciously adopted procedure. But composing with styles or genres is one of the most basic musical techniques found in television commercials, and it is easy to see why. Commercials are just about the most temporally constrained form of artistic production in existence; the cost of air time sees to that. Except in the case of occasional blockbusters (usually, at least in Britain, from privatized industries or financial institutions), advertisers have only a few seconds to communicate their message. Musical styles and genres offer unsurpassed opportunities for communicating complex social or attitudinal messages practically instantaneously; one or two notes in a distinctive musical style are sufficient to target a specific social and demographic group and to associate a whole nexus of social and cultural values with a product.[6] Commercials often contain music that almost completely lacks 'content' as a music theorist would generally define it—that is, distinctive melodic, harmonic, or rhythmic shaping—but incorporates a discernible musical logic based on style. Another car commercial, this time for the Volvo 440 saloon, provides an example.

This commercial falls into three sections, each of which has its own musical style—though the transitions between one style and another are intentionally de-emphasized. First we see the car stationary, as in a showroom; the camera moves around it, lingering over its name-plate and model badge (Fig. I.15). The music is atonal, electronic, hi-tech, space-age, depersonalized; it evokes the qualities of Swedish engineering, underscoring a voice-over that speaks of the car's 'stylish good looks' and 'tenacious handling'. Next we see the car on the open road (Fig. I.16). As it overtakes slower-moving traffic, we hear electronic timbres that mirror the quality of the 440's acceleration; otherwise the music sounds acoustic, but all that you can hear clearly is the drumbeat, in a kind of stripped-down rock style. (By 'stripped-down' I mean that the music embodies the features necessary for the recognition of genre, but otherwise has little or no distinctive musical content.) At first it is up-tempo, matching the speeding car. But the tempo decreases as the car brakes sharply to allow a family of ducks to cross the road (Fig. I.17). This introduces the third and last section. As the car comes to a stop,

Fig. I.15

Fig. I.16

⁶ David Huron has discussed the role of music in targeting commercials in 'Music in Advertising: an Analytic Paradigm', *Musical Quarterly*, 73 (1989), 557–74: 566–7. There is in addition an extensive literature dealing with advertising music from the standpoint of marketing theory, but its relevance for present purposes is constrained by the broad-brush, and indeed essentializing, nature of its engagement with the music. (Examples may be found in *International Journal of Advertising*, *Psychology and Marketing*, and *Journal of Advertising Research*; see also Craig M. Springer, 'Society's Soundtrack: Musical Persuasion in Advertising' (Ph.D. diss., Northwestern University, 1992). My thanks to Ian Mathias-Baker, doctoral student at the University of Southampton, for bringing this literature to my attention.)

| Fig. I.17 | Fig. I.18 |

the camera cuts to a shot of a little girl asleep on the back seat; her toy duck falls to the floor but, restrained by her seat-belt, the little girl hasn't even been woken by the emergency stop (Fig. I.18). And as we see her, we hear music in an again stripped-down style, but this time classical; it is melodic, tonal, and played on strings and woodwinds. (Advertisers frequently use woodwind-dominated timbres when they want to evoke domestic, family values.) Finally, as the Volvo logo appears on the screen, the voice-over concludes: 'All this for under £10,000. The Volvo 440. . . . *Think* what you could be saving.' This slogan, of course, neatly links the ethical considerations on which the commercial has focused with the financial ones that bulk large in the purchase of any car.

In this way, the central section of the commercial, when the car is on the move, is flanked by two sections in which it is stationary. This is just the same structure as in the Citroen commercial, except that the moving and stationary sections are inverted. In fact, all the commercials I have discussed have a tripartite story-line, as shown in Figure I.19. At the same time, this symmetrical structure is in each case complemented by some kind of process that continues throughout the commercial. In the Citroen commercial this process is essentially dialectical, leading to a synthesis of technology and human values; whereas in the Walkers and Prudential commercials the processive aspect takes the form of the posing and solving of a problem. There are various ways in which music can fit into such a tripartite plan; it can be used to empha-

	A	B	A
Volvo	stationary	moving	stationary
Citroen	moving	stationary	moving
Walker's, Prudential	reality	fantasy	reality

Fig. I.19

size structure or process, or to combine elements of the two. In the Walkers commercial, the music essentially falls into the same pattern as the story-line, ABA—although, as I mentioned, the final playground music does incorporate some features from the fantasy music in the central section. In other words, it emphasizes structure, but not entirely at the expense of process. By contrast, the music in the Citroen and Prudential commercials does not fall into an ABA pattern; it is through-composed, continuing and evolving throughout the entire commercial. It is, in other words, primarily aligned with process.

How does the music of the Volvo commercial fit into this interpretive framework? The short answer is that it combines structural and pro-cessive elements. As I said, there are three styles of music, correspond-ing to the three sections of the story-line, so to that extent the music is aligned with the structure. In fact, it goes a little further than this. Although the music of the first and last sections is quite different in practically every way, they both include a distinctive melodic figure that rises and falls; in each case it appears on the same notes (E–A–G♯). But its effect is quite different; whereas it first appears in an atonal con-text, it is subsequently integrated within the final cadence (Ex. I.7). In

Ex. I.7

this way, what is in itself an element of structure, a motivic identity that contributes to the ABA pattern, serves to emphasize the changing context, and hence the processive quality of the music. And it is the alignment of the music with process that is most important in terms of creating the message of this commercial, of constructing its meaning. For although there are three separate sections of music in three sepa-rate styles, there is a continuous process running through them. The opening music is atonal and electronic, while the final music is tonal and uses natural instruments; the music in the middle lies somewhere between these extremes. Figure I.20 represents the way in which this musical process is aligned with the overall message of the commercial.

The bottom line of Figure I.20 is what this commercial is all about: a message that is strikingly similar to Citroen's (and to many other car commercials, for that matter). The Volvo 440, it is saying, offers tech-nological sophistication. It offers all the handling and acceleration you

Structure	A	B	A
Process	atonal	→	diatonic
	electronic	→	natural
	and thus		
	technological	→	human

Fig. I.20

would expect from a prestige manufacturer. But it doesn't *just* offer technological sophistication. It offers braking to match its acceleration; it complements performance with safety. When you choose Volvo, then, you demonstrate your maturity, balancing the allure of high technology with social concern. (This message is, of course, very much in line with Volvo's distinctive positioning within the market.) In this way, like the Citroen commercial, the Volvo one articulates a kind of dialectical argument: the 440 provides a synthesis of those characteristics that are mutually exclusive in lesser cars. And, through its predominantly processive orientation, the music plays a major role in creating this message, in making it persuasive, in mediating it. But I think it may add an extra message of its own. At the beginning of the commercial, and again at the very end, there is a low, electronic tone. To my ears, at least, it is unmistakably reminiscent of the low, electronic tone that has for some years been a consistent feature of BMW commercials, where it is clearly meant to evoke the values of high technology. In the context of a commercial that stresses human values, the coincidence of this tone with the slogan '*Think* what you could be saving' strongly suggests that Volvo's advertisers are hoping to communicate a sub-verbal, almost subliminal message: *Volvo, the thinking person's BMW.*

Multimedia and Meaning: A Preliminary Sketch

It is not just the messages of the commercials that are subliminal. In a sense, the music is too. That is to say, viewers rarely hear the music as such; they are rarely aware of it as an entity in itself. (The exception to this is the jingle, which can take on a life of its own; but there are no jingles in the commercials I have been discussing.) Music transfers its own attributes to the story-line and to the product; it creates coherence, making connections that are not there in the words or pictures; it even engenders meanings of its own. But it does all this, so to speak, silently.

This phenomenon is well recognized among theorists of film music. Claudia Gorbman calls her book on film music *Unheard Melodies*, in order to stress the way that music—and in particular underscore music—disguises its participation in the diegetic illusion: 'Were the subject to be aware . . . of its presence as part of the film's discourse', she says, 'the game would be all over.' And later she speaks of Hollywood cinema working 'toward the goal of a transparent or invisible discourse'.[7] In saying this, she is using the vocabulary of deconstruction, and the deceptive translucency of music is a recurrent theme in the deconstructionist literature. As Derrida and de Man have shown, music may give the appearance of going directly from the heart to the heart, to borrow Beethoven's famous words,[8] but in reality no musical style is unmediated. To put it another way, music is the discourse that passes itself off as nature; it participates in the construction of meaning, but disguises its meanings as effects. Here is the source of its singular efficacy as a hidden persuader.

Because of this, unravelling the role of music within the larger discursive structure of a film or a commercial—making it audible, as Gorbman might say—involves taking up a conscious critical stance. To borrow Gorbman's image, it involves opting out of the game. But in the study of both film and the commercials, and indeed of any multimedia art-form, there is a significant methodological problem to be surmounted. In my analysis of music and meaning in the commercials, I have had frequent recourse to words such as 'projecting', 'highlighting', and 'underlining'. We use these words a lot when we talk about music. When we talk about performances, we say that they project (or fail to project) the music's structure. When we talk about songs, we say that the composer highlights a poet's choice of words or underlines their meaning. But there is a danger in this terminology, widespread as it may be. When we use such terms to describe song, we imply that the music is supplementary to the meaning that is *already* in the words.[9] And Gorbman makes the same complaint in relation to film music; the terms we use to describe it, she says, 'erroneously assume that the image is autonomous'.[10] What does she offer as an alternative? 'If we must summarize music–image and music–narrative relationships in two words or less', she says, '*mutual implication* is more accurate.' But it is possible to be a little more specific if we think of the relationship

    [7] Claudia Gorbman, *Unheard Melodies: Narrative Film Music* (Bloomington, Ind., 1987), 64, 72.

    [8] The autograph of the Kyrie of Beethoven's *Missa Solemnis* bears the inscription 'Vom Herzen—Möge es wieder—zu Herzen gehn!' (From the heart—may it return to the heart). For a discussion of Derrida and de Man on music, with references, see Christopher Norris, *Deconstruction: Theory and Practice* (London, 1982), 34.

    [9] On the logic of the supplement as applied to song, see Lawrence Kramer, 'Musical Narratology: A Theoretical Outline', *Indiana Theory Review* 12 (1991), 141–62: 154 ff; reprinted in Kramer, *Classical Music and Postmodern Knowledge* (Berkeley, 1995), 98–121: 111 ff.

    [10] Gorbman, *Unheard Melodies*, 15. I shall return to what I term 'expression theory'—the idea that meaning is contained in a dominant medium and 'expressed' by ancillary media—in Chs. 2 and 3.

between words and pictures, on the one hand, and music, on the other, in terms of denotation and connotation.[11]

What I mean by this is that words and pictures deal primarily with the specific, with the objective, while music deals primarily with responses—that is, with values, emotions, and attitudes. As an illustration of this, consider the first commercial I discussed, Citroen's appropriation of the *Marriage of Figaro* overture. The words and the pictures present a counterpoint of images of nature and technology, art and science. They tell a story. But, by themselves, they tell it incoherently; what ties the commercial together into a convincing whole is the music, through the associations and values that it brings to the story and its ability to enforce continuity. That is to say, the connotative qualities of the music complement the denotative qualities of the words and pictures. Or, to put it another way, the music interprets the words and pictures. And in doing this it plays the same role that music has played since the earliest days of the cinema, where (in Gorbman's words) it 'masks contradictions, and . . . draws the spectator further into the diegetic illusion'.[12]

Music, then, does not just project meaning in the commercials; it is a source of meaning. As I have tried to show, it generates meanings beyond anything that is said (and sometimes anything that *can* be said) in words. Some of these meanings come, as it were, ready-made, such as the genre references of the Volvo commercial. But this does not apply to those 'purely musical' relationships of continuity and discontinuity, implication and realization, that play so crucial a role in the mediation of advertisers' messages. In an attempt to formulate a general theory of musical meaning, Daniel Putnam has described how 'the contour of instrumental music, with its broad yet recognizable strokes, "fits" the contour of those broad emotions in life which, as feeling-states of the organism, can be independent of particular situations and can be transferred to a variety of diverse objects'.[13] His point is that we don't generally experience emotions in the abstract; we experience them in relation to specific objects in specific contexts (for instance, you might be jealous of your partner, or of someone else's, but you cannot just be jealous). And this provides an attractive model of what happens in the commercials, where the broad expressive potential of musical sounds acquires specific meaning by virtue of its alignment with words and pictures—through its transfer, in other words, to a variety of diverse

[11] I return to issues of denotation and connotation in Ch. 3.
[12] Gorbman, *Unheard Melodies*, 59.
[13] Daniel Putnam, 'Why Instrumental Music Has No Shame', *British Journal of Aesthetics*, 27 (1987), 59; Peter Kivy cites and discusses this passage in his *Music Alone: Philosophical Reflections on the Purely Musical Experience* (Ithaca, NY, 1990), 176. By 'objects' Putnam means emotional, or formal, objects (see below, pp. 89–90).

objects. But if this is valid, then it follows that music in the abstract—Kivy's 'music alone'—doesn't have meaning. What it has, rather, is a *potential* for the construction or negotiation of meaning in specific contexts. It is a bundle of generic attributes in search of an object. Or it might be described as a structured semantic space, a privileged site for the negotiation of meaning.[14] And if, in the commercials, meaning emerges from the mutual interaction of music, words, and pictures, then, at the same time, it is meaning that forms the common currency among these elements—that makes the negotiation possible, so to speak.

But of course the commercials are just one arena for such negotiation of meaning. Exactly the same applies to the relationship between music and words in song. And perhaps more significantly, it applies equally to the relationship between music and the vast quantity of words that are written *about* music. For there is something extraordinary about the sheer extent of the literature on music. Consider that on the one hand, musicians constantly reiterate that music cannot be captured in words, and that, on the other hand, and just as constantly, they write metaphorical or technical commentaries on music, using words to do what they say cannot be done. The apparent paradox disappears if we see the words not as trying to duplicate or substitute for the music, but as complementing it, resulting in a counterpoint between word and music, denotation and connotation. By virtue of this counterpoint, the music's potential for meaning is given specific realization; to use Putnam's term, the words mediate the transfer of music into meaning, into communication, into discourse. And to say this is certainly to blur, and perhaps to erase, the distinction between music and its interpretation. It is to recognize the constitutive role of interpretation, and, more specifically, of verbal interpretation, in the play of representations that we call musical culture. It is, in short, to see musical culture as irreducibly multimedia in nature. To put it in a nutshell: music is never 'alone'.[15]

If this is correct, then it becomes obvious why the traditional question 'What does music mean?' has resulted in such a cacophony of unsatisfying answers. The question treats meaning as if it were an intrinsic attribute of sound structure, rather than the product of an interaction between sound structure and the circumstances of its reception. It asks about discursive content in the abstract, when such content is negotiated only within specific interpretive contexts. It is, in short, an aesthetician's version of 'How long is a piece of string?'

[14] See pp. 93–7 below for a full discussion of what I term the 'affordance' model of musical meaning.

[15] I return in the Conclusion to the issues raised in this paragraph.

1 Synaesthesia and Similarity

IN THE MOST INCLUSIVE SENSE, music is anything that somebody decides to call music; there is no a priori need to be judgemental about it. But analysing music, at least in the sense that analysis is practised and institutionalized in Western or Westernized academia, necessarily involves something over and above this; it involves a sense of commitment. To analyse music is to be committed to the premiss that music is in some sense more than just a pile of notes; indeed, it is precisely the difference between a pile of notes and a piece of music that constitutes the topic of analysis. But we can be more specific than that. To analyse music is also to be committed to the idea that we perceive the notes in terms of the relationships between them: we perceive each note as influencing, and being influenced by, other notes—or at any rate, if we do not, it is hard to see what we could be analysing. In a nutshell, we analyse the interaction between the elements of the music: that is what analysing music means. And exactly the same applies to multimedia. To analyse something as multimedia is to be committed to the idea that there is some kind of perceptual interaction between its various individual components, such as music, speech, moving images, and so on; for without such interaction there is nothing to analyse.

We can push the analogy between analysing music and analysing multimedia a bit further than this. When we analyse music, we are dealing with commensurable elements; pitches, rhythms, and dynamics, that is to say, can be related directly to other pitches, rhythms, and dynamics. And from there we can go on to conjecture about the more incommensurable relationships *between* categories—to ask how, in a given style, genre, or piece, pitches relate to rhythms or rhythms to dynamics. In principle it is possible to do exactly the same with multimedia: to analyse the relationships within each medium, and then to draw out relationships between one medium and another. In other words, we might think of each medium as an independent variable, and look for the relationships between these variables that hold in any given context (and indeed, that is just what I shall be doing later in this book). The kind of speculative theorizing that underpinned early twentieth-century experimentation in multimedia, however, did not proceed in anything like this manner. The starting-point, rather, was what might be described as an acontextual, essentializing one. What, people asked, are the intrinsic connections that hold between the various different media (musical sound, written or spoken text, moving images, and the rest)? What, in a word, are the *correspondences* between them?

It was, after all, in his poem of that very name—'Correspondances', from *Les Fleurs du Mal* (1857)—that Baudelaire famously proclaimed that 'Les parfums, les couleurs et les sons se répondent'. His words echo those of an earlier writer on whose ideas he consciously drew: E. T. A. Hoffmann, who wrote in his *Kreisleriana* that 'Not only in dreams, but also in that state of delirium which precedes sleep, especially when I have been listening to much music, I discover a congruity of colours, sounds, and fragrances.'[1] And Rimbaud itemized some examples of such congruity in his equally famous 'Sonnet des Voyelles', the opening line of which is 'A noir, E blanc, I rouge, U vert, O bleu'; the remainder of the text fleshes out these correspondences. The last stanza, for instance, reads

> O, suprême Clairon plein des strideurs étranges,
> Silences traversés des Mondes et des Anges. . .
> O l'Oméga, rayon violet des Ses Yeux![2]

It was Baudelaire's 'Correspondances' that gave Symbolism its name (one of its lines reads: 'L'homme y passe à travers des forêts de symboles'), and Rimbaud's sonnet is equally emblematic of the preoccupation of Symbolist writers, painters, and musicians with the hidden correspondences between different sensory phenomena. Indeed, these two poems probably represent the best known incursions into literature of synaesthesia, the extensively documented tendency for an input in one sensory mode to excite an involuntary response in another. (The word itself was coined, in the French form *synesthésie*, in 1892.[3]) Such sensory correspondences were seen as providing a window on to the world that lay beyond the senses, and the Symbolist preoccupation with synaesthesia flourished in a rich and heady context of numerology, theosophy, and other more or less occult studies (indeed, Enid Starkie

---

[1] David Charlton (ed.), *E.T.A. Hoffmann's Musical Writings:* Kreisleriana, The Poet and the Composer, *Music Criticism* (Cambridge, 1989), 105. The chain of derivation does not stop there: as Charlton explains, the first part of Hoffmann's sentence echoes Gotthilf Heinrich Schubert's statement that 'In dreams and already in that state of delirium which usually precedes sleep, the soul seems to speak a language quite other than its usual one'. For Baudelaire's knowledge of Hoffmann, see Enid Starkie, *Baudelaire* (Harmondsworth, 1971), 271.

[2] 'O, the great Trumpet strange in its stridencies, / The angel-crossed, the world-crossed silences: /—O the Omega, the blue light of the Eyes!' (trans. Muriel Rukeyser; quoted in Sergei Eisenstein, *The Film Sense*, trans. and ed. Jay Leyda (London, 1968 [1943]), 76).

[3] By Jules Millet (cf. Alan Bullock, Oliver Stallybrass, and Stephen Trombley (eds.), *The Fontana Dictionary of Modern Thought*, rev. edn. (London, 1988), 838). For overviews of the topic, including psychoneural aspects, see Richard E. Cytowic, *Synaesthesia: A Union of the Senses* (New York, 1989) and Simon Baron-Cohen and John Harrison, *Synesthesia: Classic and Contemporary Readings* (Oxford, 1996).

has suggested that Rimbaud's sonnet may be, among other things, an alchemical allegory[4]. But there was a scientific, or quasi-scientific, element as well; speculation about the correspondences between colour and music, in particular, tied in with a tradition deriving principally from Newton, which attempted to link the two directly as parallel manifestations of universal laws of vibration. In his classic article 'Colour and Music' in the *Oxford Companion to Music*,[5] Percy Scholes was scathing about such amalgams of natural science and the supernatural, heaping particular scorn on the early twentieth-century British composer-turned-herbalist, Cyril Scott. And David Kershaw mischievously, but accurately, captures the tenor of composers like Scott when he refers to their 'fond belief that they express some eternal verities, that they grant access to esoteric vibrations which it is the composer's mission to divulge to the less sensitive and well-endowed'.[6]

But synaesthesia is a phenomenon of psychology as well as one of cultural and artistic history. To be sure, when Hoffmann writes (in the persona of Johannes Kreisler) of a coat whose colour 'was in C sharp minor, so in order to give those seeing it some peace of mind I had a collar made for it in the colour of E major',[7] it would seem reasonable enough to dismiss this as a rather extravagant literary device (Edward Lockspeiser called it 'a fantasy which must be described as thoroughly absurd'[8]). And elsewhere Hoffmann wrote, hardly less extravagantly: 'The fragrance of deep-red carnations exercises a strangely magical power over me; unawares I sink into a dream-like state in which I hear, as though from far away, the dark, alternately swelling and subsiding tones of the basset-horn.'[9] But here it is possible to cite similar, and certainly no less extravagant, associations from the psychological literature. In his classic case-study *The Mind of a Mnemonist*, the Russian psychologist Alexander Luria described some experiments he made with his subject, S.:

Presented with a tone pitched at 250 cycles per second and having an amplitude of 64 decibels, S. saw a velvet cord with fibers jutting out on all sides. The cord was tinged with a delicately pleasant pink-orange hue. Presented with a

[4] Enid Starkie, *Arthur Rimbaud* (London, 1973), 163–7.

[5] Percy Scholes, 'Colour and Music', in Percy Scholes (ed.), *The Oxford Companion to Music*, 9th edn. (London, 1955), 200–8: 208; citations below refer to this edition. Scholes's article was reprinted, essentially without change, in Denis Arnold (ed.), *The New Oxford Companion to Music* (Oxford, 1988), i. 424–32.

[6] David Kershaw, 'Music and Image on Film and Video: An Absolute Alternative', in John Paynter *et al.*, *Companion to Contemporary Musical Thought* (London, 1992), i. 467–99: 477.

[7] Charlton (ed.), *Hoffmann's Musical Writings*, 130.

[8] Edward Lockspeiser, *Music and Painting: A Study in Comparative Ideas from Turner to Schoenberg* (London, 1973), 75.

[9] Charlton (ed.), *Hoffmann's Musical Writings*, 105. For a discussion of Hoffmann's synaesthesia see R. Murray Schafer, *E. T. A. Hoffmann and Music* (Toronto and Buffalo, 1975), 149–56.

tone pitched at 500 cycles per second and having an amplitude of 100 decibels, he saw a streak of lightning splitting the heavens in two. When the intensity of the sound was lowered to 74 decibels, he saw a dense orange color which made him feel as though a needle had been thrust into his spine.[10]

S. also saw words as having their own colours, and according to Lawrence Marks, author of a book-length study of synaesthesia and related psychological phenomena, by far the commonest form of fully-fledged synaesthetic correspondence is that between words and colours. S.'s word–colour synaesthesia, however, was a little anomalous. For him, vowels made words lighter or darker; the colours of words came from their consonants.[11] In the dominant form of word–colour synaes-thesia, by contrast, it is the vowels that produce an impression of colour. The most widespread experience of synaesthesia, in other words, is exactly the one on which Rimbaud's poem was based.[12]

Or was it? 'Voyelles' is something of an object lesson in the pitfalls that attend the interpretation of synaesthetic correspondences, for (as Marks points out) Rimbaud claimed a few years later that he '*invented* the colour of vowels'.[13] And an invented correspondence is hardly a synaesthetic one in the sense in which I have been using the term: a sensory impression spontaneously resulting from another sensory input. (Even more surely, it is not a revelation of universal laws!) It would appear, then, that Rimbaud's vowel–colour correspondences were not real in a psychological sense, but fictive—in the same sense as, for instance, the elaborate correspondences between music and liqueurs which Huysmans concocted in *A Rebours*, which do not in the least resemble any case of synaesthesia in the psychological literature, and which Huysmans may therefore be assumed to have fabricated in order to lend an exotic, *fin de siècle* atmosphere to his novel. But the story of 'Voyelles' is not quite so simple, for in 1934 it was discovered that the vowel–colour combinations of Rimbaud's sonnet are almost identical to those that appeared in a widely distributed spelling book which Rimbaud is believed to have used as a child.[14] It looks, then, as if Rimbaud's correspondences *were* after all real, so to speak, to him. But they were purely contingent. And that helps to explain why his spe-cific associations between vowels and colours are so idiosyncratic;

[10] Aleksandr R. Luria, *The Mind of a Mnemonist: A Little Book about a Vast Memory*, trans. Lynn Solotaroff (London, 1969), 23. The film-maker Sergei Eisenstein, whose critique of synaesthesia I dis-cuss later in the chapter, met S. and described him in *The Film Sense*, 118–19.

[11] Eisenstein, *Film Sense*, 119.

[12] Lawrence E. Marks, *The Unity of the Senses: Interrelations among the Modalities* (New York, 1978), 87.

[13] Starkie, *Arthur Rimbaud*, 164; my emphasis. Rimbaud's claim is in 'Une Saison en Enfer', pub-lished in 1873, two years after the publication of 'Voyelles'.

[14] The article reporting this appeared in *La Nouvelle Revue Française*, 1 Oct. 1934; for a discus-sion see Starkie, *Arthur Rimbaud*, 165.

Marks's analysis of the literature indicates that there is some measure of agreement between individuals as regards which vowels go with which colours, but only two of Rimbaud's five associations conform to Marks's pattern.

Marks explains the general correlation between vowels and colours in terms of sound quality; there is, he suggests, a direct correlation between the sound frequency that characterizes a vowel and the brightness of the colour associated with it: that is to say, its position on a scale from black to white.[15] In other words, he is saying that hue as such does not seem to associate directly with vowel sound; it associates only at second hand, via brightness, and that helps to explain the scatter in the data concerning vowel–colour associations. And precisely the same applies to associations between musical pitches and colours. 'Everybody tends to have his own scheme for ascribing colours,' Marks says. 'Nevertheless, one point where virtually all synesthetes agree is on brightness. Regardless of the hue, the higher the note's pitch, the brighter the visual image.'[16] Such associations would probably be fairly reliable if, in musical contexts, we were primarily concerned with classifying notes in terms of their position within the entire auditory range. But in terms of the major–minor system, and in terms of the way in which we talk about music, the most salient identifications are those of pitch-class, not pitch; we locate notes within a pitch spiral, not a single linear dimension. And the dimension of dark to light will not map on to a spiral. The result is a more or less total lack of agreement among synaesthetes as to what notes have what colours, and this is something to which I shall return.[17]

Fully-fledged synaesthetic perception, in other words, typically exceeds anything that may be derived systematically from the sensory input; this explains its lack of intersubjectivity, and in consequence its idiosyncratic, not to say bizarre, quality. ('[I]t would appear', Jonathan Bernard remarks, that 'the more particularized and definite the reported responses of an individual, the greater the disparity with those of others.'[18]) But at this point we need to distinguish fully-fledged synaesthesia—what Luria observed in S., what Hoffmann described, and what I shall refer to as 'synaesthesia proper'—from a phenomenon that I shall call 'quasi-synaesthesia', which is much more limited in its characteristics, but much more widespread in its occurrence. Almost everybody, if asked, will agree that the sound of a flute in a high register is brighter,

---

[15] Marks, *Unity of the Senses*, 89–91. [16] Ibid. 90.

[17] A concise summary of synaesthetic associations with music may be found in Kenneth Peacock, 'Synesthetic Perception: Alexander Scriabin's Colour Hearing', *Music Perception*, 2 (1985), 483–505.

[18] Jonathan Bernard, 'Messiaen's Synaesthesia: The Correspondence between Color and Sound Structure in his Music', *Music Perception*, 4 (1986), 41–68: 42.

or lighter, than that of a tuba, which by comparison is darker and heavier—or, to go back to correlations of vowels and colours, that 'i' is brighter, or lighter, than 'u', which by comparison is darker and heavier. This does not mean that almost everybody has a visual sensation of bright light or a bright colour when they hear a flute or an 'i', and of a dark colour when they hear a tuba or a 'u', as might be the case with a true synaesthete; it means that, if asked, most people will *judge* that the one goes with the other. The dimensions of intersubjective concurrence that underlie the idiosyncrasies of synaesthesia proper, then, are in general shared with non-synaesthetic subjects. As Marks puts it, 'dimensions that are linked cross-modally in synesthesia tend also to be linked in non-synesthetic forms of analogy.'[19]

I shall return to the issue of quasi-synaesthesia in Chapter 2, where I will suggest that it forms one of the essential enabling mechanisms of multimedia. Historically, however, it is synaesthesia proper that has stimulated and, by way of a kind of rationalization, been invoked by the pioneers of multimedia. In this chapter I offer case-studies of two pioneering experiments in multimedia, Skriabin's *Prometheus* and Schoenberg's *Die glückliche Hand*, preceded by an outline of a particularly well-known example of synaesthetic perception. All three have been quite fully documented by previous writers, and my purpose in reviewing them is to extract what can be learnt from them about the general principles of multimedia. To cut a long story short, I shall argue that, in the end, the similarities between synaesthesia proper and the cross-media relationships of multimedia count for less than the differences between them. Synaesthesia provides some hints as to what multimedia is; but, perhaps more importantly, it supplies an illuminating model of what multimedia is *not*.

The Colour Hearing of Olivier Messiaen

Of course, Messiaen's music is not multimedia in any literal sense (or at least, it is no more so than any other music). But some of his scores bear colour designations attached to particular passages, usually chords or chord sequences; in the preface to *Couleurs de la Cité céleste* he wrote that 'the form of the work depends entirely on colours', and he subsequently explained: 'I have noted the names of these colours on the score in order to communicate the vision to the conductor, who will, in turn, transmit this vision to the players he is conducting; it is essential, I would go so far as to say, that the brass "play red", that the woodwind "play blue", etc.'[20] In interviews Messiaen expanded upon these hints

[19] Marks, *Unity of the Senses*, 99.
[20] Quoted and translated by Robert Sherlaw Johnson, *Messiaen* (London, 1975), 166–7.

in such a way as to suggest that the music we hear is only half of the multimedia experience he imagined, a kind of one-dimensional shadow of a multi-dimensional whole. In an authoritative article on the subject of Messiaen's synaesthesia, Jonathan Bernard quotes from an interview that Messiaen gave during the 1960s:

I am . . . affected by a kind of synopsia . . . which allows me, when I hear music, and equally when I read it, to see inwardly, in my mind's eye, colors which move with the music, and I sense the colors in an extremely vivid manner. . . . For me certain complexes of sound and certain sonorities are linked to complexes of color, and I use them in full knowledge of this.[21]

The last clause of this quotation is perhaps the most striking, because it suggests that colour represents an essential, and not merely a peripheral, component of the music; this is a disquieting thought, given that Messiaen's colour hearing is entirely idiosyncratic, and I shall return to it. Bernard, however, focuses on the correlation to which Messiaen refers between sound and colour complexes, and the greater part of his article is taken up with an attempt to discover the rationale underlying the colour labels through analysing the musical contexts with which they are associated. (In effect, he is taking up Messiaen's own challenge: 'Obviously one should be able to prove this relationship scientifically,' said Messiaen, 'but I cannot.'[22]) His argument is quite intricate, but for present purposes we can make do with a fairly rough-and-ready simplification of it.

Bernard's first finding is that Messiaen's colour–sound associations are highly consistent; the same chords or chord complexes normally carry the same labels in different contexts. (This is exactly what the psychological literature about synaesthesia would lead one to expect.) Having established this, Bernard goes on to correlate colour labels with the modes of limited transposition on which Messiaen's early musical language was based. He finds that colours are indeed associated with the modes, but that each transposition of each mode has a different colour association. So far, then, colour is associated with absolute pitch, or at least absolute pitch-class, rather than with intervallic make-up. But as he turns to the more recent music, in which the modes of limited transposition play a less dominant role, Bernard discovers a quite different principle of colour association: it is linked with specific chord

---

[21] Bernard, 'Messiaen's Synaesthesia', 41–2; the quotation is taken from Claude Samuel, *Conversations with Olivier Messiaen*, trans. Felix Aprahamian (London, 1976), 16–17. (This passage also appears in a more recent translation: Olivier Messiaen, *Music and Color: Conversations with Claude Samuel*, trans. E. Thomas Glasow (Portland, Ore., 1994), 40–1). The term 'synopsia' refers, of course, to the visual (optical) nature of the correspondence; a variety of terms are used to describe particular kinds of synaesthesia (chromesthesia, colour hearing, and so forth), but they tend to be used inconsistently, and I am therefore avoiding them.

[22] Messiaen, *Music and Color*, 41.

spacings, regardless of transposition. Neither principle of association can be collapsed into the other; Messiaen's synaesthesia seems to have two independent sources. And, for Bernard, the fact that Messiaen's colour labels cannot be reduced to a single music-structural principle means that they have great potential as an analytical tool: they allow him to link passages that have common labels, but which a conventional analytical approach would see as different, and to distinguish formations that general-purpose analytical methods would see as identical. (Set theory, for instance, is sensitive neither to transposition nor to intervallic make-up, and accordingly throws together formations whose colour associations are quite different.) In this way what he calls Messiaen's 'private, interior light show' becomes, in Bernard's hands, the basis of an analytical method that reflects not just the sound of the music for us, but the way in which Messiaen himself experienced it. It provides a uniquely privileged perspective from which to evaluate such purely musical issues as, for instance, the strength of modal influence in Messiaen's later music.[23]

All this skirts a very obvious issue: given that we can't see Messiaen's private light show, *can* we experience Messiaen's music properly? Or is what we can hear akin to the sound-track for a film the pictures of which are lost? As I said above, it is the idea of Messiaen choosing his sounds 'in full knowledge' of their colour associations that prompts such questions, and there are a number of instances where Bernard suggests that considerations of colour may have given rise to a particular musical feature.[24] Nor are Messiaen's own comments on the subject particularly reassuring. What is the conductor to make of Messiaen's directions about bringing out the colours in *Couleurs de la Cité céleste*? (Is he or she meant to shout 'Not blue enough' to the woodwinds? How is she or he to *know* whether their playing is blue enough?) And what is a pianist meant to do when confronted by the footnote in *Catalogue des oiseaux* which reads: 'The chords ought to have a sonority akin to a stained-glass window with orange dominating and complemented by specks of blue'?[25] Again, with reference to the complex, stratified textures of the 'Strophes' from *Chronochromie*, Messiaen points out how the various note-values are associated with chords of quite different colours (milky-white embellished with orange and gold, for instance, or 'frankly red'), and adds: 'Whether juxtaposed or superimposed, all permutations will be brought to the fore by chord colorations,

[23] Bernard, 'Messiaen's Synaesthesia', 61. Bernard has summarized and extended his analysis in a later publication: 'Colour', in Peter Hill (ed.), *The Messiaen Companion* (London, 1995), 203–19.

[24] See in particular ibid. 60: 'Conceivably at least some of the modal choices may have been made to reinforce this effect of enveloping greyness', and 62: 'it is quite likely, in fact, that Messiaen has stepped outside the modal system specifically to obtain this colour.'

[25] Johnson, *Messiaen*, 119.

color serving to show the divisions of time.'[26] But who will it show them to? If, as Bernard says, 'the constantly changing colors are vital to perception of the differences between the various durations',[27] where does that leave us, the listeners?

And then there is 'Miyajima et le tori', the fifth of Messiaen's *Sept Haikai*, which (Messiaen says) is an evocation of

the most beautiful landscape in Japan . . . a mountainous island with a hill covered in *matsu* (a very green Japanese pine . . .); . . . a magnificent white and red Shinto temple, facing the blue sea—and what a blue!—and a *torii* (a portico, extremely simple in form, tinted red). You can imagine all these mingled colors, the green of the Japanese pines, the red and white of the Shinto temple, the blue of the sea, the red of the *torii*—That's what I wanted to translate almost literally into my music; this piece is really red and blue, and I added even more colors to it—gray and gold; orange, pale green, and silver; red, lilac, and violet-purple—by combining different instrumental sounds and timbres.[28]

If we cannot hear these colours, if we cannot hear the musical representation, can we really claim to have heard the music at all? To ally the question of perceptibility in Messiaen's music with the issue of musical representation, however, is to suggest that the question may not matter very much in the final analysis; most music outside the Western absolute-music tradition purports to represent in some manner, but few listeners are unduly worried at the lack of consensus among philosophers and aestheticians as to how music can represent, and indeed whether it can properly be said to do so at all. Besides, we wouldn't be interested in Messiaen's synaesthesia if we weren't interested in his music in the first place, and we wouldn't be interested in his music if we couldn't derive sufficient pleasure and interest from what we can hear, rather than see, in it. To that extent (as Jean-Jacques Nattiez might put it), whatever the poietic significance of the distinctions that colour labels allow Bernard to make, they don't impinge esthesically, that is to say, on our experience of the music.

But there is a better reason than either of these for jibbing at the idea that Messiaen's music represents a multimedia event the visual dimension of which is unfortunately inaccessible to us. We can approach it by means of Scholes's observation that people can cope with much more rapid changes in sound than they can in colour. He cites complaints about the Rimington colour organ, an invention of the late nineteenth century which enabled colours to be 'played' by means of a piano-style keyboard. 'When the keys are played at all rapidly', a con-

---

[26] Messiaen, *Music and Color*, 136.   [27] Bernard, 'Messiaen's Synaesthesia', 65.
[28] Messiaen, *Music and Color*, 137–8.

temporary critic wrote, 'the effect is almost blinding.'[29] Now Messiaen's colour chords often change at a rate that would surely induce the effect of which Rimington's critic complained. Does that mean that Messiaen was almost blinded by his own music, then? It is true that Messiaen spoke of the 'dazzlement' induced by sound and colour, but for him it was a spiritual and not a physiological experience (indeed he associated it with Thomas Aquinas's maxim 'God dazzles us by excess of truth').[30] As Messiaen was himself aware, the colours he experienced when he listened to, or conceived, music were not real colours that had some-how been internalized. They were *imagined* colours; to borrow Roger Scruton's distinction, they were not colours he saw, but colours he 'saw'. Or, to put it another way, they consisted in the grafting of visual attributes on to a perception that remained in essence musical—some-thing that becomes very clear as Messiaen describes the effects that give rise to dazzlement: 'blue, red, violet, orange, green spirals, which move and turn with the sounds, at the same speed as the sounds, with the same opposition of intensities, the same conflicts of duration, the same contrapuntal twists as the sounds'. There can, then, be no question of a genuine combination of, or interaction between, sound and colour in his music; real sounds cannot interact with imaginary colours. And this means that Messiaen's music cannot function as a model for multimedia, which, by definition, consists of the perceived interaction of real sounds and *real* colours. In other words, multimedia is not simply exter-nalized synaesthesia. Synaesthesia, or at any rate quasi-synaesthesia, may be an enabling condition for multimedia, but it is not a sufficient one.

There is a larger conclusion to be drawn from this as well: the analy-sis of multimedia needs to be grounded, at least in the first instance, on the plane of reception rather than that of production. (The limitation of Messiaen's synaesthesia as a model of multimedia lies precisely in the distinction between the poietic and the esthesic.) In a sense we have gone round in a circle and returned to our starting-point: multimedia lies in the *perceived* interaction of media. And if the example of Messiaen underlines the significance of the word 'perceived' in this formulation, the next case-study will underline that of 'interaction'.

---

[29] Scholes, 'Colour and Music', 205; another account, which includes almost exactly the same formulation and is evidently based on the same sources, may be found in A. Eaglefield Hull, *A Great Russian Tone-Poet: Scriabin*, 2nd edn. (London, 1920), 224–6. Rimington was Professor of Fine Arts at Queen's College, London.

[30] See Almut Rössler, *Contributions to the Spiritual World of Olivier Messiaen* (Daisburg, 1986), 63–4.

Skriabin's Colour Hearing and *Prometheus*

Messiaen's synaesthesia, to judge by the composer's own account, was involuntary; he did not invent his colour–sound associations (in the way that Rimbaud claimed to have invented his vowel–colour associations, but perhaps did not); nor could he choose to 'see' a given chord in one way or another. To describe such perception as synaesthetic is to describe it as, in effect, hard-wired. But this criterion, perhaps easy enough to establish in the psychological laboratory, can become problematic when applied to such historical instances of synaesthesia as Skriabin's colour hearing—if, indeed, such a term can be properly applied to Skriabin. The focus for study in this case is Skriabin's fifth symphony, *Prometheus* (otherwise known as *Le Poème du feu*), which includes a part for a *Tastiera per luce*, or colour keyboard. The *luce* part is written in standard music notation using a treble clef, mainly in two parts though at one point in three; but the published score is remarkably coy about how it is to be realized. In the first place, it is not clear whether the colours were meant to be realized by concealed lights, flooding the auditorium, or whether the colours were to be projected on a screen. Charles Myers, a Cambridge professor who interviewed Skriabin in 1914, said the former; but such performances as include the light part at all have usually featured the latter.[31] The second source of doubt arises from the fact that the score nowhere says what specific colours the notated pitches are actually intended to correspond to. This, fortunately, was clarified in 1978, when a copy of the printed score bearing Skriabin's annotations was acquired by the Bibliothèque Nationale, Paris, including among other things a full table of colours.[32]

There are three principal sources for Skriabin's specific associations between colours and sounds. One is the annotated score of *Prometheus*; the other two are articles published respectively by Myers and by Leonid Sabaneev. Sabaneev conducted a whole series of psychological experiments in which Skriabin took part (along with Rimsky-Korsakov and

[31] The best source of information on performances of the *luce* part is Hugh Macdonald, 'Lighting the Fire', *Musical Times*, 124 (1983), 600–2, an article written to mark a performance at the Leeds Festival for which Macdonald collaborated in the lighting design; because of this, it has a practical orientation unmatched by other writings on the subject. (He has particularly interesting things to say regarding the differentiation of the faster- and slower-moving *luce* parts.) The whole subject of Skriabin's lighting is plunged in a paradoxical obscurity. As an illustration, Macdonald's statement that the first (Moscow) performance of *Prometheus*, in 1911, had no lighting since the planned apparatus was 'not ready', and that the first performance with lighting was the 1915 one in New York, has somehow to be reconciled with an article by Leonid Sabaneev which was published in 1911 and speaks of 'Those who listened to the *Prometheus* with the corresponding light effects' (see n. 46 below). Contemporary critics explicitly stated that the New York première of *Prometheus* (which Hull seems to imply used a Rimington colour organ) involved colours projected on a screen (*Great Russian Tone-Poet*, 225–6).

[32] Macdonald, 'Lighting the Fire', 600–1. The catalogue number of the score is Rés. Vma 228.

many less illustrious musicians).[33] Each of these sources gives a slightly different correlation of colours and sounds, but fortunately the variations are small enough that for present purposes we can ignore them. It is clear that for Skriabin it was keys, rather than individual notes or timbres, that possessed colours. In effect, he mapped the colour wheel on to the circle of fifths, beginning with C major (red), G major (orange), D major (yellow), and so on, then passing by means of enharmonic equivalence from the sharp side to the flat side, and so returning through F (dark red) to C.[34] (If the chart in Sabaneev's article in *Music & Letters* is to be believed, Skriabin did not associate colours with minor keys.) Now there is a long history of association between colours and keys, and it is notorious that there is a general lack of agreement between the colour–key associations advanced by different musicians. While Skriabin considered C major red, his fellow countryman Rimsky-Korsakov considered it to be white; and though both Russians agreed that D major was yellow, this brought them into conflict with a relatively consistent tradition in early nineteenth-century Germany that the yellow key was E major.[35] (For what it is worth, my personal view is that E major—Liszt's holy key—is a light, metallic blue.)

The conflicts between such associations, which it would be easy to multiply both endlessly and pointlessly, do not mean, however, that there is no rhyme or reason behind them. In her book on key characteristics up to the middle of the nineteenth century, Rita Steblin provides a considerable amount of information regarding the association of colours and keys, and she does so in the context of a kind of

[33] Myers published the results of his interview in 'Two Cases of Synaesthesia', *British Journal of Psychology*, 7 (1914), 112–17. Sabaneev published a general account of his experiments in 'The Relation between Sound and Colour', *Music & Letters*, 10 (1929), 266–77. He also contributed an article on *Prometheus* to the *Blaue Reiter* almanac: 'Scriabin's "Prometheus"', in Wassily Kandinsky and Franz Marc (eds.), *The Blaue Reiter Almanac*, trans. Henning Falkenstein, ed. Klaus Lankheit (London, 1974), 127–40. An editorial footnote on p. 131 paraphrases a further article published in *Music* (Moscow), 9 (1911). In his 'Synesthetic Perception', Peacock cites other Russian-language publications by Sabaneev.

[34] One uncertainty which arises out of this, and which I have not seen discussed in the literature, is what register signifies in the *luce* part. On the mapping principle, any F♯, for instance, ought to signify the same colour. But the slower voice of the *luce* rises from f♯ to f♯', while the faster voice includes a number of 'pitches' outside this range. It would be simplest, of course, to assume that octave-related notes *were* in fact identical (as was apparently the case with the Rimington colour organ; see Hull, *Great Russian Tone-Poet*, 224), and that Skriabin was guided by notational convenience or the appearance of musical voice-leading.

[35] Another Russian, Serge Koussevitsky, who conducted the first performance of *Prometheus*, added to the confusion by proclaiming that 'Surely for everybody sunlight is C major . . . And F♯ is decidedly strawberry red!' (*The Observer*, 4 June 1922; quoted in Peacock, 'Synesthetic Perception', 493). It is worth pointing out that in Sabaneev's experiments, 78 per cent of the participants (who were presumably mainly Russians) agreed with Skriabin and Rimsky-Korsakov that D major was yellow, and the same number agreed with Koussevitsky that C major (along with D major) was the most brilliant key ('Relation between Sound and Colour', 275).

structural history of key.[36] In a nutshell, she charts the decline of a primary opposition between major and minor keys, and the rise of a principle that combines the binary opposition of sharp versus flat with the cycle of fifths. The various associations of keys, including emotional and anecdotal associations as well as colour, can be seen as articulated around these historically changing structural models. In this context, Skriabin's synaesthesia may be seen as in part historically determined; his mapping of the colour wheel on to the cycle of fifths differs from the early nineteenth-century schemes, and conforms with later thinking, in that it passes effortlessly from the blue of F♯ major to the violet of D♭ major. Reflecting his compositional assumption of enharmonic equivalence, in other words, Skriabin saw the cycle of fifths as a true *circle* of fifths, and hence isomorphic with the colour wheel.

But what might be termed the cultural, as opposed to the psychological, aspect of Skriabin's colour hearing goes further than this. As Sabaneev puts it,

I know that originally he [Skriabin] recognised clearly no more than three colours—red, yellow, and blue, corresponding to C, D, and F sharp respectively. The others he deduced rationally, as it were, starting from the assumption that related keys correspond to related colours; that in the realm of colour the closest relationship coincides with proximity in the spectrum; and that as regards tonalities it is connected with the circle of fifths. Skryabin simplified the problem to the extreme, rationalising it prematurely, and possibly destroying thereby the vitality of the association, which for him became a habitual one.[37]

In referring to the association as a habitual one, Sabaneev is pointing out that any association between two phenomena, however arbitrary or contingent, may acquire a degree of psychological reality simply by virtue of being continually reinforced—through conditioning, in other words. But his comment about destroying the vitality of the association implicitly questions how far Skriabin's associations of keys and colours were genuinely perceptual at all, other than in the case of C major, D major, and F♯ major. And here there is a further complicating factor. In the course of his experiments, Sabaneev found that for many subjects the most consistent associations were between colours and the *names* of keys; if subjects heard music in D major but were told it was in D♭, they would ascribe to it whatever colours they associated with D♭. This kind of divergence did not occur, of course, with subjects who had absolute pitch, like Skriabin. The suspicion persists, however, that even in such subjects the association of colour and key is not a direct

---

[36] Rita Steblin, *A History of Key Characteristics in the Eighteenth and Early Nineteenth Centuries* (Ann Arbor, 1983).

[37] Sabaneev, 'Relation between Sound and Colour', 273. Myers adds B major, corresponding to whitish-blue, to Sabaneev's list of spontaneous associations.

one, but is mediated by verbal categorization. All this qualifies, if it does not undermine, the extent to which Skriabin's associations can be described as genuinely spontaneous—as 'colour hearing' in the same sense as Messiaen's.

In Sabaneev's disapproval of Skriabin's 'premature rationalisation' of his own synaesthesia, we may perhaps hear the voice of the scientist whose subject has gratuitously perturbed the phenomenon under investigation. (Towards the end of his *Music & Letters* article, Sabaneev spells out what he wants to discover: 'not a simple, fortuitous association . . . but an organic connection between the sensations of sound and colour' constituting 'a conformity to law'.[38] From this perspective, Skriabin was in effect tinkering with the laws of nature.) From a music-theoretical or aesthetic point of view, however, there is no compelling reason why we should share Sabaneev's negative reaction. If in *Prometheus* Skriabin systematized the relationship of sound and colour in a way that goes well beyond any perceptual given, then exactly the same kind of criticism might be made of Schoenbergian serialism (or, for that matter, the quasi-serial construction of Skriabin's Seventh Sonata). But to say this is not to invalidate either Skriabin's or Schoenberg's compositions, because compositional methods are not theories of perception, at least in any scientifically intelligible sense of the word 'theory'.[39] At the same time, the relative lack of perceptual salience in the visual structure in *Prometheus*, even as the composer experienced it, might lead us to expect the visual component of the work to be effectively subordinate to the auditory one. And there are several ways in which this can be seen to be the case.

For one thing, the very fact that the *luce* part is notated on a musical stave subordinates colour to musical principles. There may be an isomorphism between the colour wheel and the circle of fifths, but the division of the colour wheel into twelve equal segments that results from the adoption of musical notation has no privileged basis in perception; in terms of colour, that is to say, the division is arbitrary.[40] What, then, does it mean when the slower *luce* part rises through a series of pedal points from f♯ to f♯¹? The general idea seems clear; there is a single revolution, so to speak, of the colour wheel. Expressed in

---

[38] Ibid. 272–3.

[39] Readers who consider this formulation excessively flip may refer to Nicholas Cook, 'Music Theory and "Good Comparison": A Viennese Perspective', *Journal of Music Theory*, 33 (1989), 117–41, or *idem*, 'A Theorist's Perspective on Perception', in Rita Aiello (ed.), *Musical Perceptions* (New York, 1994), 64–95.

[40] In his article 'Colour and Music', Scholes provides details of a number of nineteenth-century and early twentieth-century colour keyboards, some of which (including the Rimington colour organ) divided the spectrum into twelve 'semitones'. Such practices might be seen as an updating of Newton's division of the light spectrum into seven parts on the model of the diatonic scale.

musical terms, the rise takes the form of a whole-note scale (according to Faubion Bowers, this 'represents the breathing in and breathing out of the Brahman, the evolution of the race by steps'[41]), between which are interpolated a number of chromatic notes: B, D♭, and E♯, the durations of which are shorter than those of the whole-tone scale steps. The notation makes it look as if these interpolations are simply intervening values between the main ones, something along the lines of a written-out glissando. But of course the effect in terms of colour is quite different; a semitone rise, such as from E♯ to F♯, represents a dislocation of nearly 180° on the colour wheel, corresponding in Skriabin's terms to the transition from dark red to saturated blue. It is hard to see any internal rationale for such a staggered colour sequence, and equally hard to discern any compelling link between the lower *luce* part and the structure of the music. The impression remains, then, that Skriabin has simply subordinated his colours to a principle that is not so much musical as notational, and that he has done so without regard to its perceptual effect.

If the lower *luce* part has no readily discernible relationship to the musical structure, quite the opposite is true of the upper (and more rapidly moving) part. Scholes notes that the *luce* part 'often coincides with some note or notes in the musical score, and occasionally faithfully follows the bass'.[42] But the relationship is in fact much tighter than this. It turns on the six-note 'mystic chord' on which the musical language of *Prometheus* is based; the faster *luce* part simply replicates the root of the 'mystic chord' transposition that appears at the same time in the music.[43] (Such an association, of course, implies that Skriabin saw the mystic chord as less a chord than a key, or, more precisely, a scale-set.) Any analyst who knew this could, then, reconstruct the faster line of the *luce* part on the basis of the orchestral score alone. In this way, as Peacock points out, the use of colour does exactly what Skriabin claimed in his discussion with Myers: it literally 'underlines the tonality; it makes the tonality more evident'.[44] Or, to put it another way, it provides a visual analysis concurrently with the music. It duplicates the musical information through a direct translation to another medium, without adding any additional information of its own. (In his *Blaue Reiter* article, Sabaneev explains that because 'undeveloped' media such as light and smell cannot 'express the will directly', they are necessarily subordinate to music, word, and plastic movement;

---

[41] Faubion Bowers, *The New Scriabin: Enigma and Answers* (Newton Abbot, 1974), 191.

[42] Scholes, 'Colour and Music', 208.

[43] For a systematic explanation of this relationship, following the set-theoretical analysis of Clemens-Christoph von Gleich, see James Baker, *The Music of Alexander Scriabin* (New Haven, 1986), 259.

[44] Quoted in Peacock, 'Synesthetic Perception', 496.

'their purpose is resonance, strengthening the impression of the primary arts'.[45]) And it is because the *luce* part has, in this sense, a purely supplementary role that it makes perfect sense to perform the music without the light part—as Skriabin himself said in the score. Indeed, that is how most performances of *Prometheus* have taken place, and according to Scholes the general opinion after the New York première, which included the *luce* part, was that 'the music gained nothing from the use of the colour effects'.[46]

Why might this have been? The obvious reply might be the one I explored in relation to Messiaen: the divergence between the poietic and the esthesic, between what Skriabin experienced (or intended to be experienced) and what actually *is* experienced by audiences who do not share Skriabin's particular variety of colour hearing. But three factors complicate this reply. The first is that, as we have seen, Skriabin's own synaesthesia was limited to keys built on three (or possibly four) out of the twelve pitch-classes of the chromatic scale; Skriabin may have believed in the occult correspondences of colour and sound (Eaglefield Hull called *Prometheus* 'the most densely theosophical piece of music ever written'[47]), but it is hard to believe that he would intentionally set out to create a work that even he was incapable of perceiving properly. The second factor follows on from this: it appears that the equipment of the *tastiera per luce* did not actually exist at the time when Skriabin composed the music of *Prometheus*. Skriabin had discussed such a machine with his friend Alexander Mozer, who was a professor of electromechanics at the Moscow School for Higher Technical Training, and had been assured by Mozer that it could be made. But that seems to be as far as the project had gone, and consequently the compositional incorporation of colour effects must have been essentially

---

[45] Sabaneev, 'Scriabin's "Prometheus" ', 131. In *Music and Color*, Messiaen speaks in very much the same way of the 'natural resonance' that links colours to sounds.

[46] Scholes, 'Colour and Music', 208. According to Hugh Macdonald, 'critical response on those rare occasions in modern times when *Prometheus* has been performed with colour effects has noted the incapacity of changing colours, even of coloured shapes, to hold our attention for twenty minutes' (*Skryabin* (London, 1978), 57). By 1983, however, Macdonald seems to have changed his mind, for he calls it 'the most musically successful of a number of attempts to create an art of moving colour' ('Lighting the Fire', 600). Similarly, Sabaneev wrote in his 1911 article that 'Those who listened to the *Prometheus* with the corresponding light effects admitted that the musical impression was in fact absolutely equaled by the corresponding light lighting. Its power was doubled and increased to the last degree. This happened despite a very primitive lighting, which produced only an approximation of the colors!' (paraphrased in an editorial footnote to Sabaneev, 'Scriabin's "Prometheus" ', 131). And Hull cites a review of the New York première in the *Musical Courier* which began by saying that the colours 'had no possible connection with the music', but went on to compare this with the 'divided attention' of opera, and concluded that 'This *Prometheus* music of Scriabin is not at all extraordinary or absurd when heard under the conditions imagined by the composer' (*Great Russian Tone-Poet*, 227).

[47] Hull, *Great Russian Tone-Poet*, 192.

speculative rather than empirical.[48] Both these factors, then, tend to diminish the poietic significance of colour in *Prometheus*. They confirm that it was conceived primarily as a musical composition, and not as Hull described it: 'a dual Symphony of Sound and Colour—two Symphonies at once in fact'.[49]

The final factor, by contrast, concerns the esthesic dimension, and it suggests that we should not be too ready to write off the possibilities for meaningful combinations of colours and sounds. Even if audiences do not share Skriabin's particular associations between colours and sounds, even if they do not possess the absolute pitch that may be the pre-condition for any such perceptual associations, this does not mean that they cannot respond to *changes* from one colour to another—to the rhythm such changes articulate, and to the patterning that emerges from colour repetitions. The same applies to relationships of intensity; when Sabaneev says that 'According to the composer's idea the whole hall is filled with blinding rays at the same time that all the forces of the orchestra and the chorus are mobilized and the main theme is played by the trumpets against the background of broad orchestral and organ harmonies',[50] he is describing an alignment of light and sound that could hardly be more readily perceptible. And here there is an essential difference as against the situation with Messiaen's music, where there simply *is* no literal experience of colour. Provided of course that the light show is there at all, the colours in *Prometheus* are really *there*; they change and pattern themselves, and increase or decrease in intensity, just as Skriabin intended. All that is different is that Skriabin's specific associations between the colours and the roots of the concurrent 'mystic chords' will appear arbitrary to most listeners. At most they might perhaps acquire a certain degree of motivation from their consistent employment within the context of this particular composition.

To understand why the *luce* part adds little to the experience of *Prometheus*, then, we do not need to invoke the relationship between what Skriabin conceived and what audiences see or hear. There is a much simpler explanation: the *luce* part literally *does* add little; for while the slower part has no discernible relationship to what is heard, the faster part simply duplicates information that is already present in the

[48] See Hull, *Great Russian Tone-Poet*, 191, and Bowers, *New Scriabin*, 82. Macdonald says that in the Skriabin Museum in Moscow there is a circular board with painted light bulbs on it that is supposed to have been used by Skriabin during the composition of *Prometheus*, but he adds witheringly that 'the chances that [the bulbs] are sufficiently antique . . . are remote' ('Lighting the Fire', 600).

[49] Hull, *Great Russian Tone-Poet*, 226.

[50] Sabaneev, 'Scriabin's "Prometheus" ', 140.

music.[51] In neither case is there a substantial degree of perceptual *inter-action* between what is seen and what is heard—which means that, in a significant sense, *Prometheus* does not belong to the history of multimedia at all. And to say this is to suggest that there is a definite limit to what the phenomenon of synaesthesia can tell us about multimedia, because synaesthesia consists precisely of the duplication of information across different sensory modes. To demand something other than duplication is to go beyond the bounds of synaesthetic correspondence.

Schoenberg's *Die glückliche Hand*

Die glückliche Hand, Schoenberg's nearest approach to a *Gesamt-kunstwerk*, undoubtedly does belong to the history of multimedia. Predictably, then, the extent to which it is genuinely grounded in synaesthetic perception is open to significant doubt. Completed in 1913 after a protracted genesis, but not performed until 1924, *Die glückliche Hand* is an expressionist drama in the Strindbergian mould. As Alan Lessem points out, however, the drama is shaped by 'architectonic recurrences, parallels, and symmetries'[52] rather than the stream-of-consciousness process of *Erwartung*; it is not so much a psychological drama as a symbolical and mythological one. The stage personae have universal designations: the Man, who is the central character, is complemented by the Woman, who veers between two characteristically Romantic roles, the source of artistic inspiration and the *femme fatale*. In the second role she elopes with the Gentleman, a figure reminiscent of the objectionably elegant Englishman of Wagner's story 'A Pilgrimage to Beethoven'. (Commentators have not been slow to connect the drama's evident misogyny with the events of 1908, the year of Schoenberg's first sketches for *Die glückliche Hand*, when the composer's wife Mathilde temporarily left him for the painter Richard

---

[51] There is one sense in which this is not true. Since it is normal to perceive colour but not pitch in absolute terms—i.e. to recognize red as red, but not C major as C major unless some special context is provided for the identification—the *luce* part makes it possible to observe large-scale recurrences of 'mystic chord' transposition in a way that, for most listeners, the sound by itself does not. The result is, in principle, to give immediate access to aspects of structure that otherwise require analysis. (The equivalent in the classical repertory would be a light show that represented the tonic in blue, say, and the dominant in red, with other keys having their own colours, so that large-scale tonal patterning was visible at a glance.)

[52] Alan Lessem, *Music and Text in the Works of Arnold Schoenberg* (Ann Arbor, 1979), 119. The final (1926) version of Schoenberg's libretto is given in English in Jelena Hahl-Koch (ed.), *Arnold Schoenberg, Wassily Kandinsky: Letters, Pictures and Documents*, trans. John Crawford (London, 1984), 91–8. Although the words of the opening and closing choruses might have been thought to make it sufficiently clear, Schoenberg specifically emphasized the parallelism between the opening and closing scenes, which, as he put it, was 'meant to say: etcetera, every time the same again' (from Schoenberg's unpublished response to the critic Petschnig, trans. in Ena Steiner, 'The "Happy" Hand: Genesis and Interpretation of Schoenberg's *Monumentalkunstwerk*', *Music Review*, 41 (1980), 207–22: 217).

Gerstl.[53]) Finally, a half-hidden chorus comments on the drama, chiding the Man for the betrayal of his calling. *Die glückliche Hand* is a thinly disguised allegory of the true artist's need to rise above such worldly concerns as the carping of critics and the pursuit of beauty as conventionally conceived; it represents a kind of half-way house between *Die Meistersinger* and *Moses und Aron*.

The stage action, such as it is, is complemented not only by music (scored for full orchestra), but by mime, costume, the stage set, and lighting. The last three all involve carefully co-ordinated use of colour, which fulfils a variety of roles. Some of these might best be described as symbolic. Philip Truman sees a recurrent association of red with the Man, as against the combination of different colours with the Woman (this, he says, 'reflects, no doubt, the Woman's "multicoloured", inconstant personality'[54]); he also points out that the former is associated with the use of the cello and the latter with solo violin, often accompanied by other instruments. The semiotic principle involved in this is essentially that of leitmotivic recurrence, and Truman implies that Schoenberg's use of colour is effectively subordinated to established musical principles when he writes that 'the colour element is a useful, additional aid in following the symbolism and the musical organization of a score that lacks a conventional grammar in its atonality and comparative formlessness'.[55] To say this is to suggest that colour in *Die glückliche Hand* serves very much the same function as colour in *Prometheus*: to clarify what is already there in the music. And if the argument I have been developing in this chapter is correct, that would in turn suggest that *Die glückliche Hand* is in a significant sense something less than—or at any rate other than—multimedia. In order to avoid such a conclusion, we would need to show that the relationship between colour and sound is not the direct one that Truman's description indicates.

Lessem (and, closely following him, Truman) suggests another and perhaps more significant Wagnerian precedent for *Die glückliche Hand*: the productions of *Tristan und Isolde* and other music dramas that were mounted at the Vienna Opera while Mahler was musical director. (Schoenberg saw the production of *Tristan* in the summer of 1903.[56]) In these productions Mahler collaborated with the stage designer Alfred

---

[53] John C. Crawford, '*Die glückliche Hand*: Schoenberg's *Gesamtkunstwerk*', *Musical Quarterly*, 60 (1974), 583–601: 584; *idem*, '*Die glückliche Hand*: Further Notes', *Journal of the Arnold Schoenberg Institute*, 4 (1980), 69–76: 74; Philip Truman, 'Synaesthesia and *Die glückliche Hand*', *Interface*, 12 (1983), 481–503: 487; but see Joseph Auner's arguments to the contrary in 'Schoenberg's Compositional and Aesthetic Transformations 1910–13: The Genesis of *Die glückliche Hand*' (Ph.D. diss., University of Chicago, 1991), 10–14.

[54] Truman, 'Synaesthesia and *Die glückliche Hand*', 496.   [55] Ibid. 497.

[56] Steiner, ' "Happy" Hand', 212.

Roller,[57] and different-coloured lights were used in order to symbolize the developing psychological content of the drama. The effect was sufficiently complex for a contemporary critic, Oskar Bie, to refer to it as 'Lichtmusik'.[58] Lessem, and Truman, go on to explain that Mahler and Roller were much influenced in this by the writings of Adolph Appia, who attacked the traditional realistic staging of Wagnerian music dramas, arguing that 'One could restore Wagner's essential conception . . . by eliminating external props and trappings and by projecting on the stage only the inner drama as it is experienced by the protagonists'.[59] It would perhaps be going too far to suggest that, for Appia, the staging (including, of course, the lighting) should serve the same function that Wagner assigned to the orchestra in *Oper und Drama*: that of saying what words cannot express, creating a sense of foreboding, and invoking remembrance. But a full integration of the staging in the dramatic process is certainly suggested by a lighting effect that Appia conceived for Tristan's monologue in Act III of *Tristan*, which Lessem describes as 'a light crescendo-diminuendo which, matching Tristan's rising expectations and relapse into despair, bears a direct relation to Schoenberg's own idea in the third scene of *Die glückliche Hand*'.[60]

The idea to which Lessem refers is the famous 'Lighting Crescendo' which takes place in bars 125–53 of *Die glückliche Hand*, and represents a climactic integration of colour, musical structure, instrumentation, and dramatic content. In the libretto, Schoenberg described the 'Crescendo' as follows:

As [the stage] darkens, a wind springs up. At first it murmurs softly, then steadily louder (along with the music).

Conjoined with this wind-crescendo is a light-crescendo. It begins with dull red light (from above) that turns to brown and then a dirty green. Next it changes to a dark blue-gray, followed by violet. This grows, in turn, into an intense dark red which becomes ever brighter and more glaring until, after

[57] The link with Roller is strengthened by the fact that Schoenberg suggested him as a possible scene designer for the proposed film version of *Die glückliche Hand*—though in third place, after Kokoschka and Kandinsky (undated letter, probably from 1913, to Emil Hertzka, trans. in Hahl-Koch (ed.), *Arnold Schoenberg, Wassily Kandinsky*, 101). Auner also stresses the possible influence of the anti-naturalistic dramatic productions of the Munich Artists' Theatre, which opened in 1908 ('Schoenberg's Compositional and Aesthetic Transformations', 231–3); other dramatic parallels are discussed by Hahl-Koch in *Arnold Schoenberg, Wassily Kandinsky*, 161–4.

[58] Steiner, ' "Happy" Hand', 212.

[59] Lessem, *Music and Text*, 101. In view of Wagner's own preference for realistic staging, it is clear that Appia's talk of restoring Wagner's essential conception was of a piece with Wagner's talk about realizing Beethoven's true intentions when he rescored the Ninth Symphony. What was at issue was not what Wagner and Beethoven intended, but what Appia and Wagner respectively thought they *ought* to have intended.

[60] Ibid. 101. Lessem is summarizing a passage from Appia's *Die Musik und die Inscenierung* (Munich, 1899).

reaching a blood-red, it is mixed more and more with orange and then bright yellow; finally a glaring yellow light alone remains. . . .

During this crescendo of light and storm, the MAN reacts as though both emanated from him. He looks first at his hand (the reddish light); it sinks, completely exhausted; slowly, his eyes grow excited (dirty green). His excitement increases; his limbs stiffen convulsively, trembling, he stretches both arms out (blood-red); his eyes start from his head and he opens his mouth in horror. When the yellow light appears, his head seems as though it is about to burst.[61]

Unlike the symbolic associations to which Truman refers, the 'Crescendo' involves the co-ordination of *processes* across different sensory modes and compositional media. It follows the scene in which the Man has created an elaborate diadem with a single blow of his hammer; in terms of the Schoenbergian aesthetic of artistic expression, which can more or less be assimilated to the Romantic distinction between the beautiful and the sublime, this represents a travesty of the artist's mission. (In particular, the striking idea of the single hammer blow resonates with Romantic conceptions of the flash of inspiration in which all the details of an artistic work are conceived at once, commonly seen as the emblem of the very genius that Schoenberg's Man betrays.) The 'Crescendo', then, corresponds to the Man's reaction to this betrayal and the attempt to recapture his artistic integrity, an inner struggle that issues in the exteriorization of his emotions.[62] This psychological process is represented most obviously by the sustained crescendo of the music, which builds up by stages from the triple pianissimo ostinato of bar 125 (low flute, bassoon, and harp) to the triple fortissimo fanfare for three trumpets in bar 148. The musical crescendo is not just a matter of dynamic markings, however; it is composed into the musical texture, which is at first diffuse, then congeals into a kind of figure–ground model, and becomes thicker and more homogeneous as the crescendo reaches its climax.[63] Running in parallel with all this is the lighting, which builds up from black through a succession of different reds interspersed with other colours to orange and finally a piercing yellow, coinciding with the trumpets. The overall parallelism of the processes within the various media is obvious enough: from pianissimo to fortissimo, from diffuse to homogeneous, from black to piercing yellow. But it is also possible to provide evidence that Schoenberg intended

---

[61] Taken from the translation of the libretto in Hahl-Koch (ed.), *Arnold Schoenberg, Wassily Kandinsky*, 96.

[62] In a lecture that Schoenberg gave in connection with a 1928 performance of *Die glückliche Hand* in Breslau, trans. in ibid. 102–7, Schoenberg indicated that the passage also expresses the Man's premonitions of his sexual betrayal by the Woman (p. 106).

[63] Lessem provides a motivic table illustrating the rhythmic aspect of this process (*Music and Text*, 114). Convenient tabulations of the 'Crescendo' as a whole may be found in both Crawford, 'Schoenberg's *Gesamtkunstwerk*', 586–8, and Truman, 'Synaesthesia and *Die glückliche Hand*', 498–9.

a more detailed parallelism, in particular as regards the co-ordination of colour and instrumentation, and it is here that the issue of colour–sound synaesthesia arises—though only, perhaps, at a remove.

Virtually all commentators on *Die glückliche Hand* have emphasized the relevance to it of Schoenberg's relationship with the painter Wassily Kandinsky, who was the leading spirit behind *Der blaue Reiter* (a group of expressionist artists that also included Franz Marc); and Kandinsky's abstract stage composition *Der gelbe Klang*, which dates from 1909, perhaps provides the closest parallel to *Die glückliche Hand* in terms of what Schoenberg himself described as 'the renunciation of any conscious thought, any conventional plot'.[64] The relationship between Kandinsky and Schoenberg began with a letter that Kandinsky wrote after hearing a concert of Schoenberg's music in January 1911, to which Schoenberg wrote a cordial reply. The two met in the autumn of that year, and remained in touch on a regular basis until 1914, as well as sporadically thereafter.[65] It was at this time that Schoenberg was most active as an artist, and the first exhibition of *Der blaue Reiter*, held in Munich in December 1911, included paintings by Schoenberg; in addition he contributed an essay and a song ('Herzgewachse', Op. 20) to the group's almanac, also called *Der blaue Reiter*, which was published in 1912. It is significant that the almanac also included the essay by Sabaneev on Skriabin's *Prometheus* which I have already cited; synaesthetic correspondences between colour and music, and more generally between sight and sound, played a major role in the philosophy of art which Kandinsky was developing throughout this period, and which received its definitive statement in his book *Über das Geistige in der Kunst*, also published in 1912.[66] In this book, Kandinsky described Skriabin's attempt to synthesize sight and sound as 'elementary', and outlined a much more comprehensive—and indeed metaphysical—theory of their relationship. Although avoiding numerological

[64] The text of *Der gelbe Klang* was published in the *Blaue Reiter* almanac, as 'The Yellow Sound: A Stage Composition', 207–24; alternative trans. in Hahl-Koch (ed.), *Arnold Schoenberg, Wassily Kandinsky*, 117–25. The music, by Thomas von Hartmann, was apparently no more than sketched, and was in any case lost during the Russian Revolution (ibid. 158–9). This abstract drama, of which more shortly, included the same coloured costumes and lights as *Die glückliche Hand*, and Kandinsky's epigrammatic indications of the music include a number of references to instrumental colours, though specific associations of colour and timbre are not spelt out. Schoenberg's comments on *Der gelbe Klang*, which he said pleased him 'extraordinarily', may be found in his letter to Kandinsky of 19 Aug. 1912 (in ibid. 54); it seems clear from what Schoenberg says that it was through the almanac that he first came to know of Kandinsky's drama.

[65] See ibid. 135–40, and the letters trans. therein.

[66] Wassily Kandinsky, *Über das Geistige in der Kunst* (Munich, 1912); English trans.: *On the Spiritual in Art*, ed. Hilla Rebay (New York, 1946). Many of Kandinsky's basic aesthetic premisses are also expressed in the articles he contributed to the *Blaue Reiter* almanac ('On the Question of Form' and 'On Stage Composition', 147–87 and 190–206 respectively; another translation of 'On Stage Composition' (by John Crawford) may be found in Hahl-Koch (ed.), *Arnold Schoenberg, Wassily Kandinsky*, 111–17).

speculation, Kandinsky was much influenced by theosophical thought,[67] and the starting-point for his theory is that the universe consists essentially of the play of vibrations, and that these vibrations have a fundamentally spiritual significance. Or, to put it another way, colour and sound are primary attributes of the spiritual. The Pythagorean notion of the music of the spheres lies unmistakably in the ancestry of Kandinsky's notion of the spiritual sound; he differentiates it from the 'neural' sound that we hear, but at the same time stresses the intimate linkage of the two.[68]

Über das Geistige is predicated on the same aesthetic premiss as *Die glückliche Hand*: that the proper subject for art is not what is conventionally defined as the beautiful, but something higher and more ethically charged—what Kandinsky calls the spiritual, and what both he and Schoenberg identified with a sense of 'inner necessity'. And Kandinsky's philosophy becomes a philosophy of *art* to the extent that he demonstrates the parallel realization of this spiritual quality in perceptible sound and in colour. Truman points out that Kandinsky makes frequent references to Goethe's colour system, as expressed in his *Farbenlehre*, and that like Goethe, Kandinsky 'correlates colour not only with sounds, but senses, thoughts, actions, temperaments, etc.'.[69] The crucial point, however, is that Kandinsky borrows the basic structure of his theory from Goethe. As Goethe put it,

Colour and sound do not admit of being compared in any way, but both are referable to a higher formula; both are derivable, though each for itself, from a higher law. They are like two rivers that have their source in one and the same mountain, but subsequently pursue their way, under totally different conditions, in two totally different regions, so that throughout the course of both no two points can be compared.[70]

Another way to visualize this would be a triangle, with Kandinsky's 'spiritual' (Goethe's 'higher law') at the apex; understood this way, sound and colour do not relate directly to one another, but relate indirectly through a common relationship with the spiritual. There is no question, then, of mapping the structures of sound and colour on to one another, in the manner of Skriabin's mapping of the colour wheel onto the circle of fifths. Instead, sound and colour correspond to one another in so far as they embody the same ultimate meaning.[71]

---

[67] For a brief outline of theosophical influences on Kandinsky and Schoenberg, with references, see Hahl-Koch (ed.), *Arnold Schoenberg, Wassily Kandinsky*, 144–5.

[68] For a concise exposition of Kandinsky's philosophy of art, see Jerome Ashmore, 'Sound in Kandinsky's Painting', *Journal of Aesthetics and Art Criticism*, 35 (1977), 329–36.

[69] Truman, 'Synaesthesia and *Die glückliche Hand*', 489.

[70] From *Zu Farbenlehre*; quoted by Scholes, 'Colour and Music', 204.

[71] Schoenberg, then, was entirely in conformity with Kandinsky's thinking when he said in the Breslau lecture that 'In reality, tones, if viewed clearly and prosaically, are nothing else but a

In the course of his book, Kandinsky gives his metaphysical concept of the spiritual a more practical orientation in terms of artistic expression by setting out the emotional properties of different sounds, specifically instrumental timbres, and colours. He also provides a table that places the colours in ascending order of emotional intensity (table III in *Über das Geistige*). And this is where the specific compositional link with *Die glückliche Hand*, and in particular with the 'Lighting Crescendo', comes in. There is, in the first place, a similarity between the sequence of colours in the 'Crescendo' and in Kandinsky's table; both begin with black, and pass through increasingly intense reds to orange and yellow.[72] More compellingly, there is a high level of coincidence between the instrumental timbres that Kandinsky associates with these colours and those in Schoenberg's score: Schoenberg, like Kandinsky, couples the violin with green, deep woodwinds with violet, drums with vermilion, the lower brass instruments with light red, and the trumpet with yellow. And when read in terms of Kandinsky's emotional characterizations, this colour–sound sequence results in an emotional trajectory that is entirely consistent with the action of *Die glückliche Hand*, beginning with apathy and passing through mounting passion to excitement, strength, and finally an unbalanced state bordering, as Kandinsky says, on insanity. Was Schoenberg, then, simply composing with Kandinsky's colour–sound tables in hand, just as, in later life, he composed with tables of row-forms in hand?[73]

The issue of influence as between Kandinsky and Schoenberg is complicated by issues of chronology. Until recently, it was believed that the two had met earlier than 1911—in 1909, or even perhaps 1906—and there was accordingly a general assumption that Schoenberg's experiments in multimedia drama had been prompted by Kandinsky's.[74] When it was established that they did not in fact meet or even know of each other's work until 1911, this assumption was naturally reversed;

particular kind of vibrations of the air. As such they indeed make some sort of impression on the affected sense organ, the ear. By being joined with each other in a special way, they bring about certain artistic, and, if I may be permitted the expression, certain spiritual impressions' (trans. in Hahl-Koch (ed.), *Arnold Schoenberg, Wassily Kandinsky*, 105). There is also a link with what Jann Pasler, borrowing the terminology of commentators on Baudelaire, calls 'vertical' correspondences between sense impressions and the world of ideas, as opposed to 'horizontal' correspondences between the senses ('Music and Spectacle in *Petrushka* and *The Rite of Spring*, in Jann Pasler (ed.), *Confronting Stravinsky: Man, Musician, and Modernist* (Berkeley, 1986), 53–81: 59).

[72] The principal differences are Schoenberg's interpolation of red between black and brown and his omission of blue. The latter can presumably be explained by the inappropriateness in terms of the action of *Die glückliche Hand* of the peaceful, celestial qualities Kandinsky ascribed to blue.

[73] Martha Hyde, 'The Format and Function of Schoenberg's Twelve-Tone Sketches', *Journal of the American Musicological Society*, 36 (1983), 453–80.

[74] See Hahl-Koch (ed.), *Arnold Schoenberg, Wassily Kandinsky*, 137, 152; both Lessem (*Music and Text*, 58–62) and Crawford ('Schoenberg's *Gesamtkunstwerk*') work on the basis of this erroneous dating.

'the dates of the letters', says Jelena Hahl-Koch, 'show the impossibility of such an influence'.[75] But here we come to another chronological confusion. It was until recently believed that Schoenberg composed much of the music of *Die glückliche Hand* soon after completing the libretto, in 1910, whereas it is now known that most of the music dates from no earlier than 1912.[76] This effectively reopens the question of influence where compositional details are concerned, as in the case of the colour–timbre associations in the 'Lighting Crescendo'. Lessem observes that Schoenberg's 'independence from Kandinsky seems assured by the fact that his scenario for *Die glückliche Hand* was completed eighteen months before the publication of Kandinsky's book'.[77] But, as Joseph Auner has pointed out, the scenario (what I have been calling the libretto) of the 'Crescendo' specifies the colours, but not the instruments associated with them. And whereas this is one of the passages which Schoenberg apparently *did* sketch at an early stage, he comprehensively revised it in 1912—by which time he is known (on the evidence of his letters to Kandinsky) to have read *Über das Geistige*.[78] In particular, the passage corresponding to 'dirty green' is assigned in the original sketch to woodwinds and trumpet; the introduction of the solo violin (marked 'extended' in the score), paralleling Kandinsky's association of green with 'peaceful, extended, medium range tones of the violin', dates from the final revision. There is good reason to believe, then, that whereas Schoenberg and Kandinsky arrived independently at the idea of an expressionist stage composition, the specific correlations between colour and musical timbre in *Die glückliche Hand* do, after all, reflect Kandinsky's influence.

[75] Hahl-Koch (ed.), *Arnold Schoenberg, Wassily Kandinsky*, 160. Crawford adds in a rather desperate Translator's note that 'Even though the influence of Kandinsky on Schoenberg's text for *Die glückliche Hand* is a chronological impossibility, the synesthetic ideas of the two men regarding equivalent colors, instrumental timbres and emotions are so similar as to suggest that both were influenced by a common, earlier source' (ibid. 198 n. 86). But he suggests no candidates.

[76] 'Soon it will be three years old', Schoenberg wrote in a letter to Kandinsky dated 19 Aug. 1912, 'and it is still not composed' (trans. ibid. 54). For a discussion of the compositional chronology see Auner, 'Schoenberg's Compositional and Aesthetic Transformations', 113–35, summarized in his fig. 7 (p. 114). There is a final chronological complication when it comes to making comparisons between *Der gelbe Klang* and *Die glückliche Hand*: whereas most of the former was written in 1909, the published version includes additions made in 1912 (Hahl-Koch (ed.), *Arnold Schoenberg, Warsily Kandinsky*, 159–60).   [77] Lessem, *Music and Text*, 100.

[78] Auner, 'Schoenberg's Compositional and Aesthetic Transformations', 123–4. Curiously, Auner contradicts his own suggestion that 'Schoenberg discarded the original CV [*Compositions Vorlage*] sketch in order to allow him to better integrate Kandinsky's color–timbre parallels' (p. 124) when he argues that 'The fact that there is no indication of color in [the revision], unlike the original CV sketch, suggests that with the decline in his faith in intuition Schoenberg was less concerned with the synaesthetic aspect of the work' (p. 351). The CV sketch is reproduced in Harald Krebs, 'New Light on the Source Materials of Schoenberg's *Die Glückliche Hand*', *Journal of the Arnold Schoenberg Institute*, 11 (1988), 123–41: 139 (ex. 8g). Krebs offers a purely musical interpretation of the revisions in 'The "Color Crescendo" from *Die Glückliche Hand*: A Comparison on Sketch and Final Version', *Journal of the Arnold Schoenberg Institute*, 12 (1989), 61–7.   •

But of course this brings with it a thoroughly problematic implication. It seems clear that Kandinsky was a spontaneous synaesthete;
when he listened to *Lohengrin*, he said, vivid colours 'stood before my
eyes. Wild, almost crazy lines were sketched in front of me.'[79]
Schoenberg, on the other hand, never claimed anything of the sort (and
even if he had possessed such synaesthesia, the chances of his
colour–sound associations coinciding with Kandinsky's would have
been vanishingly small). And whereas sound–colour correlations were
a lifelong preoccupation for Kandinsky, as they were for Skriabin, they
seem to have been more of a one-off experiment for Schoenberg—as if
he was just dabbling with an idea that happened to be in the air at the
time. If the colour–sound combinations in *Die glückliche Hand* have their
origin in synaesthetic perception, then, it appears to have been not
Schoenberg's but somebody else's. We might call this 'synaesthesia by
proxy', or (if it is not a contradiction in terms) 'cultural synaesthesia'.

Eisenstein's Critique

Kandinsky was an emigré Russian (quite improbably, he studied law
and political economy at the University of Moscow), and the notion of
cultural synaesthesia gains credibility from the extent to which the phenomenon, or at least the attempt to use it as a basis for artistic experimentation, was associated around the turn of the century with Russia.
(One might even suggest that, as a historical phenomenon, synaesthesia migrated from Germany to France around the middle of the nineteenth century, and from there to Russia.) So it is appropriate at this
point to invoke the critique of such attempts that another Russian,
Sergei Eisenstein, offered some 30 years later in his classic text, *The Film
Sense*. Astonishingly, Eisenstein's almost wholly negative critique,
which once again focuses on colour correspondences, occupies over a
quarter of the book.[80] And what gives this critique particular value in
the present context is that it enables us to isolate key aspects of the co-
ordination of media in *Die glückliche Hand* that deviate significantly from
synaesthesia-based models.

Kandinsky is one of the main butts of Eisenstein's criticism. Eisenstein
quotes two whole pages of *Der gelbe Klang*, and comments witheringly
that 'The contents of this work cannot be satisfactorily conveyed, due

---

[79] Trans. in Hahl-Koch (ed.), *Arnold Schoenberg, Wassily Kandinsky*, 149; see also the brief discussion (with references) of Kandinsky's synaesthesia on p. 151.

[80] Claudia Widgery, who is clearly uncomfortable with the prominence of arguments about
synaesthesia in Eisenstein's text, points out that they were 'undoubtedly sparked by the emergence
of color technology in a medium that had been limited to black and white for most of three decades'
('The Kinetic and Temporal Interaction of Music and Film: Three Documentaries of 1930's America'
(Ph.D. diss., University of Maryland, College Park, 1990, UMI order no. 9121449), 39–40).

to the total absence of content'.[81] Again, he complains that people like Kandinsky 'propose an aimless, vague, "absolutely free" inner tonality (*der innere Klang*), neither as a direction nor as a means, but as *an end in itself*, as the summit of achievement'.[82] What Eisenstein is objecting to is the abstract quality of *Der gelbe Klang*; it is a play of pure colours, sounds, and sensations, sometimes allied to isolated representational images (some 'intensely yellow giants . . . with strange, indistinct, yellow faces',[83] a yellow flower, rocks), but never in the service of any kind of narrative process. Now it is a basic part of Eisenstein's concept of montage, which I shall discuss in Chapter 2, that different media relate to one another through shared qualities, and in particular through shared emotional qualities; to this extent Eisenstein's theory of cross-media relationships is very like Kandinsky's. But for Eisenstein these abstract relationships articulate the essentially distinct contents of individual media. A crowd of people on a screen and a musical sound-track may be linked through a rhythmic or kinetic pattern, but each medium retains its own specificity. By contrast, Kandinsky eliminates virtually everything except the abstract qualities that the various media have in common. This is in line with his belief that, as Ashmore puts it, 'in realistic painting it is not the outer surfaces or shells of physical objects which are important. . . . [A]ll physical things, if reduced to vibrations, will disappear and . . . what remains will be the plastic elements in a pure state.'[84] 'Such a method', Eisenstein protests, '*consciously attempts to divorce all formal elements from all content elements*; everything touching theme or subject is dismissed, leaving only those extreme formal elements that in *normal creative work* play only a partial role.'[85]

Such disagreement might perhaps be expected in the encounter between a film-maker and an abstract painter. Nevertheless, it allows us to identify an essential difference between *Der gelbe Klang* and *Die glückliche Hand*. Lessem draws what he calls an 'important distinction' between the Wagner productions of Alfred Roller and Schoenberg's expressionist drama: in the former, he says, 'the symbol functions as an abstraction of a reality which is commonly known and which provides the explanatory framework through which the meaning of the symbol can be understood. . . . The Expressionists, on the other hand, minimalized the framework around the vision and, thus, the distinction

[81] Eisenstein, *Film Sense*, 93.
[82] Ibid. 92–3; emphases original, as in all subsequent quotations from *Film Sense*.
[83] Kandinsky, 'Yellow Sound', 213.
[84] Ashmore, 'Sound in Kandinsky's Painting', 333, 334.
[85] Eisenstein, *Film Sense*, 95. Elsewhere Eisenstein compares such a feat of abstraction with the behaviour of a madman whom Diderot described; the madman 'holds a blade of shiny yellow straw in his hand', says Eisenstein, 'and he shouts that he has caught a sunbeam'. And he adds: 'This madman was an ultra-formalist' (p. 111).

between the inner and the outer world.'[86] Now this description fits *Der gelbe Klang* very well. But it does not fit so well with Schoenberg's drama, with its clear narrative organization (however circular) and its unities of time and place (however mythically universalized). It jars with Schoenberg's statement, admittedly made nearly 20 years later, that he disliked 'what is called "stylized" decoration[s] (what style?) and always want to see a set done by the good old experienced hand of a painter who can draw a straight line straight and not model his work on children's drawings or the art of primitive peoples'.[87] And it is altogether controverted by some of the directions contained in Schoenberg's libretto, especially in the third scene, where, in a grotto that looks 'something between a machine shop and a goldsmith's workshop, several WORKERS are seen at work in realistic workingmen's dress. (One files, one sits at a machine, one hammers, etc.) . . . In the middle stands an anvil, near it a heavy hammer.'[88] According to Crawford, such directions betray a 'conflict between the allegorical/symbolic nature of the drama and the often naturalistic concept of the stage setting'; Hahl-Koch goes further, disparaging them as 'crass collisions' and 'formal blunders'.[89] But in making such a criticism, these critics are implicitly privileging the Kandinsky viewpoint over the Eisenstein one, according to which it is the divergence between different media that gives meaning to their juxtaposition. The conflict to which they refer may, in other words, have been exactly what Schoenberg intended, and to say this is to highlight a major distinction between Schoenberg's thinking and Kandinsky's.

A second main theme in Eisenstein's critique of synaesthesia is that much of what passes as synaesthetic association is not in fact synaesthetic at all (in the sense of 'an effect immediately communicated to the soul', as Kandinsky put it in *Über das Geistige*[90]), but cultural and

---

[86] Lessem, *Music and Text*, 101.

[87] From a letter dated 14 Apr. 1930 to Ernst Legal of the Kroll Opera in Berlin, concerning a proposed production of *Die glückliche Hand*; trans. in Hahl-Koch (ed.), *Arnold Schoenberg, Wassily Kandinsky*, 99.

[88] Ibid. 95.

[89] Crawford, 'Schoenberg's *Gesamtkunstwerk*', 589; Hahl-Koch (ed.), *Arnold Schoenberg, Wassily Kandinsky*, 160. A rather similar complaint was made as early as 1910—on the basis of the libretto— by the dramatist Hermann Bahr, who told Schoenberg that the Gentleman brought 'an unpleasantly real day-to-day character into the work whose effect through its compression is otherwise that of eternity' (quoted in H. H. Stuckenschmidt, *Schoenberg: His Life, World, and Work*, trans. Humphrey Searle (New York, 1977), 124). Schoenberg's demand in his letter to Emil Hertzka, concerning the proposed film version of *Die glückliche Hand*, that the visualization convey 'the basic unreality of the events . . . The utmost unreality!' (trans. in Hahl-Koch (ed.), *Arnold Schoenberg, Wassily Kandinsky*, 100) is sometimes cited in this connection, but is misleading when taken out of context. Schoenberg is talking not about abstraction but about effects of trick photography ('For instance, in the film, if the goblet suddenly vanishes as if it had never been there, just as if it had simply been forgotten, that is quite different from the way it is on the stage, where it has to be removed by some device').

[90] Auner, 'Schoenberg's Compositional and Aesthetic Transformations', 229.

historical. He piles instance upon instance in which rational explanations can be given for the supposedly intrinsic meanings of colours. For instance, he says, yellow was one of the favourite colours of Greek and Roman civilization; accordingly, early Christianity associated it with paganism, and hence with treachery (Judas Iscariot was painted in yellow garments) and, by association, jealousy.[91] And after a succession of such demonstrations he concludes gleefully: 'These are the "mystic" sources from which the symbolists tried to extract "eternal" colour meanings, and determine the irrevocable influences of colours on the human psyche.'[92] Eventually, however, he turns this argument in a positive direction. He begins by retrenching a little: 'purely physical relations do exist between sound and colour vibrations,' he says, and traditional associations, whatever their origin, 'may serve as an impetus, and an effective one at that, in the construction of the colour-imagery of the drama'.[93] But these relationships can be no more than a starting-point: 'In art it is not the *absolute* relationships that are decisive, but those *arbitrary* relationships within a system of images dictated by the particular work of art. The problem is not, nor ever will be, solved by a fixed catalogue of colour-symbols, but *the emotional intelligibility and function of colour will rise from the natural order of establishing the colour imagery of the work, coincidental with the process of shaping the living movement of the whole work.*'[94] Or, to put it in a word, these associations are contextual: '*we ourselves decide which colours and sounds will best serve the given assignment or emotion as we need them.*'[95]

And of course to say this is to establish an immediate link with what Milton Babbitt has always wanted us to call the 'contextual' nature of Schoenberg's post-tonal but pre-serial style—a style whose underlying principle is that the meaning of any compositional element derives from what, borrowing from Eisenstein, we might call a system of sounds dictated by the particular work of art. (Serialism can be seen as an extension of this principle.) Lessem specifically comments on the importance in *Die glückliche Hand* of 'identifiable motivic contents which, through repetition and variation, acquire referential meanings determined by recurring dramatic contexts'.[96] In the same way, Schoenberg's triadic correspondences of colour, instrumental timbre, and emotional meaning may conform with Kandinsky's pronouncements of their metaphysical nature, but that is not to say that their perceptual effects in *Die glückliche Hand* derive from their immanent qualities, or even from their traditional associations. But neither is it to say that immanent qualities or traditional associations are wholly irrelevant to the signifi-

[91] Eisenstein, *Film Sense*, 102; he is drawing his information from Havelock Ellis.
[92] Ibid. 106.   [93] Ibid. 119, 122.   [94] Ibid. 120.   [95] Ibid. 122.
[96] Lessem, *Music and Text*, 119.

cation established within a given compositional context; they might *motivate* contextual signification, or in Eisenstein's words 'serve as an impetus' for it. The 'Lighting Crescendo', for instance, would surely tend to turn into a 'Lighting Diminuendo' if it went from yellow to black instead of from black to yellow, because of the difference in brightness between the colours, not to mention the traditional associations of black with death and yellow with sunlight and vitality (as well as treachery and jealousy). Eisenstein's point, however, is that the influence of context is in general likely to outweigh immanent qualities or traditional associations; that is why, as he says, a given colour 'not only evades being given a single "value" as an *absolute* image, but can even assume absolutely *contradictory* meanings, *dependent only upon the general system of imagery that has been decided upon for the particular film*'.[97]

But perhaps the most interesting consequence of Eisenstein's critique of synaesthesia in general, and Kandinsky's system of correspondences in particular, has to do with the specific patterns of alignment between media. As we have seen, Skriabin's more or less mechanical association of colour and key in *Prometheus* was based on the assumption that the one medium should be congruent with the other, and Sabaneev's distinction between primary and secondary arts (a distinction which Schoenberg echoes in his Breslau lecture[98]) effectively turned this into a theoretical principle. Any other alignment would simply be a misalignment, a kind of mathematical error.[99] The same applies to Kandinsky's scheme; if compositional alignments of colours and instrumental timbres reflect the metaphysical affinities between them—if colours and timbres derive their meaning from their common source in vibration—then it is hard to see in what context it might make sense to set a particular colour with a timbre that does not belong with it.[100] (The whole idea of the music of the spheres, after all, is based on the idea of harmony, of congruence.) There is, so to speak, no middle ground between a relationship of congruence and no relationship at all. But if 'we ourselves decide which colours and sounds will best serve the

[97] Eisenstein, *Film Sense*, 120–1.

[98] He contrasts the role of less 'complicated' dynamic elements such as the sound of the wind machine with that of 'the higher type of elements', including music and coloured lights (trans. in Hahl-Koch (ed.), *Arnold Schoenberg, Wassily Kandinsky*, 106).

[99] The same principle is inherent in Messiaen's complaint about a ballet which he once saw, in which music in G major was accompanied by violet lighting: 'the colour violet and the key of G major produce an absolutely appalling dissonance!,' he wrote. '[I]t clashed terribly and made me sick in my stomach' (Messiaen, *Music and Color*, 42).

[100] There are a few instances in *Der gelbe Klang* of inverted tensional morphologies (e.g. in Picture 3, 'As the light increases, the music becomes lower and darker . . . When the light is most intense, the music has faded away entirely', in Kandinsky and Marc (eds.), Blaue Reiter *Almanac*, 219); they come mainly in the passages which Kandinsky added in 1912. But Kandinsky does not theorize such morphologies, and consequently such inversions fall outside the framework of his synaesthetically based theory.

given assignment or emotion as we need them', to repeat Eisenstein's words, then the nature of the relationship between different media becomes a perfectly legitimate matter of compositional choice. Eisenstein makes this point over and over again in his book. 'Modern esthetics is built upon the disunion of elements,' he says, quoting from René Guilleré; accordingly, 'Matching of picture and sound . . . may be built upon a combination of unlike elements, without attempting to conceal the resulting dissonance between the aurals and the visuals.'[101] And he adds: 'This occurs frequently.'[102] To say this is not to suggest that the two media should simply go their own way (as, for instance, in John Cage's and Merce Cunningham's collaborations), however; the media may correspond with one another or they may not, Eisenstein says, but 'in either circumstance the relationship must be *compositionally controlled*'.[103]

And again this proves to be a valid way of seeing Schoenberg's score. Admittedly, because of the lack of inherent perceptual salience in the colour–sound–emotion associations, it is hard to know how far instances of non-correspondence between them should be seen as genuine—which is to say, intentional—examples of what might be called the oppositional alignment of media. Lessem points out significant discrepancies between the emotional characteristics Schoenberg appears to associate with some colours (green and violet) and Kandinsky's characterizations of them.[104] But are these really oppositional alignments? Or is it just that Schoenberg decided to characterize these colours differently from Kandinsky? In view of these difficulties of interpretation, it is fortunate that, in the lecture on *Die glückliche Hand* which he gave in Breslau, Schoenberg addressed precisely this issue. He explained how he had purposely incorporated elements of difference within the generally parallel alignment of elements in the 'Lighting Crescendo':

[T]his crescendo is clothed externally in the form of an *increasing pain*. But this clothing is only an outer husk, only a line of demarcation. This can be discerned most clearly in the fact that the light and also the colors, and particularly the music, follow paths that by no means lead so directly upward as those of the wind machine or other dynamic elements. These last are less suited to more complicated developments and therefore remain limited to a straight line, to a direct ascent. . . . The play of light and of colors, however, is not based *only* on intensities, but on values that can only be compared to pitches.[105]

---

[101] Eisenstein, *Film Sense*, 80, 72.
[102] Despite this, as we shall see in Ch. 2, Eisler vehemently attacked Eisenstein for always insisting on congruence between sound and pictures.
[103] Eisenstein, *Film Sense*, 72.
[104] Lessem, *Music and Text*, 102–3; see also p. 223 nn. 111, 114.
[105] Hahl-Koch (ed.), *Arnold Schoenberg, Wassily Kandinsky*, 106.

Elsewhere in the Breslau lecture, Schoenberg described *Die glückliche Hand* as '*making music with the media of the stage*'; this, he explained, meant 'that *gestures, colors* and *light* are treated . . . similarly to the way tones are usually treated—that music is made with them; that figures and shapes, so to speak, are formed from individual light values and shades of color, which resemble the forms, figures and motives of music'.[106] As soon as the combination of music with other media is described in this way, the assumption that there should be congruence between them is revealed as no more than that—an assumption, and thus one option amongst others. In his account of the 'Lighting Crescendo' Schoenberg seems to be describing, if not a 'counterpoint' between the various media (to borrow the standard term used by film critics to describe oppositional scoring), then at least a kind of multimedia heterophony. This is as much as to say that he is ascribing the effect of the 'Crescendo' not only to the evident similarity between its various components, but also to a significant play of difference between them. And this is where he departs crucially from the synaesthetically based models of Kandinsky. In 'On Stage Composition', his preface to the published version of *Der gelbe Klang*, Kandinsky discussed the theoretical possibility that different media 'could run in entirely separate, externally different directions'.[107] But the word 'externally' gives the game away: in terms of inner, spiritual meaning the assumption of congruence remains intact, and the effect of Kandinsky's formulation is to deny significance to the external differences. It is rather like the familiar music-analytical ploy of stripping off the differentiated surface of the music like so much wrapping-paper.

The less *Die glückliche Hand* seems to have to do with synaesthesia, the more it seems like a viable model of multimedia. Synaesthesia is predicated upon low-level relationships; that is why, as I said, the translation of Skriabin's music in *Prometheus* into coloured light is an entirely mechanical process which any analyst could carry out (indeed, a suitably programmed computer could do it). But the same could not be said of *Die glückliche Hand*. As I have explained, Schoenberg and Kandinsky saw colour and sound as related to one another not directly, but through their common association with transcendent spiritual or emotional values. The music in *Die glückliche Hand* does not exhaust the signification of the colours, any more than the colours exhaust the signification of the sound; no mechanical translation from the one to the other is possible. Instead both media, together and in conjunction with

---

[106] Ibid. 105, 106–7 (emphases Schoenberg's). A contemporary critic ('Dr H. H.') described the original production in terms that fit nicely with Schoenberg's formulation: it was, he said, 'as if the musician had burst open his score, conquering new systems for it' (quoted, ibid. 156).

[107] Kandinsky and Marc (eds.), Blaue Reiter *Almanac*, 206.

the other elements of Schoenberg's *Gesamtkunstwerk*, converge upon a cumulative meaning which is emotional and, in the broadest sense, dramatic. Whereas synaesthesia is predicated on similarity, then, multimedia is predicated on difference; what distinguishes Schoenberg from Kandinsky is his explicit awareness of this—though, to be sure, the few remarks in his Breslau lecture fall far short of a theoretical formulation. But, as Eisenstein pointed out in relation to film music, multimedia is not predicated *just* on difference, and that is why the kind of correspondence that I have described as quasi-synaesthetic constitutes a necessary, though not a sufficient, condition for the emergence of perceived interactions between media. In the next chapter, then, I shall follow Eisenstein's lead and focus on the specific relationship between similarity and difference that forms the basis of multimedia.

2

Multimedia as Metaphor

Eisler's Error

As we saw in Chapter 1, Eisenstein rejected synaesthetic correspondences as a viable basis for the relationship between music and moving pictures, and emphasized instead the need to forge associations between the two media within the context of the individual film. But how is this to be done? Eisenstein's model of music–picture relationships turns out to be less different from Kandinsky's than the acerbic nature of his critique of the painter might suggest. Like Kandinsky's, his basic model of cross-media relationships seems to be triadic: picture and music are related not directly, but by virtue of something that they both embody. And at first sight this something is not very different from the 'inner sound' which, for Kandinsky, unified sound and colour; indeed, there is one place in *The Film Sense* where Eisenstein actually talks about 'the unified "inner sounding" ' of a sequence in his film 'Alexander Nevsky'.[1] Similar terms are scattered throughout the book, and sometimes they suggest what might be dubbed the occult nature of music–sound relationships: Eisenstein speaks at one point of 'a "hidden" inner synchronization', and at another of the ' "secret" of those sequential *vertical correspondences* which, step by step, relate the music to the shots *through an identical motion* that lies at the base of the musical as well as the pictorial movement'.[2] The consistent, and otherwise unmotivated, use of inverted commas in these quotations—'inner sounding', 'hidden', 'secret'— perhaps signals a tension in Eisenstein's thinking; it is as if he wants to have it both ways, harping on the occult nature of music–sound relationships but not committing himself to it. It is hardly surprising, then, that Eisler accused Eisenstein of obscurantism. His manner of thinking, Eisler complained, is 'both too narrow and too vague'; worse still, it is 'formalistic'.[3]

Eisenstein did, however, make it quite clear what he meant by the 'identical motion' linking pictures and music; he even provided a

---

[1] Eisenstein, *Film Sense*, 125.

[2] Ibid. 70, 136; the second quotation relates to his concept of 'vertical montage', which I discuss below (pp. 84–5). Examples of other similar terms include 'inner process' (p. 37); 'inner synchronization' (p. 70); 'inner unity' (p. 71); 'inner harmony' and 'inner tonality' (both p. 92).

[3] Hanns Eisler [and T. W. Adorno], *Composing for the Films* (New York, 1973 [1947]), 67. I shall return to the question of whether it is Eisler's or Adorno's voice that we hear in such passages.

diagram of it.[4] Figure 2.1 shows part of the notorious analysis of twelve shots from 'Alexander Nevsky' on which the final chapter of *The Film Sense* centres, and the bottom line of the analysis, labelled 'Diagram of Movement', represents the common element between the pictures and Prokofiev's music—what at one point in the chapter (and this is perhaps the most descriptive of Eisenstein's many terms) is referred to as the 'inner movement' of the film.[5] The way in which this 'inner movement' relates to pictures and music may most easily be seen in relation to the last three shots in Figure 2.1. In shot III there is a cloud that curves upwards towards the right hand of the frame (the second bottom line, labelled 'Diagram of Pictorial Composition', clarifies the relevant features of the shots), and this corresponds to the rising tremolando arpeggiation in the middle of the musical texture; in this way the rising curve of the 'Diagram of Movement' equally represents the motion of the picture and the music. In shot IV, by contrast, there is an absence of 'inner movement'; the flat horizon corresponds to the repeated D♯s of Prokofiev's score. Shot V should be more or less self-explanatory.

I called Eisenstein's analysis 'notorious', for it has certainly stirred up a hornet's nest of controversy among critics.[6] As might be expected, the controversy has focused on Eisenstein's strange parallel between the left-to-right motion of the music and a left-to-right reading of the individual frames; we only call the cloud in Shot III 'rising', after all, because we are reading it from left to right. Eisler claims that the fallacy lies in the use of musical notation; what the analysis proves in reality, he says, is that 'there is a similarity between the *notation* of the music and the [picture] sequence. . . . The similarity between the music and the picture is indeed indirect, suggested by the graphic fixation of the music; it cannot be perceived directly, and for that reason cannot fulfil a dramatic function.'[7] But this objection misses the mark; music is experienced through time, and a rising arpeggio is indeed perceived as 'rising', so to that extent the left-to-right notational representation is

---

[4] Unnumbered folding leaf at the end of *Film Sense*. Fig. 2.1 represents just under half of Eisenstein's entire diagram—five out of the twelve shots, to be precise.

[5] Eisenstein, *Film Sense*, 126.

[6] Among them Eisler, *Composing for Films*, 152–7; Widgery, 'Kinetic and Temporal Interaction', 42–57; Royal S. Brown, *Overtones and Undertones: Reading Film Music* (Berkeley, 1994), 134–8; and Roy M. Prendergast, *Film Music, A Neglected Art: A Critical Study of Music in Films*, 2nd edn. (New York, 1992), 223–6.

[7] Eisler, *Composing for Films*, 153. Prendergast concurs ('what the graph proves is that there is a similarity between the *notation* of the music and the picture sequence', *Film Music*, 225), and so does Widgery, whose analysis is otherwise much more accurate in locating the problem: 'Evoking the visual representation of the standard Western musical score as bearing any relation to the composition of a frame of film other than one of graphic convenience is insupportable' ('Kinetic and Temporal Interaction', 47).

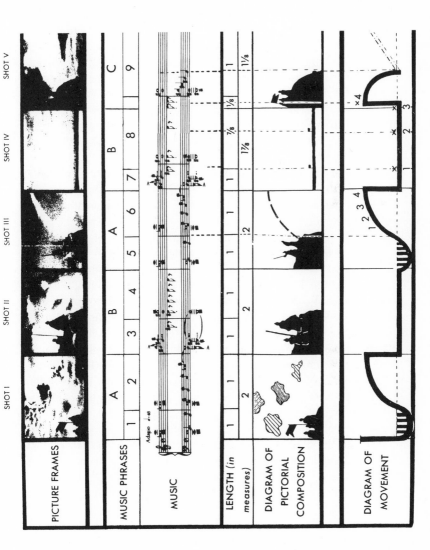

Fig. 2.1 Eisenstein's analysis of a sequence from 'Alexander Nevsky'. Illustration from *The Film Sense* by Sergei Eisenstein, © 1942 by Harcourt Brace & Co., and renewed 1969 by Jay Leyda, reprinted by permission of the publisher.

perfectly true to experience. The problem lies rather in the association of this diachronic motion with the reading of the individual picture frame. There is certainly a difficulty concerning 'graphic fixation' in Eisenstein's analysis, but it has to do with the way in which the sequence of pictures is represented, as a strip that goes from left (before) to right (after); it is this, if anything, that gives plausibility to the idea that we can also read the individual frames in the same manner—an idea that becomes particularly counter-intuitive when it results in a falling 'inner movement' marking the transition from the right of one frame to the left of the next (as in Shots III and IV). Faced with so apparently bizarre an approach, critics have generally been able to do little more than express their astonishment at the great director's failure to grasp elementary perceptual principles; for Claudia Widgery it amounts simply to 'faulty . . . observation'.[8]

Puzzling as Eisenstein's analysis may be, it is possible to see in Widgery's judgement an element of what Royal Brown has referred to as the 'overlay of the Hollywood mentality onto Eisenstein/Prokofiev'.[9] For one thing, Eisenstein makes it clear in *The Film Sense* that he thinks of pictorial composition very much along the lines of the classical painterly tradition, one of the aims of which was to guide the viewer's eye along predetermined routes. 'The art of plastic composition', he says, 'consists in leading the spectator's attention through the exact path and with the exact sequence prescribed by the author of the composition.'[10] Seen this way, the visual composition of a shot (and this is particularly likely to be the case in a sequence of stills) inevitably involves relations of before and after, and if this idea seems unfamiliar today, it is perhaps merely a measure of the extent to which film theory has subordinated principles of visual composition to issues of narrativity. The main point, however, is that Eisenstein goes out of his way to stress that not all film can be analysed on the exact model of this particular sequence. Each of the twelve shots in it is specifically composed in such a manner as to lead the eye from left to right, he explains (the only exception is Shot IX, which is experienced as a deviation from this norm), and he adds: 'This peculiarity permitted the arrangement of our diagram in the way you see it.'[11] He is not claiming, then, that

[8] Widgery, 'Kinetic and Temporal Interaction', 52. An exception is Royal Brown, who comments promisingly that 'What Eisenstein's critics fail to perceive here, I feel, are the nonliteral implications of this director/theoretician's enthusiastically literal analysis' (*Overtones and Undertones*, 137). But Brown's explanation of what Eisenstein meant ('during the time it takes that fourth shot from the "Alexander Nevsky" sequence to go by, the eye perceives a particular graphic rhythm that *corresponds* to a particular musical rhythm in Prokofiev's score') is no clearer than the original (what is a 'graphic rhythm' unless it can be expressed as a specific mapping of line against time?), and depends on the very concept of synaesthetic correspondence that Eisenstein was at pains to refute.

[9] Brown, *Overtones and Undertones*, 138. [10] Eisenstein, *Film Sense*, 148.

[11] Ibid. 154.

there is a general principle that we read pictures from left to right, any more than there are universal synaesthetic correspondences; once again, it is a matter of the individual context—a matter of composition rather than psychology. It is true, of course, that there has been a tendency for critics to impute an unwarranted generality to this analysis owing to its prominent position in one of the classic texts of the cinema; but it is hardly fair to censure Eisenstein for having chosen an atypical example in the interests of overcoming the perennial problem of representing a dynamic visual and aural experience on the printed page.

I would suggest that the relatively superficial oddity of Eisenstein's equation of left-to-right movements in music and film has had the effect of diverting attention from far more fundamental problems inherent in Eisenstein's way of conceiving music–picture relations, problems which are equally evident in Eisler's approach. As I said, for Eisenstein the link between music and picture lies in the 'inner movement' which they both embody, which is represented at the bottom of Figure 2.1. Now this is not just a graph of motion, but a graph of emotion; it represents the ' "seismographical" curve of a certain process and rhythm of *uneasy expectation*', a '*generalized graph* of the sequence's emotional content'.[12] Eisler, predictably, is uncomfortable with such loose talk about emotions and moods ('It is hardly an exaggeration', he pronounces primly, 'to state that the concept of mood is altogether unsuitable to the motion picture as well as to advanced music'[13]). He also offers a more objective alternative to Eisenstein's obscurantist concept of 'inner movement': 'The concrete factor of unity of music and pictures', he says, 'consists in the gestural element.' It is not obvious, however, that the difference between 'gesture' and 'inner movement' is very much more than rhetorical; Eisenstein, after all, introduced his concept of 'inner movement' by referring to 'the ability of each of us . . . to "depict" with the movement of our hands that movement sensed by us in some nuance of music'.[14] And Eisler sets out what is in effect Eisenstein's triadic model of music–picture relationships with exemplary clarity: '[T]he unity of the two media is achieved indirectly; it does not consist in the identity between any elements, be it that between tone and color or that of the "rhythms" as a whole. The meaning or function of the elements is intermediary; they never coincide *per se*.'[15] Faced with this kind of concurrence, one might reasonably wonder what it is about Eisenstein's theory or practice that Eisler was so opposed to.

The central issue in Eisler's critique is how far the relationship between picture and music should be, to use Eisler's terms, one of

[12] Ibid. 165, 166. [13] Eisler, *Composing for Films*, 69.
[14] Eisenstein, *Film Sense*, 130. [15] Eisler, *Composing for Films*, 70.

similarity or one of contrast—what writers on film today generally refer to as parallelism as against counterpoint.[16] As we saw in Chapter 1, in *The Film Sense* Eisenstein repeatedly refers to the possibility of counterpoint between picture and music; yet Eisler's principal objection to the 'Alexander Nevsky' sequence, and to the practice of film music in general, is its relentless pursuit of parallelism: 'Why should the same thing be reproduced by two different media?,' he asks.[17] He even attacks Eisenstein's attacks on parallelism. One of Eisenstein's attacks is directed at the coupling of the Barcarolle from Offenbach's *Tales of Hoffmann* with the image of 'a pair of lovers embracing against a background of Venetian scenery'.[18] Such a '*narrowly representational comprehension of music*', says Eisenstein with his habitual emphases, leads inevitably to 'visualizations of a most platitudinous character'.[19] And he continues:

But take from these Venetian 'scenes' only the *approaching and receding* movements of the water combined with the reflected *scampering and retreating play of light* over the surface of the canals, and you immediately remove yourself, by at least one degree, from the series of 'illustration' fragments, and you are closer to finding a response to the *sensed inner movement* of a barcarolle.

Eisler's response is, in effect, that one degree isn't enough. 'Such a procedure does not transcend the faulty principle of relating picture and music either by pseudo-identity or by association,' he grumbles; 'it merely transfers the principle to a more abstract level, on which its crudeness and redundant character are less obvious.'[20] What Eisler clearly wants to assert is a contrary principle—a principle based on what he calls 'the insurmountable heterogeneity of these media'.[21] His problem, as I see it, is that he lacks the conceptual framework necessary for the articulation of such a principle.

Eisenstein defends counterpoint in the abstract; but the closer he comes to concrete analysis, the more his vocabulary becomes one of similarity and even identity. I have already quoted his reference to the '*identical motion* that lies at the base of the musical as well as the pictorial movement', and his analysis of the sequence from 'Alexander Nevsky' revolves entirely around the demonstration of such cross-media isomorphism. In his commentary Eisler, confusingly, becomes

---

[16] For an outline history of these terms, with references, see Widgery, 'Kinetic and Temporal Interaction', 23; see also the classic 'Statement on the Sound-Film by Eisenstein, Pudovkin, and Alexandrov' included as Appendix A of Sergei Eisenstein, *Film Form: Essays in Film Theory*, trans. Jay Leyda (London, 1951), which demanded among other things 'an ORCHESTRAL COUNTERPOINT of visual and aural images' (p. 258).

[17] Eisler, *Composing for Films*, 66.

[18] Ibid. Eisler describes this as a scene from an actual film; Eisenstein, however, appears to be referring only to an association mentioned in Piotr Pavlenko's novel *Red Planes Fly East* (Eisenstein, *Film Sense*, 125–6).

[19] Eisenstein, *Film Sense*, 126.   [20] Eisler, *Composing for Films*, 67.   [21] Ibid. 74.

more royalist than the King, and criticizes Eisenstein for being insufficiently true to his own principles: 'If static picture details are to be so pedantically translated into music,' says Eisler, 'the pedantry should at least be consistent, not practiced one moment and forgotten the next.'[22] He complains, for instance, that Prokofiev's score repeats itself when the pictures do not; he complains that the music does not 'distinguish between panoramic views and close-ups'—as did his own score for 'Rain', he adds.[23] The reference is to one of a series of experimental sound-tracks that Eisler composed between 1940 and 1942, under the auspices of a project funded by the Rockefeller Foundation; the aim was to explore the use of new musical resources in the cinema. A number of commercial studios and independent producers provided film material for the purpose, and in the Appendix to *Composing for the Films* Eisler includes an account of the sound-tracks that were produced and the conclusions to be drawn from them. The most elaborate of these sound-tracks, he says, was the one he composed for Joris Ivens's 1929 film 'Rain', and he provides the score of one complete section of it, together with a synopsis of the film and a detailed commentary. As Eisler explains, the music is dodecaphonic and scored for the same instrumental combination as *Pierrot Lunaire*; indeed, he dedicated it to Schoenberg when it was issued as an independent composition (*Fourteen Ways of Describing Rain*, Op. 70).

The fundamental task of the film composer, says Eisler, is 'to compose music that "fits" precisely into the given picture; intrinsic unrelatedness is here the cardinal sin'.[24] By 'fits' Eisler means precise temporal synchronization; one of his main complaints about the 'Alexander Nevsky' sequence is that Prokofiev's music does not fit well enough in this sense. Eisler, by contrast, seems to have proceeded in a manner more closely related to the classical Hollywood approach when scoring 'Rain', first determining the 'hits'—the points that require synchronization between picture and music—and then using the resultant hit list as the basis of the music's formal structure.[25] Within this temporal framework, there are a number of parallelisms between picture and music. The first, as mentioned in the previous paragraph, is the distinction between panoramic views and close-ups; the piano theme in bars 3–4 of Eisler's score is consistently associated with close-ups of the

---

[22] Ibid. 155.   [23] Ibid. 154.   [24] Ibid. 70.

[25] '[T]he details of the classical sonata technique, especially those pertaining to the utmost motif economy and permanent variation, are retained, while the traditional architecture is replaced with the form of the picture' (ibid. 152–3); elsewhere Eisler refers to 'building complete form structures according to the specific requirements of the given film sequence, and then "filling-in"' (p. 96). This model of the formal process is reminiscent of the idea, disseminated by Schoenberg himself, that many of his atonal works borrowed their formal structures from their texts (the difference, in the case of 'Rain', being that the music is dodecaphonic instead of freely atonal).

effects of the wind. Again, an image of leaves floating in a pond coincides with a new musical figure at bar 57. '[A]ccordingly', says Eisler, when the image reappears the same musical figure comes back (bar 73). Then there are what might be termed conventionally iconic links. In bar 45, for instance, 'a violin figure, with trills almost like a faint noise, reproduces the wind,' while 'the shaking of the boughs is translated into an incidental piano phrase'; a few bars later, 'The complex rhythm of the accompanying piano and cello reproduces the syncopated, gust-like rhythm of the picture.'[26] And finally there are what might be termed iconicities of process; the first drops of rain, at bar 63, are given a 'drastically simple reproduction by means of coupled piano seconds', and the musical texture thickens into a tremolando as the rain turns into a steady downpour (from bar 81 to the end).

The difficulty is not so much in understanding the principles behind Eisler's scoring, but in understanding how they are meant to conform to the principles set out in his text. The correlation between the music and the panorama–close-up distinction works just as he described it in his commentary on 'Alexander Nevsky'; the problem, of course, is that this was a *negative* commentary, outlining and condemning the pedantic translation of picture into music. Eisler's practice both here and in the musical 'reproduction' of wind and rain is open to his own question: why should the same thing be reproduced by two different media? And how can it possibly be maintained that '[T]he meaning or function of the elements is intermediary; they never coincide *per se*', when the linkage of sound and picture is so unremittingly descriptive? What, indeed, are we to make of the fact that Eisler has chosen for the primary analytical demonstration of his approach to film scoring—his equivalent, as it were, of Eisenstein's sequence from 'Alexander Nevsky'—a film that so assiduously avoids issues of meaning or narrative content, thus lending itself unproblematically to the superficially descriptive scoring characteristic of nature and wildlife films?[27] Such questions only serve to underline the one that Claudia Gorbman pointedly asks in her well-known book on film music: 'what could Eisler have done in scoring *Mildred Pierce*?'[28]

It is always possible to explain away the inconsistencies of *Composing for the Films* on the basis of its problematic joint authorship.[29] Although the book was originally published under Eisler's name alone, in an English translation, a postscript added by Adorno to the 1969 German

[26] Eisler, *Composing for Films*, 149, 150.
[27] For a brief but illuminating comparison of the characteristics of scoring in nature and narrative films, see Widgery, 'Kinetic and Temporal Interaction', 386.
[28] Gorbman, *Unheard Melodies*, 109.
[29] See Martin Marks, 'Film Music: The Material, Literature, and Present State of Research', *MLA Notes*, 36 (Dec. 1979), 282–325: 321.

language edition (and translated in the 1971 reprint of the original English language edition) explains that this was because Adorno had withdrawn his name from the book for personal and political reasons. When a German language edition was published under Eisler's supervision in 1949, Adorno continues, Eisler made a large number of changes, all of them for the worse; most of these were blatantly political, but 'He even toned down strictly musical details, such as a critical comment on Prokoffief's Alexander Newsky score'.[30] If, as this suggests, the critique of 'Alexander Nevsky' in the original edition reflected Adorno's views more than it did Eisler's, then who knows if the same may not be true of the general aesthetic principles laid down in chapter 5? How much of the book can we in fact rely on as an undiluted expression of Eisler's views, other than (presumably) the account of his own sound-track for 'Rain'?

But the issue of the joint Eisler/Adorno authorial persona may be beside the point if, as I have suggested, the fundamental problem in *Composing for the Films* is a conceptual one. Like Eisenstein—like Kandinsky—Eisler has only one fundamental model for the relationship between different media, and it is identity. 'True unity presupposes spiritual subjectivity', says Eisler (he is quoting Hegel),[31] and the source of such unity lies in the spiritual (Kandinsky), emotional (Eisenstein), or gestural (Eisler) quality that is embodied in each medium. This is not to say that the parallelism of sounds and images which embody these qualities represents the only possible manner in which different media may be combined; if the picture gestures up, so to speak, the music can always gesture down. The point, however, is that this does not represent an alternative *principle*; seen this way, oppositional scoring, as its designation implies, represents merely the opposite of parallelism. It is the inversion of a principle, a parasitic concept, and its practice represents no more than the exception that proves the rule. Both Eisenstein and Eisler, then, assert the principle of counterpoint, but fail to theorize it; they reject the principle of synaesthesia, but cannot escape its language.[32] Both Eisenstein and Eisler, in short, end up going round in circles because they are trying to use a language predicated on similarity in order to articulate a principle predicated on difference.

---

[30] Eisler, *Composing for Films*, 168.   [31] Ibid. 65.

[32] Eisler in effect reduces Eisenstein's chapter on synaesthesia to two sentences when he condemns 'the foundation of sects which dwell . . . on the affinity between certain colours and sounds and which mistake their obsessions for *avant-garde* ideas. Arbitrarily established rules for playing with the kaleidoscope are not criteria of art' (ibid. 64–5).

The Metaphor Model

Bernard Hermann, Hitchcock's collaborator, managed to reduce the basic principles of the classical Hollywood film score to just five sentences:

I feel that music on the screen can seek out and intensify the inner thoughts of the characters. It can invest a scene with terror, grandeur, gaiety, or misery. It can propel narrative swiftly forward, or slow it down. It often lifts mere dialogue into the realm of poetry. Finally, it is the communicating link between the screen and the audience, reaching out and enveloping all into one single experience.[33]

I would like to draw attention to two features of the initial sentence in this quotation. There is, first, the linguistic link between the 'inner thoughts' that the music seeks out and intensifies and the 'inner movement' or 'inner process' on which Eisenstein's thinking is based; the difference, of course, is that in Eisenstein's case the 'inner' refers to an intrinsic (and in some way 'hidden' or 'secret') property of the film itself, whereas in Hermann it refers to something extrinsic and, in a sense, more straightforward—the characters that the film constructs. And second, there is the striking image of the music 'seeking out' these thoughts, searching as it were through the visual image in order to uncover its potential for signification, penetrating through the visible to the meaning that is embedded within it. The films that Hermann scored are full of just this kind of music–picture interaction.

A good example, because everyone can remember it, is the sequence from 'Psycho' where Marion is driving through the rainstorm—the sequence that ends as the lights of Bates Motel appear through the rain and Marion comes slowly to a stop. Hermann's angular, repetitive music does not connect in a literal manner with anything that is visible on the screen; it does not obviously synchronize, for instance, with the regular rhythm of the wiper blades, or the irregular rhythms outlined by the lights of the oncoming cars. And whereas its busy quality, its high level of activity, could be seen as corresponding to the speed of the car and the rain, the music continues at its own pace as the car slows down and stops.[34] Rather than corresponding to anything that is visible, the music jumps the diegetic gap, so to speak, 'seeking out' and uncovering the turmoil in Marion's mind, and thus transferring its own qualities to her. Its angular contours embody her unease; the repetitions and the constricted quality of the orchestration create an obsessive quality, rather like when you go over the same thing again and again in your mind. The process works the other way round, too;

---

[33] From Tony Thomas, *Film Score: The View from the Podium* (South Brunswick, NJ, 1979), 143; quoted in William Penn, 'Music and Images: A Pedagogical Approach', *Indiana Theory Review*, 11 (1990), 47–63: 47.

[34] Unlike the music in the Volvo commercial described in the Introduction to Part I.

heard in the context of the film sequence, the music acquires a specifically sinister quality that it does not have by itself. And the result of
these reciprocal interactions is to create a bond of empathy between
audience and film character—the 'communicating link' to which
Hermann referred.

This account of the familiar working of music in the narrative cinema illustrates the principle of difference that is lacking in the
Eisenstein/Eisler model of film music. The music is not simply more or
less similar to the pictures, in the static manner of Eisensteinian correspondence. Instead, the relationship between music and pictures has a
dynamic, processive character, passing from difference at one level to
similarity at another; by virtue of jumping the diegetic gap, as I put it,
the music signifies in a manner that is qualitatively different from the
pictures, and the issue of parallelism or counterpoint accordingly takes
on a quite different aspect. Now it is not my intention to argue that any
adequate model of cross-media interaction must be predicated on the
notion of cinematic diegesis. (That would contradict one of the aims of
this book, which is to counteract the dominance of approaches derived
from film theory in the analysis of musical multimedia in general.) But
the interaction exemplified in the narrative cinema is a convenient
illustration of what needs to be captured in a more generalized model
of multimedia; what we need to do is to reduce this interaction to its
essentials. And that is essentially what was attempted by Sandra
Marshall and Annabel Cohen in an unusual contribution to the sparse
experimental literature on the perception of multimedia.[35] Their experiment was based on a two-minute abstract animation which dates back
to the 1940s and which, as the authors explain,

elicits a predictable interpretation by almost all viewers. In the film, three figures, a large triangle, a small triangle, and a small circle, move in and about a
rectangular enclosure that opens and closes via a hinged line segment. The relations among the moving shapes elicit specific attributions of personality (e.g.,
the large triangle is typically referred to as being aggressive).[36]

[35] Sandra K. Marshall and Annabel J. Cohen, 'Effects of Musical Soundtracks on Attitudes toward
Animated Geometric Figures', *Music Perception*, 6 (1988), 95–112. Further related experiments are
reported in Annabel J. Cohen, 'Association and Musical Soundtrack Phenomena', *Contemporary
Music Review*, 9 (1993), 163–78, and in Valerie J. Bolivar, Annabel J. Cohen, and John C. Fentress,
'Semantic and Formal Congruency in Music and Motion Pictures: Effects on the Interpretation of
Visual Action', *Psychomusicology* 13 (1994), 28–59. This special issue of *Psycomusicology*, which was
guest edited by Cohen (and which, in fact, appeared in 1996, when the present book was in press)
provides a representative selection of current empirical approaches to the perception of multimedia.
See also Carol L. Krumhansl and Diane Lynn Schenck, 'Can Dance Reflect the Structural and
Expressive Qualities of Music? A Perceptual Experiment on Balanchine's Choreography of Mozart's
Divertimento No. 15', *Musicae Scientiae*, 1/1 (1997), 63–85.

[36] Marshall and Cohen, 'Effects of Musicial Soundtracks', 96. The film was developed by F. Heider
and M. Simmel, 'An Experimental Study of Apparent Behavior', *American Journal of Psychology*, 57
(1944), 243–59.

Marshall and Cohen's strategy, then, was to compare how viewers evaluated each of the three 'characters' when they saw the film under two different circumstances: with and without music. They also compared the effect of two different (and, it has to be said, rather basic) musical accompaniments, composed by one of the authors. Finally, they tested viewers' responses to the music when heard by itself and to the music when heard together with the film, in each case using the semantic differential technique.[37]

There is no need to summarize Marshall and Cohen's article in detail; much of it contributes to the reassuring conclusion that music does indeed affect how we experience film—and, as we saw in 'Psycho' (but as is rarely mentioned in the film music literature), vice versa. The general tendency was what common sense might suggest: ratings for different media converge when the media are combined, and 'a soundtrack with a higher level on one dimension will lead to a high level of this dimension in some other aspect of the film'.[38] All this might suggest that when media are combined, the result is a simple mixture of responses, an averaging out of the various individual properties contributed by each medium. But Marshall and Cohen made various discoveries that do not fit such an interpretation. One concerns the evaluative dimension: the music that received the higher evaluative rating by itself received the lower evaluation when heard with the film. The obvious conclusion to be drawn from this is that when the music is evaluated in the context of the film, one of the relevant criteria is goodness of fit with the pictures; this is clearly an emergent property, not one that could be predicted from the evaluation of the music and the film by themselves. The second such finding is that on the activity dimension, the music affected the various film 'characters' in contrary ways; the music that resulted in higher activity ratings for the large triangle and circle resulted in a lower activity rating for the small triangle, and vice versa.[39] It seems, to borrow Hermann's words again, as if the music sought out and intensified different characteristics of each of the geometric protagonists. Or, to put it another way, there was a different fit between the music and each of the film characters. Again, then, we are dealing with an emergent property—an attribution that is

[37] The semantic differential technique aims to obtain reliable data regarding the affective properties of a stimulus by asking for a number of individual judgements which are then mapped on to three dimensions of variance: evaluation, potency, and activity. (In Marshall and Cohen's experiment the evaluative dimension, for instance, was based on the judgements nice/awful, good/bad, beautiful/ugly, and pleasant/unpleasant.) Between them, these three dimensions are believed to capture the most important attributes of affective response (Charles E. Osgood, George J. Suci, and Percy H. Tannenbaum, *The Measurement of Meaning* (Urbana, Ill., 1957)).

[38] Marshall and Cohen, 'Effects of Musical Soundtracks', 108.

[39] This finding was consistent with a separate preliminary experiment, and was also replicated in a follow-up to the main experiment.

negotiated, so to speak, between the two interacting media in light of the individual context. And such effects cannot be subsumed within a model based on the simple mixing or averaging of the properties of each individual medium.

Marshall and Cohen accordingly put forward a model for the inter-action of music and film in their experiments that is based on the concept of ascription (Fig. 2.2).[40] They explain this diagram by saying that 'if music through structural similarity directs attention to feature "a" of the film and provides information about connotation "x", then connotation "x" may become associated with feature "a" '. Elsewhere they remark that 'Associations of the music (x) are *ascribed* to (a)'.[41] Another way of expressing this is that if the respective attributes of the two media intersect (as indicated by the shaded segment in Fig. 2.2), then some or all of the remaining attributes of the one become available as attributes of the other. And in talking about 'availability' in this context, I am echoing Marks's account of metaphor, the 'secret' of which, he says, 'lies in the fact that once an analogy is made between A and B, a whole gamut of associated meanings also becomes available. Not only is B like A in a certain way, but any and all of A's properties now

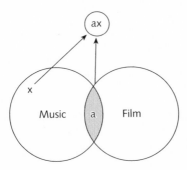

Fig. 2.2

© 1988 by the Regents of the University of California. Reprinted from *Music Perception*, Vol. 6 (1988), 109, Fig. 8b, by permission

[40] Marshall and Cohen, 'Effects of Musical Soundtracks', 109, fig. 8(b); ©1988 by the Regents of the University of California and reprinted from *Music Perception*, Vol. 6, by permission. For a critique of Marshall and Cohen's 'Congruence-Associationist' model see George Sirius and Eric F. Clarke, 'The Perception of Audiovisual Relationships: a Preliminary Study', *Psychomusicology* 13 (1994), 119–32. The issue of interaction (as opposed to simple additive relationships) between sound and image remains controversial in the experimental literature; Sirius and Clarke's experiment (which was based on Marshall and Cohen's) is typical both in failing to find clear evidence of interaction, and in seeking to explain this in terms of the inadequacy of the stimulus materials employed.

[41] Ibid. 110, 109; emphases added.

become fair game to be absorbed into B.'[42] Seen in this light, Figure 2.2 can be considered a structural representation of metaphor; and what I propose in this chapter is that metaphor may be seen as a viable model of cross-media interaction in general. I shall indicate what this proposal amounts to by outlining some of the characteristics of metaphor in its root sense—as a linguistic device—before entering into more detail as regards what it might entail when applied to multimedia.

The pre-condition of metaphor—and, if I am right, of cross-media interaction—is what I shall call an *enabling similarity*. One of the metaphors that George Lakoff and Mark Johnson discuss in their book on the subject is LOVE IS WAR. The metaphor is a viable one—it makes sense—because love and war have attributes in common: both involve two (or more) parties, and both may feature conquest, planning, strategic retreats, and so forth. (LOVE IS A POT OF NOODLES is just about viable as a metaphor, since love could be said to provide emotional sustenance— it is possible to imagine a pot noodle commercial based on this idea— but the intersection is more limited. LOVE IS A GECKO is ridiculous because there is no readily perceptible intersection between the two terms.) The meaning of the metaphor, however, does not lie in the enabling similarity; it lies in what the similarity enables, which is to say, the *transfer of attributes* from one term of the metaphor to the other. In the case of LOVE IS WAR, for instance, the transference goes like this:[43]

LOVE IS WAR
War is $\{x, y, z\}$

Therefore, LOVE IS $\{x, y, z\}$

where $\{x, y, z\}$ can refer to any or all of the attributes of war. And the meaning of this transference lies precisely in the potential for change in the perception of love that results from imposing the attributive grid of war upon it. In other words, as Lakoff and Johnson say, 'the metaphor gives love a new meaning'.[44] Rather than simply representing or repro-

---

[42] Marks, *Unity of the Senses*, 252–3. In *Metaphors We Live By* (Chicago, 1980), George Lakoff and Mark Johnson offer an even more basic definition of metaphor that is appropriate to the present context: 'The essence of metaphor is understanding and experiencing one kind of thing in terms of another' (p. 5). The path I am traversing in this and the previous chapter—essentially, from synaesthesia to metaphor—is broadly parallel to that taken in both Marks's book and Lakoff and Johnson's; in each case there is a progression from relatively literal to increasingly creative associations of ideas.

[43] The notation is adapted from Lakoff and Johnson, *Metaphors We Live By*, who term this a metaphorical entailment. Lakoff's and Johnson's approach has been further refined and extended by Mark Turner and Gilles Fauconnier, among others; for recent overviews of what is often referred to as 'conceptual blending' see Turner, *The Literary Mind* (New York, 1996) and Turner and Fauconnier, 'Conceptual Integration and Formal Expression', *Journal of Metaphor and Symbolic Activity* 10 (1995), 183–203. Music theorists who have availed themselves of these ideas include Lawrence Zbikowski (to whom I owe this reference) and Janna Saslaw.

[44] Ibid. 142 (with reference to the more complex metaphor LOVE IS A COLLABORATIVE WORK OF ART).

ducing an existing meaning, it participates in the creation of a new one. (It does not simply make sense but *makes* sense, so to speak.) It was in order to convey precisely this that I described the meaning resulting from the interaction of music and picture in Marshall and Cohen's experiment as emergent; one could say the same about the interaction of music and moving pictures in 'Psycho', or indeed about any cross-media interaction. Understood in this way, emergence is a defining attribute of multimedia.

At one level it is easy to see how this metaphor model might be applied to multimedia. A convenient way of illustrating this is through something which, if not multimedia, is next door to it: the record sleeve, which couples sound with image, and which (like the music video) occupies an unstable middle ground between marketing and aesthetic experience.[45] Chandos, for instance, have coupled Tchaikovsky's Second Symphony, recorded for the first time in its original version, with a painting by the nineteenth-century artist S. A. Mokin entitled 'Stepan Razin's Appeal' (Fig. 2.3).[46] The coupling has what might be called an immediate factual justification: both painting and symphony are products of nineteenth-century Russia. And both painting and symphony evoke national sentiment: Mokin contributes to the construction of a national history through the representation of a distant event of heroism,[47] while Tchaikovsky inserts Russian folk-song into the flagship genre of Western art music (and the soubriquet 'Little Russian' makes the nationalist connotation explicit). But the linkage goes deeper. The calligraphic detail of Mokin's painting consists of a multitude of small gestures, and evokes folk art, or maybe the Persian miniature tradition; so does the border. There is, in this way, a conscious attempt to get away from the large, perspectively organized composition of the Western fine art tradition. At the same time, however, the figures in the foreground are modelled three-dimensionally, and the heroic pose of Stepan Razin, with sabre uplifted, is more than a little reminiscent of David's celebrated (and highly idealized) painting of Napoleon crossing the Alps. The result is a rather self-conscious and slightly awkward combination of the characteristics of Russian folk art and Western fine art, the underlying purpose of which is the construction of a distinctively Russian cultural identity. And all this transfers readily to Tchaikovsky's 'Little Russian' Symphony, which attempts to build a large symphonic structure out of the brief, repetitive units of Russian

---

[45] I have discussed the phenomenon of the classical record sleeve in more depth in 'Domestic *Gesamtkunstwerk*', from which the following examples are drawn. Figs. 2.3–5 are taken from the collection of the Department of Music, University of Southampton; hence the library plates and insiglia.

[46] Chandos ABRD 1071.

[47] Stepan (Stenka) Razin was the leader of a Cossack uprising in the late 1660s, which commanded widespread popular support and admiration, though it ultimately came to nothing.

Fig. 2.3 Sleeve of Chandos ABRD 1071, incorporating 'Stepan Razin's Appeal' (S. A. Mokin)

folk-song. The painting and the symphony carry out the same kind of cultural work.

Given that sound and image are not literally experienced together, it might be better to speak of analogy here than metaphor. But the structure is the same; there are self-evident enabling similarities between the painting and the symphony, in particular the unities of time and place. There are also attributes which are relatively obvious in the painting—they can be seen almost at a glance—and which transfer meaningfully to the symphony: the construction from small, repetitive units and the uneasy fit between these and the Western models of composition whose influence is nevertheless evident, together with the cultural work that is being accomplished. In this way, the juxtaposition of image and music spells out the following metaphorical syllogism (in which I replace the IS of the verbal metaphor with the sign ↔, meaning 'is equivalent to'):

MUSIC ↔ PAINTING

PAINTING ↔ {made up of repetitive units, rejects Western tradition, constructs national identity, etc.}

Therefore, MUSIC ↔ {made up of repetitive units, rejects Western tradition, constructs national identity, etc.}

Of course it might be argued that the juxtaposition is meaningful only because the music already has these attributes, so there is similarity, but not transference. There are two answers to this. One is that the very fact of juxtaposing image and music has the effect of drawing attention to the properties that they share, and in this way constructing a new experience of each; the interpretation is in this sense emergent. The other, perhaps better, argument, however, is that once the metaphorical alignment has been made, new attributes appear: the lack of chiaroscuro in Mokin's painting, for instance, can be compared to the distinctive use of instrumental timbre—what might be called the lack of light and shade—in Tchaikovsky's orchestration, and it is the act of comparison that constructs this attribute of Tchaikovsky's orchestration as such. (It is only the alignment with the painting, in other words, that causes the absence of what we might now call chiaroscuro-like properties in Tchaikovsky's orchestration to emerge.)

But I can make these emergent properties clearer by drawing a comparison between a record sleeve that does little more than duplicate the qualities of the music with which it is coupled and one which, like the Mokin painting, gives rise to new meaning. CBS couple Bernstein's recording of the *Pulcinella* Suite with Picasso's drawing 'Pierrot et Arlequin' (Fig. 2.4).[48] The coupling is an obvious one; the date is right, the iconography is right, and the association of Picasso and Stravinsky is familiar almost to the point of banality. Moreover, Picasso's drawing shares many qualities with Stravinsky's music: suppleness, transparency, spontaneity, and a sense of play. In this way the painting duplicates the most self-evident qualities of the music. The trouble is that this is really all it does; it does not, in other words, address qualities of the music that are less obvious, or that might even be considered problematic, in the way that a slightly later coupling by the same record company does (Fig. 2.5).[49] Here we have the same association of painter and composer; the date is again right, and there is still a musical connection (the painting is entitled 'The Three Musicians'), although the painting does not bear upon the story of *Pulcinella*.[50] What it *does* bear upon, however, is (as I have described it elsewhere)

the principal musical issue of *Pulcinella*, which is the relationship between Pergolesi's music and Stravinsky's adaptation of it. In effect, it draws a parallel between the techniques of synthetic cubism and the recompositional devices that Stravinsky employs. It suggests an aesthetic whereby familiar objects are

---

[48] CBS BRG 72040.

[49] Columbia 33CX 1949 (dated 1965, whereas CBS BRG 72040 is dated 1962).

[50] This, of course, is particularly understandable in that, as the layout shows, the *Pulcinella* Suite is subordinated to the *Symphony in Three Movements*, and the spine reads 'Symphony in Three Movements, etc.'. (In Fig. 2.4, by comparison, the *Pulcinella* Suite is listed first.)

Fig. 2.4 Sleeve of CBS BRG 72040, incorporating 'Pierrot et Arlequin' (Picasso)

broken up into their parts and reconstituted in unfamiliar ways. It encompasses the juxtaposition of materials of extraneous origins and natures. It operates by allusion rather than explicit statement. And it subordinates all this to the overriding stylishness, the quality of *chic*, that characterizes both Picasso's and Stravinsky's work.[51]

In other words, the coupling of image and sound contextualizes, clarifies, and in a sense analyses the music. It instigates a new, or at any rate a deepened, experience of the music, and it is because of the effect of image upon sound—because of the interaction between the two—that record sleeves are, as I put it, at least next door to multimedia (the more so, of course, when you consider the words as well). But any juxtaposition of music and static images is very different from such multimedia genres as commercials, films, and music videos. What might an enabling similarity look (or sound, or feel) like when music is synchronized with moving images and words? And what kind of perceptual synthesis might it give rise to?

<hr />

[51] 'Domestic *Gesamtkunstwerk*'.

Fig. 2.5 Sleeve of Columbia 33CX 1949, incorporating 'The Three Musicians' (Picasso)

Similarity and Difference

The previous chapter provided the main part of the answer to the first question: multimedia depends heavily on quasi-synaesthetic correspondences. As I said there, practically everyone—not just synaesthetes—agrees that the sound of a flute in high register is 'brighter' than that of a tuba; conversely, the tuba has a bigger sound—not necessarily louder, but bigger—than the flute. According to Marks, brightness and size are the two most general, most robust examples of such cross-sensory correspondence, but there are any number of others; for instance, in a famous experiment Wolfgang Köhler, the Gestalt psychologist, found that when asked to match two nonsense words ('maluma' and 'takete') with two visual shapes, almost all his subjects matched 'maluma' with a round shape, and 'takete' with an angular one.[52] And whereas experiments like Köhler's involve the making of a conceptual judgement, the same correspondences are involved when

---

[52] Summarized in Marks, *Unity of the Senses*, 77–8. One of Marks's principal aims is to explain such responses by showing how these quasi-synaesthetic qualities—brightness, volume, angularity—may be mapped on to the physical dimensions appropriate to each sensory mode. There is a near relation of Köhler's demonstration in Chuck Jones, 'Music and the Animated Cartoon', *Hollywood Quarterly*, 6 (1945–6), 364–70: 368–9; the words are now 'tackety' and 'goloomb', while the drawings have become rather more elaborate.

people see films or watch music videos. 'Fantasia', for instance, is full of examples of direct perceptual correlations of this sort; indeed, the section in which the Sound Track is coaxed on stage, and which in a sense outlines the agenda of the film, is based almost exclusively upon correlations of visual and auditory size and brightness. Andrew Goodwin has provided a host of similar examples from music video, ranging from a synthesizer solo illustrated through 'computer-manipulated imagery of tiny globes whose scale reflects the "small" sound of the keyboard'[53] to broad parallels of mood—the use of black and white film, for instance, to bring out (seek out?) qualities of pain and loss in the music. Other examples of parallelism at this more general level might include the repetitious, calligraphic patterning shared by Mokin's painting and Tchaikovsky's 'Little Russian' Symphony and the music at the beginning of the Volvo commercial described in the Introduction to Part I, with its hi-tech sheen.

All these examples of enabling similarity can be described as iconic in one way or another, although the nature of the iconic relationship varies widely. In some cases it inheres in an apparently literal sensory resemblance—as in 'Fantasia'—whereas in others it involves connotative qualities (the quality of pain and loss shared by music and black-and-white film, in a context where colour is the norm).[54] Properly speaking, one should perhaps use an even more general term, such as 'enabling equivalence', since relationships other than the iconic can, on occasion, suffice for metaphorical transfer; the juxtaposition of onion domes and Tchaikovsky's music, much favoured by record companies, is a purely symbolical one, while the linkage between the ubiquitous images of artists on record sleeves and the music within is, in an admittedly indirect sense, indexical. But it is probably fair to say that iconic relationships in multimedia overwhelmingly outnumber others, and of these by far the most important are those that involve time. The reason for this is easy to see, if a little harder to explain. It is rather like the difference between absolute and relative pitch. A bright colour may correspond to a bright sound in an absolute sense, but what is much

[53] Andrew Goodwin, *Dancing in the Distraction Factory: Music Television and Popular Culture* (London, 1992), 65, referring to Cyndi Lauper's 'Girls Just Want to Have Fun'. It should be mentioned that Goodwin uses the term 'synaesthesia' in a very loose sense; his examples of 'Synaesthesia in the Video Text' (pp. 60–8) consist not only of correspondences that I would term quasi-synaesthetic, but also of contextual associations that really have nothing to do with synaesthesia at all.

[54] Metaphor often involves shared affective features overriding contrary denotative features, as for instance in the Citroen commercial discussed in the Introduction to Part I and again below. Marshall and Cohen suggest something similar when they refer to 'structural' similarities resulting in the transfer of 'connotation'. But Marks warns against any assumption that this is an invariable rule: 'often what is shared is a mutual *connotation* of good or bad, strong or weak, active or passive' (*Unity of the Senses*, 215, emphasis added; for experimental confirmation see Bolivar, Cohen, and Fentress, 'Semantic and Formal Congruency in Music and Motion Pictures', 44).

more salient is the relationship between a darker and a brighter colour, on the one hand, and a darker and a brighter sound, on the other.[55] The temporal alignment of such relationships, then, results in the most perceptible and immediate of all cross-media configurations: parallelisms of process. No doubt that is one reason why everyone picks out the 'Lighting Crescendo' as the most effective example of multimedia in *Die glückliche Hand*.

It is also why television commercials, which by their nature must exploit the most efficient means of communicating meaning fast, are so often organized in terms of such processes. Again, this can be illustrated by the Volvo commercial, which I described as organized around processes that are at the same time musical (in the technical sense) and semantic: ATONAL → DIATONIC, ELECTRONIC → NATURAL, and thus TECHNOLOGICAL → HUMAN.[56] How might this be represented in terms of the metaphorical model I have been outlining? ATONAL → DIATONIC and ELECTRONIC → NATURAL refer to dimensions of musical structure (what we might loosely describe as 'tonality' and 'sonority'); each is a process articulated through time. And these processes are aligned with that of the commercial's typically compressed verbal and visual narrative—a narrative that begins with the car in the showroom, represented as a gleaming object of desire, but progresses to social concern. For the Volvo driver, it is saying, material values are ultimately subordinate to human ones; safety (of both the ducks and the little girl) comes first. TECHNOLOGICAL → HUMAN, then, represents a semantic core upon which both the musical and the narrative dimensions converge. These values, more or less explicitly represented in the words and pictures, are easily enough read from the music by virtue of the temporal alignment between musical and narrative processes; the enabling similarity between the processes is partly iconic (as I pointed out, the hi-tech sheen of the electronic music matches that of the car) and partly symbolic, as in the association of woodwinds and family values.[57] And the establishment of this intersection between the music and the pictures makes it possible for the advertiser's message to 'absorb' (to use

---

[55] This is another way of arguing, with Eisenstein, for the importance of contextual organization as against the 'eternal' correspondences affirmed by Kandinsky and other synaesthetically influenced artists (see pp. 52–3 above).

[56] See Fig. I.20.

[57] In the atonal/diatonic dimension the threads of signification are perhaps beyond untangling. They range from the historical association of the diatonic with the pure and the chromatic with artifice (a classic example is *Parsifal*) to the widespread, if academically disreputable, intuition that tonal music is 'natural', while atonal music sets itself against nature. And maybe there is an iconic link between atonal dissonance and the tension of material desire on the one hand, as against diatonic consonance and personal integration on the other. For present purposes what matters is the existence of similarity or equivalence, rather than its precise source.

Marks's word) all the music's other attributes, at the same time strengthening the processive quality of the narrative, deepening the connotative story that it tells, and contributing powerfully to the construction of the implied protagonist of the commercial: you, the present or future Volvo owner.

So far, I have been describing rather abstract processes in music, processes whose significance emerges only from the analysis of individual contexts. The most fundamental iconicity between music and other media, however, is much more familiar and general. That music embodies movement is an intuitively plausible proposition; why otherwise should listening to it prompt that kinetic excess which overflows into anything from the tapping of a foot to the most frenzied dance? And of course it is axiomatic that the moving images of the cinema involve movement; etymologically that is what 'cinema' means. From this it follows that any alignment of music and moving image that reaches a threshold of similarity between the two can readily effect a transference of kinaesthetic qualities between one and the other. The interesting thing, which is very important for the analysis of multimedia, is that the extent of this enabling similarity may, in fact, be unexpectedly limited. William Penn refers to the way in which the steps of a march seen on a screen can seem to synchronize with the music even when the tempo is quite different.[58] He is referring to Georges Méliès's film 'Le Voyage dans la lune', which dates from 1902; but a more accessible example is the 'Dance of the Hours' sequence from 'Fantasia'. If it is viewed with the sound switched off, the absurdly balletic qualities of the ostriches—the crispness and precision of their movements, even the spring in their steps—evaporate. In themselves, the pictures are simply not very rhythmic. It is not, then, the synchronization of elaborately rhythmic pictures with the music that makes the ostriches dance the way they do. Instead, a limited but sufficient degree of similarity between pictures and music enables the pictures to 'sop up' (another of Marks's terms[59]) the rhythmic qualities of the music, and the result is that you *see* those qualities in the image. It all amounts to a kind of ventriloquism.

But what is generally claimed of the association of music and movement goes well beyond this. In essence the claim is exactly what Eisenstein asserted: by embodying motion, music embodies emotion. In her dissertation, Claudia Widgery documents the idea that we empathize with other people's feelings or experiences through 'an inner imitation of them "in the mind's muscle" '[60]—that is to say, through

---

[58] Penn, 'Music and Images', 58.   [59] Marks, *Unity of the Senses*, 197.

[60] Widgery, 'Kinetic and Temporal Interaction', 117. Her quotation is from Edward B. Titchener, *Experimental Psychology of the Thought Processes* (New York, 1909), 21.

internalized movement or gesture. In other words, gesture is the invisible intermediary between music and emotion. And then she exclaims, in a refreshing burst of common sense,

Applying the motor aspects of empathy just discussed to the effect on the viewer of certain music for film requires something of a leap of the imagination. After all, the filmgoer does not usually stand up in the theater and imitate the motions of the people on the screen—although the facial expressions of theatergoers can be very revealing.[61]

Against such common sense, one can only cite the name of practically every philosopher, aesthetician, or music theorist who has written on music and the emotions: such notorious adversaries as Hanslick and Wagner, Scruton and Nattiez, have all agreed on some version of this apparently extravagant notion, along with Schenker, Sundberg, Langer, Kivy, and countless others.[62] If authority can lend credence to any theory, this is it, and after her moment of spirited disbelief, Widgery reverts to the conventional language of visceral responses to music.

I have no more intention than Widgery of challenging the theory, although I shall return to the issue of music and emotion in the last part of this chapter. But it is worth distinguishing between some of the different ways in which music can embody movement, since each gives rise to a different kind of cross-media interaction. First, there is the kinesis that results from the combination of rhythm, harmony, dynamics, and other musical elements in a given musical context; this is a straightforward iconicity of process, illustrated for instance by the Sound Track sequence from 'Fantasia' or any number of music videos. (It is a music–picture relationship of this kind that Eisenstein described in his 'Alexander Nevsky' analysis.) The remaining two types of kinesis I want to identify are both more abstract, but in different ways. One might be called a 'kinesis of genre'; I am thinking, for instance, of the conventional dance types of classical music,[63] where a perceptible

[61] Widgery, 'Kinetic and Temporal Interaction', 118.

[62] Eduard Hanslick, *On the Musically Beautiful: A Contribution towards the Revision of the Aesthetics of Music*, trans. Geoffrey Payzant (Indianapolis, 1986), 11; Richard Wagner, *Opera and Drama*, in *Prose Works*, trans. William Ashton Ellis (London, 1892–9), ii. 317–23; Roger Scruton, 'Notes on the Meaning of Music', in Michael Krausz (ed.), *The Interpretation of Music: Philosophical Essays* (Oxford, 1993), 193–202: 199–202; Jean-Jacques Nattiez, *Music and Discourse: Toward a Semiology of Music*, trans. Carolyn Abbate (Princeton, 1990), 118–21; Heinrich Schenker, *Free Composition*, ed. and trans. Ernst Oster (New York, 1979), i. 4; Johan Sundberg, 'Speech, Song, and Emotions', in Manfred Clynes (ed.), *Music, Mind, and Brain* (New York, 1982), 137–50: 146; Suzanne K. Langer, *Philosophy in a New Key* (Cambridge, Mass., 1942), 226–7; Peter Kivy, *The Corded Shell: Reflections on Musical Expression* (Princeton, 1980). Additional references may be found in Stephen Davies, *Musical Meaning and Expression* (Ithaca, NY, 1994), 230, and (with specific reference to multimedia) William H. Rosar, 'Film Music and Heinz Werner's Theory of Physiognomic Perception', *Psychmusicology* 13 (1994), 154–65.

[63] See Wye Jamison Allanbrook, *Rhythmic Gesture in Mozart* (Chicago, 1983).

music–picture parallelism might be achieved through the pictures conforming to the overall kinetic quality of the dance movement, rather than as a result of moment-to-moment synchronization. (The same applies to the dance types of popular music.) The other is the kinesis inherent in structural process—the kind of large-scale patterning of implication and realization that music analysts are concerned with. And here exemplification is more effective than description.

In any literal sense, the music of the Prudential commercial I discussed in the Introduction to Part I[64] has as little to do with the pictures and the words as does Hermann's music for the driving sequence in 'Psycho'. In 'Psycho', the explanation was obvious: the music seeks out the protagonist, Marion, and reveals (or rather constructs) her state of mind. In the same way, the Prudential music seeks out the ultimate author constructed by the commercial—the invisible corporate identity of Prudential, the repository of the caring, paternal authority that the flesh-and-blood father of the commercial lacks—and imbues Prudential with its own attributes: the reassuring solidity of the counterpoint between melody and bass, the consoling qualities of the pellucidly diatonic harmony and the unhurried tempo. But the music has additional connotative attributes that inhere at the level of overall structural process. There is the regular, boxes-within-boxes structure, with two-bar phrases subsumed into four-bar periods, and with the imperfect cadence of bar 4 being answered by the perfect cadence of bar 8; all this encodes qualities of balance and control. Then there is the effortlessly directed ascent to the final tonic supported by the most unproblematic cadential progression in the entire classical repertory, II–V^7–I. This large-scale rhythm of implication and realization is felt just as viscerally, to borrow Widgery's term, as any other instance of musical kinesis. In the Prudential commercial, there is nothing in the words or pictures to correspond with this; the transfer of attributes takes place at a global level. The music's balance and control, then, encode Apollonian values that rise above the sometimes Dionysian qualities of the commercial's young protagonist. Its effortlessness whispers confidentially that you can relax when Prudential is in charge. And, as I said in the Introduction to Part I, its logic and inevitability make Prudential the natural solution to all your problems.

The metaphor model means that the starting-point for analysing musical multimedia remains where everyone has always assumed it is: similarity. But the point is that it is now *only* a starting-point. Eisenstein criticized Kandinsky for pursuing abstract correspondences between music and colour 'as *an end in itself*, as the summit of achievement, as

---

[64] See Ex. I.5.

finality'.[65] Exactly the same criticism—that it is pursued as an end in itself—might be made of Eisenstein's own pursuit of cross-medium similarity, and perhaps also of Eisler's rather half-hearted attempts at oppositional scoring.[66] The metaphor model, by contrast, invokes similarity not as an end, but as a means. Meaning now inheres not in similarity, but in the difference that similarity articulates by virtue of the transfer of attributes—the difference that results from seeing love as war, or from seeing the pictures of 'Psycho' through the grid of Hermann's music. And it is at this point that the central shortcoming in Eisenstein's and Eisler's way of thinking about multimedia becomes evident. Eisenstein wrote: 'We can speak only of what is actually "commensurable" i.e., the movement lying at the base of both the structural law of a given piece of music and the structural law of the given pictorial representation'; beyond such shared movement, he implied, different media are simply incommensurable.[67] Eisler (or maybe Adorno) attempted to raise such incommensurability to a principle, writing of the 'insurmountable heterogeneity' of music, pictures, and words, and concluding that 'the aesthetic divergence of the media is potentially a legitimate means of expression, not merely a regrettable deficiency that has to be concealed as well as possible'.[68] The point, however, is that it is only by virtue of what is 'commensurable'—that is, enabling similarity—that signification can be drawn out of heterogeneity, and only by virtue of the 'divergence' of media that there is anything for the similarity to enable. Metaphor provides a model for the two-way interaction of commensurability and heterogeneity, similarity and difference, in the absence of which Eisler's (Adorno's?) ringing aesthetic proclamation collapses into little more than a wish-list.

Just how, then, does difference give rise to signification in multimedia? The best way to answer this is to make some comparisons. The quasi-synaesthetic correspondences between pictures and music in Eisler's score for 'Rain' do not result in substantial attribute transfer; the effect (at least in so far as one can reconstruct it from reading *Composing for the Films*) is of a rather static congruence or conformance between the two. On the other hand, the Citroen commercial discussed in the Introduction to Part I exploits very much the same quasi-synaesthetic correspondences, and here there is a very obvious attribute transfer. As I said there, the picture and sound editing associate the speeding car and Mozart's music in such a way that the vivacity, power, and cultural prestige of the music (its activity,

[65] Eisenstein, *Film Sense*, 93.
[66] For a convenient summary of these see Widgery, 'Kinetic and Temporal Interaction', 71–8.
[67] Eisenstein, *Film Sense*, 128.   [68] Eisler, *Composing for Films*, 74.

potency, and evaluative properties, if you like) are transferred whole-sale to the product.[69] Why the difference? It is hard to know how to answer this question; there is no limit to the number of potentially relevant factors. But it seems likely that part of the answer lies in the sheer extent of the congruence between pictures and music in 'Rain'; it is as if too many of the music's attributes are already there in the picture, so that not enough remains to be transferred from music to picture. The same can certainly be said of the Sound Track sequence from 'Fantasia', except that this time the situation is just the other way round: the visuals have little to add to what is already there in the music (apart, perhaps, from a few colours). By contrast, the attributes which the Citroen pictures and the *Marriage of Figaro* overture have in common barely scrape the surface of Mozart's music; a weighty burden of signification, a prodigal excess of meaning, remains to be transferred to the product. In the same way, the multiple asymmetries between the music, pictures, and words in the Prudential commercial ensure that each medium has, so to speak, much to offer the others. Going back to Marshall and Cohen's diagram (Fig. 2.2), what seems to be required for the emergence of signification in multimedia is exactly what they have shown there: a *limited* intersection of attributes, as opposed to either complete overlap or total divergence.

Emergence

Eisenstein left a memorable portrait of how Prokofiev watched the film for which he would produce the music, often, says Eisenstein, by the very next day:

Although we used to watch these rushes in the dark, I could still catch glimpses of Prokofiev's hands on the arms of the chair, those enormous strong hands, which would wield the keys with fingers of steel when in a wild frenzy of inspiration he used to plunge at the keyboard that would shake beneath them. . . . As the film progressed Prokofiev's long unerring fingers, full of nervous sensitivity, started to move up and down the arms of his chair like a relentless Morse code receiver.[70]

And he continues: 'Was Prokofiev "marking out the beat"? No. . . . He was measuring out the structural pattern in which the length and

[69] For parallel accounts of metaphorical transference in television commercials see Thomas McLaughlin, 'Figurative Language', in Frank Lentricchia and Thomas McLaughlin (eds.), *Critical Terms for Literary Study*, 2nd edn. (Chicago, 1995), 80–90: 88; Hroar Klempe, 'Music, Text, and Image in Commercials for Coca-Cola', in John Corner and Jeremy Hawthorn (eds.), *Communication Studies: An Introductory Reader*, 4th edn. (London, 1993), 245–54.

[70] Sergei Eisenstein, 'P R K F V', in James L. Limbacher (ed.), *Film Music: From Violins to Video* (Metuchen, NJ, 1974), 159–63: 160.

rhythm of individual episodes are interwoven.' In Eisenstein's terms, then, he was abstracting the 'inner movement' of the music. And Eisenstein's description provides a model for the process of selection that is involved in any alignment of media. If you were to hear the music of the Volvo commercial by itself, for instance, it is quite unlikely that you would hear its TECHNOLOGICAL → HUMAN message in the manner that I have described; ATONAL → DIATONIC and ELECTRONIC → NATURAL are just two out of an indefinite number of dimensions of variance that the music embodies. These particular dimensions become salient in this particular context because they intersect with the more overt TECHNOLOGICAL → HUMAN message of the words and pictures. The alignment of the other media with music, that is to say, induces a specific perceptual selection from its available attributes. Marks speaks of the 'plurisignificance' of speech sounds,[71] meaning by this that a given low-level property (for example, a formant frequency) may give rise to different cross-media correspondences in different contexts; by analogy, one might think of music—and perhaps any other medium—as having a potential for sig-nification which is much broader than anything that can be realized in any given context. What matters, from this point of view, is not so much the signification that is 'in' the sound, but rather the potential for signification that it may support by virtue of specific intersections with other media. Seen thus, signification becomes a function of con-text; it is, in a word, performative.

Again, this is something that is implicit in the metaphor model. Any metaphor, say Lakoff and Johnson, 'highlights certain features while suppressing others'.[72] Indeed one of the main points they make in their book is that, through its built-in metaphors (MONEY IS A RESOURCE, THE MIND IS A MACHINE, and so on), language—our language, any language—nat-uralizes a certain way of seeing the world, ruling out alternatives through rendering them literally inconceivable. As they put it, 'The acceptance of the metaphor, which forces us to focus *only* on those aspects of our experience that it highlights, leads us to view the entail-ments of the metaphor as being *true*'.[73] What is at issue here is the dis-tinction between the classical view of language as a means of reproducing reality and the more contemporary view that sees it as a principal means by which reality is constructed. Thomas McLaughlin expresses this with particular clarity when he describes language as 'not a simple process of naming preexisting objects and states but a sys-tem through which we give meaning to the world'.[74] We can conclude

---

[71] Marks, *Unity of the Senses*, 81.
[72] Lakoff and Johnson, *Metaphors We Live By*, 141.
[73] Ibid. 157.
[74] McLaughlin, 'Figurative Language', 86.

this sketch of the metaphor model of multimedia, then, by exploring the distinction between the reproduction and the construction of meaning. Two points come out of this; one concerns what I have termed the emergent nature of multimedia, while the other concerns the language we use in analysing it.

When he describes his collaboration with Prokofiev in 'Alexander Nevsky', Eisenstein stresses the unpredictable nature of cross-media alignment. When he and Prokofiev put the music and the pictures together, he says, they sometimes 'had effects we were totally unprepared for'.[75] It just isn't possible to set up general rules, he explains; 'the relations between the "pictures", and the "pictures" produced by their musical images, are usually so individual in perception and so lacking in concreteness that they cannot be fitted into any strictly methodological "regulations".'[76] Or, putting it another way, everything depends on context. And in saying this, Eisenstein is revealing the influence of montage theory. The basic principle of montage theory is, as Eisenstein explains, that '*two film pieces, of any kind, placed together, inevitably combine into a new concept, a new quality, arising out of that juxtaposition*'.[77] Eisenstein is critical of much of the work that resulted from taking montage theory too literally, but affirms that 'the juxtaposition of two separate shots by splicing them together resembles not so much a simple sum of one shot plus another shot—as it does a *creation*. . . . [T]he result is qualitatively distinguishable from each component element viewed separately.'[78] This is the exact point I made about the combination of music and image in Marshall and Cohen's experiment, the effect of which was not a mixing or averaging of the individual properties of the two media, but something qualitatively different—'a "third something"', as Eisenstein himself termed it.[79] In itself, of course, montage theory is not a theory of multimedia. But Eisenstein, like his contemporary Pudovkin,[80] extended the original concept of montage to include what he called 'vertical montage': that is to say, the

[75] Eisenstein, *Film Sense*, 125.

[76] Ibid. 128.

[77] Ibid. 14; Eisler quoted this passage approvingly in *Composing for Films*, 71 n. 6. Elsewhere Eisenstein stressed that montage involved the collision rather than (as Vsevolod Pudovkin insisted) the linkage of elements (*Film Form*, 37). There is an apparent affinity between montage theory and the Surrealists' concept of juxtaposition (a concept which the Surrealists traced back to Lautreamont), as well as with Arthur Koestler's concept of 'bisociation' (*The Act of Creation* (London, 1964)).

[78] Eisenstein, *Film Sense*, 17.

[79] Ibid. His mention of 'a "third something"' resonates curiously with Barthes's account of 'the third meaning' in his essay of that name (Roland Barthes, *Image, Music, Text*, trans. Stephen Heath (London, 1977), 52–68), the subtitle of which is 'Research Notes on Some Eisenstein Stills'. But perhaps it is all coincidence, since Barthes's 'third' follows on from what he calls informational and symbolic meanings (in effect, denotative and connotative).

[80] See Widgery, 'Kinetic and Temporal Interaction', 22–3.

montage of sound and picture. 'There is no fundamental difference', he wrote, 'in the approach to be made to the problems of purely visual montage and to a montage that links different spheres of feeling—particularly the visual image with the sound image.'[81]

Montage theory, then, provided Eisenstein with the basis for what was surely the first model of multimedia to do justice to its emergent properties. Yet Eisenstein failed to take the consequences of this conception fully on board. In the song 'Oh ocean-sea, Oh sea of blue' from *Ivan the Terrible*, he says, the different lines of Prokofiev's music embodied different aspects of the sea (the light flickering across the water, the billowing of the waves, and so on), but 'together they recreated, not copied; they brought to life, rather than imitating life'.[82] Such language is absolutely consistent with the emergent quality of multimedia—with the way in which, to refer back to the metaphor model, it constructs rather than reproduces meaning. But elsewhere Eisenstein forgets himself, so to speak, and his words fall back into the classical language of reproduction: 'realistic fullness', he says during his analysis of the twelve shots from 'Alexander Nevsky', can be achieved 'only when [the] frames are filled with a plastic *representation* that is composed according to the most *generalized* graph of our theme.'[83] And a few lines later he refers to the 'growing intensity of varying *representations*' in the various dimensions of the music. But there is a problem here. According to montage theory, meaning arises directly from the juxtaposition of sound and picture; according to the metaphor model (which aims to provide a general explanatory framework for such effects of juxtaposition), it arises from the intersection between sound and picture and the corresponding transfer of attributes. Neither approach is consistent with the idea that the 'inner movement' shown in Figure 2.1 is in some sense prior to its 'representation' in music and picture. Such a conception hypostatizes 'inner movement', ascribing to it a reality in some shadowy domain of existence that depends neither on its being seen nor on its being heard.[84]

Such obscurantism might be expected to attract Eisler's condemnation, and he duly explains that, while Eisenstein was right to identify the essential role of gesture in music–picture relations,

---

[81] Eisenstein, *Film Sense*, 63–4. A few pages later, Eisenstein writes even more suggestively that '*in principle* these sound–picture relationships do not differ from relationships within music' (p. 68). I do not know whether it would be going too far to see an affinity between Eisenstein's principle of vertical montage and Schoenberg's principle of the identity of the horizontal and vertical dimensions of musical space.

[82] Eisenstein, 'P R K F V', 161.

[83] *Idem, Film Sense*, 166.

[84] Even more problematic is a formulation which Widgery cites from Roger Sessions's *The Musical Experience of Composer, Performer, Listener* (Princeton, 1950), 15: 'The gestures which music embodies are, after all, invisible gestures; one may almost define them as consisting of movement in the

The function of music . . . is not to 'express' this movement—here Eisenstein commits an error under the influence of Wagnerian theories about the *Gesamtkunstwerk* and the theory of artistic empathy—but to release, or more accurately, to justify movement. . . . [Music's] aesthetic effect is that of a stimulus of motion, not a reduplication of motion. In the same way, good ballet music, for instance Stravinsky's, does not express the feelings of the dancers and does not aim at any identity with them, but only summons them to dance.[85]

In the same way, he seems to be implying, good film music does not express the feelings of the characters or aim at any identity with them—does not seek out their inner thoughts or create a communicating link with the audience, to borrow Hermann's terms once again. Eisler's anti-Hollywood stance, his Brechtian opposition to the utopias of cinematic diegesis, lies barely concealed under the surface of his writing. But there is a philosophical rather than an ideological sense in which Eisler's critique is beyond criticism. To see the music as expressing the characters' inner thoughts is to naturalize the latter, to suggest that they have some kind of priority over the music. It is to reduce the music to a kind of supplementary role, underlining or projecting something that already exists. It is, in short, to collude with Hollywood in its creation of the 'transparent or invisible discourse' of which Gorbman spoke.[86] In reality, music—like any other filmic element—participates in the *construction* of cinematic characters, not their reproduction, just as it participates in the construction, not the reproduction, of all cinematic effects. We shall see in the next chapter that this apparently modest distinction assumes a quite disproportionate role in analysing musical multimedia, and that 'expression theory', if it may be called that, is one of the main reasons why existing models of multimedia are in general so inadequate.

Multimedia and Meaning

I have been using the words 'emotion' and 'meaning' with some freedom, suggesting that sounds, pictures, and words may be aligned with one another on the grounds of shared emotional properties, and conversely that meaning emerges from such alignments. Such freedom might seem premature considering that there is no generally accepted

---

abstract, movement which exists in time but not in space, movement, in fact, which gives time its meaning and its significance for us' ('Kinetic and Temporal Interaction', 114). Davies quotes and criticizes a similar formulation by Victor Zuckerkandl (*Musical Meaning and Expression*, 234).

[85] Eisler, *Composing for Films*, 78. Once again, Eisler's (Adorno's?) theory is out of line with his (Eisler's) practice; note the repeated use of the word 'reproduce' in the description of the relationship between visual and musical movement in 'Rain' (p. 64 above).

[86] See above, p. 21.

theory of how music expresses emotion or, more generally, how music means—or even, in some circles, *whether* it does so in any usefully discussable sense. The purpose of this section is not to solve the problem of musical meaning, but simply to outline as much of a working model as we need for the purposes of analysing musical multimedia. And my starting-point will be an approach which now seems to command a reasonable degree of consensus among philosophers of the British empirical tradition, and which is most fully represented in the writings of Stephen Davies and Peter Kivy.[87]

We should start by recognizing the constraints of this approach. When Davies uses the word 'meaning' in the title of his recent book, he isn't referring to meaning as it is constructed by, say, cultural studies or reception theory. He means the expression of emotion. And when he uses the term 'musical', he means the same as Kivy explicitly indicates in *his* title: 'the purely musical experience' or, more concisely, 'music alone'. Davies even elevates the assumption of music's autonomy to a methodological principle for the analysis of multimedia: 'The contribution music might make in song, opera, film and the like are clear', he says, 'only if one is aware of the strengths and weaknesses, so to speak, of music in its most abstract setting.'[88] This is rather reminiscent of the Hanslickian strategy of infinite deferral that music theorists have traditionally used as a defence against engagement with issues of musical meaning: there is no point in thinking about music's referential meaning, the argument goes, until we have a complete understanding of its immanent structure (which is to say, never). In fact, the whole framework of Kivy's and Davies's approach is Hanslickian; Kivy's term 'music alone' actually comes from the first chapter of Hanslick's *On the Musically Beautiful*.[89] It might seem surprising that the currently dominant theory of musical expression should be based on a work notorious for its insistence that, as Joseph Margolis puts it, 'music could not be more than mere "sound and motion" '.[90] But such surprise is occasioned largely by a widespread misreading of Hanslick, whose essential argument was not that music cannot occasion profound feeling, but that such feeling is not the proper subject-matter for aesthetics. Instead

---

[87] See esp. Davies, *Musical Meaning and Expression*; Kivy, *Music Alone*; idem, *Corded Shell*.

[88] Davies, *Musical Meaning and Expression*, p. xi.

[89] Hanslick, *On the Musically Beautiful*, 2: 'Music alone among the arts still seems incapable. . . .' The phrase is more effectively isolated in the classic translation by Gustav Cohen (*The Beautiful in Music: A Contribution to the Revival of Musical Aesthetics* (New York, 1974), 17: 'Music alone is unable. . . .') Of the two translations, Payzant's (based on the 8th edn. of Hanslick's book, 1891) is generally to be preferred for accuracy, and Cohen's (based on the 7th edn., 1885) for period and literary quality; in what follows I use Cohen's as the source of my quotations.

[90] Joseph Margolis, 'Music as Ordered Sound: Some Complications Affecting Description and Interpretation', in Krausz (ed.), *Interpretation of Music*, 141–53: 142.

of denying music's expressive properties, Hanslick stresses them, but regards them as antithetical to beauty. And if we put on one side the argument about beauty, we shall find in Hanslick's book not only the essentials of the Kivy/Davies approach to musical expression, but also a suggestion of how we can go beyond the self-imposed limitations of that approach.[91]

Like Kivy and Davies, Hanslick rejects what are today generally called the 'expression' and the 'arousal' theories of musical meaning; that is to say, he does not believe that music derives its meaning either from what the composer intended to express when writing it or from what listeners feel when listening to it.[92] Again like Kivy and Davies, he locates the core of musical expression in its kinetic qualities, which, he says, reproduce the dynamic properties of

the ideas of love, wrath or fear. . . . Which of the elements inherent in these ideas . . . does music turn to account so effectually? Only the element of *motion*—in the wider sense, of course, according to which the increasing and decreasing force of a single note or chord is 'motion' also. This is the element which music has in common with our emotions, and which, with creative power, it contrives to exhibit in an endless variety of forms and contrasts.[93]

But as Kivy has suggested in an eloquent pair of essays that explore the affinities and contrasts between Hanslick's thinking and his own,[94] Hanslick's discussion of musical expression becomes increasingly tenuous from that point on. It is as if Hanslick saw these motions as somehow impinging directly on the nervous system, giving rise to the unreflective feelings which Hanslick, with his aesthetician's hat on, ruled out of the court of beauty. Kivy's and Davies's theory—it is hardly

[91] I want at this point to anticipate a possible source of confusion. Hanslick declares at one point that we should never describe music as 'expressing' emotion (*The Beautiful in Music*, 75), on the grounds that we can only apply emotional terms to music in a figurative sense, but then goes on to do just this (most notoriously when he speaks of the 'expression of passionate grief' in *Orfeo ed Euridice*, discussed below, p. 94). Equally, Davies argues that we should describe music as 'possessing' emotional properties rather than 'expressing' them, and criticizes Kivy's careless talk of music expressing emotion (*Musical Meaning and Expression*, 261); but just four pages later, we find him saying that music does not just present emotions, but comments on 'the emotions so expressed' (and after all, what did he call his book?). Strictly speaking, then, none of the authors I am discussing thinks one should speak of music expressing emotion, but in practice all of them do, and so shall I.

[92] 'Aesthetically speaking, it is utterly indifferent whether Beethoven really did associate all his works with certain ideas. We do not know them, and as far as the composition is concerned, they do not exist.' '[T]he time-honoured axiom of the theorists: "Grave music excites a feeling of sadness, and lively music makes us merry," is not always correct. If every shallow Requiem, every noisy funeral march, and every whining Adagio had the power to make us sad, who would care to prolong his existence in such a world?' (Hanslick, *The Beautiful in Music*, 84–5, 138). For a comprehensive discussion of these theories, see Davies, *Musical Meaning and Expression*, Ch. 4.

[93] Hanslick, *The Beautiful in Music*, 38.

[94] 'Something I've always Wanted to Know about Hanslick' and 'What was Hanslick Denying?', in Peter Kivy, *The Fine Art of Repetition: Essays in the Philosophy of Music* (Cambridge, 1993), 265–75, 276–95.

worth distinguishing them at the level of detail I am offering—accepts Hanslick's premiss, but generalizes it. Music, says Davies, presents what he calls 'emotion characteristics in appearances'; it sounds sad in exactly the same sense that willow trees and St Bernard dogs look sad—not because they *are* sad, but because there is a certain resemblance between their appearance and that of a sad person.[95] (In other words, the sadness of willows, St Bernards, and music is not the revelation of an inner state of mind but a public, observable trait.) In music the principal source of this iconicism is, as we might expect, motion. As Davies puts it, 'Motion is heard in music, and that motion presents emotion characteristics much as do the movements giving a person her bearing or gait.'[96] Music is sad, then, not in a literal sense, nor because the composer was sad when he or she wrote it, nor even because it makes us sad, but because it 'presents the outward features of sadness'.[97]

For Kivy, the idea that music can in this sense possess sadness—that sadness is therefore an intrinsic property of the music—is what separates his own conception of musical expression (and Davies's, of course) from Hanslick's. This thesis, he says, 'is of fairly recent vintage, the product mainly of contemporary analytic philosophy'.[98] All the same, Hanslick got remarkably close to such a formulation; 'We are perfectly justified in calling a musical theme grand, graceful, warm, hollow, vulgar,' he wrote, 'but all these terms are exclusively suggestive of the *musical* character of the particular passage.'[99] But where Hanslick definitely anticipates Kivy and Davies, and contemporary analytic philosophy in general, is in his cognitive theory of the emotions. Hanslick outlines this in the context of an argument that music cannot express an emotion like love. 'The feeling of *love*', he says, 'cannot be conceived apart from the image of the beloved being, or apart from the desire and the longing for the possession of the object of our affections. It is not the kind of psychical activity, but the intellectual substratum, the subject underlying it, which constitutes it *love*.'[100] In today's parlance, Hanslick is speaking of the formal object of an emotion; he is saying that since music cannot convey that object, it cannot express emotion at all. Kivy and Davies accept Hanslick's premiss, but are less sweeping in the conclusions they draw from it. Instead of concluding that music cannot express emotion, they conclude that it cannot express those emotions that require formal objects—like love, perhaps, and certainly

---

[95] Davies, *Musical Meaning and Expression*, 227–8, 240. As Davies points out (with apparent bitterness), both Kivy and he have used the example of St Bernards to make this point.

[96] Ibid. 229. [97] Ibid. 239.

[98] Kivy, 'What was Hanslick Denying?', 279.

[99] Hanslick, *The Beautiful in Music*, 74. [100] Ibid. 34.

like pride or jealousy (as I said in the Introduction to Part I, you cannot just wake up feeling jealous; you have to feel jealous of someone or
something). And they draw a distinction between these higher emotions which require objects (what, following Julius Moravcsik, they call
'Platonic attitudes'[101]) and the more generalized emotions that do
not—emotions like happiness and sadness. It follows that music cannot
express pride or jealousy (and on Hanslick's criteria the same applies to
love), but it *can* express happiness and sadness.

We can summarize the Kivy/Davies theory of musical expression,
then, by saying that music can present the appearances of emotions like
happiness and sadness, but it cannot express more complex, 'higher'
emotions. Moreover, its inability to present formal objects means that
it can express emotions only in their generic aspects; Davies hypothe-
sizes that 'what distinguishes the species within these genera is the
nature of their formal objects'.[102] Or, as Schopenhauer put it in *The
World as Will and Representation*,

> Music does not express this or that particular and definite pleasure, this or that
> affliction, pain, sorrow, horror, gaiety, merriment, or peace of mind, but joy,
> pain, sorrow, horror, gaiety, merriment, or peace of mind themselves, to a cer-
> tain extent in the abstract, their essential nature, without any accessories, and
> so also without the motives for them.[103]

And from this it should follow that music cannot present nuances of
happiness and sadness; it cannot, for instance, distinguish sadness from
depression, dejection, or gloom. (In Kivy's colourful phrase, 'a piece of
music can be mournful but not neurotically mournful over the death
of a canary.'[104]) Predictably, however, musicologists have found this
notion that music can express only unnuanced emotion unpalatable,
and a leisurely debate on this issue took place between Kivy and
Anthony Newcomb at four- or five-year intervals throughout the
1980s. It achieved little more than to underline the differing priorities
of musicology and philosophy.[105] In his response to Newcomb, Kivy
essentially reiterated his position: music can express gross emotional
properties, but in the absence of formal objects it cannot express subtle
emotional properties (and Davies concurs[106]). Kivy also complained
that Newcomb's counter-examples were ones in which, as in opera,

---

[101] Kivy, *Music Alone*, 175; Davies, *Musical Meaning and Expression*, 214.

[102] Davies, *Musical Meaning and Expression*, 226.

[103] Arthur Schopenhauer, *The World as Will and Representation*, trans. E. F. J. Payne (New York, 1969), i. 261.

[104] Kivy, *Music Alone*, 174.

[105] Anthony Newcomb, 'Sound and Feeling', *Critical Inquiry*, 10 (1984), 614–43, was a response to Kivy's *Corded Shell*; Kivy replied in *Sound Sentiment* (Philadelphia, 1989).

[106] Davies, *Musical Meaning and Expression*, 251.

words were aligned with music: words, he says, can turn gross emotional properties into subtle ones, so that Newcomb was no longer talking about pure music.

This, it seems to me, shows where the weak point in the Kivy/Davies model of musical meaning lies. In *Music Alone*, Kivy points out that passages in Mahler's symphonies, 'even those having no titles or textual associations', have sometimes been said to be 'expressive of the "neurotic" '. And he adds: 'But if music can be expressive of the neurotic, then, where it is also mournful, why not neurotically mournful? And does this not show, contrary to what I have been claiming, that music can be expressively very specific?'[107] (No mention, thankfully, is made of canaries.) Similarly, he continues, the 'dignified and stately' opening of Elgar's First Symphony could quite justifiably be heard as 'expressive of the pride of an imperial race at the apex of its power. . . . Yet pride is just one of those emotions I have identified as paradigmatic of the Platonic attitudes and, therefore, something music cannot be expressive of.' Kivy's response to both counter-examples is the same: the music might be heard this way, to be sure, but 'only by someone acquainted with the composer and his social milieu'.[108] And if we hear the music this way, in the light of contingent knowledge, we are no longer hearing it as pure music, as 'music alone'. For Kivy, that is the end of the argument. To me, however, it seems more like the beginning, because it raises the question: do we *ever* hear music alone, and if we do, can we be justified in regarding this as the paradigm case of musical listening? A negative answer to both these questions is suggested by the fact that our musical culture invests a great deal of time and effort in an apparent attempt to ensure that we *don't* hear music alone—to ensure that we know that Mahler was neurotic, that is to say, and that Elgar epitomized the values of the British Empire in its Indian summer before the First World War.

Let us suppose that the music, heard in isolation, fails to convey Mahler's neuroticism and Elgar's imperial swagger; it merely sounds mournful, dignified, or stately. That might set limits to the efficacy of music if we were accustomed to employ it as a system for communicating information, along the lines of the talking drums of Africa. But it has very little to do with the practice of music in the Western art tradition, where an entire publication industry has been brought into being precisely to make good this lack; I am thinking, for instance, of the classical music magazines that are burgeoning on high street newsagents' shelves, as well as the informative booklets without which no classical CD release would be complete. And the result of this

---

[107] Kivy, *Music Alone*, 178.   [108] Ibid. 180.

blending of sound and word is that we hear into the music, so to speak, what perhaps couldn't be heard out of it were we (in the interests of scientific experimentation) to make a dedicated attempt to hear it 'alone'. Moreover, it is a striking fact of music history—though one that doesn't seem to get into the history books—that the historical rise of autonomous instrumental music, Kivy's 'music alone', coincided with the evolution of the analytical programme note and the music appreciation text. It is as if the words that had been excised from the music had to find an alternative outlet; or as if what was repressed from musical consciousness emerged in a kind of cultural subconscious, if not a conscious subculture. Scott Burnham brings out the paradox in this nineteenth-century reconfiguration of musical culture when he says that 'music no longer in need of words now seems more than ever in need of words'.[109] Equally paradoxical is the idea that the paradigmatic, the most culturally privileged, audition of music alone is the one that is accompanied by printed material (whether an analytical programme note or a score).[110] Pure music, it seems, is an aesthetician's (and music theorist's) fiction; the real thing unites itself promiscuously with any other media that are available.

'From its own resources,' wrote Schopenhauer, 'music is certainly able to express every movement of the will, every feeling; but through the addition of the words, we receive also their objects, the motives that give rise to that feeling.'[111] In Wagner's hands, Schopenhauer's almost Hanslickian formulation becomes the basis of a fully-fledged theory of operatic multimedia: 'that which is utterable in the speech of Music', says Wagner, 'is limited to feelings and *emotions*. . . . What thus remains unutterable in the absolute musical tongue, is the exact definement of the *object* of the feeling and emotion, whereby the latter reach themselves a surer definition.'[112] Instead of seeing 'the absolute musical tongue'—music alone—as serene in its aloofness and self-sufficiency, Wagner emphasizes its craving for verbal completion, a craving that he expresses through the explicitly sexual image of the 'fertilizing seed'. As Frank W. Glass says in the book for whose title he borrowed this phrase, Wagner 'saw music and poetry uniting in opera in an act of love in which poetry was the masculine partner and music, the femi-

---

[109] Scott Burnham, 'How Music Matters: Poetic Content Revisited', in Nicholas Cook and Mark Everist (eds.), *Rethinking Music* (Oxford, forthcoming), 193–216. I shall return to this issue in the Conclusion.

[110] Perhaps it would be more accurate to say that this is the second most culturally privileged model of musical listening; the top of the pile would be represented by the recumbent figure of Brahms on his sofa, enjoying a fine performance of *Don Giovanni*, an experience of music in which no veridical sensory processes are involved whatsoever.

[111] Schopenhauer, *World as Will and Representation*, ii. 449.

[112] Richard Wagner, 'A Communication to my Friends', in *Prose Works*, i. 267–392: 364.

nine'.[113] I shall return in the next chapter to the essentializing impulse that is evident in Wagner's characterization of the components of multimedia. The point I want to make here is that music's urge towards consummation by the word (and the allusion to Suzanne Langer's image of music as 'unconsummated symbol' is wholly appropriate in this context) is deeply embedded in the very tradition for which Hanslick, Kivy, and Davies act as apologists.

Such consummation works exactly in the way that Kivy indicated in his response to Newcomb: words transform gross emotional properties into subtle ones. And they do so, in part, by supplying the formal objects to the emotions embodied in the music and thus nuancing them—so transforming the mournful quality of Mahler's music into an expression of neurosis, or turning the dignity and stateliness of Elgar's into an expression of imperial self-confidence. But perhaps the clearest examples of this kind of union between sound and word are the biographical interpretations of Beethoven's symphonies which were widespread during the nineteenth century, and which constructed a musical protagonist to whom the emotions in the music could be assigned. To take just one example, Franz Fröhlich, one of the earliest interpreters of Beethoven's Ninth Symphony, understood the palpable conflict and grief of the first movement to represent Beethoven's struggle with deafness; he even explained the particular emotional nuances of different passages of the music (bars 1–30 express in succession tender longing, heroic strength, tragic pathos, and the perception of joy), commenting that all this added up to a portrait of an uncommonly powerful personality. Fröhlich's influential reading became part of a nineteenth-century tradition of interpretation (dominated, incidentally, by Wagner), which not only nuanced the gross emotional properties of the music, but helped to stabilize the reception of a composition that contemporary listeners found notoriously problematic.[114] Fröhlich's narrative analysis—and the others that followed—fulfilled the functions that Barthes groups together under the term 'anchorage':[115] directing the interpretation of a limitlessly polysemic text, controlling the proliferation of meaning, and easing the transition of sound into discourse. To

[113] Frank W. Glass, *The Fertilizing Seed: Wagner's Concept of the Poetic Intent* (Ann Arbor, 1983), 3. The sexual connotations of Wagner's image emerge particularly clearly when he adds that 'only can this marriage prove a fruitful one, when the Musical-speech allies itself directly to its kindred elements in Word-speech; the union must take place precisely *there*, where in Word-speech itself there is evinced a mastering desire for real utterance of Feeling to the senses' ('Communication to my Friends', 364).

[114] For overviews see Robin Wallace, *Beethoven's Critics: Aesthetic Dilemmas and Resolutions during the Composer's Lifetime* (Cambridge, 1986); Nicholas Cook, *Ludwig van Beethoven: Symphony No. 9* (Cambridge, 1993); David Levy, *Beethoven: The Ninth Symphony* (New York, 1995).

[115] Roland Barthes, 'Rhetoric of the Image', in *Image, Music, Text*, 32–51: 38–40. In 'Domestic *Gesamtkunstwerk*', I outline the way in which record sleeves play a similar role.

trace the reception of the Ninth Symphony through responses like Fröhlich's is to see musical meaning in the making.

In a characteristically intimate aside, Kivy describes 'that scourge of middle age: waking up in the middle of the night with a vague and disturbing feeling of anxiety over nothing in particular, which pretty soon finds more than enough of the usual objects to fasten upon—unpaid bills, unexplained pains, ungrateful children, unwanted troubles'.[116] If a theory of multimedia is to be extracted from Kivy and Davies, then this is it: the indefinite emotions embodied in the music promptly fasten upon the objects that are supplied by words or images or any other media, and so the gross emotional properties of the music are contextualized and nuanced. Without denying the validity of this model of music as unnuanced emotion, I would like to complement it with the opposite model: music as emotionless nuance. Once again it is Hanslick who suggests the way. In *The Beautiful in Music*, he discusses the famous aria 'Che farò senza Euridice' from Gluck's opera *Orfeo ed Euridice*, in which Orfeo bewails his loss of Euridice to the underworld. At a time when thousands were moved to tears by this aria, Hanslick says, a contemporary of Gluck pointed out that 'precisely the same melody would accord equally well, if not better, with words conveying exactly the reverse'.[117] To be sure, he concedes, 'music certainly possesses far more specific tones for the expression of passionate grief', a statement that confirms (if confirmation is needed) Hanslick's belief in the expressive properties of music.[118] But we can't solve the puzzle by blaming the composer for writing ineffective music, he continues; of all composers it is Gluck who has the highest reputation for dramatic accuracy, and generations have hailed this very aria as a triumph in the expression of supreme grief. Yet musical settings like this, 'when considered apart from the text, enable us at best to *guess* the feeling that they are intended to convey'. And at this point Hanslick makes a telling analogy: such settings, he says, 'resemble a silhouette, the original of which we recognize only after being told whose likeness it is'.[119]

In structural terms, the model of musical meaning that this suggests is very much the same as the unnuanced emotion model I discussed earlier. But the content, so to speak, is just the other way round. Hanslick is not saying that the words supply a subtle emotional identi-

[116] Kivy, *Music Alone*, 165. Kivy puts forward this model of objectless emotion in the course of his exposition of 'arousal' theory, which he rejects, but subsequently incorporates it into his 'possession' theory (p. 175).

[117] Hanslick, *The Beautiful in Music*, 48.

[118] In 'Something I've always Wanted to Know about Hanslick', Kivy argues that in this passage Hanslick gives the lie to his own thesis that music cannot express emotion, since his complaint is that Gluck wrote music that expressed the *wrong* emotion.

[119] Hanslick, *The Beautiful in Music*, 49.

fication for the gross emotional properties already in the music; he is saying that the words supply the gross emotional identification. In which case, what does the music do? The silhouette analogy supplies the answer: once you know who it is a silhouette of, you see the individual in terms of the particular graphic characteristics, exaggerations, or clarifications of the silhouette. The silhouette, in other words, nuances your perception of the individual, and in the same way the music nuances the emotion that is presented in the words. And this interpretation of Hanslick is confirmed by other remarks scattered through his book. After arguing that love must have a formal object, he observes that 'love may be gentle or impetuous, buoyant or depressed, and yet it remains love. . . . [M]usic can express only those qualifying adjectives, and not the substantive, love, itself.'[120] Again, he says that music cannot express 'the whispering of love, or the clamour of ardent combatants', and explains: 'The *whispering* may be expressed, true; but not the whispering of "love"; the *clamour* may be represented, undoubtedly; but not the clamour of "ardent combatants".'[121] All this is reminiscent of what Kivy said about neurotic mourning over dead canaries. But again, it is the other way round. Kivy assumes that the music embodies the basic emotion but not its nuancing; Hanslick is saying that it embodies the nuancing but not the emotion.

In multimedia contexts like film and television commercials it is easier, I think, to find examples of music functioning as emotionless nuance than as unnuanced emotion. After all, words and pictures in the cinema almost invariably supply the gross emotional identifications; the role of the music is generally to structure and inflect the emotion, and in particular to give greater definition to its passage through time. Again, consider the music in the Walkers crisps and Volvo commercials that I described in the Introduction to Part I, neither of which has any clear emotional identity in its own right. Each, however, throws into relief the message of the words and pictures with which it is aligned, not just lending continuity and conviction to that message but helping to construct it by means of the binary oppositions and processive structures that I outlined. It is as if the music provided a kind of ready-made truth table, a logical framework into which any message could be inserted and made to seem persuasive or even inevitable. In *The Composer's Voice*, Edward T. Cone quotes W. J. Turner's wonderfully evocative comparison between the expressive potential of Mozart's music and 'a still, bright, perfect, cloudless day. . . . Such a day does not provoke or in the faintest degree suggest one mood rather than another. It is infinitely protean. It means just what you mean. It is

120 Ibid. 35.   121 Ibid. 33.

intangible, immaterial—fitting your spirit like a glove.'[122] That is how the music of these commercials seems: empty of meaning, but ready to accommodate any meaning that is aligned to it, or even to create meaning where there was none. And Cone himself puts forward a quite similar model of how, as he puts it, 'the content of songs emerges from the mutual relations of words and musical gestures, and from the light they throw on each other'. Indeed, he compresses the point I have been trying to make into nine words when he says that 'musical gestures lack signification, but they can be significant'.[123]

Where I have spoken of the music accommodating the meaning of words, Cone speaks of appropriation: 'music', he says, 'does not express emotions but appropriates them.'[124] By this he means that music 'sops up' the meaning of the words, to borrow Marks's term again, and that in this way it realizes some of its 'expressive potential'. Indeed, he goes on to suggest that the fundamental role of words in songs is to 'exemplify', to specify and so render tangible, the expressive properties of the music to which they are set. But there are two related ways in which I think Cone's formulation stands in need of clarification. One is that the idea of exemplification suggests that meanings already exist in the music, if only latently; this contradicts the premiss that meaning in multimedia is emergent—a premiss with which Cone himself concurs ('the content of songs *emerges* from the mutual relations of words and musical gestures').[125] The second aspect of Cone's model that needs clarifying concerns the concept of 'appropriation', which carries an implication rather like Turner's cloudless day image: it suggests that any music might be able to express anything. Cone does not mean to imply this; on the contrary, he says quite specifically that 'a piece of music allows a wide but not unrestricted range of possible expression'.[126] But the concept of 'appropriation' does not articulate this structured relationship. J. J. Gibson, however, had a word that does: he referred to the structured interaction of an organism and its environment as 'affordance'. If we speak of music affording meaning to words, or of words affording meaning to music, then in either case it is apparent that we are speaking of some kind of intersection between the attributes of each medium. It might seem as if you could insert any

---

[122] Edward T. Cone, *The Composer's Voice* (Berkeley, 1974), 173. The quotation is from W. J. Turner, *Mozart: The Man and His Works* (New York, 1938), 380–1.

[123] Cone, *Composer's Voice*, 166, 165.   [124] Ibid. 166.

[125] A source of confusion in discussions of musical meaning is the conflation of the meaning assumed to reside 'in' the music, as potential, and the meaning that is realized in any given situation. I would argue that only the latter, as emergent, should properly be called 'meaning'; the other might be called 'expressive potential' (Cone), 'semantic potentiality' (Nattiez, *Music and Discourse*, 126), or potential for signification.

[126] Cone, *Composer's Voice*, 166.

message into the musical framework of the Walkers crisps commercial, but that is not really the case; as I explained in the Introduction to Part I, there is a structural isomorphism between the music and the narrative. And this is what enables the musical affordance of meaning.

'Sops up', 'intersection', 'enables': this is the same vocabulary I used to outline the metaphor model of multimedia. And it is perhaps obvious that the model of meaning that I have been outlining is, in effect, an application of the metaphor model. The Kivy/Davies approach to musical meaning, predicated on the concept of 'music alone', is highly reminiscent of the synaesthesia-based model of multimedia that I ascribed to Eisenstein and Eisler; it is based on the same static idea of similarity, interpreted here as an iconicity between musical motion and Davies's 'emotion characteristics in appearance'. The model of meaning in multimedia that I have put forward is based on the same similarity. But, like the metaphor model, it goes beyond this. Music may contribute what Kivy calls gross emotional properties to the interaction of different media, or it may modify the emotional properties contributed by other media; that is to say, it may function as unnuanced emotion or as emotionless nuance. For that matter—and this is a possibility I have not discussed—it may contribute in ways that relate not so much to emotions as traditionally categorized, but rather to such affective qualities as activity, potency, and evaluation. But whatever music's contribution to cross-media interaction, what is involved is a dynamic process: the reciprocal transfer of attributes that gives rise to a meaning constructed, not just reproduced, by multimedia.

3

Models of Multimedia

IN THIS CHAPTER I put forward three basic models of multimedia. The intention is to provide an inventory of the ways in which different media can relate to one another, together with an associated terminology for describing them, and I shall outline the three basic models with reference to some of the examples of multimedia encountered so far in this book. But the models and the vocabulary associated with them also provide a framework for reviewing the theoretical content of existing writings on multimedia—in which I include traditional interpretations of song and opera, as well as accounts of relatively marginalized or more recent multimedia genres such as film and music video. The chapter is essentially organized in two passes, then, with the first section functioning as a kind of exposition, and the remainder developing the three basic models in counterpoint with the existing literature. There is no recapitulation.

Three Basic Models

Figure 3.1 represents the relationships between what I see as the three basic models of multimedia, which I am calling conformance, complementation, and contest. I have characterized multimedia as predicated on a distinctive combination of similarity and difference; so it is logical that the three models should be related through what I call the similarity test and the difference test (shown by the triangles).

The **similarity test** is based on the distinction that Lakoff and Johnson make between consistent and coherent metaphors. They make this distinction in the course of a discussion of metaphors that are clearly related to one another but not identical. One of their examples is LOVE IS A JOURNEY; this lies behind such metaphorical expressions as 'This relationship is a dead-end street', 'We've gotten off the tracks', and 'Our marriage is on the rocks'.[1] These expressions, in Lakoff and Johnson's terminology, are **coherent**, because they are all variants of LOVE IS A JOURNEY; in this sense they 'fit together'. But there is another sense in which they do *not* fit together, because each interprets LOVE IS A JOURNEY in a different manner. 'This relationship is a dead-end street' aligns love with a car trip, and to this extent it is quite distinct from the railroad comparison of 'We've gotten off the tracks' or the sea voyage

---

[1] Lakoff and Johnson, *Metaphors We Live By*, 45.

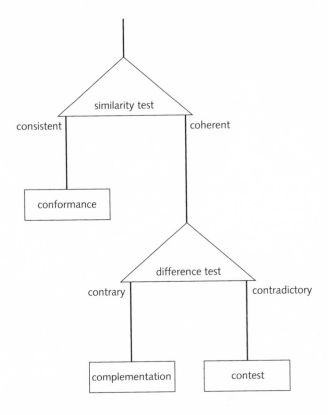

Fig. 3.1

comparison of 'Our marriage is on the rocks'. On the other hand, 'Our marriage is on the rocks' comes to the same thing as 'This relationship is foundering', because both expressions are based on the alignment of love with a sea voyage; in Lakoff and Johnson's terminology, these expressions are **consistent**. We might generalize Lakoff and Johnson's distinction by saying that coherence allows for differential elaboration as between the levels of a hierarchy; the expressions 'This relationship is a dead-end street' and 'Our marriage is on the rocks' elaborate the underlying metaphor LOVE IS A JOURNEY in different ways, and therefore relate to one another only at a remove: that is to say, through their common derivation from LOVE IS A JOURNEY. By contrast, the narrower category of consistency excludes such differential elaboration; there is no metaphorical difference between 'Our marriage is on the rocks' and 'This relationship is foundering', and in this way the two expressions relate directly to one another (as well as to LOVE IS A JOURNEY).

The first stage in the identification tree shown in Figure 3.1, then, is to ask whether the component media of a given instance of multimedia are consistent with one another in a sense that is parallel to Lakoff and Johnson's. (The clumsy expression 'instance of multimedia' reflects the lack of a term that is applicable across different media in the way that 'piece', for instance, applies to music; in future I shall abbreviate it to IMM.) This is a filter test the effect of which, if passed, is to establish that the IMM is **conformant**. It is not hard to find instances of conformance between media pairs within IMMs. The faster *luce* part in Skriabin's *Prometheus*, for instance, is consistent with the music, in that it corresponds to the sequence of 'mystic chord' roots; the music elaborates that sequence, while the faster *luce* part does not, but there is no element of incompatibility between the two. The slower *luce* part, on the other hand, does not relate in any such direct manner to the music, so that colour–sound relations in *Prometheus* cannot be said to be conformant overall. Again, Eisenstein explained the sequence of twelve shots from 'Alexander Nevsky' in a manner that stressed the conformant relations between pictures and music:[2] each, he claimed, embodies the same inner motion, and it is this conformance that Eisler made the object of his critique. But a moment's reflection will show that the 'Nevsky' sequence is not really an example of conformance at all, in the sense in which I have defined it. The pictures and the music elaborate the inner motion in quite distinct ways, and the result is to create a relationship of semantic difference between them (as against the synaesthetic identity which Eisenstein himself attacked[3]). And this differential elaboration establishes an asymmetry between the two media; the diegetic identification prompted by the pictures means that it is natural to speak of the music projecting the content of the pictures, but not of the pictures projecting the content of the music.

Where an IMM is conformant, or where the relations between the constituent media of an IMM are conformant, it should be possible to invert such statements without change of meaning; it makes as much sense (indeed, it makes just the same sense) to speak of the upper *luce* part in *Prometheus* projecting the music, as of the music projecting the upper *luce* part. Again, one might equally well speak of the coloured lights in Kandinsky's *Der gelbe Klang* projecting the stage action, or the stage action projecting the music, or the music projecting the colours; that is what it means to say that all the constituent media of *Der gelbe Klang* are conformant with one another, and that *Der gelbe Klang* is an instance of conformance overall. As Kandinsky envisaged it, each medium of *Der gelbe Klang* is congruent with each of the others; it

---

[2] See p. 58 above.   [3] See pp. 53–4 above.

embodies the same spiritual content. And the abstract, non-representational quality of the staging—its reduction, as far as possible, to a play of colours and shapes in motion—means that there is a minimum of differential elaboration as between the different media (although it is impossible to tell how far this may have been the case with Hartmann's music, since this has not survived). Here the relevant comparison is the one I offered in Chapter 1 with Schoenberg's *Die glückliche Hand*: Schoenberg deliberately incorporated elements of difference between the media of his *Gesamtkunstwerk*, ranging from the non-conformant structures within the general parallelism of the 'Lighting Crescendo' to the narrative organization of the drama and the realistic stage setting for which the score calls. In other words, the constituent media of *Die glückliche Hand* are elaborated differentially. There is no direct congruence between them; they are congruent only at a remove, by virtue of deriving from the same underlying emotional and spiritual content. As an IMM, in short, *Die glückliche Hand* is coherent, not consistent.

We can draw two related observations from this discussion, of which the first is of a technical nature. As I have explained,[4] Kandinsky conceived intermedia relationships as *triadic*; a colour corresponds to a sound inasmuch as both correspond to an underlying emotional or spiritual meaning. We can, then, distinguish this triadic variety of conformance from what might be called the unitary and dyadic varieties.[5] *Dyadic* conformance means that one medium corresponds directly to another, in the way that the faster *luce* part of *Prometheus* corresponds to the sequence of 'mystic chord' roots. (The term 'dyadic' does not, of course, mean that there can be only two constituent media; it means that there is a direct, pair-wise relationship between each medium and each of the others). *Unitary* conformance, by contrast, means that one medium predominates, and that other media conform to this. It is notorious, for instance, that Goethe preferred Corona Schröter's setting of *Erlkönig*, which Carolyn Abbate describes as 'hardly more than a bit of patterned melody for the recitation of each verse',[6] to Schubert's. A strophic song setting like Schröter's, says Abbate, 'introduces no alien

---

[4] See above, Ch. 1, p. 46, and Ch. 2, p. 57.

[5] To avoid confusion, I should distinguish this from the kind of triadic relationship illustrated by the joint relationship of 'This relationship is a dead-end street' and 'Our marriage is on the rocks' to LOVE IS A JOURNEY, which is an example of coherence, not of conformance. The point is that, as I said, there is no direct relationship between 'This relationship is a dead-end street' and 'Our marriage is on the rocks', whereas in Kandinsky's system there are direct relationships between colour and sound as well as between each and the corresponding emotional or spiritual meaning. Structurally, therefore, there is no difference between triadic and other varieties of conformance; 'unitary', 'dyadic', and 'triadic' represent different ways of conceptualizing the same structure. One might refer to them as modal categories.

[6] Carolyn Abbate, 'Erik's Dream and Tannhäuser's Journey', in Groos and Parker (eds.), *Reading Opera*, 129–67: 134.

element—a reading—but rather collaborates with the poem, helping the words to shout out their own sounds'. And this is confirmed by Goethe's praise for the settings of Carl Friedrich Zelter, which he described as 'so to speak, identical with my songs'.[7] Goethe's ideal, then, was unitary conformance, although it is doubtful whether there can really be any such thing as a song setting that introduces literally no qualities of its own, and I shall argue in the next section that genuine instances of unitary conformance are vanishingly rare. Indeed—and this is the second observation—conformance is a much less frequently encountered category of IMM than the existing literature might lead one to suppose; it is telling that my principal example of conformance, *Der gelbe Klang*, survives only in a fragmentary form (and I have suggested that, if the music still existed, it might prove not to be conformant at all). The importance of conformance, in other words, is not so much as an overall model of multimedia, but as a model of the relationship of constituent media within an IMM.

When considered overall, then, most IMMs prove not to be consistent; they fail the similarity test. As Figure 3.1 shows, this leads to the second test, which I have termed the **difference test**. This test is based on the two fundamental relationships of differentiation embodied in Greimas's narrative grammar and represented most clearly in his 'semiotic square'.[8] These relationships are **contrariety** and **contradiction**, of which the latter (like 'consistency' in the case of the similarity test) is the narrower, or 'marked', term.[9] This means that just as the similarity test was a test for consistency, so the difference test is a test for contradiction. A successful outcome establishes the IMM in question as an instance of contest, while the default category is complementation. And as before, the best way to introduce these categories is by examining the test in operation.

Contrariety might be glossed as undifferentiated difference; contradiction implies an element of collision or confrontation between the opposed terms. All the commercials I discussed in the Introduction to Part I exemplify difference between their constituent media; words and pictures are generally aligned with one another and share the same narrative structure, but each medium elaborates the underlying structure in a different way. And I emphasized the way in which the music characteristically introduces connections or connotations of its own,

---

[7] Quoted in Cone, *Composer's Voice*, 20.

[8] Introductions to Greimas's semiology and its musical applications may be found in Raymond Monelle, *Linguistics and Semiotics in Music* (New York, 1992), and Eero Tarasti, *A Theory of Musical Semiotics* (Bloomington, Ind., 1994).

[9] In the sense of Michael Shapiro's markedness theory (for a convenient introduction see Robert Hatten, *Musical Meaning in Beethoven: Markedness, Correlation, and Interpretation* (Bloomington, Ind., 1994), 35 ff.).

reinforcing and nuancing the processive structure in the Volvo and Walkers crisps commercials, the connotations of cultural prestige in the Citroen commercial. None of these, however, involves outright contradiction; the differential elaborations of the various media mesh together, rather than colliding with one another. This is not the case, however, with the Prudential commercial. As I explained, words and pictures collide in the puns on 'cutting' grass and records, and 'packing' cereals and packing them in at Wembley; or, to put it more precisely, the puns articulate a collision between the different levels of signification, with the lexical similarity masking a semantic contradiction. (That is how all puns work.) And the same applies to the music, both in terms of the striking disjunction between its formal structure and that of the commercial's narrative structure, and in terms of the outright contradictions between the classical music we hear and the rock music we see. The story of conflict and resolution which the commercial tells is in this way realized performatively in the conflicted, if ultimately harmonious, relations between sound and sight.

These contradictions, then, establish the presence of significant elements of **contest** within the Prudential commercial. The term 'contest' is intended to emphasize the sense in which different media are, so to speak, vying for the same terrain, each attempting to impose its own characteristics upon the other. One might develop the analogy by saying that each medium strives to deconstruct the other, and so create space for itself. Any IMM in which, as in the Prudential commercial, one or more of the constituent media has its own closure and autonomy is likely to be characterized by contest; IMMs that involve the addition of a new medium to an existing production are a particularly rich source of examples. (Madonna's video 'Material Girl', which superimposes fully elaborated cinematic diegesis upon a previously released song, and which I discuss in Chapter 4, is a good example; so is Godard's cinematic adaptation of Lully's *Armide*, discussed in Chapter 6.) In this, as in other respects, contest lies at the opposite extreme from conformance. Conformance begins with originary meaning, whether located within one medium or diffused between all; contest, on the other hand, ends in meaning. And as the association of conformant models with synaesthetic and metaphysical speculation demonstrates, conformance tends towards the static and the essentialized, whereas contest is intrinsically dynamic and contextual.

The mid-point between these two extremes is represented by the third model of multimedia, **complementation**, which Figure 3.1 represents in negative terms as that which exhibits neither consistency nor contradiction. It is possible, however, to characterize complementation more positively. It might be compared to the 'separate spheres' model of gender relations that was current in the nineteenth century: the difference between the constituent media of an IMM is recognized—this is what distinguishes complementation from conformance—but at the same time the conflict between them that characterizes the contest model is avoided because each is assigned a separate role. (Lawrence Kramer expresses a similar point in more memorable language when he writes that the different media 'can only confront each other across the locked gate of semiotic difference'.[10]) The theory of classical Hollywood film, for instance, asserts that pictures and words tell stories, which music cannot, but that music does what pictures and words cannot: 'seek out and intensify the inner thoughts of the characters', as Bernard Hermann put it,[11] and 'invest a scene with terror, grandeur, gaiety, or misery'. Kramer's 'locked gate', in other words, does not prevent the transfer of attributes between the constituent media. But the example of the Hollywood film shows something else as well: the idea of complementation easily turns into an assumption of primacy. Music in the films may have been seen as doing what pictures and words could not do, but it was still assumed to be subordinate to the diegesis. Ernest Lindgren states flatly that 'music in the film is a servant art'.[12] Of course, the comparison with gender relations might have prepared us for this silent transition from an egalitarian concept of interaction to one of hegemony, and I shall return to this in the next section.

The 'separate spheres' model of complementation is an *essentializing* one: pictures, words, and music are each seen as having their own intrinsic properties, and much of the literature on song, opera, and other multimedia genres is taken up with the rehearsal of these properties (as will become abundantly clear by the end of this chapter). There is, however, a second variety of complementation, which is *contextual* rather than essentializing. Here, to return to the image I used earlier, different media are seen as occupying the same terrain, but conflict is avoided through the existence of what might be called mutual gaps. Songs, for instance, might be expected to epitomize contest, for it is axiomatic that they involve the addition of music to a text that not only existed prior to the music, but was usually conceived as a self-sufficient entity.[13] In some cases, and certainly in the most interesting ones from an analytical point of view, the result is conflict between the

---

[10] Lawrence Kramer, *Music and Poetry: The Nineteenth Century and After* (Berkeley, 1984), 17.

[11] See Ch. 2, p. 66 above.

[12] Ernest Lindgren, *The Art of the Film* (London, 1948), 139. John Wiley uses a related image to characterize the relationship between music and dance: 'Music is only an accomplice' (*Tchaikovsky's Ballets: Swan Lake, Sleeping Beauty, and the Nutcracker* (Oxford, 1985), 8).

[13] This statement applies to the classical art song; the addition of words to an existing melody, or the concurrent genesis of both, is of course much more widespread in such genres as Renaissance contrafacta or popular song.

media and the emergence of new meaning. Nevertheless, as has been frequently observed, composers often select their texts for their 'musical' properties, as for instance the allusive and epigrammatic poems of Heine. In this context, 'musical' does not so much mean 'like music' as 'ready for music'; the prime characteristic of such a text is what might be called its 'gapped' nature. Of course, reader-response criticism sees *all* texts as characterized by gaps, zones of indeterminacy that allow readers to fill in the missing aspects and so interpret the text in the light of their own experience and inclination.[14] The 'musical' or 'music-ready' text is the same, only conspicuously so; it has, so to speak, music-shaped gaps. ('The author of the text', wrote Schoenberg, 'must save space on the surface for music to occupy.'[15]) Conversely, one might speak of classical Hollywood film music having 'diegesis-shaped gaps', in the sense of its lack of thematic identity and structural autonomy (I am thinking in particular of Hermann's scores). Indeed, the same might be said of the Volvo and Walkers crisps commercials that I discussed in the Introduction to Part I, as well as of the literally 'gapped' music of the Citroen commercial, where the landscape shots were edited in between the successive phrases of Mozart's music. In all such cases, complementation results not from the properties of words, pictures, or music *per se*, but from the way in which they are manipulated within a specific context.

Whether essentializing or contextual, complementation is readily associated with the successive phases of multimedia production. The classical Hollywood film, for instance, was in general virtually complete before it was passed on to the composer for scoring; the composer's job was understood as one of complementing what was already there in the words and pictures, which is, of course, highly consistent with the assumption that the music should be, as Lindgren put it, a servant art. Similarly, in song, the addition of music to an existing poetic text corresponds to the idea that words and music have complementary functions, though here there is less agreement regarding the issue of dominance. Such successive production, normally involving a number of individuals, is equally characteristic of the contest model. The visuals of music videos used to be invariably, and are still generally, superimposed upon existing songs; while in 'Fantasia' Disney's artists were adding images to music that was in some cases several centuries old. The difference is that, in the contest model, the emphasis is more overtly on the point of reception rather than that of production—on the

---

[14] See e.g. Wolfgang Iser, *The Act of Reading: A Theory of Aesthetic Response* (Baltimore, 1978).

[15] Foreword to *Texte* (Vienna, 1926), trans. in Hahl-Koch (ed.), *Arnold Schoenberg, Wassily Kandinsky*, 89. (*Texte* was an omnibus publication of the libretti for *Die glückliche Hand, Totentantz der Principien, Requiem,* and *Die Jakobsleiter.*)

esthesic rather than the poietic level, to use Nattiez's terminology. And the reason for this is perhaps obvious. With its radical deconstruction of the component media and its generation of new meaning, contest covers its own traces, eradicates its own past; for this reason I see it as the paradigmatic model of multimedia.

Conformance, by contrast, is hardly a model of multimedia at all, if (as I maintain) multimedia is to be defined in terms of the perceived interaction of different media. One might, at the risk of a gratuitous multiplication of terminology, use the term 'multimedia' for all combinations of media, regardless of their experiential effect, while reserving the term 'intermedia' for those instances where such interaction is to be found (which is to say, complementation and, above all, contest).[16] But what is more germane is to observe that, as I said, instances of overall conformance, as opposed to the conformance of individual media within a multimedia whole, are vanishingly rare. Overall conformance is like Jerrold Levinson's category of 'juxtapositional' hybrid art-forms, in which 'the objects or products of two (or more) arts are simply joined together and presented as one larger, more complex unit. . . . [T]he contributing elements . . . form a whole by summation and not by merging or dissolution of individual boundaries.'[17] In poietic terms, Levinson's category makes perfectly good sense. In esthesic terms, however, it is in effect a null category, because aligned media are *always* perceived as interacting with one another (even if, in the limiting case, one medium is only perceived as an unwanted interference in relation to another). Indeed, something similar might be said, if with less force, of complementation; it is hard to instance an IMM in which there is positively no element of conflict or contradiction between the constituent media. Applied literally, then, the similarity and difference tests might lead to the conclusion that contest is to all intents and purposes the only category of multimedia. A more sensitive application, however, will distinguish between the different roles played by different media within any IMM, and will characterize the relative preponderance of conformance, complementation, and contest.

[16] Although not used by her, the term 'intermedia' is suggested by Claudia Stanger's coining of the term 'intertext' in a parallel context ('The Semiotic Elements of a Multiplanar Discourse: John Harbison's Musical Setting of Michael Fried's "Depths" ', in Steven Paul Scher (ed.), *Music and Text: Critical Inquiries* (Cambridge, 1992), 193–215: 214).

[17] Jerrold Levinson, 'Hybrid Art Forms', *Journal of Aesthetic Education*, 18/4 (Winter 1984), 5–13: 8–9; the article is reprinted, with a few additional end-notes, in *idem*, *Music, Art, and Metaphysics: Essays in Philosophical Aesthetics* (Ithaca, NY, 1990), 26–36. Levinson's other categories, which can readily be applied to multimedia, are 'synthesis or fusion' (in which there is interaction between the products of each art and their relative contributions are roughly equal) and 'transformation' (which accounts for other instances of interaction).

Primacy and Expression Theory

The existing literature of multimedia suffers, as I see it, from two associated problems: the terminological impoverishment epitomized by film criticism's traditional categorization of all music–picture relationships as either parallel or contrapuntal, and a largely unconscious (and certainly uncritical) assumption that such relationships are to be understood in terms of hegemony or hierarchy rather than interaction. These assumptions go back as far as the theorization of multimedia can be traced, which is to say to ancient Greece. In his *Republic*, Plato described the relationship between text and music (which, historically, is the main source of multimedia theory) in terms of the language of conformance: 'the foot and the melody', he wrote, should 'conform to . . . man's speech and not the speech to the foot and the melody'.[18] The second part of the sentence shows that when Plato says 'conform' he means what I have called unitary conformance, and this becomes even clearer when he adds that 'the harmony and rhythm must follow the words and not the words these'. And unitary conformance has been the dominant model of inter-media relationships ever since. Peter F. Stacey has provided a concise but meaty synopsis of music–text theory from Plato's time to the present century,[19] and it would be redundant to reiterate the successive statements he quotes from Guido, Zarlino, Galilei, Monteverdi, Gluck, and (of course) Goethe, among others, all of whom assert the primacy of the text and the need of the music to 'serve' it, as Gluck said—a term that links in turn with Lindgren's description of film music as a 'servant art'.[20]

But Stacey provides two important glosses on the story. The first is that he traces an overall change in emphasis from conformance at the level of words (as in Plato, Guido, and Zarlino) to conformance at the semantic level; 'the important thing' in song setting, according to Goethe, 'is to put the listener into the mood that the poem establishes'.[21] And Stacey links this migration of conformance from the lexical to the semantic level with the reversal in text-music relations that

[18] Trans. in Oliver Strunk (ed.), *Source Readings in Music History* (New York, 1950), 7.

[19] Peter F. Stacey, 'Towards the Analysis of the Relationship of Music and Text in Contemporary Composition', *Contemporary Music Review*, 5 (1989), 9–27. Stacey begins his account with the two quotations from Plato that I have just cited.

[20] 'I have striven to *limit* the music to its true function, which is to *serve* the poetry expressively while following the stages of the intrigue', from Gluck's preface to *Alceste* (trans. taken from Michel Poizat, *The Angel's Cry: Beyond the Pleasure Principle in Opera* (Ithaca, NY, 1992), 55). Gluck's words are echoed even more closely by Miklos Rosza's maxim that, in the cinema, 'Music serves the drama' (quoted in Penn, 'Music and Images', 63).

[21] Letter of 2 May 1820, quoted in Stacey, 'Relationship of Music and Text', 12. Roger Parker provides a further gloss on this story by tracing a parallel development from Momigny to late Verdi—in other words, from the beginning to the end of the nineteenth century ('On Reading Nineteenth-Century Opera').

ensued in the nineteenth century. He cites Schopenhauer's maxim that 'the text . . . should never leave a subordinate position, in order to make itself the chief element and the music a mere means of expressing it'. The rationale for this is that, as Schopenhauer goes on to say, 'music expresses the quintessence of life and its events'.[22] In other words, music embodies pure meaning; the culmination of the migration from lexical to semantic conformance, then, establishes the primacy of music and consequently the subordinate status of the text. And this explains Liszt's prediction, which Stacey also quotes, that 'the masterpieces of music will absorb the masterpieces of literature'.[23] In one sense, then, we may speak of a diametric change in thinking on music–text relations; the Platonic assumption of the primacy of text, publicly challenged in the 'Querelle des Bouffons', yielded in the nineteenth century to that of music. But to say this is at the same time to emphasize the continuity of approach from Plato to Liszt. The conceptual model in operation—unitary conformance—does not change; all that happens is that the primary and subordinate terms flip over, so to speak. I shall soon return to this.

The second point that Stacey makes is an even more fundamental one: the practice of text setting has rarely conformed to the theory. 'The surviving fragments of Greek music', he says, 'point to a discrepancy between theory and practice': melodic structure not infrequently overrides the patterns of speech.[24] In the medieval period too, he says, 'there would appear to be a substantial gap between theoretical statement and compositional practice'.[25] And in later periods discrepancies between what was said and what was done became notorious. Michel Poizat points out that *Alceste*, the opera in the preface to which Gluck spoke of music serving the poetry, owes its popularity largely to its enclosed and reprised arias, which contradict Gluck's own principles.[26] And everyone has pointed out that none of Wagner's music dramas adheres fully to the principles adumbrated in *Oper und Drama*.

All these features, I would maintain, can be found in the current literature on multimedia: the assumption of unitary conformance, the flipping over of primary and subordinate media, and the discrepancies between theory and practice. Here, as in several other areas of musi-

---

[22] Schopenhauer, *World as Will and Representation*, quoted in Stacey, 'Relationship of Music and Text', 13. Wagner repeats Schopenhauer's words almost verbatim in his essay on Liszt's symphonic poems: the musician, he says, 'sublimates whatever lies within [life] to its quintessence of emotional-content—to which alone can Music give a voice, and Music only' ('On Franz Liszt's Symphonic Poems', in *Prose Works*, iii. 249).

[23] Quoted by Stacey, 'Relationship of Music and Text', 13; trans. from Franz Liszt, *Gesammelte Schriften* (Leipzig, 1882), iv. 58.

[24] Stacey, 'Relationship of Music and Text', 10.   [25] Ibid.

[26] Poizat, *Angels' Cry*, 57; he is reiterating an observation by Jacques Bourgeois.

cology, the writings of Joseph Kerman have played a key role. In the introduction to his highly influential text *Opera as Drama* (the title of which carries an unmistakable implication of rewriting Wagner), Kerman makes the following memorable statement:

Of the many current partial attitudes towards opera, two are most stultifying: the one held by musicians, that opera is a low form of music, and the one apparently held by everyone else, that opera is a low form of drama. These attitudes stem from the exclusively musical and the exclusively literary approaches to opera.[27]

One could hardly ask for a more ringing attack on the idea of unitary conformance, or more generally on the idea that either text or music should be the servant of the other. But Kerman seems to find it hard to adhere to his own position. Two sentences later, he quotes Edward Cone's statement that 'In any opera . . . we must always rely on the music as our guide toward an understanding of the composer's conception of the text. It is this conception, not the bare text itself, that is authoritative in defining the ultimate meaning of the work.'[28] And using this unambiguous statement of the primacy—the ultimate authority—of music as a kind of shield, Kerman sets out his own view: 'The final judgement, then, is squarely musical, but not purely musical, any more than it is purely literary.'[29] Turning as it does on the distinction between 'squarely' and 'purely', Kerman's formulation is as obscure as Cone's is clear, but its basis in the concept of primacy seems evident enough.

'It is not by reading Kerman's introduction', writes Peter Kivy (who perhaps finds this formulation as cryptic as I do), 'that we come to understand what his thesis is, but by reading what he says about individual operas and how he values them.'[30] And Kivy goes on to make a comparison between his and Kerman's views on *Così fan tutte*. For Kerman, there is a contradiction between the psychology of the text and that of the music: Da Ponte's libretto is all about the shallowness of human emotion, whereas Mozart, being Mozart, wrote music of uncanny psychological depth. As Kivy summarizes Kerman, the consequence is that 'whereas *Figaro* is a perfect work from the point of view of opera as drama, *Così* is a flawed one'.[31] When he says 'from the point of view of opera as drama', Kivy is distinguishing Kerman's approach

[27] Joseph Kerman, *Opera as Drama* (New York, 1956), 21.

[28] Ibid. 21–2. He gives the source as Cone's 'The Old Man's Toys: Verdi's Last Operas', *Perspectives USA*, 6 (1954).

[29] Kerman, *Opera as Drama*, 22.

[30] Peter Kivy, *Osmin's Rage: Philosophical Reflections on Opera, Drama, and Text* (Princeton, 1988), 257.

[31] Ibid. 258.

from his own, which he terms 'drama-made-music'. *Così*, he suggests, is in effect a sinfonia concertante on the stage; the characters have so little depth because they are not individuals but types (*the* soprano, *the* heroic tenor, and so on), and the plot is simply an excuse for the symmetrical permutations and combinations of the voices. 'If what happens in *Così fan tutte* is not "impossible",' writes Kivy, 'it is certainly "improbable" in the extreme.'[32] But for Kivy that is not the issue. From the point of view of opera as drama-made-music, Kivy continues, Da Ponte's text is 'the quintessentially musical libretto, and the opera that Mozart made of it his ultimate triumph. It gave his musical fantasy almost complete freedom, because Da Ponte's plot was a purely musical design—a purely musical "story".' For Kivy, then, *Così* ('and I mean it', he adds, 'to stand for all operatic works') is purely, and not just squarely, musical; Kivy could hardly be more explicit in his adherence to the principle of primacy.

Susan Youens has put forward an interpretation of Debussy's *Pelléas et Mélisande* that is like Kivy's interpretation of *Così* in that it, too, emphasizes the musical rather than literary qualities of Maeterlinck's text. Like Kivy, Youens stresses the depersonalization of the characters: 'Destiny's place in the play', she says, 'is so disproportionately large that the dramatis personae dwindle by comparison. . . . The tighter Destiny's grip on the principal figures, the less they are able to explain what they do or say.'[33] Indeed, they 'live at a frontier where language falters because it is unsuited to express the knowledge that matters most'.[34] And this is because Destiny lies beyond verbal explanation; it is music, says Youens, that is 'the voice of Fate'.[35] As a drama paradoxically predicated on the inadequacy of words and the impossibility of effective action, then, *Pelléas* is the archetype of Kivy's drama-made-music, asserting (as Youens puts it in her final sentence) music's 'primacy over words'. It is, so to speak, the ultimate embodiment of Schopenhauer's and Liszt's belief in the primacy of music. Now what is revealing about Youens's interpretation is that it is a mirror image of the interpretation Kerman offered in *Opera as Drama* (which, as it happens, Youens conspicuously omits to mention). Kerman agrees that the characters are depersonalized, but adds an immediate value-judgement: 'this play, this opera, suffers from the chronic disease of dramas constructed essentially out of ideas instead of persons and their progress.'[36] The result, he continues, is that 'fate extinguishes the play. . . . [U]ltimately Maeterlinck

---

[32] Peter Kivy, *Osmin's Rage: Philosophical Reflections on Opera, Drama, and Text* (Princeton, 1988), 261.

[33] Susan Youens, 'An Unseen Player: Destiny in *Pelléas et Mélisande*', in Groos and Parker (eds.), *Reading Opera*, 60–91: 84–5.

[34] Ibid. 71.   [35] Ibid. 88.   [36] Kerman, *Opera as Drama*, 189.

was defeated by his paradoxical effort to convey dramatically the meaninglessness of action.' And this, for Kerman, constrains what can be achieved by the opera; 'in the end', he says, 'the libretto is the limitation.'[37] The reason for this lies in the relative primacy of music and text: the music of *Pelléas*, he says, 'supports the play, never trying to do more than clarify it or make it more vivid or credible'. In short, 'the primary dramatic articulation is literary rather than musical.'[38]

Youens's and Kerman's interpretations of *Pelléas*, then, are diametrically opposed, which is to say that they are in essence the same interpretation except that everything is reversed. We might reasonably be suspicious of a principle of primacy that flips so easily from one extreme to the other; in particular, we might question the rootedness of this principle in any empirical reality. It is harder to be sure about the relationship between Kivy's and Kerman's interpretation of *Così*. If Kivy is right in characterizing Kerman's interpretation of *Così* as the opposite of his own, Kerman is in effect advocating the primacy of text—in other words, the same relationship of unitary conformance between the two that Kivy advocates, only the other way round. But then it would be hard to describe such an interpretation as even 'squarely' musical. What is clear, however, is that Kerman is advocating a conformant relationship between text and music, since what he is objecting to is the contradiction between the psychology embodied in each. And the essential commensurability between Kerman's and Kivy's approach is reflected in Kivy's conclusion that *Così*, and opera in general, should be understood in terms of both opera-as-drama *and* drama-made-music: 'both ways are right,' he says; 'both ways are rewarding, and as interpretations both are more or less consistent with the text.'[39] In one sense this conclusion is admirable: instead of a single fixed interpretation predicated on either the primacy of text or that of music, we can keep our interpretations mobile by oscillating between the primacy of the one and that of the other. In another sense, however, such a stratagem might be seen as little more than a means of disguising the inadequacy of a theoretical approach to multimedia that is predicated on primacy, and more generally on conformance, rather than on interaction.

In the first section of this chapter, I referred to the distinction between unitary, dyadic, and triadic conformance as a modal one,[40] meaning by this that each embodies the same structural model but with a different emphasis. From this point of view, one of the problems with most current explanations of multimedia is that primacy, which is a modal category, is treated as if it were itself a structural model. I can clarify this by showing how the idea of primacy—which may be glossed

---

[37] Ibid. 174.   [38] Ibid. 173.   [39] Kivy, *Osmin's Rage*, 261.   [40] See above, n. 5.

as the assumption that a given IMM may be most readily understood in terms of one of its constituent media—may be incorporated within any of the three basic models of multimedia. Up to now, we have been dealing with primacy in its guise as unitary conformance; in the interests of plain English we might call this *amplification*,[41] since the effect is to enhance the meaning that is already present in a given medium through the conformance with it of one or more other media, without the entailment of any relationship of difference between them. (Kerman's claim, then, is that Debussy's music amplifies Maeterlinck's libretto, and that in essence that is all it does.) In the first section, however, I also mentioned primacy in the context of complementation, giving as an example the assumption that pictures and music have different roles in the cinema, but that the role of music is a subordinate one. We might now term this *projection*, implying the extension of meaning into a new domain, but without the collision of signification that defines contest. (Hermann's music for 'Psycho', then, projects the dramatic and emotional qualities of Hitchcock's pictures.) In the case of contest, primacy implies antagonism, resistance, struggle; I shall term this *dominance*. That is what Kerman is describing when he says of *Wozzeck* that 'In certain scenes the music coheres with great force, producing a curious schizophrenic effect in relation to the firmly literary form established by the naturalistic dialogue.'[42]

It should be clear from this that to assert the primacy of one medium over another is not to offer a theoretical model for their relationship. I shall offer, but not develop, the suggestion that Kerman's and Kivy's opposed readings of *Così* each embody a different aspect of what is most adequately viewed as a contest between text and music. (On such an interpretation, the contradictory psychologies of which Kerman complains can be seen as marking out the terrain in dispute.) Not surprisingly, then, elements that rightly belong to different structural models weave confusingly in and out of the existing literature on multimedia. Paul Robinson, in his self-consciously 'deconstructive postscript' to a collection of studies focusing on libretti, tilts iconoclastically at what he calls 'the imperialistic textualism of today's literary culture', insisting that 'an operatic text really has no meaning worth talking about except as it is transformed into music.'[43] The libretto, he seems to be saying, can at most amplify the meaning of the music. And in any case, he points out, it is usually impossible to hear the words—they are in a for-

---

[41] This term is used by Andrew Goodwin (*Dancing in the Distraction Factory*, 87–8), though not in quite the same sense.

[42] Kerman, *Opera as Drama*, 226.

[43] Paul Robinson, 'A Deconstructive Postscript: Reading Libretti and Misreading Opera', in Groos and Parker (eds.), *Reading Opera*, 328–46: 329, 341–2.

eign language, they are covered up by the orchestration, and worst of all they are sung.[44] But it is not long before we find him describing what he calls the 'libretto-in-hand' reading of opera. He writes:

This, I suspect, is the way that we listen to opera most often. . . . What is going on here, I believe, is in fact a dual process: on the one hand listening, on the other reading, which through years of practice become fused in our minds into a more or less unitary experience. In fact, we become convinced that we actually hear words that are in reality being fed to us by our eyes.[45]

This is intended to substantiate his point that the words don't matter since we can't hear them. But in reality it undermines his original point; we would hardly bother with the libretto unless the verbal input contributed to the experience, and that contribution must necessarily be located in the difference between the music and the words. If the two media are so closely fused that it can be hard to tell them apart, that reflects not the overwhelming of one medium by the other, but rather the reciprocal interweaving of signification that characterizes complementation. (It follows that if we still wanted to think of the music as primary, we would now speak of the words projecting its meaning.) The difference between what Robinson is describing and what he purports to be describing becomes obvious if we compare his 'libretto-in-hand' reading with Poizat's account of a related situation:

Every opera lover knows at first-hand the experience of the libretto falling out of his hands: you are listening to a recording of your favorite opera, installed comfortably in an easy chair, book in hand so as to follow better the subtleties of inflection, the expressivity of the interpretation. Inevitably, if the work is beautiful and the interpretation good, certain passages will wrest your attention from the printed words: you lean back in your chair and lose yourself in listening, for all the world oblivious of the printed text. It is then that the libretto falls from your hands.[46]

As I read it, Poizat's tale outlines a transition from the initial complementation of sight and sound through a stage of contest until, with the 'wresting' of attention away from the printed words, music overwhelms word, and the libretto drops to the floor. This is a timely reminder that inter-media relationships are not static but may change from moment to moment, and that they are not simply intrinsic to 'the IMM itself', so to speak, but may depend also upon the orientation of the recipient.

But we need to look to film theory for the clearest indications of what happens when an impoverished vocabulary for inter-media relationships is treated as if it were a source of structural models. In Chapter 2 I described how Eisenstein and Eisler were trapped by the language of

---

[44] Ibid. 329.   [45] Ibid. 342.   [46] Poizat, *Angel's Cry*, 36.

similarity; they asserted, but could not theorize, the principle of differ-ence. Translated into the traditional language of film criticism, this equates with the distinction between parallelism and counterpoint, of which the second is not a genuine principle at all—or, as I would now prefer to designate it, a structural model—but simply the negation of parallelism. (One could make a similar critique of musicological lan-guage; when Brian Ferneyhough advocates 'the project of consciously composing *against* the words', he is simply inverting what he refers to as the traditional 'representation of textual connotations in parallel musical guise',[47] while Roger Parker complains that writers on nine-teenth-century opera treat the concept of dramatic irony as an 'escape clause' that excuses them from theorizing any music–text relationship other than similarity.[48]) But of course the concepts of parallelism and counterpoint do not exhaust what film critics wish to say, and the result is that the terms become loaded with more signification than they can bear. Kathryn Kalinak illustrates this by means of a quotation from Béla Balász:

Thus the sound film in its most recent development no longer seeks to illustrate passions seen in the pictures, but to give them a parallel, [and] different musi-cal expression. The visible reflection of the picture and the audible manifesta-tion in the music of the same human experience thus run parallel without being dependent upon each other.[49]

Parallel but different, parallel without being dependent: it sounds as if Balász is talking about complementation, but the terminology is far from clear, and Kalinak points out that 'the very meaning of parallelism shifts from one sentence to another'. And against Balász's usage we can set that of George Burt, according to whom, 'In filmmaking, the drama is the primary concern; music performs a complementary role.'[50] We could translate this into the innocuous statement that music projects the film; the two media are complementary, but the film is primary. But just a few pages later he tells us that 'When music and film are com-bined, they interact contrapuntally. Interaction is the key aspect.'[51] Is Burt contradicting himself? Probably not, provided we assume that he is using the term 'contrapuntal' to refer to complementarity. But this of course means that he is using 'contrapuntal' to mean the same thing that Balász meant when *he* said 'parallel', despite the fact that the terms

[47] Brian Ferneyhough, 'Speaking with Tongues. Composing for the Voice: A Correspondence-Conversation', *Contemporary Music Review*, 5 (1989), 155–83: 161.

[48] Parker, 'Verdi through the Looking-Glass', 295.

[49] Kathryn Kalinak, *Settling the Score: Music and the Classical Hollywood Film* (Madison, 1992), 16. The source of the quotation is Balász's *Theory of Film: Character and Growth of a New Art*, trans. Edith Bone (London, 1952), 236.

[50] George Burt, *The Art of Film Music* (Boston, 1994), p. viii.   [51] Ibid. 6.

are supposed to be opposites. The possibilities for confusion under such circumstances are endless, and it is hard to avoid the impression that the impoverished language of traditional film criticism has meant not just that readers cannot always be sure what writers are saying about music–film relationships, but that the writers are sometimes not sure themselves.

In contemporary film criticism's attack on the terminology of parallelism and counterpoint, however, the confusion resulting from an impoverished vocabulary plays only a subsidiary role. The principal criticism is that, as Kalinak puts it, 'Classical theory depends upon the assumption that meaning is contained in the visual image and that music either reinforces or alters what is already there.'[52] In other words, it is predicated on what, in Chapter 2, I termed 'expression theory': the assumption that music in the film simply represents a meaning that already exists, rather than participating in the construction of that meaning. ('When *tremolo* strings are heard,' Kalinak writes, 'the music is not *reinforcing* the suspense of the scene; it is part of the process that creates it.'[53]) The problem is a broadly linguistic one. 'While it is relatively easy to discard the concepts of parallelism and counterpoint,' says Kalinak, 'it is much more difficult to abandon terminology that sustains attendant assumptions about the transcendence of the image and the dependence of the music in relation to it. Language that suggests music reinforces, emphasizes, contradicts, or alters the image falls into this trap.'[54]

The issue, however, is not so much the primacy of the image, but rather primacy *per se*; the terminology about which Kalinak complains is, after all, equally capable of being used either way (so that in the case of music video, for instance, it might seem just as natural to talk about the images reinforcing, emphasizing, contradicting, or altering the music). The problem lies in an approach that begins by identifying one medium as the origin of meaning, and uses this as the measure of other media through a series of pair-wise judgements of similarity or dissimilarity. There is nowhere that such an approach can locate the emergence of new meaning. That is why we can do justice to multimedia only by means of a theory that is based on the concept of attribute transfer, and on the structural framework within which such transfer takes place. Once again, it is complementation and contest that prove to be critical in analysing musical multimedia.

[52] Kalinak, *Settling the Score*, 29. Michel Chion makes the same point in *Audio-Vision: Sound on Screen* (New York, 1994), 38.

[53] Ibid. 31.　　　　　　　　　　　　　　　　　　　　[54] Ibid. 30.

The Seeds of Conflict

It is perhaps evident by now that how we theorize multimedia is not simply a technical matter: it reflects broad cultural and even philosophical orientations. What I have called 'expression theory', which has its origin in Plato's pronouncements on the correct relationship between words and music, can be linked with what Joanna Hodge has called the 'platonic' view of art—a view that she contrasts with the 'constructivist' view, and which might reasonably be considered to be a view not just of art, but of the relationship between discourse and reality. Hodge explains what she means by the 'platonic' view by reference to the 'picture' theory of meaning that Wittgenstein set out and criticized in *Philosophical Investigations*.

The focus of Wittgenstein's argument is the assumption of the 'picture' theory that language, as a means of communicating information between individuals, reproduces a meaning that already exists in some private, pre-linguistic reality. Wittgenstein's point is that any such private, inaccessible reality cannot serve as an explanation of the observable behaviour of language. As Hodge puts it, 'this reference back to an occult domain [has] absolutely no explanatory power, since the explanation is offered in terms of a domain which remains, inevitably, occult.'[55] And from this it follows that 'The wrong picture of meaning is the picture whereby words and sentences are taken to represent a reality lying outside that sentence'.[56] Applied to art, this corresponds to classical aesthetics with its emphasis on representation (whether in the form of platonic transcendence or mimetic realism) and absolute values. By contrast, the right way is to see language as 'a system through which we give meaning to the world', to repeat the description by Thomas McLaughlin that I quoted in Chapter 2.[57] This corresponds to Hodge's 'constructivist' view of art, which sees it as 'making available new ways of constituting our sense of reality',[58] and which emphasizes contingency and context. What is particularly germane is Hodge's reading of classical aesthetics as a historically specific construction that attempts to pass itself off as universal—as 'somehow the natural and obvious way to set up the appreciation of art', in Hodge's words.[59] Classical aesthetics, then, is ideological in the key sense of disguising its own mediating role. Exactly the same might be said of 'expression theory', and of the terminology of reinforcing, emphasizing, contradicting, and altering that it engenders, all of which is grounded on the principle of an originary meaning which art, multimedia or otherwise, repro-

---

[55] Joanna Hodge, 'Aesthetic Decomposition: Music, Identity, and Time', in Krausz (ed.), *Interpretation of Music*, 247–58: 250.

[56] Ibid. 249.

[57] See above, p. 83.

[58] Hodge, 'Aesthetic Decomposition', 255.

[59] Ibid. 253.

duces. Maybe the linguistic trouble starts with the very word 'medium', which (despite Marshall McLuhan's best efforts) immediately implies a distinction from 'message'.

It is perhaps also evident that the prevalence of what might be called hegemonic models in multimedia theory—the idea that one medium must be primary and others subordinate—resonates with socio-political structures that are deeply embedded in Western culture. Indeed, the homologies are so self-evident that to spell them out would be to court banality. There is, however, a more technical, and rather less obvious, respect in which thinking about multimedia reflects broader ideological currents, and this involves the essentializing nature of most accounts of complementation. As is often the case, the issue emerges with particular clarity in film theory. Kalinak traces the idea that sight and sound have fundamentally different phenomenologies to Plato (of course) and Aristotle. 'Already in place in the ancient world', she says, 'was a paradigm for understanding sensory perception which connected the eye to the ordering structure of consciousness and posited the ear as free from such mediation.'[60] She cites the precisely parallel finding of Helmholtz that, in contrast to the intellectual mediation of sight, music is apprehended directly, 'without any intervening act of the intellect'.[61] And the same idea has been expressed with specific reference to film music by composers ranging from Elmer Bernstein and Aaron Copland[62] to Eisler, according to whom the ear is 'archaic' by comparison with the eye. 'To react with the ear,' he remarks, 'which is fundamentally a passive organ in contrast to the swift, actively selective eye, is in a sense not in keeping with the present advanced industrial age and its cultural anthropology.'[63] Writers like Claudia Gorbman and Claudia Widgery stress the slow response of the ear as compared to the eye.[64] Conversely, David Kershaw points out how visual activity, by itself, remains 'flaccid' by comparison with 'the acoustic vigour of sounding rhythms; it lacks the "edge" which sound enjoys, for it has no transient bite'. When coupled with sounds, however, visual rhythms 'spring forward from the screen with a quite remarkable immediacy, vitalized, dynamic, and organic'.[65]

It is difficult to talk about complementation without drifting into sexual imagery, and Kershaw's vocabulary conveys the same associations that Wagner made explicit in his image of the 'fertilizing seed', which

[60] Kalinak, *Settling the Score*, 22.
[61] Hermann Helmholtz, *On the Sensations of Tone*, trans. Alexander Ellis (New York, 1954), 3; quoted in Kalinak, *Settling the Score*, 23.
[62] Kalinak, *Settling the Score*, 212 n. 9.
[63] Eisler, *Composing for Films*, 20; though it sounds more like Adorno talking.
[64] Gorbman, *Unheard Melodies*, 11–12; Widgery, 'Kinetic and Temporal Interaction', 142.
[65] Kershaw, 'Music and Image on Film and Video', 488.

I discussed in Chapter 2.[66] Wagner is talking about the relationship between music and words, whereas Kershaw is talking about images, but there is a more striking difference: for Wagner it is the word that does the consummating, whereas for Kershaw it is music. And against Kershaw's implicit gendering of music and image, one might set John Shepherd's diametrically opposed and quite explicit characterization: 'Male hegemony', he says, 'is essentially a *visual hegemony*,' and the binary opposition of sight and sound means in turn that '*the very fact of music*, based as it is on the physical phenomenon of sound, constitutes a serious threat to the visually mediated hegemony of scribal elites'—a formulation that links the word, too, with masculinity, and so ends up by reproducing Wagner's gendering of word and music.[67] In this permutating chain of essentializations, according to which intrinsic characteristics are attributed variously to gender, sensory mode, and artistic media, one thing remains invariant: the logic of complementarity, of which Wagner's formulation is the *locus classicus*. I have already linked Wagner's concept of the fertilizing seed with Schopenhauer's identification of music with emotions and words with their objects; this lies behind Wagner's characterization of the operatic orchestra's ability to articulate, as Frank Glass puts it, the things that words cannot express: emotional gesture, remembrance, and the sense of foreboding.[68] Cone has elaborated Wagner's insight into a theory of song, according to which words and music respectively convey conscious and unconscious thought.[69] And Youens interprets *Pelléas et Mélisande* in exactly the same way when she says that the depersonalized protagonists' 'unconscious words and actions issue not from autonomous human wills but from the external agency of Fate'[70]—of which music, as we know, is the voice.

As far as I am aware, Kerman was the first musicologist to characterize the complementarity of words and music in terms of denotation and connotation,[71] although he does not go very far towards theorizing these terms. As I explained in the Introduction to Part I, they refer respectively to the objective and attitudinal properties of their referent.

[66] See above, p. 92.

[67] John Shepherd, *Music as Social Text* (Cambridge, 1991), 156, 159. The same gendering is expressed by Walter Murch in his foreword to Chion's *Audio-Vision*: he speaks of film as a marriage between King Sight and Queen Sound (p. viii).

[68] Glass, *Fertilizing Seed*, 47–9; see Ch. 1, p. 43 above.

[69] Cone, *Composer's Voice*, 31; the link with Wagner becomes explicit on p. 35. Taking Cone's theory as his starting-point, but apparently without knowledge of its origins in Wagner, Kivy has asked what it is that the operatic orchestra expresses, and after complex argumentation comes up with precisely Wagner's original answer: 'It is, quite simply, *expressive gesture and bodily movement*' ('Opera Talk: A Philosophical "Phantasie" ', in *Fine Art of Repetition*, 137–59: 156).

[70] Youens, 'Unseen Player', 70. Youens builds her interpretation on the basis of Maeterlinck's own distinction between what he called dialogue of the first and second degrees (p. 67).

[71] Kerman, *Opera as Drama*, 15.

(John Fiske and John Hartley make the distinction by saying that 'A general's uniform *denotes* his rank . . . , but *connotes* the respect we accord to it.'[72]) Applied to opera, then, the identification of word with denotation and music with connotation suggests the kind of layered, non-competitive relationship which I have termed 'complementation'; music says what words cannot, and words what music cannot, so that each medium makes good what would otherwise be a lack in the other. In practice, of course, things are not quite so simple. Kerman refers to the 'frank Italian convention whereby words and reason yield, at a dramatic crux, to the emotional expression of music handled in its own terms' (later he describes this as the 'chief source of power' of opera in general),[73] so suggesting the same kind of diachronic transition from complementation to contest that Poizat described from the recipient's point of view.[74] But the basic idea that 'each art makes explicit the dimension that the other leaves tacit', as Lawrence Kramer expresses it,[75] lies at the heart of any concept of complementarity in multimedia.

I want to draw two observations out of this. The first concerns the essentialism of practically all discourse on denotation and connotation in multimedia. Kerman, like practically everyone else, sees words as denotative and music as connotative; denotation and connotation, in other words, are posited as intrinsic attributes of the respective media. Film critics characterize music in exactly the same way, contrasting it variously with 'the film' or 'the drama', by which they mean a composite of words and pictures. And in the Introduction to Part I, I described cross-media interaction in television commercials in exactly these terms. At the same time, though, such essentialism cannot be defended in principle. Roland Barthes, whose essays on the semiology of photography contain the classic accounts of denotation and connotation, defines these terms as representing, respectively, primary and secondary signification. Going back to Fiske and Hartley's example, we could say that it is only because it denotes his rank (this is primary signification) that the general's uniform can connote our respect for it (secondary signification). Richard Middleton has complained that, in their 'rush to interpretation', too many writers discuss connotation—

[72] John Fiske and John Hartley, *Reading Television* (London, 1978), 44.
[73] Kerman, *Opera as Drama*, 58, 230.   [74] See above, p. 113.
[75] Kramer, *Music and Poetry*, 6. Kramer himself offers a variant on denotation and connotation, speaking of the complementarity of connotation and combination (p. 5). By 'combination' he means the structural dimension of music or poetry. He sees music as centrally combinatory and peripherally connotatory, whereas poetry is the other way round; music and poetry are in this sense mirror images of one another. Kramer's emphasis on the combinatory properties of music links with the emphasis which many writers about film place on the diachronic continuity and cohesiveness of music as against the characteristic disjunction of the pictures (see e.g. Kalinak, *Settling the Score*, 47, and Widgery, 'Kinetic and Temporal Interaction', 236–7).

secondary signification—without pausing first to think about the primary signification on which it must be based.[76] And when we think of denotation and connotation in this way, it becomes clear that the same medium may denote on one occasion and connote on another. Barthes observes that whereas in most contexts (say a car repair manual—not that this is a very Barthesian example) the images illustrate the text, in the case of a press photograph caption it is the other way round: 'it is now the words which, structurally, are parasitic on the image.'[77] If words and images can denote in one context and connote in another, then it is obvious that denotation and connotation are not attributes of one medium or another, but functions which one medium or another may fulfil in any given context.

My second observation is a further-reaching one. While complementation is undoubtedly a valid model of cross-media interaction, the real thing is rarely as neatly demarcated as the theory might suggest; complementation constantly teeters on the verge of contest. Wagnerian music drama is a good context in which to make this point.'The manner in which we all evaluate opera still depends a good deal on Wagnerian criteria,' writes Roger Parker;[78] and his point could perhaps be generalized to multimedia in general, for most of the points I have been making in this chapter are directly applicable to Wagner. We have, for instance, the same assertion of primacy, but confusion about its direction; it has often been observed that in *Oper und Drama* Wagner insisted that the dramatic text was primary and music only a means towards an end, whereas towards the end of his life—and possibly as a result of reading Schopenhauer—he insisted on the primacy of music. Glass, however, suggests that there is really no contradiction at all, and that what Wagner meant to assert was not the primacy of the text but that of the drama—'not the dramatic poem,' as he famously said in 'Beethoven', 'but the drama that moves before our very eyes, the visible counterpart of Music'.[79] Seen this way, we would have not primacy but what I have called triadic conformance; text and music are linked not only directly but through their common affinity with the dramatic essence, what one might call the abstract drama, which Wagner

[76] Richard Middleton, *Studying Popular Music* (Milton Keynes, 1990), 220.

[77] Roland Barthes, 'The Photographic Message', in *Image, Music, Text*, 15–31: 25.

[78] Parker, 'Verdi through the Looking-Glass', 291.

[79] Richard Wagner, 'Beethoven', in *Prose Works*, v. 112; see Glass, *Fertilizing Seed*, 23, 77. A related contradiction surrounds Wagner's notorious statement in *Zukunftsmusik* that the music was predetermined by the poem. Abbate offers a similar reconciliation of Wagner's meaning in 'Opera as Symphony, a Wagnerian Myth', in Carolyn Abbate and Roger Parker, *Analyzing Opera* (Berkeley, 1989), 92–124: 98 ff. Another symptom of the same contradiction is Wagner's simultaneous description of the first edition of the *Ring* libretto as a 'poetic work' and a 'draft for that intended actual work of art' (see Arthur Groos, 'Appropriation in Wagner's *Tristan* Libretto', in Groos and Parker (eds.), *Reading Opera*, 12–33: 17).

referred to as the 'poetic intent'.[80] (This produces a logical problem, however, if one assumes—as Wittgenstein, Hodge, and McLaughlin would lead one to assume—that this abstract drama is in fact constructed precisely by the text and the music; the implication is that text and music are, in part, reflecting themselves, resulting in a kind of regress. The same problem arises when writers on film talk about the relationship between the film and the music, as if the music were not already part of the film.)

But perhaps it is a mistake to view Wagner's theory in terms of conformance at all. Wagner, after all, wanted naturalistic staging in his music dramas, just as Schoenberg did in *Die glückliche Hand*, and it is only the producers in the Roller tradition who have objected to the 'conflict between the allegorical/symbolic nature of the drama and the often naturalistic concept of the stage setting', as Crawford put it, and tried to impose a Kandinsky-like synaesthesia upon his music dramas.[81] What this indicates is that it was not Wagner's aim to eliminate the difference between media; he saw text and music as coherent, not consistent, and accordingly he saw the relationship between text and music as mediated through their common but partial linkage with the abstract drama. (Seen this way, the relationship between text, music, and drama is the same as that between 'This relationship is a dead-end street', 'Our marriage is on the rocks', and LOVE IS A JOURNEY.[82]) And when, in *Oper und Drama*, Wagner spoke of the 'perfect union' of words and music, he was thinking of union in the sexual sense that underpins the idea of complementation. We are dealing, then, not with an incestuous sameness but with the attraction of opposites. If Wagner gave the first comprehensive theoretical articulation of complementation theory, in effect spelling out the concepts of denotation and connotation without using the labels, it is only natural that we should understand his music dramas on this basis, as William Kinderman does when he writes: 'In works such as the last acts of *Siegfried* and *Götterdämmerung*, the manifold interrelationships in the tonal structure of the whole are regulated by a musical hierarchy, and this hierarchy coincides with and reinforces a hierarchy of dramatic values.'[83] Textual and musical hierarchies work in step with one another, then; each medium elaborates the same underlying structure in its own specific manner.

[80] Glass, *Fertilizing Seed*, 3–4.

[81] See above, pp. 42–3. It follows that the many writers who have taken Wagner to be the epitome of synaesthetic fusion have misunderstood him; for instance Eisenstein, of all people, lists him together with Skriabin among those who have 'dreamt of this ideal' (*Film Sense*, 74).

[82] See above, n. 5.

[83] William Kinderman, 'Dramatic Recapitulation in Wagner's *Götterdämmerung*', *19th-Century Music*, 4 (1980), 101–12: 108, quoted in Abbate, 'Opera as Symphony', 95 n. 11.

Abbate, who quotes Kinderman, is scathing about this kind of neat analytical packaging, which appeals, she says, 'to the commonplace that Wagner's genius expressed itself in both musical and dramatic ideas, each completely satisfying, the two woven together into a perfect whole'.[84] For Abbate, the separation of the spheres of text and music, denotation and connotation, can never be complete; the two can never really work in step. Her vocabulary is instead a vocabulary of contest. She speaks constantly of intrusion; text intrudes upon music, and music upon text.[85] As the music begins to hear the story told by the poetry in Erik's dream (from *Tannhäuser*), she says, it succumbs to anarchy. The Conspiracy Scene from *Götterdämmerung* begins the same way, but 'here, the symphonic overwhelms and defeats the poetic'.[86] There is, then, neither a neat separation nor a natural hierarchy between music and the word. Music is 'pulled awry by a text with which it cannot be at peace'; in short, the two media are 'at war'.[87] And other writers use the same vocabulary of contest to characterize all opera. For Peter Conrad, for instance, 'Words and music are united by antagonism. Opera is the continuation of their warfare by other means.'[88] And such conceptions of opera as contest are by no means restricted to the modern (or post-modern) age. Hanslick saw music and drama as 'mutually destructive', and compared opera to a constitutional government 'whose very existence depends upon an incessant struggle between two parties, equally entitled to power'; the result was 'continual acts of trespass or concession'.[89] And as early as the turn of the nineteenth century, Momigny had characterized the relationship of the media in language which, for all its urbanity, perhaps still carries an undertone of violence when he asked 'Can Poetry agree in every detail with Music?', and answered, 'No: in this amiable alliance, as in marriage, the contracted parties must make mutual sacrifices.'[90]

But we can be a little more specific in tracing the slippage from complementation to contest. As I said early in this chapter, a characteristic of complementation is the 'gapped' text—the text that leaves space for the medium with which it is to cohabit (to use an apt term of Katherine Bergeron's[91]). The text in question need not, of course, be literary. Eisler spoke of the need to avoid extended use of *Lied*-style melody in

[84] Abbate, 'Opera as Symphony', 95.   [85] See e.g. ibid. 110, and *idem*, 'Erik's Dream', 147.

[86] 'Erik's Dream', 167; 'Opera as Symphony', 118.

[87] 'Opera as Symphony', 95; 'Erik's Dream', 131.

[88] Peter Conrad, *Romantic Opera and Literary Form* (Berkeley, 1977), 178.

[89] Hanslick, *The Beautiful in Music*, 59.

[90] J.-J. de Momigny, *Cours complet d'harmonie et de composition* (3 vols., Paris, 1803–6), ii. 622; quoted and trans. in Parker, 'Verdi through the Looking-Glass', 291. This, of course, links neatly with Murch's explicitly gendered characterization of film (see above, n. 67).

[91] Katherine Bergeron, 'How to Avoid Believing (while Reading Iago's "Credo")', in Groos and Parker (eds.), *Reading Opera*, 184–99: 190.

film music on the grounds that it would interfere with the visuals and result in 'obscurity, blurring, and confusion';[92] and he was describing not an oppositional style of scoring but the standard practice of composers like Hermann. But pre-compositional gap-making, if it can be called that, is most clearly seen when an existing text is adapted for cohabitation, and in most cases it is a literary rather than a musical text that is adapted. The most evocative account of this process that I know is that of the composer Robin Holloway, who speaks of the way in which large literary works have to be 'not merely "cut into ribbons" but melted down and reconstituted in quintessence, differently intended . . . transformed into something made to receive and require music'.[93] Such pre-compositional gap-making seeks out in advance the terrain that may be disputed between media, and as far as possible eliminates it; that is how it ensures, or at least favours, complementation. But of course multimedia does not always (indeed does not usually) involve the use of such adapted, gapped texts, and in such cases contest becomes inevitable. Elsewhere Holloway talks of the problem of setting poetry like Geoffrey Hill's, which (as he puts it) is 'so *finished*, wrought and worked-over to a point of self-fulfilment which gives music no foothold or entry'.[94] In such cases assault becomes the only option; the composer has, so to speak, to batter his or her way into the text, creating breaches in its defences and shattering its autonomy. And indeed Holloway has given an account of how he resolved a prolonged composition impasse in setting Marvell's 'On a drop of dew' when he abandoned his original plan to amplify or project Marvell's meaning, and instead wrote music that ' "denied" the poem's sense'.[95]

The most complete vocabulary of contest is the one that Lawrence Kramer develops in his book on music and poetry in the nineteenth century.[96] He begins by discarding traditional accounts of song that treat the music as no more than 'a supplementary expression of poetic meanings'. A better model, he says, is Cone's idea of song as 'the appropriation rather than the imitation of a text'. But, like Abbate, he stresses the element of antagonism that this involves: 'the poetry and music will

---

[92] Eisler, *Composing for Films*, 42. Royal Brown offers a number of pertinent observations about the gapped nature of film music, including its syntactic discontinuity (*Overtones and Undertones*, 94).

[93] Robin Holloway, 'Word—Image—Concept—Sound', *Contemporary Music Review*, 5 (1989), 257–65: 257–8. An interesting theoretical account of a comparable process, influenced by Greimas, may be found in Claudia Stanger's 'Semiotic Elements of Multiplanar Discourse', which describes how the composer John Harbison created a pluri-isotopic ('musical') text for his song cycle *The Flower-Fed Buffaloes* in parallel with the mono-isotopic text of Judge Learned Hand's address 'The Spirit of Liberty'.

[94] Robin Holloway, 'Setting Geoffrey Hill to Music', *Contemporary Music Review*, 5 (1989), 33–5: 33.

[95] Robin Holloway, 'Notes on Setting a Poem of Marvell', *Contemporary Music Review*, 5 (1989), 185–8: 188.

[96] Kramer, *Music and Poetry*, ch. 5 ('Song'), from which the following quotations are taken.

pull the voice in different directions,' he says, and so 'the music appropriates the poem by contending with it'.[97] Ultimately the music must do violence to the text: 'Song . . . is not a refined way to throw language into high relief. It is a refined form of erasure.' And he goes on to illustrate such erasure by means of examples from Beethoven, Schubert, and Brahms, and to distinguish three processes involved in it: expressive revision (when the music subverts the poem through its incongruity), imitation (when the music corresponds only superficially to the poem, so creating an area of semantic indeterminacy), and structural dissonance (when the music denies 'its expressive support in a crucial way or at a crucial moment'). Kramer's vocabulary is powerful, and his deconstructive readings are incisive; if a criticism is to be made, it is that they silently embody the very words-to-music approach which was meant to be being deconstructed. When he discusses 'Erlkönig' or Schoenberg's *The Book of the Hanging Gardens*, he begins with the text, extracts its narrative and connotative content (by this I mean something similar to what I called Wagner's 'abstract drama'), measures the music against it, and—in a deconstructive turn—shows how the music subverts, inverts, or erases that content. What he does *not* do is read the music in a systematic manner for its own discontinuities or aporias; his basic model of text–music relations, then, is one of subverted dominance. Kramer's approach is naturalized by its chronological framework—after all, the texts of these songs were written first—and indeed it *is* natural, in the sense that the sharing by the poem and the commentary of a common textual medium creates an entirely unavoidable complicity between them.

For Kramer, then, as for Abbate, multimedia tends towards contest, and contest tends towards the destruction of media identity. What is represented as an essentialized contest between media—the war between music and words—can often, however, be seen more accurately as a contest between different levels of signification. The term 'levels' applies in different ways to different media; in the case of music, I am thinking primarily of structural level (in any of the conventional music-theoretical senses), while the corresponding axis in language extends from the lexical to the semantic. But in either case the same principle applies, and this is the principle that I referred to at the beginning of this chapter as differential elaboration. Different media are just that: different. As Luciano Berio says, 'their syntactic differences are irreducible.'[98] It is possible to link media robustly at one level of hier-

---

[97] The link with Abbate becomes most overt when he speaks of the 'volatile interplay between two attempts to be heard—that of the music and that of the poem' (ibid. 169). Like Poizat, Kramer interprets the interplay of text and music in fundamentally psychoanalytical terms.

[98] Luciano Berio, interviewed by Umberto Eco, 'Eco in Ascolto', *Contemporary Music Review*, 5 (1989), 1–8: 7.

archy, as for instance in the parallel crescendo of light and sound in *Die glückliche Hand*.[99] But the principle of differential elaboration means that a relationship of processive similarity established at one hierarchical level will result in difference at another; which is why attempts to force media into close superficial alignment (for instance, by cutting film to music) have the paradoxical effect of emphasizing the difference between the two media. In other words, you can have similarity at an underlying level, which entails difference at a surface level, or similarity at a surface level, which entails difference at an underlying level, but you cannot have similarity (or difference, I am inclined to add, but that is a different point) at all levels. It is not surprising, then, that the historical debate about multimedia is essentially a sustained quarrel about the right level at which to align media.

If Stacey is right that the period from ancient Greece to the nineteenth century saw a gradual ascent of alignment from the lexical level to the semantic, from the surface level to that of superordinate structure, then it stands to reason that the chronic complaint has been, as Stacey summarizes Galilei, that 'the principles of mimesis were being applied too automatically and at too low a level'.[100] The same complaint was still being made in the 1920s, directed now at low-level 'punning' relationships between silent films and the music that was played along with them.[101] The conventional wisdom, then, has always been what Schoenberg said in his essay 'The Relationship to the Text': 'Apparent superficial divergencies can be necessary because of parallelism at a higher level.'[102] And this rule is only confirmed by the divergences from it that have frequently been made in the pursuit of self-conscious anomaly. 'Punning' alignments of media are commonplace in television commercials, such as the Prudential one I described in the Introduction to Part I, and are most often used to counteract the potential banality of the advertiser's message. They also feature prominently in the video of Madonna's 'Material Girl', where the effect is to destabilize the hierarchy of the media.[103] But perhaps the most sustained historical example of the intentional inversion of Schoenberg's principle is provided by the repertory of operatic depictions of madness.

[99] See above, pp. 43–5. [100] Stacey, 'Relationship of Music and Text', 11.

[101] Kalinak, *Settling the Score*, 55. The transition from silent film to talkie is a remarkable story in terms of levels of alignment, with an almost overnight reversal from the high-level alignment of the silent film, based on mood, to a low-level alignment based on the temporal synchronization (and with ludicrous attempts to 'justify' the use of music in terms of the diegesis), culminating finally in an industry practice that generally cultivated the middle ground between these extremes; see chs. 3–4 of Kalinak's book.

[102] Arnold Schoenberg, *Style and Idea* (London, 1975), 144. Schoenberg's use of the word 'apparent', particularly in conjunction with the word 'necessary', can be related to the impulse of most twentieth-century theorizing about music to explain away appearances and so reveal a deeper, hidden reality; cf. Eisenstein's references to 'hidden' and 'secret' correspondences (see above, p. 57).

Ellen Rosand's study of such depictions identifies as a crucial technique the alignment of text and music at too superficial a level: Sacrati and Monteverdi create the sense of madness by attaching music to words, not meanings, resulting in a setting that is at the same time 'madly literal' and 'irrationally obtrusive and dominant';[104] while Handel lets his musical devices run riot, so creating dramatic anarchy. 'Opera itself', Rosand concludes, 'can be said to be generically mad, for its double language provides a perfect model for the splitting or fragmentation of character.'[105] And the means by which this is achieved is the creation of a hierarchy whose levels are at war with one another.

Multimedia and Autonomy

The association which Rosand documents between media hierarchy and reason perhaps carries the clue to the strangely charged ethical dimension that attaches to much discourse about multimedia. Eisler's association of the Wagnerian (or supposedly Wagnerian) idea of 'fusion', and the Hollywood tradition of film scoring that was explicitly based on Wagnerian principles, with the 'domain of synaesthesia, the magic of moods, semi-darkness, and intoxication',[106] reflects the principles of Adorno's culture critique, which demanded a critical, deconstructive reading alert to the deceptions of apparently self-evident meaning. This, too, explains Brecht's insistence that, as he put it,

So long as the expression 'Gesamtkunstwerk' (or 'integrated work of art') means that the integration is a muddle, so long as the arts are supposed to be 'fused' together, the various elements will all be equally degraded, and each will act as a mere 'feed' to the rest. The process of fusion extends to the spectator, who gets thrown into the melting pot too and becomes a passive (suffering) part of the total work of art. Witchcraft of this sort must of course be fought against. Whatever is intended to produce hypnosis, is likely to induce sordid intoxication, or creates fog, must be given up.[107]

Kershaw echoes such language in his article on music and the abstract film when he condemns the 'fawning dependency of visual image on sound' that results from too tight a co-ordination of the two; any such 'simplistic one-to-one relationship', he says, results in 'the one becoming a mere embellishment, a condiment to the other'.[108] And the lan-

---

[103] See Ch. 4 below.

[104] Ellen Rosand, 'Operatic Madness: A Challenge to Convention', in Scher (ed.), *Music and Text*, 241–87: 264.

[105] Ibid. 287.　　　　　　　　　　　　　　[106] Eisler, *Film Sense*, 72.

[107] John Willett (ed. and trans.), *Brecht on Theatre: The Development of an Aesthetic* (London, 1964), 37–8.

[108] Kershaw, 'Music and Image on Film and Video', 488, 485.

guage of all these statements is more than a little reminiscent of Hanslick, who said of listeners who looked to music for a merely emotive experience that 'a good cigar, some exquisite dainty, or a warm bath yield . . . the same enjoyment as a Symphony'.[109] (Such listeners, he continues, would do better to use chloroform than music, and so would have no need 'for stooping to the vulgar practice of wine-bibbing, though it must be confessed', he adds, 'that this, too, is not without its musical effects'.)

Why the strikingly moralistic and even prurient language? In Kershaw's case it is perhaps merely a rhetorical hangover from critical theory (allied, incidentally, to a Schoenbergian or Kandinskian inheritance: 'It is vital', he remarks, 'that each medium be permitted to develop according to its own "inner necessity" '[110]). But in Hanslick's case the explanation has to be different, and it lies in what can only be called the 'ethics of autonomy'. When Abbate and Kramer speak of the state of war between music and language, they do so with a kind of deconstructionist glee: they are indulging in a post-modernist celebration of the inversion and collapse of established hierarchies of signification. When Hanslick says the same, he means exactly the opposite. '[T]he rigour with which music is subordinated to words', he says, 'is generally in an inverse ratio to the independent beauty of the former'; that is why there is 'a perpetual *warfare* between the principles of dramatic nicety and musical beauty'.[111] In so far as the word intrudes upon music, then, music loses its own voice, and hence it must be defended against such intrusion. For this reason, 'A good opera composer . . . will always allow the claim of *Music* to prevail, the chief element in the Opera being not dramatic, but musical beauty.'[112] As I read him (and it has to be admitted that no reading of Hanslick can ever be much more than a personal interpretation), Hanslick's primary concern is to maintain the autonomy of music, and in principle I suppose that of other media, in the alignment of one medium with another. He is advocating, in other words, a complementation model based on the differential elaboration of each medium—the very theory of opera, ironically, which Wagner put forward in his image of the fertilizing seed. But if Abbate is right, Wagner's theory was not a good representation of his own practice, which instead tended towards contest and consequently the deconstruction of the structural hierarchy of each participating medium. Read this way, Hanslick's book is an accurately targeted assault on the Wagnerian music drama.

I have explained the autonomy but not the ethics. This, however,

---

109 Hanslick, *The Beautiful in Music*, 125.
110 Kershaw, 'Music and Image on Film and Video', 483.
111 Hanslick, *The Beautiful in Music*, 57, 58.   112 Ibid. 59–60.

follows easily enough. Romantic aesthetics associated structural unity with creative genius (the outstanding symbol of this is Schenker's fervent espousal of Mozart's and Beethoven's descriptions of the moment of inspiration in which their works were revealed to them, complete in every last detail—descriptions which have subsequently been shown to have been fabricated[113]). And it associated both structural unity and creative genius with artistic value. Anything that impinges upon structural unity—and for Hanslick that meant any cross-media contest—must therefore diminish artistic value, or reduce art to entertainment or mere hedonism (this is where Hanslick's cigars, dainties, and warm baths come in). It is easy to see, then, that as long as Romantic aesthetics persisted—and it still does in rock music, if not elsewhere—the alliance of one medium with another is bound to attract suspicion in much the same way (and for much the same reasons) that musical arrangements and transcriptions were widely seen as disreputable during the first half of the twentieth century. When music videos were first introduced, rock die-hards saw them as intruding upon the authenticity of the musical experience and the authority of the musicians.[114] Such late twentieth-century responses merely replicate old arguments that good music or good writing cannot but be defamed through union with another medium ('I hate to believe', said Rilke of his own poetry, 'that there could be any room left over for another art'[115]), and that therefore the only art that welcomes the embrace of another is bad art: in the mid-1830s Bellini wrote that 'a good *dramma per musica* is the one that does not make good sense'.[116] And just before he describes film music as a servant art, Lindgren states equally flatly that 'Music which is so good that it calls attention to itself at the expense of the film is out of place.'[117]

I have described contest as the paradigmatic model of multimedia; it follows, then, that analysing musical multimedia entails dispensing with the ethics of autonomy, and with the Romantic conception of authorship which underwrites it. A basic fact about most multimedia is that it is the work of more than one author. But critics and analysts

---

[113] On Schenker, see Nicholas Cook, 'Music Minus One: Rock, Theory, and Performance', *New Formations*, 27 (1996), 23–41; on fabrication, see Maynard Solomon, 'On Beethoven's Creative Process: A Two-Part Invention', in *Beethoven Essays* (Cambridge, Mass., 1988), 126–38.

[114] 'The video "boom" is being used to try to "fix" musical meanings, close off listeners' interpretative autonomy, and at the same time focus attention on a new technology under the control of the music leisure industries and the advertisers' (Richard Middleton, 'Articulating Musical Meaning/Reconstructing Musical History/Locating the "Popular" ', *Popular Music*, 5 (1985), 41; quoted and discussed in Goodwin, *Dancing in the Distraction Factory*, 9).

[115] Rainer Maria Rilke, *Letters, 1910–1926* (New York, 1969), 246; quoted in Kramer, *Music and Poetry*, 128.

[116] Letter to Count Carlo Peopli, quoted in Parker, 'Verdi through the Looking-Glass', 297.

[117] Lindgren, *Art of the Film*, 139.

seem to go out of their way to avoid recognizing this. Kerman's principle that operas are squarely (if not purely) musical, which must imply that they are essentially the work of their composers, leads to the construction of a position of authority that is expressed most openly in the writings of Frits Noske. '[O]nce a composer is prevented from bending a librettist to his will,' says Noske, 'he is unable to display his full force as a dramatist.'[118] Elsewhere he comments on a contradiction between text and music in *Così*, and asks: 'Which of the two is speaking the truth, text or music? Of course it is the music that belies the words and not vice versa. Thus music ironically reveals the dramatic truth.'[119] In saying this, Noske is erasing the inherently dialogic nature of opera and of all multimedia, assimilating it instead to the criteria of univocality upheld by Romantic aesthetics; and what he spells out is hardly more than what traditional musicological approaches have done by implication. A principal aim of multimedia theory as I understand it, then, must be to reverse this erasure. And in technical terms, I would suggest, the principal means by which this is likely to be achieved is by analysing the way in which contest deconstructs media identities, fracturing the familiar hierarchies of music and other arts into disjointed chunks or associative chains. The remainder of this book will offer some indications as to what this might mean in practice.

[118] Frits Noske, *The Signifier and the Signified: Studies in the Operas of Mozart and Verdi* (The Hague, 1977), 195.

[119] Ibid. 102. Abbate and Parker criticize a similar formulation by Noske in their Introduction to *Analyzing Opera*, 13.

PART II

Introduction: Steps towards Analysis

'One conclusion seems to be insistent,' writes Roger Parker towards the end of his article 'Verdi through the Looking-Glass'. 'It is that . . . we can espouse no "ideal" way in which words and music will make drama together, and that we should be careful not to approach the issue with unconscious *a priori* assumptions.'[1] As I tried to show in Chapter 3—and the point applies to multimedia in general, not just to opera—the traditional language for analysing the interaction of different media is thoroughly entangled with prescription, implicit value-judgement, and unsupported generalization. One of the points of having a relatively standardized vocabulary for the description of cross-media relationships is that it makes it possible to reverse this process, so prising description apart from prescription. Where Lindgren says that music which is so good that it calls attention to itself at the expense of the film is out of place,[2] then, we might instead say that film music is normally designed to complement the words and pictures; where Plato says that harmony and rhythm must follow the words, we can say that music may amplify textual meaning (but then again, it may not). Moreover, a terminology that avoids, as far as possible, prejudging what it finds is the best insurance against the kind of critical treadmill that Parker goes on to describe: the interminable celebrations of the perfect marriage of music and words that he describes (in words which I have already quoted) as 'dispiritingly dull, encouraging us again and again to search across repertories, revealing the same generic jewels, the same kinds of skillful adaptation between words and music, music and words'. And the role of analysis, as I suggested in the Preface, is to oppose such sedimented patterns of perception, testing easy, 'with-the-grain' interpretations against other possible readings, and in this way seeking out the unconscious a priori assumptions that Parker speaks of.

I don't, of course, mean to imply that analysis should not begin with a 'naturalistic' reading of the IMM in question: that is to say, one that reflects sedimented patterns of perception. My point is precisely that this is a starting-point, which is to say that one should move away from it. But it is worth asking some basic questions before one does so, since a naturalistic perception is as valid an input into the analytical process as any other (but not *more* valid, of course). For instance, does the IMM give the impression that there is an originary meaning located within

---

[1] Parker, 'Verdi through the Looking-Glass', 305.   [2] See above, p. 128.

a specific medium, such that the other media merely express this meaning? Do there appear to be constant relationships between the various media (for instance, the 'hierarchy of discourses identified as central in the classic realist text', as Andrew Goodwin puts it[3]); or are these relationships variable and contextual? How is the recipient of the IMM positioned by virtue of any such hierarchies? And how far do they correspond to discrete stages in the production process (as in the musical setting of a pre-existent text or the scoring of a completed film), and to what might be called the 'hierarchy of authorship', whereby opera composers appropriate their libretti, to borrow Cone's useful term, while film composers remain subordinate to their directors? Finally, can these initial impressions of cross-media relationships be provisionally mapped on to the framework of conformance, complementation, and contest? And is it possible to make any generalizations regarding the level of such relationships (in terms of foreground versus background or lexical versus semantic)?

If common sense dictates that one begin with a naturalistic perception, it might also suggest that the best way to move away from it is to listen to or look at each contributory medium on its own.[4] In a television commercial, for instance, you can turn the sound down and view the pictures, and although it isn't normally possible to separate the music from the dialogue or voice-over in the same way, it is at least possible to focus attention on one as against the other. Here another set of questions comes into play, the last of which I shall return to shortly: How far does each medium create the same effect when heard or seen on its own as when experienced in the context of the IMM as a whole? Where it isn't possible to separate the media physically, is it easy to focus on one or the other, or is there a strong perceptual fusion between them? How far does each medium create the effect of being complete and self-sufficient, and how far does it seem to embody a meaning of its own? From here one might go on to analyse each medium according to whatever methods are appropriate to it, charting, for instance, patterns of openness and closure, of implication and realization, and then bringing the analysis of all of the media together to provide an analysis of the IMM as a whole. And if the effect of an IMM

[3] Goodwin, *Dancing in the Distraction Factory*, 94. Goodwin is drawing from Colin MacCabe, 'Realism and the Cinema: Notes on Some Brechtian Theses', *Screen*, 15/2 (1974), 7–27. As MacCabe puts it, 'A classic realist text may be defined as one in which there is a hierarchy among the discourses which compose the text and this hierarchy is defined in terms of an empirical notion of truth' (p. 8).

[4] This is what Chion, in the chapter of his book entitled 'Introduction to Audiovisual Analysis', calls the 'masking method' (*Audio-Vision*, 187); see also the procedure advocated by James Webster in 'The Analysis of Mozart's Arias', in Cliff Eisen (ed.), *Mozart Studies* (Oxford, 1991) 103–99: 140. Webster remarks that 'Although this method requires that the aria temporarily be treated not as a unity but as a congeries of discrete procedures, one's initial sense of artificiality soon yields to pleasure at the results?

were the sum of the effects of its constituent media, that would be all there was to analysing multimedia. But of course the argument of this book is that multimedia is to be understood as the perceived interaction of different media, and to say this is to locate the topic of analysis precisely in the divergence between the two: between the effect of the IMM as a whole, that is to say, and the sum of the effects of its constituent media. For this reason I see the analysis of the individual media, like the initial naturalistic perception of the IMM as a whole, as being no more than a starting-point, a pre-condition of multimedia analysis proper.

All analysis is poised uncomfortably between realism and reduction: the only thing as useless as an analysis which cannot be related to experience is one that does not simplify the phenomenon it purports to explain. As applied to the analysis of multimedia, this means that we need to focus on the perceived interaction of media, but that we need at the same time to simplify the plurality of relationships between them, whereby every medium is experienced in the light of every other. An obvious solution is to pair each medium with each of the others, and to read each pair each way. In other words, in a television commercial you would read the music in terms of the words and vice versa,[5] the music in terms of the pictures and vice versa, and the words in terms of the pictures and vice versa. Some of these pairings will appear much more intuitive when read one way rather than the reverse, of course; we are used to asking how film music expresses the meaning in the pictures, but not how the pictures expresses the meaning in the music. But the reverse is perfectly possible; in the experiment which I described in Chapter 2, Sandra Marshall and Annabel Cohen tested the perceived effects of pictures on music as well as those of music on pictures. And in music video, asking how the pictures express the meaning of the music may come more naturally, so to speak, than the reverse. In this way, inverting the 'natural' relationship between pictures and music—the relationship that reflects sedimented patterns of perception—means reading film on the model of music video and music video on the model of film.

Some Approaches to Media Pairing

There is a general methodological point here. Whenever one medium appears to have a relationship of primacy over another—whether in terms of production or reception—*inversion* of the relationship becomes a useful heuristic procedure. Here some specific examples may help.

[5] This corresponds loosely to two of the questions Chion proposes in audio-visual analysis: 'What do I see of what I hear?' and 'What do I hear of what I see?' (*Audio-Vision*, 192). Chion's protocol, however, does not distinguish the various elements of the sound-track, such as dialogue, music, and sound effects.

One is David Lewin's analysis of the opening of the First Act trio from Mozart's *The Marriage of Figaro*.[6] What Lewin does here, or at least what he purports to do, is to extract practical conclusions for stage direction from an analysis of the music. In other words, his basic approach is to ask not how the music expresses the staged drama, but how the staged drama expresses the music. Or, to put it more straightforwardly, he reads systematically *from* the music *to* the stage action. He observes structural features of the music (the inconclusiveness of the Count's cadence on 'Cosa sento!', for instance, or the way in which Basilio's first entry demolishes the tonic that has just been reached and thrusts the music back into the dominant), and from these observations he draws directorial conclusions: '[T]he Count', he says, 'must work hard—too hard—to achieve the eventual cadence at the end of his solo.' ('That is,' he adds, 'one feels the Count is not in control because one observes a musical problem.') Again, 'Basilio's solo wipes out the Count's labors, abandoning the Count's hard-earned tonic command and leading back to the dominant whence the Count started out in rage and confusion.'[7] And all this leads to insights which, he claims, will be very useful to the actors playing the various roles.[8] But I shall refer the reader to Lewin's original rather than attempting to reproduce his analysis in detail here. Instead, I shall offer a second example of an inverted reading, this time of a song: 'Wenn ich in deine Augen seh'', the fourth song in Schumann's *Dichterliebe* (Ex. II.1).[9]

Conventional readings of this song, which begin with the text and ask how the music expresses it, tend to lead to the conclusion that Schumann has missed the point of the poem. Heine paints an idyllic picture of love, building up to the words 'Ich liebe dich', I love you. And then, in the last line ('so muß ich weinen bitterlich'), he destroys everything that has come before. As Eric Sams puts it, 'Heine means that "Ich liebe dich" was a lie. But Schumann is innocent of innuendo. His music's meaning is not even discontent, let alone distress.'[10] Such a conclusion is natural enough if one simply works from the words to the

[6] David Lewin, 'Musical Analysis as Stage Direction', in Scher (ed.), *Music and Text*, 163–76.

[7] Ibid. 163, 168.

[8] I said above that Lewin 'purported' to draw such practical conclusions from the analysis because I suspect him of adopting the stage direction approach primarily for its value as a new, and very rich, metaphor for analytical and critical writing. In other words, I think I was being slightly naïve when, in a review of Scher's *Music and Text*, I sought to defend Lewin against Hayden White's criticisms on the grounds that 'Lewin addresses his injunctions to actors, not to scholars' (*Music & Letters*, 74 (1993), 303–306: 306).

[9] The text may be translated as follows: 'When I look into your eyes / all my sorrow and pain vanish; / when I kiss your lips / Then I become wholly well; / when I lay my head on your breast / the bliss of Heaven comes over me. / But when you say, "I love you" / I must weep bitterly.' For another inverted reading of a song by Schumann, see Kofi Agawu, 'Theory and Practice in the Analysis of the Nineteenth-century *Lied*', *Music Analysis* 11 (1992), 3–36.

[10] Eric Sams, *The Songs of Robert Schumann* (London, 1969), 111.

Ex. II.1 Schumann, 'Wenn ich in deiner Augen seh''

music: the 9–8 appoggiatura on the first syllable of 'liebe' expresses and reinforces the pain of love, while the resolution of the dissonance and the motion to the final cadence (coinciding with 'so muß ich weinen bitterlich') contains all the signs of consolation and tenderness: the secondary dominant harmonies orbiting around the tonic, the conjunct bass-line, and the strong underlying II–V–I progression which supports the measured descent of the vocal melody from B (bar 14) to the tonic, G. And at first sight a Schenkerian analysis[11] would seem to confirm all this: the word 'liebe' coincides with the motion of the *Urlinie* from $\hat{3}$ to $\hat{2}$, whose effect is heightened by the 9–8 appoggiatura (in traditional Schenkerian terminology the appoggiatura 'expresses' the structural descent), so that the remainder of the song consists of a kind of steady unwinding of the tension built into the underlying structure.[12] We have here all the makings of the kind of traditional critical interpretation that Parker deplores, yet another demonstration of 'the same kinds of skillful adaptation between words and music, music and words'— except that the music is seen as expressing an entirely literal reading of Heine's text, and hence in poetic terms a misreading of it (and an entirely uncreative one at that: nothing as complex as the anxiety of influence is at work here).

But there is something musically wrong with this interpretation, and that something emerges if we invert the conventional discourse hierarchy of song and read instead from music to words, treating the words as if they were as much part of the music as other features of the musical surface. (The piano-dominated textures of Schumann's songs in general, and the shadowy, decentred imitation between voice and piano in bars 1–5 of this song in particular, make it the more plausible to read the voice part, words and all, as a component of the overall musical texture.) On this basis, we can observe at bars 6–7 an effect that is reminiscent of the Count's first cadence in 'Cosa sento': the music works hard—too hard—to establish a definitive cadence in the subdominant, C major (particularly if the singer takes the higher *ossia* line). And just as in the case of Basilio's entry, the music slips out of the new key as soon as it has been achieved, entering a kind of tonal limbo that culminates in the directionless diminished seventh of bar 13. None of this particularly recommends itself as conventional text-setting: the emphatic cadence of bars 6–7 coincides with the words 'so werd' ich ganz und gar gesund' (Then I become wholly well), while the tonal limbo coincides with 'doch wenn du sprichst' (But when you say). What is more, the emphatic cadence of bars 6–7 virtually disappears in

---

[11] Schenker's own analysis may be found in *Free Composition*, ii. fig. 152 (1).

[12] For Schenker the song stops at bar 16; the piano postlude lies outside the fundamental structure.

a Schenkerian reduction, emerging as no more than a local passing event. The result is, to repeat Lewin's words, a musical problem: the massive rhetorical emphasis of the cadence has no structural support. If the function of the musical surface is to express underlying structure—and that is the essential principle of Schenkerian analysis—then bars 6–7 express nothing at all; structure and surface are at loggerheads. The dislocation continues up to the word 'liebe', at bar 14, where several things happen at once. The harmony suddenly re-engages with the overall tonic (it is with the II that the song perceptibly begins to end); the fall of the *Urlinie* to $\hat{2}$ links this moment back to the opening $\hat{3}$ as well as forward to the final tonic. But the operative word is 'suddenly'. There is no preparation for this decisive structural event; instead, the $\hat{2}$ over II is blurted out without warning. In the same way as bars 6–7, then, bar 14 embodies an inter-level conflict, a structural aporia.

What happens if we now move from this structural interpretation to the words, treating them as if they were, so to speak, the outer skin of the musical surface? The divergence of structure and rhetoric in bars 6–7 already withdraws authority from the emotional commitment implicit in the words; the text–music composite enacts just the opposite of the 'wholeness' to which the text refers. And the music clearly gives the lie to the affirmation of bar 14: on the surface, it seems to be saying, she loves you, but underneath that she does nothing of the sort. (Reciprocally, the coincidence of the poetic crux with that of the music highlights the lack of structural support for the musical surface; in this sense the words express the musical structure.) Schumann, in other words, has created a kind of structural parallelism between text and music. Each is elaborated in a manner appropriate to its particular medium, but in each case there is a conflict between levels: the conflict between musical structure and surface in the one case and between genuine feeling and verbal dissimulation in the other. In this way it is Sams, not Schumann, who has missed the point. And he has done so because he has not read the music as anything other than an expression of the words.

Inversion, then, guards against the kind of oversight that all too easily results from unconscious a priori assumptions; it brings to light features that are submerged or overwhelmed in a naturalistic, with-the-grain reading—and this becomes the more so in the case of IMMs which are more complex in the sense of incorporating more than two media. It also serves another, and more technical, purpose. I said in Chapter 3[13] that, in terms of Kandinsky's triadic model of cross-media relations, it makes no difference whether you see music as

---

[13] See above, p. 100.

expressing stage action, or stage action as expressing music; that is what it means to say that Kandinsky's model is one of conformance. But in the case of *Figaro* and 'Wenn ich in deine Augen seh'', it clearly makes a great deal of difference whether we read from text to music or from music to text. And that is as much as to say that in neither of these IMMs is the relationship between text and music one of conformance (on the contrary, the presence of differential elaboration in Schumann's song, coupled with the structural parallelism which I mentioned, indicates that the basic relationship is one of complementation). Inversion, then, can be seen as an application of what in Chapter 3 I called the 'similarity test': if, under inversion, the relationship between two media remains invariant, then they are consistent and not merely coherent, and so the relationship between them is one of conformance.

There are other things, apart from inversion, which it is useful to do when pairing media. One is what might be called *reading for gaps*. Earlier I referred to the possibility of reading individual media for their patterns of openness and closure, of implication and realization. In a sense that is exactly what reading for gaps means; where there is an absence of closure, or where there is an implication but not a realization, there is a gap, and this gap may play a significant role in the alignment of one medium with another. But not all gaps are gaps in themselves, so to speak: that is to say, gaps that are evident purely from inspection of the medium in which they occur. Many gaps are relational, in the sense that one medium will be seen as gapped specifically in relation to some other medium. Hollywood underscore music, for instance, does not necessarily sound gapped when heard by itself; it is typically 'gapped for speech', however, in terms of its degree of melodic prominence and rhythmic activity, and perhaps also its frequency distribution and timbral make-up. What this means is best illustrated by the reverse. Stephen Deutsch observes of Leonard Bernstein's score for 'On the Waterfront' that, in the opening sequence, 'his wonderful percussion fughetta and sax melody line seems not to make any room for the ensuing dialogue', and he adds graphically: 'One can hear the dubbing engineer holding to the faders when anyone speaks, thereby frustrating the music's intentions, which is still battling with the text.'[14] The situation Deutsch describes is, as his language makes clear, one of contest: music and words are fighting for the same terrain, and the words establish their dominance only by brute force (literally *ex machina*). By contrast, conventional underscore music is specifically composed to complement the words. And the distinction between the

[14] Stephen Deutsch, posting to the Music-and-Moving-Pictures list, 13 Nov. 1995. Much the same might be said in general of the increasingly common use of pop music, complete with lyrics, in place of underscore.

text that is designed to be gapped in relation to another medium—what in Chapter 3 I called 'pre-compositional gap-making'—and the text which becomes gapped only by virtue of contest with other media is, of course, the distinction between contrariety and contradiction. In other words, it represents an application of the difference test.

The final procedure during media pairing that I wish to mention is more explicitly analytical, and consists of looking for significant distributions of oppositions across media; accordingly I shall refer to it as *distributional analysis*. The simplest example of this is the kind of alignment between binary pairs that I illustrated in the case of television commercials: the ABA pattern shared by both the narrative and the music in the Walkers crisps commercial, for instance, or the parallel evolution of music, pictures, and words in the Volvo commercial (atonal → diatonic, electronic → natural, technological → human). But sometimes it makes sense to associate events within each medium on the basis of a number of distinct categories, or 'paradigm classes', and to correlate the patterns of distribution that emerge across the various media. This procedure, familiar to music analysts under the curiously vague name 'semiotic analysis',[15] represents an adaptation of Lévi-Strauss's procedure for the analysis of myth, and it has the unique advantage of applying equally readily to different media. The reason is that it may be applied wherever oppositions can be identified, regardless of any other attributes of the medium in question. In rap videos, for instance, distributional analysis of music and pictures can reveal how these contrasting media are organized according to the same principles. (I discuss this approach with reference to Madonna's 'Material Girl' video in Chapter 4, and in Chapter 5 I use it to analyse the fight sequence in Disney's visualization of *The Rite of Spring*.) By contrast, correlations between media-specific models—implication-realization analysis, set-theoretical analysis, and so on—can be made only indirectly: that is to say, at the level of total output (for example, through the patterns of openness and closure that they yield), or in terms of abstract structural isomorphisms.

This is not, of course, to suggest that all IMMs can be adequately analysed by means of distributional analysis; where there is differential elaboration of media, there is a need for media-specific methods of analysis (hence my use of a Schenkerian approach in analysing 'Wenn ich in deine Augen seh'', and also when discussing Godard's 'Armide'

---

[15] For brief introductions to this variety of semiotic analysis, familiar from the work of Nicolas Ruwet and Jean-Jacques Nattiez, see e.g. Jonathan Dunsby and Arnold Whittall, *Music Analysis in Theory and Practice* (London, 1988), or Nicholas Cook, *A Guide to Musical Analysis* (London, 1987). It should be noted that there are other varieties of semiotic analysis of music, but historically Nattiez-style distributional analysis has tended to monopolize the term; for a comprehensive review, see Monelle, *Linguistics and Semiotics in Music*.

in Chapter 6). Even in such cases, however, distributional analysis can be a useful procedure for establishing what there is to analyse.

Media Identities

So far I have spoken blithely of reading one medium in terms of another, as if there were no problem in deciding what 'medium' means in any particular instance. (Indeed, I have been avoiding the ostensibly fundamental issue of what a medium is since the beginning of the book, and shall continue to do so until the Conclusion.) Most writers about multimedia are content to talk about relationships between music and pictures, or in Claudia Widgery's more explicit formulation between 'overall musical kinesis' and 'the ultimate rhythm of a film'.[16] Widgery's terms do at least signal the globalizing nature of such concepts, and she coins them in the context of a discussion of the various individual parameters that can contribute to rhythmic character. Film rhythm, she explains, can result from diegetic movement (that is, from the motion of people, cars, or whatever in the depicted scene), from camera movement or zoom shots, or from the cutting of the film between one shot and another. And any or all of these may be related to the various parameters of musical rhythm: surface rhythm in its various aspects, harmonic rhythm, tonal or formal rhythm. The process of analysis, then, might be expected to have the effect of breaking down global categories such as 'music' and 'pictures' through the discovery of component parameters that contribute independently to the multimedia experience. And this is just what Widgery suggests: when we apply theoretical models of cross-media relationships to specific contexts, she says (she is talking specifically of concepts like parallelism and counterpoint), 'the process of applying them . . . has the potential of bringing to light countless additional parameters influencing the total scope of their definition.'[17] Seen this way, the identification of the functional components of a given IMM—what may conveniently be termed its 'media categories'—becomes not so much a prerequisite for analysis, but rather an analytical outcome.

But this is where analysis has traditionally become entangled with ideology. In film criticism it has generally been considered improper to attribute an independent significance to parameters such as cutting rhythm. According to Andrey Tarkovsky,

the assembly of shots . . . does not . . . create its own rhythm. . . . The distinctive time running through the shots makes the rhythm of the picture; and

[16] Widgery, 'Kinetic and Temporal Interaction', 138, 133.   [17] Ibid. 33.

rhythm is determined not by the length of the edited pieces, but by the pressure of the time that runs through them. Editing cannot determine rhythm.[18]

In other words, he is saying, cutting rhythm can express diegetic rhythm, but it cannot act as an independent variable; as Widgery puts it, 'it is the interaction of a shot's kinetic content with the timing of its cutting and the dynamics of the individual shots that precede and follow it that determines the ultimate rhythm of the film.'[19] Indeed, it was an established principle of the classical Hollywood film that cutting rhythm should not be perceptible as such: 'the ideal cutting', said Hitchcock, 'is the kind you don't notice *as* cutting' (and he went on to apply the same principle to film music).[20] What we are dealing with is, once again, Gorbman's 'transparent or invisible discourse'; cutting rhythm, camera motion, and other technical aspects of film production should efface themselves so that the viewer is aware only of the diegesis or the qualities that it connotes. Or, to put it more precisely, there is an assumption that each medium embodies a hierarchy such that signification is generated at the level of total output, and not by virtue of the independent functioning of any of its constituent parameters. We have, in fact, an exact analogue to the Hanslickian defence of musical autonomy which I discussed in Chapter 3. And in each case there is a weight of tradition—what in Chapter 3 I called an ideology—that validates and naturalizes such autonomy, together with the discourse hierarchy associated with it.

What may then, despite the apparent incongruity, be called the Hanslick/Hollywood line on multimedia assumes the integrity of the participating media. More technically, it assumes the uninterrupted differential elaboration of each medium, resulting in a global model of complementation. It is, in fact, a prime example of the 'unconscious *a priori* assumptions' of which Parker complains. It follows that, if the role of analysis is to oppose such assumptions, one should attempt to read *against* such media-specific hierarchies—against the grain, as it were—and be forced into deducing their existence only as a result of empirical resistance. But what might this mean when translated into practice? The answer falls into two halves: positive and negative. The positive part is that one should look (and listen) for direct, 'horizontal' linkages between the subordinate levels of hierarchies within different media. For instance, when in Chapter 4 I suggest that there is a direct link between cutting rhythm and musical form in 'Material Girl', the

[18] Andrey Tarkovsky, *Sculpting in Time*, trans. Kitty Hunter-Blair (New York, 1987), 117; quoted and discussed in Widgery, 'Kinetic and Temporal Interaction', 132.

[19] Widgery, 'Kinetic and Temporal Interaction', 133.

[20] Cited in Roger Manvell and John Huntley, *The Technique of Film Music*, rev. edn. (London, 1975), 50.

implication is that cutting rhythm is acting as an independent parameter, and not simply as an element within the 'ultimate rhythm' of the video as a whole. (In short, the implication is that in 'Material Girl' cutting rhythm is opaque, rather than transparent.) And the negative part of the answer follows on from this. If 'horizontal' associations between independent parameters disrupt media-specific hierarchies—if, to use Abbate's striking word, they mean that the media intrude upon one another—then one can also read against hierarchies by looking (listening) for contradictions between their levels. Perhaps the warfare between music and text that Abbate, Conrad, and Kramer have so vividly evoked could be described with increased precision and stability of terminology in terms of the relationships between levels within each medium.

In saying this, I am suggesting that in order to find ways of analysing multimedia that can be generalized from one context to another—in a word, in order to *theorize* multimedia—it may sometimes be less productive to model relationships between media directly than to do so indirectly, by way of their effects upon media-specific hierarchies. The reason is simple: whereas we have only primitive tools for modelling relationships between media as such, we have well-developed tools for analysing media-specific hierarchies, particularly in the case of music. Admittedly, these tools were developed in the service of the ideology of organicism; analysts of music are much more used to demonstrating the presence than the absence of hierarchical structure, just as they are more used to demonstrating the absence rather than the presence of syntactical gaps and discontinuities. But most analytical tools work equally well when set in reverse motion. And if both complementation and, in particular, contest entail the disruption of media-specific hierarchies, then analysing multimedia requires a sensitivity to what might be termed degenerate or decayed hierarchies—hierarchies, in other words, whose internal connections have begun to unravel, resulting in flattened, network-like structures or associative chains. It is perhaps no accident that it was the colossus of nineteenth-century multimedia, Richard Wagner, who coined the term 'motivic web' to describe a principle of musical formation that works, so to speak, from the bottom up. What is surprising is that he coined it to describe not his own music dramas, but the paradigm examples of 'absolute' music, Beethoven's symphonies. (It could admittedly be argued that when Wagner referred to Beethoven's symphonies, he was in reality always talking about his own music dramas, and in any case I shall return in the Conclusion to what I see as the problematic status of 'absolute' music.)

I referred to the motivic web as a principle that works from the bottom up; it embodies the idea of musical form emerging from a plurality of local associations between one figure and another. As such, the motivic web—and the same applies to networks and associative chains in general—represents the opposite of the top-down principle embodied in the idea of hierarchy, which begins with an image of the whole that is then elaborated through successive layers of subdivision.[21] Musical analysis, as it has developed from the time of Beethoven to the present day, has concentrated almost entirely on top-down models, principally as a result of its commitment to aesthetic values grounded (as I said at the end of the last chapter) in the twin ideas of structural unity and creative genius. The procedure I have described in the previous pages, by contrast, is resolutely bottom-up; if there appears to be an originary meaning associated with a dominant medium, then the analytical process promptly inverts it, while the protocol of pairing each medium category with every other makes it possible to chart the processes by which meaning emerges from the interaction between one medium category and another. But of course this protocol is not to be taken too literally. If it were, the analytical process would be interminable, because of its iterative nature: it begins with provisional identifications of media categories, which are refined and subdivided as a result of the pairing process, leading to revised identifications, which in turn result in further pairing processes, and so on. Moreover, the number of pairs (x factorial where x is the number of distinct categories) increases so rapidly with each new identification as to quickly become unmanageable. The protocol, then, is really only an expository tool, with limited aims that may be summarized as follows: to provide orientation, to guard against a priori assumptions, and to get the analytical process started. Before long, any IMM is likely to suggest its own ways of continuing.

---

[21] Further discussion of bottom-up and top-down models, particularly in the context of performance analysis, may be found in my article 'Music Minus One'.

Credit Where It's Due:
Madonna's 'Material Girl'

A Musicology of the Image?

DATING FROM 1985 and directed by Mary Lambert, Madonna's video 'Material Girl' quickly became something of a critical *cause célèbre*.[1] On the one hand, it was instrumental in establishing Madonna's media image as the representative of a new kind of feminism—one that combined the most traditional of feminine charms with a quite untraditional kind of independence. On the other, it played a major role in establishing Madonna's reputation in the academic world as the representative of an equally new kind of post-modernism; she was seen as an artist who composed with images and identities in almost the way that traditional musicians composed with tunes and harmonies. The result is that 'Material Girl' has become one of the most highly theorized of all music videos.

The story of Madonna is an astonishing one by any standards, and her reception in the academic world is by no means the least astonishing part of it. All the same, it is not hard to see why 'Material Girl' appealed to academics. Based on a song whose words unambiguously subordinate love to money, the video incorporates clips of Madonna in performance, but there are two factors that complicate the status of this performance. In the first place, the clips are set up as a staged routine that replicates, or parodies, Marilyn Monroe's performance of 'Diamonds are a Girl's Best Friend' from the film 'Gentlemen Prefer Blondes'; for the academic critic (though perhaps not for many of the video's intended viewers), this intertextual reference creates an effect of ironical distance between the video and the Hollywood tradition on which it draws. But then, in the second place, these clips are embedded within a rather Hollywood-like story whose message is just the opposite of the song's. The video opens with the whirring noise of a projector; two men are viewing the rushes of Madonna's performance. It turns out that the entire stage routine is part of a film production, and that Madonna is being courted by a rich suitor who appears on the set with expensive gifts. She will not allow herself to be bought, however; she succumbs instead to the producer of the film (played by Keith

[1] The video of 'Material Girl' forms part of 'Madonna: The Immaculate Collection', Warner Music Vision 7599 38214–3 (PAL), 38195–3 (NTSC).

Carradine, one of the men we saw at the beginning), who offers her daisies rather than diamonds, and ends up seducing her in a pick-up truck he has borrowed—for a price—from one of the studio hands.

There is, then, a glaring contradiction between the make-money-not-love message of the song and the romantic story in which it is embedded, whose message is that love cannot be bought. The effect is to problematize the relationship between the two Madonnas we see in the video: the actress (whom, following Ann Kaplan,[2] I shall refer to as Madonna I), and the singer played by the actress (Madonna II). To this extent, the video can be said to embody a typically post-modernist concern with issues of image and identity. And the tension between the two Madonnas clouds the transparency of representation at which films like 'Gentlemen Prefer Blondes' aimed. In this way, critics like Kaplan see 'Material Girl' as deconstructing the conventions of the classical Hollywood cinema. But at this point we need to be careful, because such critics are inclined to see virtually *all* music videos as subverting cinematic conventions. And as Andrew Goodwin and Simon Frith have pointed out, there is no a priori reason why those conventions should be assumed to be relevant to what is, after all, an irreducibly musical medium. In particular, the double address that is characteristic of music videos—the effect of which is inevitably to undermine the transparency of diegesis—is a normal feature of musical performance (any first-person musical narrative, whether rock ballad or *Lieder*, requires the singer to be at once the story-teller and a character in the story).[3] Put bluntly, Goodwin's and Frith's argument is that post-modernist critics see fragmentation, discontinuity, and heteroglossia in music videos because they don't listen to the music; one might compare this with switching off the sound during the *Nine O'clock News* and then celebrating the manner in which its visual imagery subverts narrative models of coherence. 'Strangely enough,' Goodwin observes, 'very few analysts have thought to consider that music television might resemble music.'[4]

Even fewer analysts have thought to consider that Madonna's music videos might resemble music. While critics have competed with one another to give Madonna proper credit for being 'truly avant-garde' and even for representing 'the future of feminism',[5] Susan McClary

[2] E. Ann Kaplan, *Rocking Around the Clock: Music Television, Postmodernism, and Popular Culture* (London, 1987).

[3] On double address see Goodwin, *Dancing in the Distraction Factory*, 75. The more general attack on post-modernist appropriations of music video may be found throughout Goodwin's book, and in Simon Frith, 'Afterword. Making Sense of Video: Pop into the Nineties', in *Music for Pleasure: Essays in the Sociology of Pop* (Cambridge, 1988), 205–25.

[4] Goodwin, *Dancing in the Distraction Factory*, 3.

[5] Camille Paglia, 'Madonna—Finally, a Real Feminist!', in Adam Sexton (ed.), *Desperately Seeking Madonna: In Search of the Meaning of the World's Most Famous Woman* (New York, 1993), 167–9: 167, 169; originally published in *The New York Times*, 14 Dec. 1990.

points out that 'The scorn with which her ostensible artistic focus has been trivialized, treated as a conventional backdrop to her visual appearance, often is breathtaking.'[6] The issue I want to highlight is not whether Madonna is a great singer (many of her professed fans don't think she is, and there are certainly some rough edges in 'Material Girl'), but whether one can sensibly expect to understand her videos without basing such an understanding on the music. McClary's own approach to Madonna's music (and, through it, Madonna's videos) is predicated on an association between the compulsive return to clearly established keys on the one hand and male hegemony on the other; her assumption is that by subverting the one, Madonna subverts the other. It could be argued that the establishment of keys simply isn't an issue in pop music in the way it is in common-practice classical styles, so that McClary's approach is not as telling when applied to the former as it is to the latter.[7] What is not in doubt, however, is the serious musicological attention that McClary sees as Madonna's due.

I know of no comparable examples of serious attention being given to the music of Madonna's videos. Stephen Young's self-consciously 'postmodern essay' on 'Like a Prayer'[8] is a particular disappointment in this regard; the author, a professional ethnomusicologist, refers to the music only at the end of his article, describing it as 'unambiguous . . . a mainstream contemporary pop sound with no real subtleties or surprises. As such, its role is probably a mitigating one, blunting and softening the harder edges, the more challenging content of the lyrics and video.'[9] No doubt this is true as far as it goes. But it seems to assume that (to borrow Kathryn Kalinak's words again) the music merely 'reinforces, emphasizes, contradicts, or alters' a meaning that is already contained in the words and pictures, and in this way Young's approach exemplifies the shortcomings of what I have called 'expression theory'.[10] And the apologetic tone of his characterization of the music is reminiscent of misguided attempts to justify film music according to the values of concert music, instead of theorizing its role as *film* music.[11] I

[6] Susan McClary, *Feminine Endings: Music, Gender, and Sexuality* (Minneapolis, 1991), 148.

[7] In 'Madonnathinking Madonnabout Madonnamusic', Robert Christgau praises McClary, but remarks that, 'Having established that Madonna refuses the sort of melodic resolutions that define "masculine cadential control" in the two Whitesnake songs she parses, she gives no indication that she's examined less macho pop—I'd suggest Paula Abdul before Pat Benatar—for similar structures. And those "musical affiliations . . . with Afro-American music" must stand out more when Monteverdi and Tchaikowsky are your daily bread' (in Sexton (ed.), *Desperately Seeking Madonna*, 201–7: 205; originally published in *The Village Voice*, 26 May 1991).

[8] Stephen Young, 'Like a Critique: A Postmodern Essay on Madonna's Postmodern Video *Like a Prayer*', *Popular Music and Society*, 15 (1991), 59–68.

[9] Ibid. 67.   [10] See above, pp. 86, 115.

[11] Arthur Bliss, who was primarily a composer of concert music but also worked in films, made the astonishing statement that 'in the last resort film music should be judged solely as music—that is to say, by the ear alone, and the question of its value depends on whether it can stand up to this

would argue that, in the same way, the widespread inability of commentators to find anything to say about the music of music videos may result from the lack of an adequate theoretical basis for relating what is heard to what is seen. The underlying reason for this, however, is not an inappropriate assimilation of music videos to the values of concert music, but rather the opposite: what I would see as an inappropriate disregard of those values, and indeed of any musical values at all. Even the best writing on music videos, such as Goodwin's, is undermined by the relative crudeness of its categories for the description and analysis of musical structure. Most writers (and here Goodwin is an exception[12]) do not even seem to perceive this as a problem, and the inevitable result is that music videos almost always end up being analysed as videos but not as music. As I said, 'Material Girl' is one of the most highly theorized of all music videos, but in all this literature I have yet to find a single sentence specifically about the music.

In his book, however, Goodwin coins a suggestive phrase that promises something which nobody so far has delivered: he calls the third chapter 'A Musicology of the Image'. As I understand the phrase, a musicology of the image would seek to interpret the music video as, before anything else, a musical entity; to adapt Schoenberg's phrase,[13] it would understand it as making music with the media of the video. My purpose in this chapter is to suggest how it might be possible to work from fairly basic music-theoretical concepts towards an understanding of the relationship of music to words and pictures, so—in effect—putting the music back into the analysis of music video.

test' (quoted in Manvell and Huntley, *Technique of Film Music*, 54). Musicological studies of film music still tend to embody this premiss, by implication if not explicitly.

[12] Goodwin complains that 'the analysis of the music itself remains so undertheorized. There is, for instance, no way of talking about *timbre* in traditional Western musicological terms that even begins to be adequate to its role in establishing musical meaning in pop' (*Dancing in the Distraction Factory*, 57). This last remark is fair comment, and one of the advantages of 'Material Girl' from my point of view is that its relatively static timbral profile enables me to evade this shortcoming for the purposes of diachronic analysis. A fairly detailed taxonomy for music in the analysis of video is offered by Alf Bjornberg in 'Structural Relationships of Music and Images in Music Video', *Popular Music*, 13 (1994), 51–74. His procedure is first to rate the music's potential for narrativity along a number of predetermined dimensions, and then to assess the degree to which the pictures realize this potential. While no doubt valid as far as it goes, this approach does appear unduly to prioritize one aspect of the music–picture relationship, and there is no attempt to move from technical analysis to critical reading. See also Bjornberg, 'Music Video and the Semiotics of Popular Music', in Rossana Dalmonte and Mario Baroni (eds.), *Proceedings of the Second European Music Analysis Conference*, (Trent, 1992), 379–88.

[13] In his Breslau lecture, Schoenberg referred to *Die glückliche Hand* as 'making music with the media of the stage'; see above, p. 55.

Words and Music

The song 'Material Girl'[14] was released on Madonna's second album, 'Like a Virgin' (1984); the video followed a year later. It is only to be expected, then, that there is a hierarchy within the constituent media of the video; one might express this by saying that the relationship of words to music is nested within the larger relationship of both to pictures. But to put it this way is to be not quite accurate. The division of the video into music, words, and pictures cuts across the video's functional categories; while the words of the song belong with the music, the diegetic dialogue with which the video begins belongs with the pictures. This dialogue is in effect supplanted by the song; there is no dialogue after the beginning of the song proper (by which I mean where the words begin—as opposed to the introductory groove, which underscores some of the dialogue). Or, to put it another way, word as narrative gives way to word as song. This becomes particularly salient at the important point in the narrative where the producer enters Madonna I's dressing-room with his daisies and, for the first time, receives a positive response; Madonna I smiles and says something to him, but all we can hear is the song. (This neatly inverts the opening shot of the video, where the two men are watching the rushes of Madonna's singing, and all we can hear is their dialogue.) Paradoxically, the fact that we cannot hear what Madonna says turns this into an eloquent moment: it articulates the disjuncture between Madonna I, the Madonna who speaks, and Madonna II, whom we hear singing. Diegetic narrative and song, then, function as superordinate structures within which individual media are subsumed; one might think of them as constituting parallel hierarchies. As will become clear, however, the relationship between these hierarchies is not a stable one, and in analytical terms the plot of the video is one of emergent inter-media contest. For convenience I shall organize the following discussion according to the categories of words, music, and pictures; but the real topic is the relationship between what may be termed song hierarchy and narrative hierarchy.

The song constructs a single coherent persona, the 'material girl' who defines herself through her relationships with the boys who pursue her. The complete text is reproduced below, and it has a straightforward verse–refrain organization. The verses have a consistent textual structure. In each case, there is an initial couplet that says what the boys do, while the following couplet is a commentary saying that

---

[14] Madonna frequently co-writes her songs, but this was not the case with 'Material Girl'; the song-writers were Peter Brown and Robert Rans. McClary comments that 'interestingly, two of the songs that earned her so much notoriety—"Material Girl" and "Like a Virgin"—were written by men' (*Feminine Endings*, 153).

what counts is their money; this is in each case focused around the last word of line 3—*credit, cash, interest, pennies, rich.* (There is a persistent punning relationship between human and monetary values, most obviously seen in the words 'credit' and 'interest'; I shall return to this.[15])

VERSE 1
Some boys kiss me, some boys hug me.
I think they're okay.
If they don't give me proper credit,
I just walk away.

VERSE 2
They can beg and they can plead
But they can't see the light. *(That's right!)*
Because the boy with the cold hard cash
Is always Mister Right.

REFRAIN
'Cause we are living in a material world
And I am a material girl.
You know that we are living in a material world
And I am a material girl.

VERSE 3
Some boys romance, some boys slow dance.
That's all right with me.
If they can't raise my interest
Then I have to let them be.

VERSE 4
Some boys try and some boys lie
But I don't let them play. *(No way!)*
Only boys who save their pennies
Make my rainy day.

REFRAIN
'Cause we are living in a material world
And I am a material girl.
You know that we are living in a material world
And I am a material girl.

Living in a material world
And I am a material girl.
You know that we are living in a material world
And I am a material girl.

---

[15] For John Fiske 'pennies' carries a faint homonymical resonance of 'penis', in which case 'cold *hard* cash' could also be invoked as part of this network of ambiguity ('British Cultural Studies and Television', in Robert C. Allen (ed.), *Channels of Discourse, Reassembled: Television and Contemporary Criticism*, 2nd edn. (Chapel Hill, NC, 1992), 284–326: 312–13).

Boys may come and boys may go
And that's all right you see.
Experience has made me rich
And now they're after me.

REFRAIN
'Cause we are living in a material world
And I am a material girl.
You know that we are living in a material world
And I am a material girl.

Living in a material world
And I am a material girl.
You know that we are living in a material world
And I am a material girl.

The summary transcription of the main musical materials in Example 4.1, which omits the consistent eighth-note syncopations of the verse and refrain, shows how the music of the verses, marked 'V', corresponds with the textual structure. The antecedent–consequent construction of the music brings out the parallelism of the couplets, while at same time creating contrast between them through the relationship between the half close at the end of line 2 ($\hat{3}$ over VI, bar 4) and the full close at the end of line 4 ($\hat{1}$ over I, bar 8).

The refrains consist of almost identical pairs of couplets; only the first few words differ. Here again the music (marked 'R' in Ex. 4.1) has an antecedent–consequent construction; it is in fact strikingly similar to that of the verses, sharing exactly the same cadential pattern ($\hat{3}$ over VI at the end of the first couplet, $\hat{1}$ over I at the end of the second).[16] In this way, there is a structural parallelism not only between the words and music of both the verses and the refrains, but also between the music of each. *V* and *R*, as I shall from now on call them, also share what—even for a disco number—is a highly redundant pitch organization. The downbeats of *V* spell out an underlying I^{7} arpeggio, and each of its phrases articulates a fall of a fifth (from b♭^{1} to e^1 in the first phrase, and from g^1 to c^1 in the second). Perhaps the static—even insipid—nature of the melodic construction is a pre-condition for the particularly teasing quality that Madonna draws out of this music in performance. And at the quarter-note level, there is a consistent stepwise motion that is again made up of sequences related by thirds (E–F–E–F, G–A–G–A); these lower-level sequences parallel the verbal repetitions in the first line of each verse ('*Some boys* kiss *me, some boys*

---

[16] Another cadential similarity is that in each case the VI at the end of the first couplet is approached via parallel harmony, but the direction is different: I↓VII–VI in the verses, IV–V–VI in the refrain.

Ex. 4.1 The main musical materials of 'Material Girl'

Words by Peter Brown & Robert Rans. Music by Peter Brown. © 1984 Candy Castle Music, USA. Warner/Chapell Music Ltd, London. Reproduced by permission of International Music Publications Ltd, Essex.

hug *me'*, and so on). As for *R*, it similarly arpeggiates a I chord, although here the slower pace of the melodic motion means that passing notes (the Ds) fall on some of the downbeats. But the redundancy remains; there are four essentially identical melodic rises from c^1 to e^1 (only the last falls back to c^1), and apart from the upbeat phrase to bar 5, the music is wholly contained within the ambit of the third from $\hat{1}$ to $\hat{3}$.

At the same time, there are two factors that tend to fuse *V* and *R* into a single unit. In the first place, there is a developing emphasis throughout *V* on downward motion: in the first phrase, bars 3–4 elaborate the descent from $b\flat^1$ to e^1, while the corresponding descent from g^1 to c^1 in the second phrase is prolonged to three bars (6–8). And of course the relationship between the two phrases is itself one of descent, from the e^1 that forms the terminal point of the first phrase to the c^1 of the second. *R* follows on from both of these: it inhabits the space between the e^1 and the c^1, creating a kind of zigzag contour between the two notes, and its tessitura is anomalously low (anomalously in that the refrain is generally the climactic, or at least the most striking, part of a pop song). There is, then, an overall process that encompasses both *V* and *R*: a general downward motion coupled with a diminishing pitch range, which coincides with the increasing compactness of sound resulting, in *R*, from the parallel root-position harmony in all but the last bar. The second factor that tends to fuse *V* and *R* into a single unit is rather more wide-ranging. It revolves round what is labelled *INT2* in Example 4.1: the raunchy-sounding synth melody that precedes the first verse (*INT* stands for introduction), and recurs later in the song as a bridge. Beginning with a rising fifth ($b\flat$–f^1), and progressively filling in this interval, *INT2* is in an unambiguous Mixolydian mode. The $b\flat^1$ of *V* also creates a Mixolydian quality, but here it is more ambiguous; the II–V–I cadence at the end of *V* sounds like a straight diatonic major. And in the case of *R*, with its repeated IV–V progressions, there is no doubt about the major mode. There is to this extent a consistent process—a transition from Mixolydian to major—that fuses not just *V* and *R*, but *INT2*, *V*, and *R* into a single unit.

Figure 4.1 shows how these musical materials, and others, are distributed over the course of the video as a whole, starting from the beginning of the groove. The first observation to be made is that the overall pattern of repetition clearly establishes the role of *V*, *R*, and *INT2* as paradigm classes;[17] each of those materials appears several times, with other material intervening, and in this sense functions as an independent structural unit. And the same applies to *INT1*, which

[17] See above, p. 142, for a brief explanation of paradigm classes.

Bar	1	5	9	17	25	33	40	44	52	60	68	75
			Beginning of song proper									
		INT1	INT2	V	V	R	INT2	V	V	R	R	INT2
		4	8	8	8	8	4	8	8	8	8	8
						*						*

Groove continues throughout . . . .

Fig. 4.1 Distribution of musical materials in 'Material Girl'

at its first appearance (bars 5–8) sounds like just a stage in the textural build-up to the beginning of the first verse, but subsequently recurs with the addition of new materials, as shown in Example 4.1. *V*, *R*, *INT1*, and *INT2*, then, represent the four musical paradigm classes of the song; apart from bars 117–20 (the start of the concluding section, to which I shall return), all the other musical materials are simply superimposed on one or another of these basic building blocks.

As may be seen from Figure 4.1, *V* and *R* always appear in direct succession, which might be expected in view of their adjacency on the Mixolydian–major axis that I have described; the changing weightings of *V* and *R* that result from the patterns of repetition (*V–V–R*, *V–V–R–R*, *V–R–R*) perhaps give an end-directed quality to the overall sectional structure of the song.[18] On the first two occasions that the *V–R* pair appears, it is immediately preceded by *INT2*, again as might be expected. On all three of its appearances, however, the *V–R* pair is directly *followed* by *INT2*; in this way the unambiguously diatonic major *R* is consistently juxtaposed with the unambiguously Mixolydian *INT2*. And this consistency makes it possible to think of the song's macro-structure as based on three statements of the *V–R–INT2* complex (bars 17–43, 44–82, and 91–116), with an introduction preceding the first statement (bars 1–16), an interpolation based on *INT1* between the sec-ond and third statements (bars 83–90), and a conclusion following the third statement (bars 117 to the end). As Figure 4.2 shows, such an interpretation throws particular emphasis on the interpolation at bars 83–90, which now represents the only anomalous element in an oth-erwise entirely regular musical structure based on, but amplifying, that of the text: *introduction, X, X, X, conclusion.*

What is the main conclusion to be drawn from this analysis of words and music in 'Material Girl'? It is that the structure of the music essen-

---

[18] Sectional distributions in pop music are of course inclined to be simply formulaic. However, Pat Leonard's account of working with Madonna suggests that this is not the case with her: 'We'll do something and I'll say, "Let's go to the next chorus and repeat it," and she goes, "Why? Where do these rules come from? Who made up these rules?" ' (Fred Schruers, 'Can't Stop the Girl', *Rolling Stone*, 5 June 1986, 28–60: 60; quoted in Lisa A. Lewis, *Gender Politics and MTV: Voicing the Difference* (Philadelphia, 1990), 107).

INT1	V	R	R	*INT2*	*INT1*	V	R	R	*INT2*	*coda*	*INT1*	*INT1*	*INT1*	(fade)
8	8	8	8	4	4	8	8	8	4	4	8	8	8	
				*	*				*	*				

drops out continues . . . .   (fade)

tially amplifies that of the words. The resulting song structure is highly redundant; one might call it overdetermined. And the absence of obvious areas of indeterminacy—of what one might call structural or semantic apertures—means that the song is intrinsically resistant to incorporation within another medium, at least if significant interaction between the various constituent media is to be achieved. There are, however, a couple of what might be called musical loose ends, both of which cut across the song structure as I have described it. One of these consists of a network of relationships revolving round the e^1–d^1–a^1–g^1 cadential figure in the fourth bar of *INT2*, a figure whose rising fifth (d^1–a^1) perhaps echoes the $b\flat$–f^1 in the first bar, and that stands out against the overwhelmingly stepwise melodic motion of 'Material Girl' as a whole.[19] These relationships are best presented in the form of a pitch-class table (Fig. 4.3). As may be seen, the cadence figure from *INT2* creates a connection between two melodic motifs that occupy prominent positions in the song. The first of these occurs in the passage at the beginning of the concluding section, to which I previously referred (bars 117–20); following the final *V–R–INT2* complex, it consists of four repetitions of the words 'a material', sung to the notes

Bar	5	9	17	25	33		40
	Introduction		X				
	INT1	*INT2*	**V**	**V**	**R**		**INT2**

	44	52	60	68	75
	X				
	V	**V**	**R**	**R**	**INT2**

	83		91	99	107	114	117	121	129	137
	?		X				Conclusion			
	INT1		**V**	**R**	**R**	**INT2**	*coda*	*INT1*	*INT1*	*INT1*	(fade)

Fig. 4.2

---

[19] Devotees of analysis will observe that the melodic skeleton of this figure, $b\flat$–f^1–d^1–a^1, is a tonal inversion of the underlying pattern $b\flat^1$–e^1–g^1–c which I have described in *V*; in this way a middle-ground feature of *V* (prolonged through stepwise motion) is reflected at foreground level by *INT2*.

INT2 figure	e^1	d^1		a^1	g^1
'a material' motif	e^1	d^1	c^1		
'-terial' motif			c^2	a^1	g^1

Fig. 4.3

c^1–e^1–d^1, with the repetition producing the e^1–d^1–c^1 pattern shown in Figure 4.3. (This point in the song gains enormous emphasis from the fact that, for the first and only time, the groove drops out.) The second motif takes the process of liquidating the song's title one stage further, being sung to '-terial'; the word almost turns into a melisma here. Representing one of the additions to the original *INT1* material (see Ex. 4.1), this motif is perhaps the most striking element of the conclusion; it also occurs during what I called the anomalous interpolation between the second and third statements of the *V–R–INT2* complex (bars 83–90), where it has the effect of anticipating the timeless quality of the song's ending.

The second loose end to which I referred has to do with large-scale metrical structure. 'Material Girl' is based on regular eight-bar phrases, and sounds like it. But there are some irregularities. At bars 40–3 a single four-bar phrase is interpolated. Also at bar 40, and at three subsequent points (bars 75, 114, and 117), there are one-bar elisions, marked with asterisks in Figure 4.1. The four one-bar elisions, of course, cancel out the four-bar addition. The result is that by bar 121, the first of the repeats of *INT1* with which the song fades out, the original eight-bar periodicity established at the beginning of the song proper has been restored; the surface metre is back in synchronization with the underlying metre. I am not suggesting that this is a salient aspect of the song's perception, much less an unconscious principle of compositional design working itself out through the music. If this very neat structure is more than an accident (and the laws of chance would suggest that it may be), then it is surely there because someone put it there. And this suggests a degree of compositional reflexivity that might not have been expected in what appears, at first glance, to be a more or less formula-driven disco number. As will become evident, it is not the only thing about 'Material Girl' to suggest this.

Music and Pictures

The closed, seamless nature of the song—what I referred to as its high level of redundancy—means that the video necessarily adds to what is already, in essence, a self-sufficient textual and musical structure. To put it another way, the song is not a 'visual' text, in the sense of containing gaps for the incorporation of visual elements (I am using the word 'visual' in a sense corresponding to the 'musical', or music-ready, text[20]). Under such circumstances, as I said in Chapter 3,[21] we would expect the added medium—the pictures—to create space for itself by, in effect, mounting an assault on the autonomy of the song. And the relationship of contest which this suggests is intensified through the incorporation within the 'Material Girl' video of classical cinematic codes of narrative diegesis. There is, in effect, a collision between two competing hierarchies, and I shall argue that the result is to destabilize the meaning of the words and, through them, the closure of the song as a whole. The pictures, in short, serve to open the song up to the emergence of new meaning.

But we should bear in mind Richard Middleton's warning about the dangers of a 'rush to interpretation'.[22] Before we start drawing premature conclusions about the meaning of the 'Material Girl' video, then, we need to find a systematic way of modelling the relationship between music and pictures in it. Many music videos, particularly rap videos, are constructed out of a small number of easily distinguishable visual strata (six might be a typical number), which are edited in very much the same way that the music is constructed.[23] An excellent example, current on MTV at the time I originally drafted this chapter, is 'This D.J.' by Warren G; there are recurrent shots of Warren G standing against a wall, of the musicians going past in a car, and so on, and while the distribution of these materials is not directly co-ordinated with that of the musical materials, the compositional principle is the same. In other words, both music and pictures can be understood in terms of distributional analysis, and the relationship between them can be understood as an interplay of structurally congruent media; this more or less amounts to saying that the pictures can be analysed musically. Such videos represent, in Michel Chion's striking phrase, 'visible stuff to listen to'.[24]

Can this approach be applied to 'Material Girl'? The graph at the top of Figure 4.4 reproduces the distribution of musical paradigm classes from Figure 4.1, with the addition of two non-structural occurrences of the *INT2* figure (bars 67, 106; the inverted v's show immediate repetitions of a given paradigm class, corresponding again to Figure 4.1, and I have numbered the verses). Below this, in the middle of Figure 4.4,

---

[20] See above, p. 105.   [21] See above, p. 123.   [22] See above, p. 119.

[23] In calling the distinct musical materials 'strata', as if they were there all the time and just toggled in and out of the field of vision, I am putting forward a compositional model rather similar to the one which Edward T. Cone proposed for Stravinsky's music ('Stravinsky: The Progress of a Method', *Perspectives of New Music*, 1 (1962), 18–26). And the model I am outlining here for rap videos can also be applied to the *Rite* sequence from 'Fantasia' (see below, pp. 183–7).

[24] Chion, *Audio-Vision*, 163.

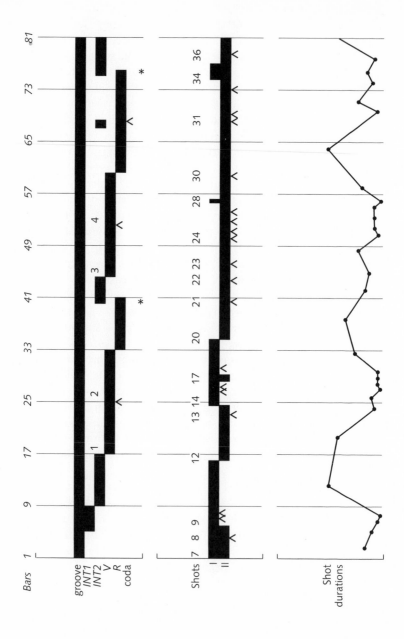

Fig. 4.4 Music and picture structure in 'Material Girl'

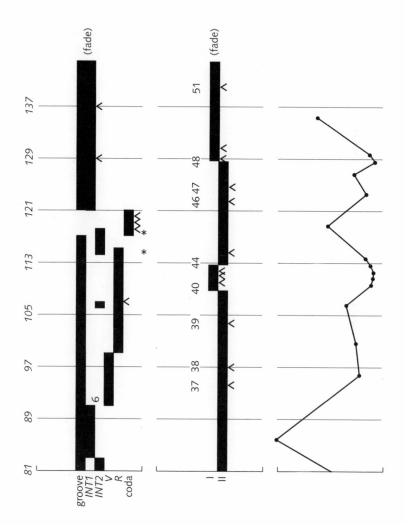

are the two clearly articulated visual paradigm classes, corresponding to the Madonna I and Madonna II levels of the narrative; for convenience I shall refer to these as the outer and inner levels respectively. The numbers above the picture line refer to individual shots (they start at 7 because the first six shots precede the beginning of the song proper); what the inverted v's mean here will become clear shortly. It may be seen that on a number of occasions the pictures simultaneously reference *both* the outer and inner levels. At the beginning of Figure 4.4, for instance, a rehearsal with Madonna II is just breaking up (or was it perhaps an actual take? [25]); her rich suitor has come on to the stage to give her a present (shot 7), and we see her thanking him rather peremptorily and leaving (shot 8). This, then, is a moment of transition between the two levels. Again, in shot 34 we see the producer watching Madonna II in performance, but the object of his gaze is, of course, Madonna I. And then there are the two brief clips that coincide with the interjections *'That's right!'* and *'No way!'* (the third line of verses 2 and 4). In the first of these (shot 17) Madonna I is sitting in the rich suitor's sports car while we hear the song performed by Madonna II; but she lip-synchs *'That's right!'*, making the words—together with their referent, 'they can't see the light'—seem as if they are addressed to her suitor. The second shot (number 28) lasts only half a bar; it shows Madonna I (you can tell it is Madonna I by the crucifix ear-rings) playing cards with one of the men from her stage routine. This is an anomalous and tantalizingly brief shot, and I shall come back to it later.

The identification of the inner and outer levels as the basic visual paradigm classes is confirmed by more abstract aspects of the video design. 'Material Girl' is dominated by two colours. One is white, the colour of Madonna I in her dressing-room (where even the phone, shown in close-up at shot 9, is white) and most conspicuously as she joins the producer at the end, wearing a white dress and carrying the white daisies that he has given her. The other is red, the colour of the stage set (including Madonna II's clothes and accessories), as well as of the rich suitor's car and gift—and also the colour of the expensive present that the producer buys Madonna I near the beginning of the video, but drops in a bin when he realizes that's not what she wants. These invariably matched reds, then, are associated not only with the 'material girl'

[25] It is impossible, or irrelevant, to distinguish between rehearsals and takes, since we never see any cameras or other cinematic apparatus. The paradoxical effect of this classical cinematic convention is to suggest that we are watching the making of the video we are watching (rather than that of some other film). But as Lewis points out (*Gender Politics and MTV*, 130), the diegetic dialogue at the beginning contradicts this by referring to the director as 'he', whereas 'Material Girl' was in fact directed by a woman. (The fact that cine film is being used—as also becomes evident in the opening scene—has no bearing upon this, being standard industry practice for high-budget music videos.)

of the song (Madonna II), but also with attempts to treat Madonna I as if she were a material girl. The symbolism is of course eminently readable: white, the colour of virgins, versus red, the colour of whores. And this opposition gains particular pertinence from Madonna's explicit statement in a well-known interview that she 'grew up with two images of women: the virgin and the whore'. She added, 'It was a little scary.'[26]

But the kind of distributional analysis to which I referred does not work so well for 'Material Girl' as it does for rap videos. Two visual paradigm classes are not enough to support patterns of distribution that are comparable with those of the music, and there is no consistent stratification within the two visual paradigm classes; different shots do not fall into easily distinguishable categories defined by subject, distance, and camera angle, diegetic or camera movement, and so forth. As a result, only limited conclusions can be drawn from a direct comparison of the visual and musical paradigm classes shown in Figure 4.4. For instance, transitions between visual levels are quite frequently within a bar or so of transitions between musical paradigm classes (bars 4–5, 16–17, 33–4, 74–6, 112–14), but by no means is this invariably the case. Perhaps, then, there is some consistent patterning of the visual transitions according to the musical paradigm classes with which they are aligned? Figure 4.5 tests for this, reconfiguring the analysis of the shots from Figure 4.4 according to the music, but the results are not compelling. To be sure, bar 2 of R twice coincides with a narratively important transition between visual levels (bars 34 and 108). And we might also observe that each complete occurrence of the V–R–$INT2$ complex (bars 17–43, 44–82, and 91–117) coincides with a movement away from and back to visual level II. But these are undeniably fragile correlations between the music and the pictures. To achieve more robust correlations, we need to take account of what are traditionally—that is, in terms of classical film theory—seen as subordinate elements of the narrative hierarchy: the rhythms created by cutting from one shot to another. That is what is indicated by the inverted v's in the middle graph of Figure 4.4 and in Figure 4.5; they are keyed to the shot numbers shown above them.[27]

We can begin with some general observations. The vast majority of cuts in 'Material Girl' are closely co-ordinated with either the metre or the phrase structure; in other words, they come either on the downbeat

[26] From the *National Times*, 23/29 Aug. 1985, p. 9, quoted in Fiske, 'British Cultural Studies', 309. The white/red symbolism of 'Material Girl' may be compared with the black/red symbolism of 'Like a Prayer' (1989), also directed by Mary Lambert (discussed in Young, 'Like a Critique', 62).

[27] In the relatively few instances where there are dissolves (which are always associated with transitions between musical and/or visual paradigm classes), the inverted v marks the point where the first image disappears.

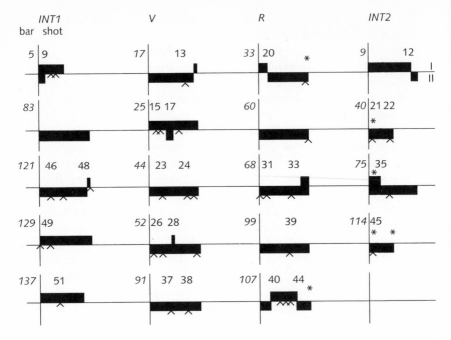

Fig. 4.5

or around an eighth note before it, matching the syncopation of the melody. This accounts for 28 out of the total of 45 cuts that occur after the beginning of the song proper, while a further 12 cuts come on the third beat of the bar, reflecting the music's cut-time quality (no pun intended). Of the remaining five cuts, one coincides with the extended lead into the refrain at bar 59 (shot 30). All this is consistent with Frith's claim that 'Most videos are cut straightforwardly to the rhythm of the song'.[28] The relationship is not, however, as direct as Frith's formulation might suggest. Straightforward cutting to the rhythm of the song might be expected to result in a series of shots of identical or near-identical length, duplicating the music's metre, phrasing, or sectional structure. But the cutting of 'Material Girl' does not duplicate these aspects of the music, and on only two occasions are there successive shots of even approximately the same length (in both cases, curiously, a sequence of three shots, each a bar long in the first case and a bar and a half in the second: shots 16–18 and 25–7). And this has a con-

[28] Frith, 'Afterword', 219. It should be noted that when I refer to the synchronization of cuts and musical beats I am dealing with a phenomenological effect; the correlations given in this paragraph were established on the basis of repeated real-time viewings of the video, not frame-to-frame analysis in an editing suite. (The same applies to the analysis of cutting rhythms in 'Fantasia' which I offer in Ch. 5.)

sequence that may at first sight seem paradoxical. In the Introduction to Part II, I mentioned that, according to classical film theory, cutting rhythms should be imperceptible; they are subsumed within the narrative hierarchy of the film. The fact that the cuts in 'Material Girl' (and indeed in music videos generally[29]) are aligned with, but do not duplicate, the rhythm of the song means that, once again, the cutting rhythms tend towards imperceptibility. But of course there is a difference. Instead of being subsumed within the narrative hierarchy, the cutting is subsumed within the song hierarchy; in effect, it becomes a parameter of the music. And to this extent the narrative hierarchy is disrupted. Or, to put it another way, the cinematic codes adopted by 'Material Girl' begin to lose their autonomy. In the contest between the narrative and song hierarchies, then, the first round goes to the song.

Now we can add some detail. Whereas Figure 4.5 does not reveal compelling associations of musical paradigm classes with transitions between the inner and outer levels, it *does* show some significant associations with cutting rhythms. In the visuals aligned with *V*, the obvious parallelism between shots 17 and 28 represents the interjections *'That's right!'* and *'No way!'*, both of which occasion shifts in visual level. If we discount these, there is a total of twelve cuts, and of these, six occur in just two locations—the downbeats of bars 3 and 7. (These of course represent corresponding points in terms of musical phrase structure.) Again, there is a significant coincidence in the cutting locations of the visuals aligned with *INT2*, where cuts within a given visual level are only found half-way through the first and fourth bars. Here there is perhaps a link with the elisions which occur at the same points in *INT2* (always at the juncture of modally dissimilar materials); the rationale would be that the same shifting quality is conveyed through visual and musical means. In the case of the visuals aligned with *R*, on the other hand, there is only a limited coincidence of cutting locations, and in the case of those aligned with *INT1* there is none at all.

There is also a quite different kind of association between cutting rhythms and the distribution of musical paradigm classes. This can be seen in the graph at the bottom of Figure 4.4, the vertical axis of which represents the duration of each shot.[30] Flurries of cuts coincide with

[29] A telling example in this context is Queen's 'Bohemian Rhapsody', dating from 1975 and regarded by many as the first music video. Almost every new musical phrase or section is aligned with a cut, and the result is that the cutting rhythm becomes intrusive; the effect is rather banal, creating a music video equivalent of mickey-mousing. By contrast, the 1992 remake of the 'Bohemian Girl' video for 'Wayne's World' conforms to what had by then become standard industry practice; the video is cut to the rhythms of the music in Frith's sense, without duplicating the phrase and section structure.

[30] The value corresponding to each shot's duration is horizontally aligned with the midpoint of the shot. The vertical and horizontal scales are the same.

each of the repeats—and *only* the repeats—of V and R (bars 25–32, 52–9, 68–75, 107–14); here the rationale would be that the high level of musical redundancy resulting from the immediate repetition is compensated by increased activity in the visuals. These flurries of cuts separate groups of longer shots, and the result is that the duration contour graph falls into a series of waves. But the graph is dominated by a single isolated shot that lasts nearly sixteen bars ('isolated' because the adjacent shots are only one and a half and three bars long respectively): shot 36. And here there is an interesting, though admittedly speculative, comparison to be made with another Madonna video directed by Mary Lambert. In his analysis of 'Like a Prayer', Stephen Young observes that the golden section of the entire video comes during its longest scene (the one in which Madonna dances in front of flaming crosses), and that this point, moreover, coincides with the golden section of that individual scene. Now searching for golden sections is often a symptom of analytical desperation, and this might be thought to be particularly so in the case of a Madonna video. But a very similar relationship is to be found in 'Material Girl': the golden section of the song as a whole comes at the end of bar 88, and this is also the golden section of shot 36. Of course, as in the case of the underlying metrical regularity I discussed earlier, it may all be just coincidence: coincidence that the golden sections of the song and the shot coincide, coincidence that something similar happens in 'Like a Prayer'—and coincidence that both videos were directed by Mary Lambert. The alternative, which is perhaps not a more extravagant hypothesis, is to think that the videos were designed that way.

Then does anything particularly significant happen in 'Material Girl' at the end of bar 88? This is the point where Madonna II throws a fur around her shoulders, which is an apt enough symbol of the 'material girl'. But what is more suggestive is that it coincides with the first appearance of the complete '-terial' motif, with its non-harmonic A resolving to G. There are several respects in which this motif, and more generally the occurrence of *INT1* to which it belongs, might be considered the structural nucleus of the song. The motif itself represents one of the 'loose ends' I discussed; it might also be seen as representing the delayed realization of several implications set up near the beginning of the song.[31] And as I mentioned, this occurrence of *INT1* represents both an anomalous interpolation into the song's otherwise regular structure (*introduction, X, X, X, conclusion*), and the interpellation into

[31] The B♭ in bar 3 of V can be understood to imply two things: a high-register C and a resolution to A. Neither occurs at the time; both are realized by the '-terial' motif. (Of course, such common-practice models of implication and realization might be considered inappropriate to a pop song like 'Material Girl'.)

it of the timeless quality of the conclusion—something that is heightened by the use of echo. A number of the song's most salient structural aspects intersect at this point, then, and their intersection is marked by a formal linkage of music and pictures that again suggests an unexpected degree of compositional reflexivity.

Pictures, Words, and Performance

The distinction I have made between the inner and outer visual levels is based on content; apart from this, my analysis of the pictures has so far been purely formal. There is a sound methodological basis for this: as I said in the Introduction to Part II, the analysis of oppositional categories and their distribution can be pursued in the same terms for music and pictures, so that the two media (or their constituent parameters) can be directly related to one another. This is not possible when it comes to visual content, where a comparable analysis of inter-media relationships would generally be possible only on the basis of some kind of external categorization (for instance, the three dimensions of the semantic differential technique[32]). On the other hand, approaches derived from film criticism, which proceed from the exegesis of narrative content to the analysis of music's role in reinforcing or subverting that content,[33] are clearly of limited value for an understanding of music videos, where the music is not intended to be inaudible ('masking its own insistence and sawing away in the background of consciousness', as Claudia Gorbman puts it[34]), but just the opposite. The pictures, after all, are ultimately there to foreground and sell the music.

In any case, the almost seamless alignment of words and music in the 'Material Girl' song means that we can focus discussion of the relationship between song and video around the words. It has frequently been pointed out that the word–picture relationships in 'Material Girl' are not straightforward. Kaplan, for instance, observes that in shot 17 (bar 28) 'Madonna lip-synches "That's right" from the "Material Girl" song—a phrase that refers there to her only loving boys who give her money—in a situation where the opposite is happening: she *refuses* to love the man who is wealthy!'[35] And immediately following this, the song says, 'they can't see the light'—words which are of course perfectly applicable to the rich suitor, but for reasons diametrically opposed

---

[32] See p. 68 above.

[33] One connection in which a traditional, leitmotivic association of musical theme and narrative diegesis could conceivably be invoked is bars 9 and 75, the only points where the full eight-bar version of *INT2* appears, in each case coinciding with the producer's scopophilic gaze. (These are also the only points where the e^1–d^1–a^1–g^1 motif mentioned earlier appears.) Interpreted this way, bars 67 and 106, the one-bar interpolations of the *INT2* figure, would express the producer's impatience.

[34] Gorbman, *Unheard Melodies*, 1.   [35] Kaplan, *Rocking Around the Clock*, 124–5.

to those given in the song. What is more, a few bars later we hear the words 'always Mister Right' just as Madonna I almost walks into the producer at the entrance of the studio—and of course, in terms of the Madonna I narrative, the producer *is* Mister Right, but again for all the wrong reasons. In each of these cases there is a superficial congruence of text and picture, while at an underlying level the two are contradictory.

The basic conception of the video is such that we would expect to find inverted alignments of this kind between the song and the outer visual level. But word–picture relationships are sometimes problematic at the inner visual level as well: that is to say, the level of the staged performance. At bar 22, which corresponds to the third line of the first verse, Madonna II rubs her fingers together to clarify which of the two possible meanings of the word 'credit' (money and respect) is intended; this seems straightforward enough. And there is a similar clarification of ambiguous lexical content at bar 55, where Madonna II puts her foot on the chest of the dancer who lies on the floor before her as she sings the words 'some boys lie' (verse 4, first line)—except that this time the gesture clearly reinforces the *wrong* meaning, for in this context 'lie' means 'tell lies'. Here, then, there is an unstable, punning relationship, if not an outright contradiction, between the words and the pictures; while this is a familiar means of simultaneously creating emphasis and humour in television commercials,[36] its use at this point in 'Material Girl' represents something of an intrusion into the conventions of staged performance.

The same instability characterizes the recurring images of material wealth that feature prominently in the staging of the song. During the first refrain, the dancers illustrate the words by holding out jewellery (shot 20), while during the second refrain Madonna II picks the dancers' pockets, thrusting the dancers aside if there is no money to be found in them, and finally holding a banknote in the air in triumph (shot 38). And again, in the final verse ('Experience has made me rich'), Madonna II reinforces the word 'rich' by thrusting out her elbows, sending a ripple through the line of dancers on either side of her; this is followed by a shot in which banknotes flutter down through the air above her (shots 37–8). But the unambiguous staging is once more problematized by the text, which continues 'And now they're after me'. The problem is that the men always *were* after Madonna II; that is what the stage action is all about, and what made it possible for the 'material girl' to become rich. The difference *ought* to be that she can now afford to relate through love instead of money. In which case, the words 'Experience has made me rich' should perhaps be understood to mean

---

[36] See e.g. the analysis of the Prudential commercial in the Introduction to Part I.

that she is not only financially secure but rich in experience, mature—which is just the opposite of what is conveyed by the fluttering bank-notes. And the resulting destabilization of the vocabulary of wealth retrospectively affects the other references to money; it suggests that the significance of 'credit' and 'interest' may not have been quite as unambiguous as the stage action made them out to be.

Given the nature of the song-and-dance routine, one can at least point with confidence to such examples of conformance between song and staging as Madonna II's aggressive hip-flick at bar 49 (on the 'I' of 'I have to let them be'), the crack of her fan as she brings it down on a dancer's head (bar 89), and the traditionally choreographed routine at bars 69–72: Madonna II and the dancers all come down the steps in strict time with the music, first two steps and then four steps per bar, ending with a turn that is co-ordinated with the beginning of the second couplet of the refrain. In one sense, this song-and-dance routine represents the most conventional aspect of the entire video, even (as I suggested) to the point of parody. But nothing in this video is ever quite what it appears, and there is another sense in which this routine is the most paradoxical element of all. This centres on what might be called the performative axis, one pole of which is the apparently unmediated presentation of the artist in performance, the other the apparently unmediated presentation of a cinematic narrative. Alternation between these poles, and often a blurring of the distinction between them, is a standard feature of music videos. In 'Material Girl', the two poles are represented respectively by Madonna II and Madonna I. But there is something anomalous about this. Performance shots usually give the viewer immediate access to the artist; they represent a means of identification with the star. In the case of 'Material Girl', however, the performance shots are distanced from the viewer, because they are embedded within the Madonna I narrative. In other words, far from appearing as an unmediated presence, the Madonna who performs on the video—Madonna II—is set up as a fictional character played by Madonna I. And the process of regression does not stop there, because the video makes it clear that Madonna I is herself no more 'real' than Madonna II.

One indication of this is shot 28 (second half of bar 55), the tantalizingly brief shot coinciding with the words 'No way!', where we see a skimpily clad Madonna I playing cards with one of the dancers from the stage routine and then bending towards him. Everything is wrong in this shot. For one thing, 'No way!' refers to the previous words, 'I don't let them play'—and here we see Madonna playing cards with one of the men to whom 'them' refers.[37] We have, then, the same kind of

[37] He is, I think, the same man whom she knocked over with her hip-flick in bar 49 and put her foot on in bar 55 ('some boys lie').

opposition between word and image that occurred at the previous inter-jection ('*That's right!*', shot 17). And just as the lip-synching of the pre-vious interjection conjoined the inner and outer levels of the narrative, so the content of shot 28 confuses them through the introduction of the dancer who otherwise belongs only to the inner level. But this time the confusion is worse, because we see the 'good' girl (Madonna I) gambling—behaviour surely more characteristic of the 'bad' girl, Madonna II. The result is to create a kind of semantic haemorrhage between the two levels of the narrative.[38] Yet the video has been set up in such a way that everything turns on the distinction between Madonna I and Madonna II; the producer succeeds where the rich suitor failed precisely because he understands the difference between them. Indeed, whereas Madonna II is the epitome of the experienced woman who can look after herself, Madonna I is literally taken for a ride by the producer, who *pretends* he can't afford expensive presents or fast cars (hence the significance of his paying a studio hand for the use of the pick-up truck at the end).[39] Here, for once, we see a Madonna who is vulnerable. But then, is Madonna I *really* duped? If the charac-ter whom I have throughout called the 'producer' is indeed the pro-ducer (and it is hard to know who else he might be, since he clearly has some involvement in Madonna I's career, and we are told that he is not the director[40]), then is it remotely plausible that Madonna I would think he was too poor to run a car of his own? Or is it enough that he is seen to indulge Madonna I's fantasies by *pretending* to be poor? In fact, is Madonna I's real aim to exercise and publicize her power over the producer by making him go through with this absurd charade?

'Material Girl' is not a Hollywood movie and it would be quite wrong-headed to look for unambiguous answers to such questions. Indeed, the point is precisely that they are unanswerable. However we read these episodes, their contradictions intrude upon the narrative that the video

[38] Kaplan sees the same in the 'very knowing manner' in which Madonna I walks to the truck at the end of the video (*Rocking Around the Clock*, 125).

[39] As pointed out by Goodwin (*Dancing in the Distraction Factory*, 99). In this light, Fiske's accep-tance of the producer's poverty at face value seems simply wrong, even if he has Madonna on his side ('British Cultural Studies', 310, 311). There is one tiny detail that suggests a still deeper dis-simulation. After arriving with Madonna I in the sports car, the rich suitor walks into the studio; as he does so, he tosses the keys to the producer (shot 19). Why? This is hardly likely to be a sponta-neous gesture of generosity; nor can the producer be reasonably expected to offer a valet service. Perhaps we are meant to assume that the suitor borrowed the producer's car to give the appearance that he had more money than he actually did. Or maybe the producer set up the (not-so-rich) suitor in the hope of catching Madonna on the rebound. . . .

[40] See Lewis, *Gender Politics and MTV*, 130. Kaplan has created a certain amount of confusion by referring to him as the 'director', which is clearly incorrect; even Goodwin contradicts himself, refer-ring to him at one point as the 'producer' and at another as the 'director' (*Dancing in the Distraction Factory*, 99).

purports to tell. And the effect of such contradictions—and here I include the contradictions between words and pictures that I discussed earlier—is to project a further, privileged position from which Madonna I may be seen to be duped, or hypocritical, or simply fictive. To this extent, the real persona constructed by 'Material Girl' is not Madonna II or Madonna I; it is an unseen, authorial Madonna whom logic compels us to call 'Madonna 0'.

In Place of Closure

Madonna has said that 'Everything I do is sort of tongue in cheek'.[41] But she has constantly been read straight by critics such as Tom Ward. In January 1985 he wrote of 'Material Girl' (the song, not the video, which had yet to appear) that

such perfectly whorish sentiments as 'the boy with the cold hard cash / Is always Mister Right' or 'Only boys who save their pennies make my rainy day' are given her cutest 'Boy Toy' treatment. Harrumph. Not to quote Marx on anybody, but a world where 'because I have money I can surround myself with beautiful women' is still an *ugly* one. Furthermore, if we were truly 'living in a material world', we would no longer allow materials to be produced and distributed in such a way that millions of 'boys who save their pennies' find their real wages steadily eroded and, periodically, their very livelihoods pulled out from under them.[42]

And Ward goes on to complain that Madonna 'hasn't the courage of her rancidly Reaganite convictions: she hedges on the stark brutalism of "Material Girl" when she tries to come on all vulnerable and abandoned for "Pretender". . . . This latter stance is particularly grating in the light of Christopher Connelly's recent *Rolling Stone* profile, which makes it amply clear who's always done the abandoning in her case.'

As Goodwin remarks,[43] what is revealing about this kind of criticism is its automatic identification of Madonna Louise Veronica Ciccone with the 'material girl' of the song. Goodwin argues that the video is designed to promote this identification by constructing 'Madonna's star identity . . . as that of Material Girl', with the purpose of 'shifting Madonna's image from that of disco-bimbo to "authentic star" '. But this is a curiously perverse argument, for two reasons. In the first place, the identification of Madonna with the Material Girl had taken place

---

[41] *National Times*, 23/29 Aug. 1985, p. 10, quoted by Fiske, 'British Cultural Studies', 309.

[42] Tom Ward, 'Opaque Object of Desire', in Sexton (ed.), *Desperately Seeking Madonna*, 28–30: 29; originally published in *Village Voice*, 8 Jan. 1985. Similarly Luc Sante describes the video of 'Material Girl' as 'crass, vulgar, obvious, charmless, and virtually definitive of the grasping zeitgeist of 1984' ('Unlike a Virgin', in Sexton (ed.), *Desperately Seeking Madonna*, 140–8: 143; originally published in *New Republic*, 20 Aug. 1990).

[43] Goodwin, *Dancing in the Distraction Factory*, 100.

before the video was made, if Ward's critique is anything to go by (and in any case, as Goodwin himself points out elsewhere,[44] singers are constantly being conflated with the characters they represent, whether they like it or not). In the second place, the 'material girl' image precisely flouts popular-musical—which is to say, Romantic—criteria of authenticity; the staging could hardly make it more obvious that Madonna II performs not in the service of her art or under the imperative of personal expression, but for the effect she has on the men around her. It would make better sense, then, to see the video as designed to do exactly the opposite of what Goodwin suggests: to deconstruct the identification of Madonna with the Material Girl. It does this in an obvious way by embedding the Material Girl within the persona of Madonna I, who values feelings above material possessions, who is generous (as when she offers her girl-friend the suitor's diamonds) where the Material Girl is grasping, and who is vulnerable where the Material Girl is heartless.[45] And one might, perhaps, give this deconstruction a gendered twist by suggesting that the 'perfectly whorish' Material Girl (to repeat Ward's phrase) represents a male construction whose complacent closure is subverted by the video—and in this context it is appropriate to recall that the song was written by two men, whereas the video is the work of two women.[46]

But a more profound deconstruction of 'Material Girl' results from the problematization of the song's authorial voice. The video's multiplication of Madonnas asserts that both the singer-Madonna and the actress-Madonna are creations of the Madonna we neither see nor hear, the author-Madonna who we know is always 'in charge', whatever the circumstances.[47] If it is true, as Lewis asserts, that Madonna has achieved the rare distinction—for a woman—of being accepted as an author by the music press,[48] then the 'Material Girl' video may be seen as one of

[44] Goodwin, *Dancing in the Distraction Factory*, 75–6.

[45] In terms of image management there might be good reason for this; Luc Sante comments that 'The reason that Madonna does not possess much intrinsic sexual appeal . . . is that she lacks any trace of vulnerability. . . . Pout and pant and writhe though she might, Madonna is not sexually convincing because her eyes do not register. They are too busy watching the door' ('Unlike a Virgin', 146–7. Not everyone would agree, of course.

[46] Of course it could be said that to counterpose the 'bad' girl, Madonna II, with the 'good' girl, Madonna I, is simply to place one construction of male hegemony against another. But then much the same has been said about Madonna's feminism in general; see e.g. Lynne Layton, 'Like a Virgin: Madonna's Version of the Feminine', in Sexton (ed.), *Desperately Seeking Madonna*, 170–94: 190–1.

[47] Asked in an interview why she appeared chained up in the 'Express Yourself' video, Madonna replied, 'Okay, I have chained myself, though, okay? No—there wasn't a man that put that chain on me. I did it myself. . . . I'm in charge, okay?' ('Madonna Interview', in Sexton (ed.), *Desperately Seeking Madonna*, 277–87: 282; broadcast on *ABC News Nightline*, 3 Dec. 1990—not 1991 as stated by Sexton, p. viii).

[48] Lewis, *Gender Politics and MTV*, 108; see also McClary, *Feminine Endings*, 149. What is at issue here is expressed graphically in an interview published (significantly) in March 1985. Madonna explains how, when she was making 'Desperately Seeking Susan' (1984), one of the studio drivers

the principal agencies by which this was achieved. And it follows from this that, although in historical terms the 'Material Girl' video is the video of the song, the effect of the video is only tangentially to project and illuminate a meaning that is already embedded in, or associated with, the song. If the staging of the song-and-dance routine generally illuminates the text, the outer narrative within which it is embedded subverts it. The collision between the song and the narrative destabilizes both. The narrative hierarchy fragments as subordinate elements are subsumed within the song—which is why I said that the first round of the contest went to the song. But the contest is not entirely one-sided, for the aberrant visualizations sometimes render the song's words ambiguous when at first they had seemed perfectly clear, opening up semantic apertures where there initially seemed to be none. The most important effect of the video narrative is not, however, to fragment the song hierarchy—as I said, one of the functions of a music video is to foreground the music—but to transpose it wholesale from one domain of reference to another. In a nutshell, the video changes the song's central topic from the construction of a character to the construction of an author. And in this way the song becomes just one element in the emergence of a new meaning that arises, in the video, out of the interaction of music, words, and pictures.

But of course the meaning of 'Material Girl' is no more circumscribed by the video than it is by the song, as can be clearly seen from the extraordinarily varied ways in which Madonna and her music have been received among such diverse groups as female versus male, gay versus straight, and academic versus teeny-bopper. The ultimate meaning of 'Material Girl', if any such thing can usefully be said to exist, is negotiated by those who love what Madonna does, or who hate it, or who are just curious about what is going on in it.

said to her, ' "I have this bet going with my friend, he told me that all the music you do was done by someone else and they picked the songs and did it all, and all they needed was a girl singer and you auditioned and they picked you. And Madonna isn't your real name and all of it is fabricated." And I said, "WHAAAAAAATT?? Are you out of your mind??!" But that's what his friend told him, and it suddenly hit me that's probably what a lot of people think. It hit me' (Laura Fissinger, 'Maybe She's Good—Ten Theories on How Madonna Got "It" ', *Record*, 4/5 (Mar. 1985), 30–6: 36; quoted by Lewis, *Gender Politics and MTV*, 108). This interpretation is highly compatible with Frith's observation that the 'obsessive use of movie quotes' in music videos—of which 'Material Girl' is obviously a prime example—represents 'a quick and easy way for musicians (and their audiences) to signal their knowingness about what is going on. . . . By acting out an obvious Hollywood scenario, musicians indicate their own detachment from the fantasy' ('Afterword', 217, 218).

5

Disney's Dream: The *Rite of Spring* Sequence from 'Fantasia'

D ISNEY HAD WANTED from the beginning to include some sort of legend of the creation, volcanoes and tidal waves and lumbering dinosaurs. He assigned his research assistants to discover some appropriate music, but all they could offer him was Haydn's *Creation*, which somehow didn't seem sufficiently epic. Disney presented the problem to Stokowksi, and Stokowski offered a bold solution.
'Why don't we do the *Sacre*' he said.
'Socker?' Disney asked. 'What's that?'[1]

I will say nothing about the visual complement as I do not wish to criticize an unresisting imbecility; I will say and repeat, however, that the musical point of view of the film sponsored a dangerous misunderstanding.[2]

Stravinsky's damning words capture the tone of academic commentary, in so far as there has been any such thing, on the film that Walt Disney believed 'would signal a new dawn for the animated cartoon'.[3] Disney's hopes were pinned not only on the technical innovations that 'Fantasia' exploited (including unprecedentedly intensive use of the studio's multi-plane cameras, which allowed independent control of several layers of animation, and a multi-speaker sound system known as 'Fantasound'), but also on the prospect of bringing works of the high art tradition to mass audiences. 'Think of the numbers of people who will now be able to hear your music,' he told Stravinsky.[4] The com-

---

[1] Otto Friedrich, *City of Nets: A Portrait of Hollywood in the 1940's* (London, 1987), 35–6.

[2] Igor Stravinsky and Robert Craft, *Expositions and Developments* (London, 1962), 146.

[3] Leonard Maltin, *Of Mice and Magic: A History of American Animated Cartoons*, rev. edn. (New York, 1987), 63.

[4] Stravinsky interviewed in *Musical Digest*, Hollywood, Sept. 1946; repr. in Vera Stravinsky and Robert Craft, *Stravinsky in Pictures and Documents* (London, 1979), 358. Claudia Widgery has pointed out the extent to which film was seen as 'an invaluable means of exposing the masses to good or new music' in the 1930s ('Kinetic and Temporal Interaction', 28). A few years later, Chuck Jones, who was director of cartoons at Warner Brothers Studios, referred specifically to the educational potential of the animated cartoon when he said that it can 'match, enhance, make credible the melodic fantasy of the composer. . . . I believe that the educational system will one day demand a library for its public schools of just such painless introductions to classic and semiclassic music' ('Music and the Animated Cartoon', 366).

poser was unimpressed: 'Well, the numbers of people who consume music . . . is of no interest to me. The mass adds nothing to art.' And Stravinsky's lofty attitude was replicated by many contemporary critics, for whom the cartoon treatment of the Western master-work tradition constituted (as Leonard Maltin puts it) a form of 'musical blasphemy'; on the other hand, Maltin continues, the masses stayed away, 'put off by the movie's highbrow connotations'.[5] When it was first released in 1940, then, 'Fantasia' fell between all the stools, and so was a commercial failure. This was fully reversed only 30 years later, in the aftermath of the Beatles' 'Yellow Submarine', when 'Fantasia' was re-released, now targeted to the new youth audience as 'the ultimate visual experience'.[6] To add a personal note, I recall queuing to see 'Fantasia' in the early 1970s, but being unable to get into the cinema.

Disney has been given little credit, by Stravinsky or anybody else, for including in 'Fantasia' as notorious a score as *The Rite of Spring*, the American première of which took place in 1924, only 14 years before Disney's decision to feature it.[7] Stravinsky's later account of his negotiations with Disney suggests that they were rather acrimonious. The request for the use of *The Rite*, he says, was 'accompanied by a gentle warning that if permission were withheld the music would be used anyway'[8] (which would have been legal since there was no American copyright for the work). And in 1960 there was a squabble in the pages of the *Saturday Review* regarding how much Stravinsky was paid (he said $5,000, Disney said $10,000), and also regarding Stravinsky's initial reactions to the film. When he was shown the first rough drawings for the *Rite* sequence in December 1939, Disney claimed, Stravinsky had 'said he was "excited" over the possibilities . . . and when shown the finished product [he] emerged from the projection visibly moved'. In reply, Stravinsky recalled that he had seen the *Sorcerer's Apprentice* sequence in negative (this makes sense, since it was the first sequence to be made), which had amused him, and he had said so. But, he continued, 'That I could have expressed approbation over the treatment of my own music seems to me highly improbable—though, of course,

[5] Maltin, *Of Mice and Magic*, 63.

[6] Ibid. 347. Maltin adds: 'Animator Art Babbitt was asked by some young people who saw the film for the first time if he and his colleagues had used drugs when they made the film thirty years before. "Yes, I was on drugs," Babbitt replied, "Ex-Lax and Pepto-Bismol!".' According to the film credits, Babbitt worked on the 'Nutcracker Suite' and 'Pastoral' Symphony sequences.

[7] The contract between Walt Disney Enterprises and Stravinsky is dated 4 Jan. 1939, and followed on negotiations about the possible use of *The Firebird* for an animated cartoon; subsequently a contract was signed for *The Firebird*, together with *Renard* and *Fireworks*, though in the event none of these was used (Stravinsky and Craft, *Stravinsky in Pictures and Documents*, 363–4).

[8] Stravinsky and Craft, *Expositions and Developments*, 145.

I should hope I was polite.'[9] One might expect the composer to be more readily amused by the Mickey Mouse treatment Disney handed out to Dukas than by the juxtaposition of his own music with prehistoric animals; 'duller than Disney's dying dinosaurs' was Stravinsky's damningly alliterative description of Karajan's recording of 'Ritual Action of the Ancestors'.[10] Yet this hardly explains the rhetorical tone of his condemnation of 'Fantasia' as sponsoring a 'dangerous misunderstanding'. The danger, as I shall argue later in this chapter, was to the image of *The Rite* as absolute music that Stravinsky had been busily disseminating since the 1920s—an image which has certainly misrepresented the work as a historical phenomenon, and arguably as a musical one too.

Stravinsky's negative reaction was no doubt prompted also by what Disney and the conductor, Leopold Stokowski, had done to the music. When he saw the film, Stravinsky says, 'I remember someone offering me the score and, when I said I had my own, the someone saying, "But it is all changed". It was indeed.'[11] There were reorchestrations—most prominently, as Stravinsky says, the transposition to a higher octave of the horn glissandi in the 'Dance of the Earth' (the result is that they sound incongruously like the trumpeting of elephants). More significant, however, was the omission of some of the component pieces of *The Rite* and the reordering of the rest, as shown in Figure 5.1 (which also lists the cuts within pieces).[12] Stravinsky's explanation for this— that the most difficult pieces had been eliminated—is probably not fair; at all events, it overlooks the rationale for the reordering. In the first place, the general pattern is retained by which fast and loud movements alternate with slow and quiet ones; in effect, the Introduction to Part II replaces the 'Spring Rounds', while the 'Dance of the Earth' takes the place of the 'Sacrificial Dance' as the final climax. And secondly, the abbreviated repetition of the opening bassoon solo at the end

---

[9] Stravinsky and Craft, *Expositions and Developments*, 146. Friedrich ascribes the comments about Stravinsky's reaction to an 'associate' of Disney, rather than to Disney himself, and adds one that really is beyond belief: 'Stravinsky . . . had even observed that the concept of the world's creation and prehistoric life were what he "really" had in mind when he wrote *Le Sacre*' (*City of Nets*, 37). This comment is perhaps the source of Ralph Stephenson's statement that the sequence 'was favourably received by the composer as a legitimate interpretation of his music' (*Animation in the Cinema* (London, 1967), 39).

[10] Igor Stravinsky and Robert Craft, *Dialogues and a Diary* (London, 1968), 88.

[11] Stravinsky and Craft, *Expositions and Developments*, 145.

[12] In Fig. 5.1 and throughout, bold type refers to rehearsal numbers in the 1967 study score (Boosey and Hawkes 19441). This cannot of course be the same as the score on which the performance in 'Fantasia' was based, which could have been either the 1921 (so-called 'first') or 1929 ('revised') edition. The variance in texts of *The Rite* is notorious, but mainly concerns rhythmic notation and details of orchestration, and for this reason is ignored here. For further information see Stravinsky and Craft, *Stravinsky in Pictures and Documents*, 526–33; van den Toorn, *Stravinsky and The Rite of Spring*, 39–56; and Louis Cyr, 'Writing *The Rite* Right', in Pasler (ed.), *Confronting Stravinsky*, 157–73.

gives the music an immediate, literal closure that is not present in Stravinsky's original score.

		Omissions
	Introduction to Part I	
13	Augurs of Spring	
37	Ritual of Abduction	
79	Introduction to Part II	**85** to **86**+2; **86**+5
91	Mystic Circles of the Young Girls	**94** (whole)
104	Glorification of the Chosen One	**112**+3 to **113**+3; **117** to **120** (whole)
121	Evocation of the Ancestors	**127**+2 to **127**+4 (replaced by timp roll)
129	Ritual Action of the Ancestors	
71+1	The Sage	
72	Dance of the Earth	
	Introduction to Part I (first 6 bars)	

Fig. 5.1 The music of the *Rite of Spring* sequence

A Close Reading

Two distinct traditions lie behind the visualizations of music in 'Fantasia'.[13] The first of these, of course, is the cartoon film with which the name 'Disney' was already synonymous in 1940. Most cartoons were shorts, with their characteristically compressed time-scales, but Disney had made the first animation feature, 'Snow White and the Seven Dwarfs', in 1938, while 'Pinocchio' was released in February 1940, a few months before 'Fantasia'. (The world première of 'Fantasia' took place on 13 November.)[14] I have no intention of offering a general history of cartoon music up to 1940; but one development during the 1930s is worth mentioning in this context: in his highly influential cartoon scores, Scott Bradley had been pioneering the reduction of mechanical sound effects to a minimum, instead creating the desired effect within the music.[15] In other words, there was a precedent, even

[13] 'Fantasia' is available on video releases Disney D211322 (PAL) and 1132 (NTSC); it should be noted that this is the original, 120-minute release, not the cut-down, 82-minute version which was made for general release. It is of course a stereo remix of the multitrack original, and for this reason the following analysis does not consider the potentially significant dimension of spatial positioning.

[14] For a Disney filmography see Maltin, *Of Mice and Magic*, 357–70.

[15] Prendergast, *Film Music*, 187–9, quoting industry commentary of the time (1937). Bradley was music director at MGM from the 1930s to the 1950s, and Prendergast describes his work in

in mainstream cartoons, for the illustration of screen action through exclusively musical means. And this in turn links with another, highly relevant precedent for 'Fantasia': the production, particularly by Disney, of cartoons based on existing music (mandating, of course, the editing of the film to the music, rather than the other way round). As early as 1929, only a year after the introduction of synchronized sound, Disney produced 'The Skeleton Dance', the first of the 'Silly Symphonies', in which the animations were linked with music by Saint-Saëns and Grieg. Another example is 'The Band Concert' (1935), the first Mickey Mouse film in colour, which featured Mickey conducting the *William Tell* overture. There was, then, what might be called an in-house tradition leading up to 'Fantasia'. Indeed, the continuity is quite explicit, for the *Sorcerer's Apprentice* sequence, featuring Mickey in the title role, was originally intended as a stand-alone 'Silly Symphony'. The decision to make it part of a full-length feature was an afterthought prompted, paradoxically, by the unprecedentedly high cost of the *Sorcerer's Apprentice* sequence; the predictable result was that 'Fantasia' resulted in an even more unprecedented overspend.[16]

The second tradition to which I referred is a more experimental, and generally European, one, involving abstract, generally hand-painted images linked to music. The best-known practitioner was probably Oskar Fischinger, whose film 'Mozart Minuet' anticipated the Bach sequence of 'Fantasia' with its images of 'waves rising up in an endless procession'.[17] The link is more than accidental, and indeed it is sometimes stated that Fischinger was one of the animators of 'Fantasia'.[18] What actually happened is that Fischinger carried out preliminary work on the 'Toccata and Fugue' sequence at the Disney studios, but

some detail; see also Ingolf Dahl, 'Notes on Cartoon Music', originally published in *Film Music*, 8/3 (May–June 1949), repr. in Limbacher (ed.), *Film Music*, 183–9. Dahl, incidentally, was one of Stravinsky's closest professional associates throughout the 1940s, and collaborated with him in the *Musical Digest* interview cited in n. 4 above; for details of their relationship see Stravinsky and Craft, *Stravinsky in Pictures and Documents*, 378–9.

[16] For the early history of 'Fantasia' see David R. Smith, '*The Sorcerer's Apprentice*: Birthplace of *Fantasia*', *Millimeter* (Feb. 1976), 18–67; Maltin, *Of Mice and Magic*, 59–60; and Friedrich, *City of Nets*, 34–7. For the overexpenditure see Smith, '*Sorcerer's Apprentice*'; Jimmie Hicks, ' "Fantasia's Silver Anniversary" ', *Films in Review*, 16/9 (1965), 529–35, according to which 'Fantasia' cost $2 million and recouped its costs in 1963; and Joe Adamson, 'Chuck Jones Interviewed', in Gerald and Danny Peary (eds.), *The American Animated Cartoon: A Critical Anthology* (New York, 1980), 128–41: 138. Jones comments that 'To call Disney a businessman is about like calling Adolf Hitler a humanitarian. He was the *despair* of the business. He made *Fantasia* [1940] for $3 million when all he had in the studio was $2 million! He kept doing things nobody believed in.' It should be remembered, though, that 'Snow White and the Seven Dwarfs' eventually grossed $8 million—'a titanic sum for a film made during the Depression', as Friedrich remarks (*City of Nets*, 34).

[17] Manvell and Huntley, *Technique of Film Music*, 182. Ch. 3 of Manvell and Huntley's book provides a useful general introduction to this tradition.

[18] See e.g. ibid. 182, and Dahl, 'Notes on Cartoon Music', 185.

left after altercations about his abstract style. (Maltin cites a contemporary account of discussions in which one of the animators snapped, 'We don't want anything like that, do we?', with another replying 'Hell, no!'[19]) Despite this, Fischinger's general style was carried forward into the final version of the Bach sequence, and there are abstract elements in some of the others—most obviously the one featuring the Sound Track.

But in general the various sequences in 'Fantasia' are *either* abstract *or* representational (in a cartoon sense, of course), and there seems to have been little attempt to impose an overall visual unity upon the film as a whole; different teams worked on each sequence, and there was little overlap in the personnel. In the case of the *Rite of Spring* sequence, however, there were apparently separate directors for the various sections;[20] and possibly as a result of this, it includes both abstract and representational animation, together with much that lies in between these extremes. This makes it a particularly appropriate focus for analysis, for, as will become clear, the nature of the relationship between music and pictures in it varies a good deal, depending largely on the abstract or representational quality of the latter. In brief, the music tends towards primacy in the sections with relatively abstract visuals, whereas there tends to be a tension between music and narrative during the more representational visualizations. In both cases, however, there is an intimate relationship between music and pictures (and after all, the rationale of 'Fantasia' as a whole is musical, not narrative). In what follows, then, I shall discuss the relationship between music and narrative in the *Rite of Spring* sequence while at the same time working from the small to the large scale.

We might start with the relationship between music and pictures which takes its name from Disney's cartoons: mickey-mousing. This refers to the kind of close synchronization between diegetic movement and sound-track that Disney developed in the 1930s (for instance, when Mickey takes a couple of steps forward and the music sounds with them), and its effect is, in a paradoxical way, to underline the arbitrariness of the link between the screen action and its musical correlate. The opening of the *Rite* sequence provides a number of comparable examples, though in a very different context. The sequence begins with a back-lit image of Stokowski conducting the bassoon solo, providing a transition from the outer world of Deems Taylor's introductory

[19] Maltin, *Of Mice and Magic*, 60–1.

[20] John D. Ford, 'An Interview with John and Faith Hubley', in Peary and Peary (eds.), *The American Animated Cartoon*, 183–91: 184. John Hubley, who worked on the initial section, states that there was one overall director, but in fact two are listed in the credits (Bill Roberts and Paul Satterfield); Hubley is credited under 'Art direction', along with Maclaren Stewart and Dick Kelsey.

voice-over.[21] The image fades, and the screen becomes black. Gradually a distant galaxy appears, fragmenting into individual stars as it comes closer. Up to **4** there is no specific synchronization between pictures and music; the bassoon and cor anglais solos, together with their decentred accompaniments, convey a sense of desolation, but the link between the media is essentially no more than one of mood. But the effect of the string pizzicati at **4** is to announce something new: in the music they introduce the D clarinet melody, while in the film a cloud of luminescent gas passes across the screen, much closer to the 'camera' (as, for simplicity, I shall call the positioning of the implied viewer) than anything seen previously. It is not that there is any very specific affinity between the cloud of gas and the clarinet theme; the basis of their association is simply the fact that they appear together. Similarly, the D clarinet motif at **2+2** is repeatedly linked with shooting stars, and what establishes the linkage is not so much the nature of the motif (though there is a certain similarity between its contour and the curving trajectory of the shooting stars) as the consistency of the association. On occasion, however, there is a clearly iconic relationship between the music and the image with which it is linked: at **5**, for instance, a small, burning star passes so close to the 'camera' that flames lick the 'camera' position, and these flames are tightly synchronized with flickering motifs in the clarinets.[22]

In all these cases, the melody–accompaniment relationship of the music corresponds to the figure–ground relationship of the visuals, and so the one articulates or clarifies the other. In particular, the gathering focus of the music, which reaches a polyphonic but highly co-ordinated climax at **11**, parallels the increasing sense of a narrative viewpoint that the film conveys; as the final shooting star plunges towards the earth and the picture dissolves into a view of shifting clouds with a distant landscape behind them, there is a definite sense that a story is beginning. There is a long pause before **12**, and the pictures from there to the end of the introduction (**13**, where 'The Augurs of Spring' begins) create the effect of a transition in exactly the same way that the music does. Clouds continue to move across the screen during the final, abbreviated repetition of the opening bassoon solo, but the string

---

[21] The text of the voice-over is as follows: 'When Igor Stravinsky wrote his ballet *The Rite of Spring*, his purpose was (in his own words) to express primitive life, and so Walt Disney and his fellow artists have taken him at his word. Instead of presenting the ballet in its original form, as a simple series of tribal dances, they have visualized it as a pageant—as the story of the growth of life on earth. It's a coldly accurate reproduction of what science thinks went on during the first few billion years of this planet's existence. So now imagine yourself out in space, billions and billions of years ago, looking down on this lonely, tormented little planet spinning through an empty sea of nothingness.' Later in this chapter I shall consider some of the issues this voice-over raises.

[22] The effect appears to have been heightened through reorchestration at this point.

pizzicati, which anticipate one of the main ostinato patterns of 'The Augurs', are marked by small puffs of light, representing volcanic explosions scattered around the mountainous landscape. The explosions appear to take place in strict synchronization with the strings' sixteenth notes (though the effect of rhythmic precision disappears if you look at the film without the music), and they stop whenever the pizzicati stop. And then, as 'The Augurs' begins, there is a cut to a medium 'shot' of volcanoes erupting, with sheets of flame and ash co-ordinated with the musical accents.

Several things combine to create a strong effect of disjunction at **13**. For one thing, Stokowski does not observe Stravinsky's eighth note equals quarter note direction; he takes 'The Augurs' slower than that would suggest, which results in a sudden musical change of gear (the effect is as if a splice has been made in the recording).[23] Again, the pictures are more unambiguously representational from **13**, with the 'camera' being now, for the first time, at ground level. And throughout 'The Augurs' there is a tightness of synchronization between pictures and music that goes beyond anything that has come before (except for the tongues of flame after **6**, which find a close volcanic correlate in the four bars before **17**, where sheets of flame are tightly synchronized with the trumpets). But the sense of disjunction perhaps comes more than anything from the cut at **13**, the first perceptible cut in the entire film, but the first of many in 'The Augurs'. The result is to create a clear sense that everything up to this point has been a single introductory gesture; in this respect we can say that the pictures work in parallel with the music. From **13** on, however, the very closeness of their relationship creates a kind of tension between them; at times the music seems to intrude upon the pictures as a result of the constant synchronization between the two. The source of this tension lies in the anti-naturalistic patterns of activity that are forced upon the volcanoes by the musical rhythm—an artificiality that reaches its height at the bar before **22**, where the fortissimo chord prompts all the volcanoes to erupt at once in neat, vertical pillars of fire. They look more like orange gas jets than volcanoes. If the effect is rather silly, this is because we do not expect to see volcanoes being choreographed; there is a tension between the visualization of the music and our representational instincts. To put it another way, the extremely tight relationship of

---

[23] There is, incidentally, a very prominent splice at **29**+6. Although the 1967 score is consistent as regards the tempo at the beginning of 'The Augurs' (there is a quarter-note equals 50 indication at **12**, and a half-note equals 50 indication at **13**), Stravinsky subsequently specified a metronome marking of 56 for 'The Augurs' (Appendix to Igor Stravinsky, *The Rite of Spring: Sketches 1911–1913* (London, 1969), 36), which would result in a perceived change of tempo, but in the opposite direction from Stokowski's.

music and pictures at a surface level results in a conflicted relationship at an underlying one.

By contrast, 70 years of cartoons have familiarized us with the idea that animals dance to music, even extinct ones.[24] It seems hardly necessary to document the kinesthetic associations that Disney's animators make between the swoop of the pterodactyls and the repetitions of the clarinet arpeggio after **87**, or the sudden flight of the archaeopteryx, which circles against the sky in time with the repetition of the first violins' phrase (after **93**). Again, at **97** the pizzicati in the lower strings bring out the balletic quality of the jogging dinosaurs (I could just as well have put it the other way round), while their heads go down to scoop the water in line with the falling fifths in the flute and solo cello at **97**+2 and **97**+4; at **98** the off-beat interjections of the low strings and bass clarinet convey the heavy tramp of the *Stegosaurus*. Or one might instance the way in which the animals stop and look up expectantly at the bars before **101** and **102**—an effect that reflects not only the change of instrumentation and the pauses in the music, but also Stravinsky's original choreographic directions for these passages (to which I shall return in the latter part of this chapter). All these are, in essence, typical examples of cartoon choreography; what makes them remarkable is only the skill with which the animators have succeeded in creating the effect that the music was composed for the animations, not the other way round. The most intensively choreographed passage, however, is the one that follows: the chase and fight between the *Tyrannosaurus rex* and the *Stegosaurus* which takes place during the 'Glorification of the Chosen One' and spills over into the 'Evocation of the Ancestors'. The patterning of both the music and the pictures is quite intricate throughout this passage, and so it is worth examining their relationship in some detail.

The animators do not, of course, overlook the most obvious suggestions of the music. At **102** the animals look up with increasing consternation, in loose synchronization with the horns' rising sevenths (the cutting rhythm quickens along with the music), while at **103,** which Stravinsky once referred to as an 'orchestral haemorrhage',[25] the 'camera' spins to the right, following the now terrified animals' gaze; on the last beat of the bar, at the climax of the 'haemorrhage', there is a cut to the *Tyrannosaurus* silhouetted against a sky riven with lightning. After a moment's shocked pause, the eleven ominous fortissimo chords begin. At first the *Tyrannosaurus* remains motionless, but on the fourth

---

[24] One might almost say 'particularly extinct ones'; almost the first animated cartoon, and certainly the first one to make a mass impact, was Winsor McCay's 'Gertie the Dinosaur' (Maltin, *Of Mice and Magic*, 5).

[25] Stravinsky and Craft, *Dialogues and a Diary*, 86.

chord it begins to advance in time with the music. On the eighth chord there is a cut to the animals turning to flee, and from **104**, the beginning of the 'Glorification', there is an extended passage made up of juxtaposed pictures of the animals fleeing and the *Tyrannosaurus* pursuing them, with the predator's vicious snaps synchronized with the equally vicious opening figure of the 'Glorification'.[26] Throughout this passage and the fight that follows, both Stravinsky's score and Disney's visualization consist of contrasted and repeated blocks of varying lengths. Figure 5.2 provides an analytical overview, with each block being designated by a letter (a, b, c) and the larger groups that they form by a roman numeral; the arabic numbers following the letters and roman numerals indicate the number of beats, measured in eighth notes.[27] Finally, the vertical lines preceding some of the blocks indicate cuts

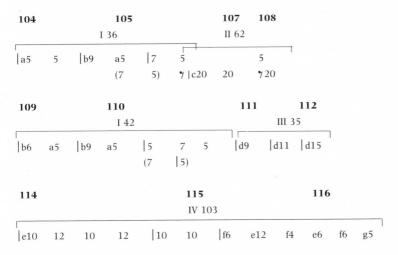

Fig. 5.2 Analytical overview of the fight sequence

[26] The *Tyrannosaurus* is today considered to have been a scavenger rather than a predator (its feeble front legs could not have been used for the kind of fighting Disney portrays); but 'Fantasia' was generally in line with scientific opinion at the time. Hicks records that Julian Huxley was hired to offer advice about protozoan life (' "Fantasia's" Silver Anniversary', 531), while Friedrich states that Chester Stock of Caltech also gave advice on the same subject, and that Disney even sent his technicians to Mount Wilson observatory to study the shapes of nebulae (*City of Nets*, 36). An exception was the depiction of the dinosaurs dying from drought. 'More likely they were frozen by the Ice Age,' said John Hubley. 'But Disney didn't want an Ice Age; he wanted a desert sequence' (Ford, 'Interview with John and Faith Hubley', 184).

[27] Where there is only an arabic number, the block is of the same type as the previous one; the (7 5) shows an alternative segmentation, depending whether the added quarter note is taken with the end of one block or the beginning of the next (it can be seen that the cuts follow a different

between shots that are co-ordinated with the beginning of that block, cuts that are not co-ordinated in this way being omitted.

We can make some general observations on the basis of this chart. For one thing, there is a contrast between the groups that are characterized by cuts at the beginnings of blocks (I and III) and those that are not (II and IV); these coincidences establish what might be termed audio-visual downbeats. The result is that groups I and III create the effect of being accented as compared with groups II and IV, giving rise to a kind of large-scale downbeat–afterbeat pattern; group II constitutes a kind of prolonged afterbeat following on the initial group I, while the more extended group IV follows on from the composite downbeat formed by the second group I and group III (that is to say, **109–12**). In this way the passage is pervaded by rhythmic expansion at a number of levels: just as each of the three 'd' blocks in group III is longer than the previous one, so group II is longer than the initial group I, and group IV is longer than the combination of the second group I and group III. On an even larger level, the passage from **109** to **116** forms a kind of extended consequent to the passage from **104** to **108**; in other words, the whole of the 'Glorification' falls into two halves, each beginning with the same material (group I), but with the second almost twice as long as the first (180 beats, versus 94). And it is worth observing that this two-part structure is more Disney's creation than Stravinsky's, for it depends both on the cutting of significant portions of the original score (as shown in Fig. 5.1) and on the large narrative structure of the sequence: **104–8** corresponds to the chase, while **109–16** corresponds to the fight between the *Tyrannosaurus* and the *Stegosaurus*.

Another significant correlation between musical and narrative structure can be observed at **114**, where the new pizzicato motif (which coincides with a sudden drop to the first 'piano' in the 'Glorification') corresponds to a new stage in the fight. After their initial, inconclusive engagement (at **111** and **112**), the *Tyrannosaurus* begins stalking the *Stegosaurus*, which at first backs away, and then both the fight and the music build up together, climaxing together at the 'Molto allargando' which, in Disney's version, leads straight into the 'Evocation'. A further observation is that the most musically repetitive part of this sequence, the six successive appearances of block 'e' from **114**, is enlivened by means of a relatively autonomous visual structure: this can be represented by the symmetrical pattern (x y z z y x), where 'x' refers to the normal positioning of the two combatants with the *Tyrannosaurus* on

---

segmentation on each occasion). This method of notation is adapted from van den Toorn, *Stravinsky and the* Rite of Spring; van den Toorn himself adapted it from Boulez's 'Stravinsky Remains' (trans. in Pierre Boulez, *Stocktakings from an Apprenticeship* (Oxford, 1991), 55–110).

104

a5

Tyr. attacks 5

b9 animals flee (from front)

 Steg. turns (from behind)

b9

a5

b6
109

Tyr. attacks . . . .

105

a5

Tyr. snaps animals flee 5

Tyr. snaps they fight 5

 7

a5 5

110

Steg. snaps

Fig. 5.3 Two parallel passages in the fight sequence

the right, 'z' to its reversal, and 'y' to the interpolated shots of the other animals watching.

But what might be seen as the most intricate interlacing of music and pictures occurs in the two 'I' groups. Figure 5.3 shows what is involved, and includes a summary of the visual content. The vertical alignment here is rather different from that in Figure 5.2: corresponding blocks appear in columns, and it can be seen that in each case the same musical materials appear in the same order, but with interpolations. The graphic representation, then, prioritizes the similarity between the two passages, and makes it possible to see how far visual similarity conforms with that of the music. On two occasions the same narrative action takes place at the corresponding musical point: the *Tyrannosaurus* attacks at **104** and **109**, while there are close-ups of it snapping at **105** and **110**+1. (There is a fairly general principle that whereas cuts between shots fall on the downbeats of the 'a' blocks, the dinosaurs' snaps are synchronized with the syncopated accents.) Elsewhere, however, the action is diametrically opposed: at **104**+2 (the 'b9' block) the animals are fleeing, and the 'camera' is in front of them; while at **109**+2 the *Stegosaurus* turns to fight, and we see it from behind. And there is a similar opposition of fleeing and fighting at **105**+1 and **110**+2 respectively.

What gives credibility to this reading is that the relationships are so definite: things are either the same, or exactly the opposite. But in a way it could hardly be otherwise. Just as the music is made up of contrasted blocks of varying durations (which is why it lends itself to this kind of graphic representation), so the visualization juxtaposes opposed images: the *Tyrannosaurus* attacking and the animals fleeing, or the *Tyrannosaurus* snapping at the *Stegosaurus* and then vice versa. Or one might reverse the direction of the argument and say that the patterning of the music resembles the film editing.[28] Either way, the combination of such music and film results in a very fertile context for the emergence of significant juxtapositions; it is perhaps not too cynical to suggest that almost *any* combination might produce perceptible and apparently intentional patterns, in much the same way that a kaleidoscope does. I am not suggesting, then, that Disney's animators carefully planned out this sequence along the lines of my analysis. What I *am* suggesting is that one of the attractions of *The Rite* as a subject for animation, and in particular one of the attractions of animating this passage in terms of a fight, is the way in which the music is constructed

---

[28] This bears upon the comparison I made in Ch. 4 between Cone's model of Stravinsky's music in terms of strata, a model that applies to much of *The Rite*, and the editing of music (especially rap) videos; see above, p. 159.

out of opposed blocks—a feature which *The Rite* shares with a great deal of Stravinsky's music.

Whereas Disney's interpretation of the 'Glorification' revolves around the patterning of musical and visual blocks, the linked volcano and tidal wave sequences (corresponding to 'The Augurs of Spring' and 'Ritual of Abduction') suggest a quite different approach: one based on relatively high-level metrical structure. The easiest way to explain this is by reference to the distinction that van den Toorn draws between what he calls 'Type I' and 'Type II' rhythmic materials in *The Rite*. Type I passages consist of the alternation of discrete blocks of different lengths; both the 'Glorification' and the 'Evocation' are examples. Type II passages, by contrast, have a steady overall metre but are made up of 'a superimposition of two or more motives that repeat according to periods, cycles, or spans that are not shared but vary independently of, or separately from, one another';[29] they often appear at points of climax, preceded by Type I passages. And van den Toorn's analytical application of these models revolves largely around demonstrating how each depends on an interplay between rhythmic irregularity (which is obvious in the shifting metric notation of Type I, but hidden in Type II) and metric regularity (which is explicitly notated in Type II, but hidden in Type I). Or, to put it another way, his analyses involve showing how the music is experienced in terms of different levels of rhythmic hierarchy being played off against one another. Following Andrew Imbrie,[30] van den Toorn proposes two contrasted types of listening strategy: 'radical' readings, based purely on surface rhythms, versus 'conservative' readings emphasizing underlying metrical continuity. Boulez's well-known analyses of *The Rite* are exclusively 'radical'; at the beginning of 'The Augurs', for instance, he follows the varying 'cells' created by the rhythmic accents, making no attempt to relate them to the notated 2/4 metre. Van den Toorn's point is that only by attempting to relate rhythm to metre, and by adjudicating between the contrary demands of each, can we do justice to the particular rhythmic dynamism that characterizes Stravinsky's music in general and *The Rite* in particular. To be sure, he says, the rhythms that Stravinsky pits against his underlying metres generally end up disrupting them, but 'it is only by pursuing a path of accommodation that insight can be gained into the nature of the disruption'.[31]

We have to adjust van den Toorn's terminology a little in order to apply it to 'The Augurs'. The opening, at **13**, does not look like Type I,

[29] Van den Toorn, *Stravinsky and the* Rite *of Spring*, 100.

[30] Andrew Imbrie, ' "Extra" Measures and Metrical Ambiguity in Beethoven', in Alan Tyson (ed.), *Beethoven Studies* (New York, 1973), 45–66.

[31] Van den Toorn, *Stravinsky and the* Rite *of Spring*, 113.

since it is notated in 2/4; but it could easily have been notated using a shifting metre instead of cross-metric accents, and the aural effect is comparable to that of more typical Type I passages, and this remains the case up to the end of **21**. By contrast, the latter part of 'The Augurs', from **28** to the end, is clearly Type II. There is no clean break between the one and the other; **22**–**7** constitute a transition between the two types. And what do Disney's animators make of all this? At first they cut with the downbeat of each new block (**14**, **14**+4, **15**, **16**, **18**); the only exception is three eighth notes before **17**, where a cut comes together with the trumpet figure (which, as I previously mentioned, is itself synchronized with the volcanic tongues of flame). But from there on there are several cuts synchronized with the beginning of melodic motifs (eighth notes after **19**, **19**+5, and **21**). There are also two cuts that coincide with the accents of the 'Augurs' chord (first eighth note of **19**+7, last eighth note of **20**+3); throughout the passage, however, these accents have received almost continual diegetic emphasis, in the form of eruptions and spurts of lava. All in all, then, the animation of the passage up to the end of **21** is predominantly 'radical'. And as such it can be contrasted with the 'conservative' interpretation that Stravinsky specified in his choreographic annotations, where he directed that 'the choreographic accents are the tonic accents of the measures, not those of the music'.[32] One can imagine Stravinsky laying against Disney the same charge that he laid (unfairly, as we shall see) against Nijinsky: 'He believed that the choreography should re-emphasize the musical beat and pattern through constant co-ordination. In effect, this restricted the dance to rhythmic duplication of the music and made of it an imitation.'[33]

The climactic chords at the end of **21** mark a major point of articulation both musically and visually; this is the point where the volcanoes all erupt at once, looking (as I said) like orange gas jets. It is also a point of articulation in narrative terms. From the beginning of 'The Augurs' up to here the film has depicted volcanic eruptions; now the focus becomes the flow of lava, with the remainder of 'The Augurs' following the lava down from the mountains to the sea. The sequence begins with a single extended shot that continues until **26**; at first the screen shows nothing but a featureless, red abstraction, but soon it is animated by calligraphic, fountain-like plumes that pick up the repetitive patterns of the music. Then, at **25**, the image coalesces into clouds, far below which a yellow crater can be seen. Up to here the music has consisted almost exclusively of one-bar repetitions grouped into four-bar phrases,

---

[32] Stravinsky, Appendix to *The Rite of Spring: Sketches 1911–1913*, 36. The wording is that of Stravinsky's 1969 commentary, not the original annotations.

[33] Igor Stravinsky and Robert Craft, *Memories and Commentaries* (London, 1960), 37.

but the flute melody at **25**—a genuine four-bar melody, not four repeated bars—strengthens the sense of emerging periodicity. At **26** there is a cut to a closer view of the crater, with ripples visible on the surface of the lava as it flows down the mountainside, and in essence the remainder of the sequence consists of parallel musical and narrative motions. As the music becomes increasingly periodic and its dynamic level and textural density grow, so the pictures follow the torrent of lava down; the climax is reached as molten rocks crash into the sea and the 'Ritual of Abduction' begins.

Although the overall pattern is clear enough, it is worth going into a little more detail about the relationship between the periodic structure of the music and the cutting of the film. The passage starting at **28** is a textbook example of van den Toorn's Type II, with eight-beat patterns in the flutes (which fragment into two-beat patterns as their sequence becomes increasingly random), three-beat patterns in the cellos and basses, two-beat patterns in the brass and violas, an approximation to one-beat patterns in the clarinets, and unmeasured trills in the bassoons. Figure 5.4 shows the cutting rhythm from here to the end of 'The Augurs'. The first two cuts (at **28** and **28**+4) correspond to the downbeats of the four-bar periodic structure[34]—what may conveniently be called hyperdownbeats—but as the trumpet tune becomes fragmented (from **28**+8) the periodicity becomes confused; all one can say is that until a beat before **31** the cuts at least fall on the metrical downbeats. From **31** to the end of 'The Augurs', however, the four-bar periodicity is secure (although it is initially complicated by the prominent off-beat horn and double bassoon at **31**). Accordingly there is a cut on the hyperdownbeat at **31**+4, but thereafter the increasingly prominent hyperdownbeats are consistently avoided; as can be seen from Figure 5.4, most of the shots consist of odd numbers of beats, and so are cut across the barline.

Is there a rationale behind all this? Three positive answers can be given. The first is that initially the cutting reinforces the emergence of periodicity (hence the cuts at the hyperdownbeats following **28** and **31**), but once the periodicity is established, the cutting plays against it. To use Imbrie's terminology, the cutting at first favours a 'conservative' reading of the music, but then migrates to the surface, and so becomes 'radical'. In other words, it appears to be broadly compatible with the kind of listening strategy that van den Toorn describes. The second answer follows on from the first: the 'play' against the underlying periodicity to which I referred takes the form of a partially autonomous cutting structure. Figure 5.4 is arranged on two levels to bring out the

[34] The music does not completely fall into four-bar (eight-beat) periods owing to the three-beat pattern of the cellos and basses. But the dominant effect is as stated.

Fig. 5.4 Cutting rhythms in 'The Augurs of Spring'

(a b a c) pattern, where (a, b, c) represent different numbers of beats; as may be seen, there are two such patterns, one on each line of Figure 5.4, with the crossover between them resulting in the (7 6 7 6) pattern between **32** and **34**. (As in the analysis of the fight sequence, I am not claiming that this pattern was consciously put there by the animators, or that it is likely to be perceived as such by any viewer; I am simply pointing out that it is there.) As for the last answer, it is the simplest and probably the most salient: there is an overall quickening of the cutting rhythm as 'The Augurs' reaches its conclusion. Fragmentation helps to build climaxes in pictures, as in sound.

In musical terms 'Ritual of Abduction' is the sustained climax to which 'The Augurs' has built, and in terms of Disney's narrative it corresponds to the tidal wave to which the preceding eruptions give rise. Here, too, it is possible to invoke a technical analysis of the music in order to explain one of the most striking features of the visualization: the black, blank screen at **46**, following on the equally blank, white screen after **45**, coinciding with what van den Toorn calls a 'wildly irregular climactic stretch' of Stravinsky's score.[35] Van den Toorn's analysis of 'Ritual of Abduction' again revolves around 'conservative' and 'radical' readings: his assumption is that the listener will try to find some regular metrical unit in terms of which the music can be parsed, perhaps the initially notated 9/8, perhaps 6/8 or some other unit. And his argument is that no such superordinate unit can be found; there *is* no consistent metrical unit higher than the eighth-note—a pulse, or *tactus*, which van den Toorn describes as 'almost impossibly rapid'.[36] What is more, it is exactly at **46** that, according to van den Toorn, the irregular metres will '*force* listeners to make at least an attempt at the eighth-note'[37]—an attempt which, he implies, can be maintained, if at all, only with significant mental (and perhaps even physical) strain.

How does this relate to Disney's animation? From the beginning of 'Ritual of Abduction' there is constant, frenetic motion, with waves surging abstractly across the screen and spiralling plumes of spray. This motion accommodates, or appropriates, the rhythmic energy of the music, but (as can be seen if the film is watched without sound) there is no determinate realization of the rhythm or even the pulse. The only exception is at **40**, where the pictures are cut tightly with the music: scenes of billowing spray coupled with the horn phrases are intercut with images of lightning behind dark clouds synchronized with the

[35] Van den Toorn, *Stravinsky and* The Rite of Spring, 108.
[36] Ibid. 110. The *tactus* is the most salient level of rhythmic regularity in music, the pulse with which people most readily tap their feet, and it is normally in the range 40 to 160 MM (p. 64). The notated tempo of 'Ritual of Abduction' is dotted quarter-note equals 132, or eighth-note equals 396.
[37] Ibid. 64.

tremolando phrases in the second violins, and the lightning seems to flicker in an eighth-note pulse. At **45** the waves peak, together with the music's registral climax; the octave glissando in the violins is visualized as the cresting of water as it crashes over a cliff. Spray surges over the 'camera' position, resulting in visual 'white-out' as all eight horns play their rising fifth figure, triple fortissimo, 'pavillons en l'air'. And then, exactly at **46**, there is a cut to a black screen, with only a small orange-red patch at the top; it looks as if the shot had been taken through water, with the orange-red patch rippling gently, completely out of time with the music. This continues until **47**, where the 'camera' begins to pan down, so that occasional patches of volcanic orange pass up the screen, flickering in time with the *sforzando* chords at bars 5, 7, and 10 after **47**.[38] Even without the benefit of a technical analysis of the music, there is a distinct impression that the visualization has in some sense 'modulated' beyond any attempt to match the frenetic foreground rhythm of the music, and now responds only to middleground accentuation. Indeed, there is a rather similar effect in the music at the end of this passage, during the final four bars of 'Ritual of Abduction': the thirty-second-note tremolandi absorb and, so to speak, dissipate the still unresolved rhythmic energy of the musical foreground. Disney's pre-emptive translation of this effect creates the illusion that, in the end, it is Stravinsky's music that is reacting to the pictures, not the other way round.

In 'The Augurs' and 'Ritual of Abduction', then, it is possible to read Disney's visualization almost as if it were an element of the music, and I shall come back to the question of what this may mean in terms of the models of multimedia which I have put forward. When it comes to structure on an even larger scale, however, it is possible to see the visuals as contributing to a level of articulation that is not present in the music at all. Early critics like Henry Cope Colles said of the original production of *The Rite* that its incidents 'follow each other without much feeling for rational sequence or climax'.[39] Even van den Toorn, after demonstrating the coherence of its characteristic pitch structures, confesses that '*The Rite* does not readily submit to the imposition of an all-embracing plot'.[40] And if we are to share the opinions of Arthur Berger and of Stravinsky himself, then the problem of coherence will have been

---

[38] Perhaps it is these points, or the flickers of lightning after **40**, that Dick Kelsey had in mind when he turned his difficulties as an art director for *The Rite of Spring* sequence into verse: 'The Rite of Spring is a moody thing / So make it dark as night, / With lots of jets and black silhouettes / But be damn sure it's light' (Maltin, *Of Mice and Magic*, 61).

[39] Henry Cope Colles, ' "Le Sacre du Printemps" at Drury Lane', *The Times*, 26 July 1913 (unsigned); repr. in François Lesure, *Igor Stravinsky, Le Sacre du Printemps: Dossier de Presse* (Geneva, 1980), 67.

[40] Van den Toorn, *Stravinsky and* The Rite of Spring, 188.

exacerbated for Disney—if, that is, it represented a problem for him at all—by the nature of Stokowski's performance. According to Berger, Stokowski's 'racy, turbulent readings' of *The Rite* had the effect of 'dragging the form into confusion',[41] while Stravinsky had just one word for the performance in 'Fantasia': 'execrable'.[42]

So what did Disney and his animators do about this? In the first place, of course, they submitted *The Rite* to the imposition of an all-embracing plot: a unilinear, chronological narrative that follows the development of the earth from its early geological history to the extinction of the dinosaurs, and finally the more recent geological events that resulted in their traces being buried within the rocks. (At times the *Rite* sequence seems to adopt the conventions of the educational film, though under a thin disguise of fantasy, as when the passing aeons are symbolized by waves of darkness that traverse the screen during the depiction of early life in the ocean.[43]) At the same time, however, the unilinear plan is overlaid by a symmetrical one: space—geological events—life—geological events—space. The last of these corresponds to the abbreviated repetition of the opening bassoon solo which Disney added. The symmetry is also rendered unmistakable by the closely parallel construction of the two geological sections, in each case beginning with cataclysmic events on the land, followed by a descent to sea-level (in the first case following the lava, in the second the rocks) and turbulent marine scenes. Even the graphic appearance of the two sea sequences, respectively aligned with the 'Ritual of Abduction' and the later part of 'Dance of the Earth', is unmistakably similar. There is also consistent use of symmetry to provide visual closure to smaller narrative sections, best illustrated by the life sequence, since it has most subdivisions, all but the first being closed in this way.[44]

But that is not all. Figure 5.5 shows the alignment of the various individual numbers of *The Rite* with Disney's scenario, and adds two further parameters which contribute to the large-scale organization of this sequence from 'Fantasia'. The first of these is colour. ('B' in Fig. 5.5 stands for blue, while 'O' stands for a range of colours from red through orange—hence the 'O'—to yellow.) Maltin has observed that 'Right from the start [and that means the early 1930s] Disney was concerned with creative use of color, not just color itself'. He instances the 1934

[41] Arthur Berger, 'Music for the Ballet', in Minna Lederman (ed.), *Stravinsky in the Theatre* (New York, 1949), 41–69: 53.

[42] Stravinsky and Craft, *Expositions and Developments*, 146.

[43] At **80**, **81**, and **82**, in each case coinciding with the same musical passage.

[44] The sea-shore sequence that begins at **83** ends just before **90** with the same backdrop it began with; the sequence of animals at peace begins and ends with prominent yawns (**90**+3, **101**+4); the *Tyrannosaurus* sequence is framed by shots of the animals looking on (**102–3**, **125**); and the extinction sequence is framed by shots of the burning sun (**128**, **139**). The third and fourth of these coincide with formal divisions in the music, and the second with a thematic repetition.

Introduction to Part I	Emergence from space	B	F
	The earth in turmoil		
The Augurs of Spring	Volcanoes,	O	F
	lava flow	O	F
Ritual of Abduction	Tidal wave	O	L
	The pageant of life		
Introduction to Part II	Protozoa,	B	R
	sea-shore	O	—
Mystic Circles of the Young Girls	Animals at peace	—	R
Glorification of the Chosen One,	Hunt and kill	B	L
Evocation of the Ancestors			
Ritual Action of the Ancestors,	Extinction	O	R
The Sage			
	The earth in turmoil		
Dance of the Earth	Earthquake,	O	F .
	sea	B	L
Introduction to Part I (abbreviated)	Return to space	—	—

Fig. 5.5 Large-scale structure in the *Rite of Spring* sequence

Silly Symphony 'The Flying Mouse', in which the colours parallel the expressive trajectory of the cartoon (an unlikely parallel with Roller and Schoenberg suggests itself at this point). But in 'Fantasia', and specifically in the *Rite* sequence, colour is used structurally. There are two aspects to this. The first can be seen from Figure 5.5: almost every section or subsection is dominated by either blue or the red-orange-yellow complex, and there is a discernible large-scale rhythm of alternation from section to section. (More precisely, single blue-dominated sections alternate with a variable number of sections dominated by red-orange-yellow, a procedure which is close to one of Stravinsky's characteristic modes of musical construction.[45]) This alternation cuts across the symmetrical patterning I described in the previous paragraph; one of the few striking distinctions between the graphics of the sea scenes in 'Ritual of Abduction' and 'Dance of the Earth' is that the former are weighted towards red, the latter to blue. As for the second aspect of the structural use of colour, this subsists simply in the compact, 'designer'

[45] e.g., the blocks at **111–12** designated in Fig. 5.2 as 'd9', 'd11', and 'd15' might be further broken down into two elements, a fixed one (x) and a variable one (y); the analysis would now read: x3 y6 x3 y8 x3 y12.

feel that the colour organization gives to the film; a very obvious parallel, discussed in the previous chapter, is provided by the music videos of Madonna and Mary Lambert.[46]

The other additional parameter shown in Figure 5.5 plays a perhaps even more fundamental role in the experience of 'Fantasia'. It is represented by the letters 'F' (for forwards) and 'L' and 'R' (for left and right, of course), and shows the prevailing motion of the film—a motion that sometimes appears to be created by camera movement, and sometimes diegetically. (There are no letters for backward motion because it is almost completely absent from the *Rite* sequence; panning up and down occur only at occasional moments, generally associated with the sun.) Again, the basic principle appears to be one of alternation; successive subsections have contrasted prevailing motions. But there is a major exception: the consistent and almost uninterrupted forward motion from the beginning of the *Rite* sequence to the end of 'The Augurs of Spring', a motion that only becomes fully evident for what it is if one watches the film without the music. The 'camera' position is initially constructed through the motion of the galaxy and other heavenly bodies towards the implied viewer (they move upwards and to the right). Since there is no such thing as absolute motion in space, it is pointless to ask whether this is constructed as camera or diegetic motion; but the distinction becomes salient as the scene changes to the earth's surface. During the volcano sequence the prevailing motion derives from the 'camera', while during the ensuing lava flow sequence it is diegetic (the lava constantly flows towards the 'camera', threatening at times to swamp it). Even on those occasions when the forward motion is interrupted, there is generally movement in another direction. As a result, the few genuinely static shots create a kind of tension; they seem to demand resolution, almost in the manner of a musical dissonance, as at **28+4**, where a static shot of a distant mountain is relieved after a few seconds as the river of lava appears at the bottom of the picture. (At this point one suddenly realizes that the trumpet tune at **28+4** sounds distinctly like one of those broad melodies that nineteenth-century composers used to depict rivers.)

This almost continual forward motion serves to draw the viewer into the narrative of the film. But it does more than that. It gives a sense of large-scale continuity and direction to the entire opening sequence of the film, binding the Introduction to Part I together with 'The Augurs of Spring'. The sense of sustained motion even spills over into 'Ritual of Abduction', in spite of the change of direction shown in Figure 5.5. Smaller processes of intensification—the build-up of both the

[46] See above, pp. 162–3.

Introduction and 'The Augurs' towards their climaxes—are subsumed within this larger directed motion. A single filmic gesture is created which reaches from the opening space sequence right up to the dawn of life. There is nothing on quite this scale in the rest of the film—or, indeed, in Stravinsky's score.

The Rite in Context

At the beginning of this chapter I referred to the image of *The Rite* as absolute music that Stravinsky was at pains to disseminate in the decades after its composition. As is well known, the original staged production of *The Rite*, with sets by Nikolai Roerich and choreography by Vaslav Nijinsky, was a *succès de scandale* in Paris, while its London reception, though on the whole cordial, was by no means rapturous. It was the concert performance of the following year, conducted like the original production by Pierre Monteux, that gave *The Rite* immediate entry into the modernist canon; Emile Vuillermoz recorded that

After the last chord there was delirium. The mass of spectators, in a fever of adoration, screamed the name of the author, and the entire audience began to look for him. An exaltation, never to be forgotten, reigned in the hall, and the applause went on until everyone was dizzy. . . . For Igor Stravinsky, the homage of unlimited adoration.[47]

Stravinsky himself called this 'a triumph such as *composers* rarely enjoy'.[48] But it was not until he saw the 1920 revival of *The Rite* with new choreography by Leonid Massine, he said, that he realized he preferred *The Rite* as a concert piece.[49] One might have deduced as much, though, from an interview that Stravinsky gave a few days before the first performance of the Massine version, in which he claimed that the pagan dances of the staged version were merely a 'point of departure (*pretexte*)' for the music. 'I wrote an architectural work,' he said, 'not a story-telling one. It was an error to approach it from the latter point of view instead of from the real meaning of the score' (the error, he implies, being Nijinsky's).[50] But the conclusion of this argument seems to be that there is no need for choreography at all; after all, if the meaning is all in the score, why stage the piece?

[47] Emile Vuillermoz, review published in *Comoedia*, 6 Apr. 1914; trans. in Stravinsky and Craft, *Stravinsky in Pictures and Documents*, 106–7.

[48] Stravinsky and Craft, *Expositions and Developments*, 143. The italicizing of the word 'composers' is, I think, a dig at Diaghilev, for a few lines later Stravinsky observes that 'Diaghilev was always verdantly envious of any success of mine outside of his Ballet' (p. 144).

[49] Ibid. 144. Stravinsky gives the date as 1921, but the Massine version ran from 15 to 27 Dec. 1920 (Lesure, *Igor Stravinsky*, 164).

[50] Michel Georges-Michel, 'Les deux *Sacre du Printemps*', *Comoedia*, 14 Dec. 1920; repr. in Lesure, *Igor Stravinsky*, 53; trans. in Lederman (ed.), *Stravinsky in the Theatre*, 24–6.

Van den Toorn takes his cue from Stravinsky. '*The Rite* was already very overtly "dance music",' he says, so that 'choreographic interpretations tended therefore to be redundant . . . and hence to degenerate into spectacle.' (The logical consequence of this statement appears to be that if music is good for dancing to, there is no point in dancing to it.) And if *The Rite* attained 'the kind of universal appeal it has now for so long enjoyed' only when it migrated from the theatre to the concert-hall, he continues, it was only conforming to the general rule: 'in modern times . . . music has succeeded as musical structure (i.e. as "music") or it has barely succeeded at all.'[51] Of course you might expect a music theorist to say that; the discipline of music theory is predicated on the assumption that music can be usefully understood as some kind of 'objective construction' (the phrase is Stravinsky's, and it again comes from the 1920 interview), and van den Toorn's analysis makes no further reference to stage productions of *The Rite*. But the same assumption was so universally shared during the decades after the First World War that it came to seem self-evident. What began as a neo-classical reaction against Romantic excess turned at first into an orthodoxy, and then, as it became transparent, an ideology. In seeking to reinterpret as absolute music what he had composed as a 'musical-choreographic work',[52] Stravinsky was reacting (and contributing) to an emerging aesthetic consensus that extended far beyond the domain of music.

The assumption of aesthetic autonomy is so deeply ingrained in the one article to have been published on 'Fantasia' in a serious academic journal as, in effect, to prejudge the conclusions that it reaches. The article is called ' "Fantasia" and the Psychology of Music', and it was published by Horace B. English, of Ohio State University, in 1942, just two years after the film was released.[53] The visualization of *The Sorcerer's Apprentice* is acceptable, English says, because Dukas conceived his music as the illustration of a story, and so 'No violence is done to the composer's intent. . . . [T]he screen is merely substituted for the stage.'[54] But it cannot be justified with the greater part of the music in 'Fantasia', which is abstract (and, though he does not specifically mention it, I have little doubt that English would have included *The Rite* in this category). The reason, English explains, is that human

[51] Van den Toorn, *Stravinsky and* The Rite of Spring, 17, 18.

[52] Stravinsky's term: Stravinsky and Craft, *Stravinsky in Pictures and Documents*, 75.

[53] Horace B. English, ' "Fantasia" and the Psychology of Music', *Journal of Aesthetics and Art Criticism*, 2 (1942–3), 27–31.

[54] Ibid. 28. A very similar argument was presented at the time of the film's first release by Franz Hoellering (untitled review in *The Nation*, 23 Nov. 1940, pp. 513–14). Hoellering adds a comment that sheds an interesting light on the cinema-going conventions of the period: 'the audience applauded exactly where it would have applauded if the score had been composed by a Hollywood musician. . . . [T]o have the Pastoral Symphony interrupted by applause for sugar-sweet centaurettes is painful' (p. 513).

psychology dictates that visual experiences inevitably dominate aural ones, and so Disney's attempts to use pictures to illustrate music are doomed to failure; they turn art music into background music. Worse than that, he continues, Disney's visualization intrudes upon listeners' freedom to interpret the music in their own way, setting itself up as *the* correct way to hear the music—whereas in reality 'There cannot be . . . any universally "correct" visual pattern for one of Bach's fugues or even for highly programmatic music.' Consequently, he concludes, 'To encourage people to look for and upon Mr Disney's or anyone else's images is to encourage them to do something in the presence of music besides respond to music, is to make them to that extent less musical.'[55]

Despite an appealing streak of common sense, English's article is an object lesson in how to get things wrong. The trouble begins at the beginning, with the confident distinction between programme and abstract music (and this is an issue to which I shall return in the Conclusion). As far as *The Rite* is concerned, however, English cannot really be blamed. Stravinsky had, after all, himself authorized the interpretation of his music as ' "music" ' (to borrow van den Toorn's pithy expression). Indeed, in his 1920 interview, Stravinsky had explained how his initial idea for *The Rite* had been a musical theme; because he was himself a Russian, he said, its 'strong and brutal manner' had suggested to him the scenario of pagan Slavic tribes—'But bear in mind', he added, 'that the idea came from the music and not the music from the idea.'[56] And all this had percolated into the American reception of *The Rite*. The day after the American première (a concert performance which took place on 31 January 1924), the *New York Times* ran a review by Olin Downes which made use of extensive quotations from the 1920 interview, including Stravinsky's account of the work's origins. Downes followed these quotations with a rather curious comment: 'That is the story, and we believe the sincere story, of the musical evolution of this extremely interesting and exciting creation.'[57] Why did Downes need to say he believed the story? Did he have reason to doubt the sincerity of Stravinsky's account of the genesis of *The Rite?* In fact, he might well have, for as Richard Taruskin bluntly puts it, 'there was hardly a word of truth in this, and Stravinsky knew it'.[58]

I have little to add to the story that Taruskin unfolds, and will do no more than briefly summarize it. In his autobiography, and again in *Expositions and Developments*, Stravinsky stated that *The Rite* began not

[55] English, ' "Fantasia" ' 29, 30–1.   [56] Lederman (ed.), *Stravinsky in the Theatre*, 24.

[57] Olin Downes, ' "Sacre du Printemps" Played', *New York Times*, 1 Feb. 1924; repr. in Lesure, *Igor Stravinsky*, 95–6.

[58] Richard Taruskin, 'The Rite Revisited: The Idea and the Source of its Scenario', in Edmond Strainchamps and Maria Rika Manietes (eds.), *Music and Civilization: Essays in Honor of Paul Henry Lang* (New York, 1984), 183–202: 184.

as a thematic idea but as a dream in which he saw a sacrificial virgin dancing herself to death. In *Expositions and Developments* he specifically added that 'This vision was not accompanied by concrete musical ideas.'[59] And when he began to work in earnest on *The Rite*, the first thing he did was to enlist the aid of Roerich in developing the scenario. The two met and discussed the project—then known as 'The Great Sacrifice'—in 1910, for on 19 June Stravinsky wrote to Roerich asking him to forward the piece of paper on which he had written down the libretto and which he had accidentally left behind.[60] But the chronology and its significance emerge most clearly from a letter that Stravinsky wrote to Roerich a year later. 'Dear Nikolai Konstantinovitch', it reads, 'I feel it is imperative that we see each other to decide about every detail—especially every question of staging—concerning our child. I expect to start composing in the fall.'[61]

Although Roerich was a painter, his special qualification for this task was that he was an acknowledged expert on the pagan civilizations that occupied what later became Russia, and Taruskin has uncovered many of the sources on which Roerich based his scenario; they range from Herodotus to nineteenth-century scholarship. What emerges most forcefully from this is the scientific accuracy of the result; far from consisting, as Disney put it, of 'a simple series of tribal dances', Roerich's scenario might be described as a work of ethnography masquerading as fantasy. Indeed, much the same might be said about Stravinsky's music. Here again the process of revision has been at work. In *Memories and Commentaries* (1960), Stravinsky specifically stated that 'the opening bassoon melody in *Le Sacre du Printemps* is the only folk melody in that work'.[62] But Taruskin's researches have not only matched the sketches for *The Rite* against existing folk tunes; he has even found the sources from which Stravinsky took some of them, while there is evidence that Stravinsky may have collected others himself.[63] And what again emerges is the scientific accuracy of the result—not in terms of the literal reproduction of folk music, to be sure, but in the consistent association of folk-derived materials with the ritual contexts to which they authentically belonged. When Stravinsky claimed in *Expositions and Developments* that 'very little immediate tradition lies behind *Le Sacre du Printemps*',[64] then, he could hardly have been more economical with the truth.

[59] Stravinsky and Craft, *Expositions and Developments*, 140.
[60] Stravinsky, Appendix to *The Rite of Spring: Sketches 1911–1913*, 27–8.
[61] Ibid. 29. [62] Stravinsky and Craft, *Memories and Commentaries*, 98.
[63] Richard Taruskin, 'Russian Folk Melodies in *The Rite of Spring*', *Journal of the American Musicological Society*, 23 (1980), 501–43. Taruskin's article reproduces a photograph of Stravinsky taking down the song of a mendicant folk-singer in Ustilug in or around 1910 (p. 507).
[64] Stravinsky and Craft, *Expositions and Developments*, 147. Admittedly this remark refers specifically to musical traditions, but even there Taruskin has demonstrated the intimate relationship

But the most relevant aspect of Stravinsky's revisionism for present purposes is what Taruskin calls the 'great and deliberate injustice' that Stravinsky did to Nijinsky.[65] At the time of the original production, Stravinsky was unstinting in his praise for Nijinsky's choreography; a fortnight after the first performance, he told an interviewer who had questioned the choreography that 'Nijinsky is an admirable artist. . . . His contribution to *Le Sacre du Printemps* was very important.'[66] And a few weeks after that he wrote to Maximilian Steinberg that 'Nijinsky's choreography was incomparable. With the exception of a few places, everything is as I wanted it. One must wait a long time before the public becomes accustomed to our language, but of the value of what we have done I am certain.'[67] (The collaborative 'we' speaks even louder than the laudatory vocabulary.) But by the time he wrote—if 'wrote' is the right word[68]—his so-called autobiography, in 1936, Stravinsky had begun to tell a different story. 'To be perfectly frank,' he said, 'the idea of working with Nijinsky filled me with misgiving. . . . His ignorance of the most elementary notions of music was flagrant. . . . When, in listening to music, he contemplated movements, it was always necessary to remind him that he must make them accord with the tempo, its divisions and values.'[69] And by the time *Expositions and Developments* was published, a quarter of a century later, the story had hardened up: ' "I will count to forty while you play," Nijinsky would say to me, "and we will see where we come out." He could not understand that though we might at some point come out together, this did not necessarily mean we had been together on the way.'[70]

The curious thing is that what Nijinsky was doing, as Stravinsky describes it, sounds very similar to what Stravinsky praised in Massine's 1920 choreography of *The Rite*. In the revisionary interview he gave before the first performance of Massine's version, Stravinsky explained it as follows:

Here is a four-beat measure, then a five-beat one. Massine might have his dancers move in a rhythm of three times three, which corresponds and makes the exact same total. . . . And he keeps up this battle, this slowing down or pre-

between Stravinsky's achievement and the context from which it emerged ('Chernomor to Kashchei: Harmonic Sorcery; or, Stravinsky's "Angle" ', *Journal of the American Musicological Society*, 38 (1985), 72–142).

[65] Taruskin, '*The Rite* Revisited', 184.

[66] Interview in *Gil Blas*, 14 June 1913; trans. in Stravinsky and Craft, *Stravinsky in Pictures and Documents*, 511.

[67] Letter of 3 July, trans. in Stravinsky and Craft, *Stravinsky in Pictures and Documents*, 102.

[68] Stravinsky's *An Autobiography* (London, 1975 [1936]) was 'largely ghostwritten by the Diaghilev acolyte Walter Nouvel' (Taruskin, 'Russian Folk Melodies', 502).

[69] Stravinsky, *Autobiography*, 40–1.

[70] Stravinsky and Craft, *Expositions and Developments*, 143.

cipitation, for two or even twenty measures, but he always comes out in accord with any section as a whole.[71]

And curiouser still (as Alice might have put it), evidence is now available that the kind of mechanical counting Nijinsky had been doing was exactly what Stravinsky had told him to do. This evidence takes the shape of the four-hand piano score which Stravinsky marked up for Nijinsky and which contains a host of remarkably detailed choreographic indications. Stravinsky gave the score to Misia Sert on the day after the first performance,[72] and only recovered it in 1967, when it was auctioned in London. Stravinsky's own transcriptions of some of the annotations were included in the Appendix to the facsimile publication of the sketches for *The Rite*, and they include many points where Nijinsky was instructed to count individual beats: 'From the beginning to here, 136 eighths', writes Stravinsky at **111** (the 'Glorification' is especially rich in such annotations), while at **43–4**, in 'Ritual of Abduction', he asks for 'trampling with each eighth. Do not attempt to count the measures.'[73]

What the choreographic annotations make quite clear is the wild inaccuracy of the statement, in Stravinsky's supposed autobiography, that 'In composing the *Sacre* I had imagined . . . a series of rhythmic mass movements of the greatest simplicity which would have an instantaneous effect on the audience, with no superfluous details or complications such as would suggest effort.'[74] On the contrary, the annotations demand the most staggeringly complex realizations, with minutely specified rhythms or metres cutting across anything that is audible in the orchestra; as Stravinsky himself wrote in his 1967 commentary on the annotations, 'The dance is almost always in counterpoint to the music.'[75] Indeed, he expressed his astonishment that he 'could have envisaged synchronization of music and choreography to such a degree, and expected any choreographer to realize it in 1913'. He went on to declare that 'this account of the choreography supersedes all others, including those testaments of my own faulty memory now permanently on exhibit elsewhere'. And elsewhere, less publicly, Stravinsky seems to have explicitly withdrawn his criticisms of Nijinsky's choreography, declaring it 'the finest embodiment of *Le Sacre*'.[76] On 24 June 1970 he actually wrote a letter to the editor of *The*

[71] Lederman (ed.), *Stravinsky in the Theatre*, 24.

[72] For a discussion of the circumstances surrounding this gift, see Stravinsky and Craft, *Stravinsky in Pictures and Documents*, 514–22.

[73] Stravinsky, Appendix to *The Rite of Spring: Sketches 1911–1913*, 41, 37.

[74] Stravinsky, *Autobiography*, 48.

[75] Stravinsky, Appendix to *The Rite of Spring: Sketches 1911–1913*, 35.

[76] From a conversation with Yury Grigorovich mentioned by Taruskin ('*The Rite* Revisited', 184 n. 4), who cites as his source Vera Krasovskaya, *Nijinsky* (New York, 1979), 272. In addition, Vera

Nation suggesting that some American ballet company should produce *The Rite* with Nijinsky's original choreography. 'I would come to see that myself,' he added.[77]

What are these annotations like? I have already mentioned that at the beginning of 'The Augurs' Stravinsky directed that the choreographic accents should be on the metrical downbeats and not the rhythmic accents. This, I suggested, corresponds to van den Toorn's 'conservative' reading. (Up to **18**, Stravinsky explains in his commentary, the dancers have been 'bobbing up and down in one place'; this is the passage where, in 1960, Stravinsky had claimed he imagined 'a row of almost motionless dancers'.[78]) After **28**, however, Stravinsky specifies cross-metres: there are to be eight bars of 3/4 (against the notated 2/4), then two bars of 2/4, followed by three further bars of 3/4 and fifteen of 2/4.[79] Now this is the passage which I earlier described as a textbook example of van den Toorn's Type II, and the 3/4 metre Stravinsky asks of the dancers corresponds with the three-beat pattern in the cellos and basses. In effect, then, the alternations between 2/4 and 3/4 mean that the dance line is migrating from one part of the rhythmic hierarchy to another—in a rather similar way, incidentally, to the trumpet melody from **28**+4, whose phrases are two, three, or four bars long and thus align themselves in varying ways with the regularly repeating elements of the texture. And Stravinsky asks for another kind of changing pattern when he directs that the choreographic accents fall on the metric downbeats at **34**, but on the second beat of each bar when the music repeats almost literally at **35**.

Stravinsky and Robert Kraft report that Stravinsky wrote a marginal note in Irina Vershinina's monograph on his early ballets, 'saying that criticism of Nijinsky's choreography had always been "unjust" ' (*Stravinsky in Pictures and Documents*, 511).

[77] The letter is reprinted in Stravinsky and Craft, *Themes and Conclusions* (London, 1972), 218. Not the least interesting aspect of this letter is the way in which it slips from saying that the recovery of the choreographic annotations 'makes possible the recreation of the ballet as it was conceived' to advocating the revival of 'the Nijinsky original'; the clear implication is that, contrary to the complaints Stravinsky had made during the intervening years, Nijinsky's choreography was a reasonably accurate reflection of what Stravinsky had specified. It is on this basis that I more or less equate the two in what follows.

[78] Stravinsky and Craft, *Memories and Commentaries*, 37; 'Nijinsky made of this piece a big jumping match,' he complains. In *Expositions and Commentaries*, he gave a more vivid impression of what it was like when he described it as a 'group of knock-kneed and long-braided Lolitas jumping up and down' (p. 143). Stravinsky's rather telegraphic annotations gain visual depth when read in conjunction with two illustrated commentaries: Pasler, 'Music and Spectacle in *Petrushka* and *The Rite of Spring*', and Millicent Hodson, 'Nijinsky's Choreographic Method: Visual Sources from Roerich for *Le Sacre du Printemps*', *Dance Research Journal*, 18 (1986–7), 7–15. Hodson's *Nijinsky's Crime Against Grace: Reconstruction Score of the Original Choreography* for Le Sacre du Printemps (Stuyvesant, NY), originally announced for publication in Winter 1993, was still not available at the time this book went to press.

[79] Stravinsky, Appendix to *The Rite of Spring: Sketches 1911–1913*, 36. Although Stravinsky explains that he has related the annotations to the rehearsal numbers in the orchestral score (p. 35), I am not clear exactly which bars he is speaking of at this point.

In 'Ritual of Abduction', too, it is possible to see some relationship between Stravinsky's choreographic annotations and the kind of rhythmic analysis that van den Toorn offers. As I explained, the focus of van den Toorn's analysis is the way in which the music refuses to be subsumed under any higher-level metrical structure than the 'impossibly rapid' eighth-note *tactus*. This links nicely with Stravinsky's direction about 'trampling with each eighth' which I have already quoted, except that the direction comes at **43–4**, a little ahead of van den Toorn's (and Disney's) point of breakdown, which is **46**. At that point (or to be precise, at **46**+1), Stravinsky directs that the dancers form into three separate groups, which implies some kind of choreographic counterpoint, and in the following bars he specifies a number of accents; these presumably fall on the downbeats, so bringing out the changing metres and conforming, in a different way, with the wholly 'radical' interpretation that van den Toorn offers of this passage. And there are later passages in the choreography which have even more complicated annotations than this. I shall outline just a few representative examples. After **53** (in the 'Spring Rounds', which Disney omitted), Stravinsky divides the dancers into five groups, writing in a separate stave for each; the individual rhythms are too complicated to describe, he says, but 'the projected phrasing of all except one of the five groups is largely independent of the musical meters'.[80] The one rhythm which *does* correspond to the music is a syncopated pattern in 4/4, consisting of one eighth-note, three quarter-notes, and another eighth-note: this is the rhythm of the bass at **53**. From **54**+1, Stravinsky directs that this rhythm should continue to receive the main choreographic emphasis—but the rhythm has now disappeared from the music. (Here, then, the dancing corresponds not to what is in the music, but to what *was* in the music and is no longer.) Finally, as an unambiguous example of choreographic autonomy, at the bar before **138** (in the 'Ritual Action'), Stravinsky initially directed that the women should dance in 29/4, but replaced this with what he calls a two-part 'canon of choreographic rhythm not underlined in the music'.[81]

In his letter to *The Nation*, Stravinsky called the recovered choreographic score of *The Rite* 'much more valuable than any commentary', on the grounds that it 'changes and deepens the interpretation of the music (especially in matters of phrasing)'.[82] The idea that the choreography might 'change' the interpretation of the music of course gives the lie to Stravinsky's insistence in the 1920 interview that the 'real meaning' of *The Rite*, as he put it, was all there in the score. In this way, it rescues the staging from redundancy, and by implication admits

[80] Ibid. 38.   [81] Ibid. 42.   [82] Stravinsky and Craft, *Themes and Conclusions*, 218.

that the regimen of musical autonomy has limits. It also raises the question of how far different visualizations may be compatible with one another: how much overlap should we expect there to be between alternative interpretations of the same score? To be more specific, what parallels, if any, can we find between the choreographic realization Stravinsky envisaged and the *Rite* sequence of 'Fantasia'?

Specific correspondences can, of course, be found; they always can. For instance, Stravinsky directs that the dancers all fall to the floor in the last bar of 'The Augurs', and it is just at this point that we see molten rocks cascading catastrophically into the sea. Again, at 'The Sage' (before **72**), Stravinsky directs that 'Everyone stands still', while at the bar before **72** (the harmonics chord) he writes, 'They all change posture';[83] these correspond respectively to Disney's eclipse sequence, with the infinitely slow movement of the moon against the face of the sun, and a cut to the lifeless landscape following the great extinction. And at the bars before **101** and **102** Stravinsky directs the dancers to stop and start again, just as Disney's dinosaurs do, while the circular motion of the dinosaurs scooping up water after **97** coincides with Stravinsky's specification of a 'bell-swinging movement'.[84] We might also draw parallels of a different kind between 'Fantasia' and Nijinsky's conception of *The Rite* as embodying 'the soul of nature expressed by movement to music. It is the life of the stones and trees. There are no human beings in it.'[85] It is this conception that led Nijinsky to aim at a style of dance which an unkind critic described as a series of 'slow, uncouth movements in which the dancers were so seemingly obsessed by the earth that they appeared unable to stand upright'[86]—and that, of course, would not be a bad description of Disney's dinosaurs. Like Nijinsky, both Roerich and Stravinsky emphasized the role of stones and rocks in *The Rite* (Stravinsky referred to its 'lapidary rhythms', and once called it a 'stone sculpture'[87]), which ties in with the geological emphasis of Disney's visualization. Finally, Disney's earthquake sequence provides about the most literal interpretation possible for 'The Dance of the Earth'.

---

[83] Stravinsky, Appendix to *The Rite of Spring: Sketches 1911–1913*, 40.   [84] Ibid. 41.

[85] Interview with Nijinsky in the *Pall Mall Gazette*, 15 Feb. 1913; repr. in Stravinsky and Craft, *Stravinsky in Pictures and Documents*, 95.

[86] Cyril E. Beaumont, *Complete Book of Ballets* (London, 1937); quoted in Eric Walter White, *Stravinsky: The Composer and his Works*, 2nd edn. (London, 1979), 215. Jacques Rivière expressed the same conception more favourably: 'Rather than glide over things in his flight the dancer comes down on them with the full weight of his body, he accounts for every one with his heavy and complete attack' (Jacques Rivière, 'Le Sacre du Printemps', *La Nouvelle Revue Française*, 7 (1 Nov. 1913); repr. in Lesure, *Igor Stravinsky*, 38–48; trans. taken from Hodson, 'Nijinsky's Choreographic Method', 9. Part of Rivière's article is trans. in Lederman (ed.), *Stravinsky in the Theatre*, 22–3).

[87] Stravinsky and Craft, *Stravinsky in Pictures and Documents*, 77, 92, and Pasler, 'Music and Spectacle', 71.

At this more general level, one basic difference between the original staging and 'Fantasia' might be put forward: Disney provides an explicit narrative—what I previously referred to as an 'all-embracing plot'—whereas Stravinsky (or rather Stravinsky/Roerich) does not. Indeed, Stravinsky said in his 1920 interview that 'There is no plot and no need to look for one. . . . *Le Sacre du Printemps* is a spectacle of pagan Russia . . . that rules out a subject.'[88] But this is a suspiciously defensive—if not self-contradictory—formulation; and conversely, if Deems Taylor's voice-over in 'Fantasia' describes the *Rite* sequence as 'the story of the growth of life on earth', it also refers to it as a 'pageant'[89]—a perhaps more accurate term that is not far removed from Stravinsky's 'spectacle'. And in reality there is not much difference between the two scenarios in this respect. In each case there is a slender narrative thread; the main difference is that the Stravinsky/Roerich scenario is circular and mythical, whereas Disney's is unilinear and historical. But even this distinction is undermined by the symmetry of the end of the 'Fantasia' sequence, with its withdrawal back into space. And the eclipse, which begins at 'The Sage' but is only completed with the return of the opening bassoon solo, also introduces an element of non-linear chronology; together with the other shots of the sun, it carries a mythical resonance that strikingly anticipates '2001: A Space Odyssey'. Perhaps, then, one could say that Disney's visualization of *The Rite* explores the affective properties of primitivism in a manner that is parallel, rather than opposed, to the original scenario. In fact, as much is suggested by the correspondences between 'Fantasia' and the emotionally loaded images contained in an interview that appeared on the day of the first performance of *The Rite*, in which Stravinsky spoke of 'the obscure and immense sensation of which all things are conscious when Nature renews its forms', 'the musical material [which] itself swells, enlarges, expands', and the 'sacred terror of the midday sun'.[90] Admittedly, all these characterizations refer specifically to the

[88] Lederman (ed.), *Stravinsky in the Theatre*, 26.　　　　[89] See above, n. 21.

[90] Igor Stravinsky, 'Ce que j'ai voulu exprimer dans *Le Sacre du Printemps*', *Montjoie!*, 29 May 1913; repr. in Lesure, *Igor Stravinsky*, 13–15; trans. in Stravinsky and Craft, *Stravinsky in Pictures and Documents*, 524–6. In his autobiography, Stravinsky made out that this article altogether misrepresented what he had said; but his own contemporary corrections to a Russian translation of the interview give the lie to this, for they are very minor. The content of the article was of course embarrassing for the absolutist Stravinsky of the 1920s, while the title (which, to be fair, was presumably not Stravinsky's) clearly became an object of infuriation; an account of the whole affair may be found in Stravinsky and Craft, *Stravinsky in Pictures and Documents*, 522–6. The reference to the 'sacred terror of the midday sun' sounds like a regression to the original conception of *The Rite* as the depiction of a midsummer ritual. As Taruskin demonstrates in '*The Rite* Revisited', this would have been more accurate historically, and the sacrificial rites on which Roerich based his scenario were in honour of the Slavic sun god Yarilo (whose name actually appeared in the programme booklet for the first performance). All this, which Disney could not possibly have known, would fit even better with the iconography of the sun in 'Fantasia', especially during the extinction sequence.

Introduction to Part I, whereas the passages with which they resonate are scattered through Disney's *Rite* sequence; but the affinity of tone is unmistakable. Seen this way, Disney's visualization of the music as the story of life becomes an alternative metaphor to that of the pagan celebration of spring.

The obvious way to conceive of the relationship between the music and its two visualizations is in terms of differential elaboration; the kinetic and affective content of the music forms a kind of substrate, which each visualization elaborates in a different manner. (Seen this way, the two visualizations are complementary to one another.) But this picture is of course incomplete, because it overlooks the *musical* elaboration and its relationship to each visualization. And it is in this relationship that the most characteristic aspect of *The Rite* as a work of multimedia is to be found. We can begin with Stravinsky's observation, which I have already quoted, that in his choreographic annotations to *The Rite* 'the dance is almost always in counterpoint with the music'— a statement that is, at first sight, entirely compatible with his statement in *Memories and Commentaries* that 'Choreography, as I conceive it, must realize its own form, one independent of the musical form though measured to the musical unit.'[91]

But we need to be careful about the word 'counterpoint'. The choreography that Stravinsky notated is contrapuntal in something closer to the musical sense of that term than the film-critical one; it refers to difference, to be sure, but within a strong framework of similarity. This is obvious when the dancers oppose the rhythmic accents of the music by duplicating its metrical downbeats, or when they duplicate one particular layer or another in a polyrhythmic texture. In each case the musical framework remains intact, and the dancing underlines one musical element or another in very much the same way as orchestration does. But it is also true when the choreographic metre is different from any that is present in the music, as after **54**, or where the dance incorporates its own autonomous structure, as in the canon around **138**. In such cases the dance constitutes a differential elaboration within the framework of the music's higher-level rhythmic (which is also to say, formal) structure; it functions more like an additional contrapuntal element than an orchestrational emphasis. And it is worth pointing out that Stravinsky intended this kind of elaboration during some of the passages of the score that seem uncharacteristically placid and regular, as after **95**, where the regular powers-of-two phrasing was to be cross-cut by three separate groups dancing contrapuntally in 5/4. It is per-

---

[91] Stravinsky and Craft, *Memories and Commentaries*, 37. This statement is more than a little reminiscent of Eisler's pronouncements regarding the relationship between music and film—pronouncements which, as we saw in Ch. 2, are hardly borne out in his own films.

haps significant that this passage falls within what, in *Expositions and Developments*, Stravinsky described as the weakest section of *The Rite*. The suggestion is that what was good in the context of a 'musical-choreographic work' was not so good as absolute music.

I referred to such contrapuntal choreography as an 'additional' element. But that is, in a way, misleading; if there is one thing to be learned from the genesis of *The Rite*, it is that the choreography, along with other aspects of the staging, constituted an integral part of the compositional process. ('The music and the ballet were composed together,' wrote Nijinksy; 'they were born at the same time.'[92]) And if the dance was composed according to the same rhythmic principles as the rest of the music—which is in essence what I have been arguing—then the choreography becomes structurally indistinguishable from any other musical element; when Jann Pasler says that in *The Rite* dance is 'another dimension of the music', we should take her words quite literally.[93] It follows from this that to speak of the relationship between 'music' and 'dance' in *The Rite* is also misleading to the extent that it suggests a relationship between two distinct things; depending on the level to which we refer, there is either only one thing (because music and dance together constitute a single hierarchy), or else an indefinite number, since any element of the music may relate directly to any element of the choreography. In this way, Nijinsky's statement that 'I put all of my energy into choreographing the dance according to the idea and the spirit of the music, in such a manner that the ballet does not appear to be stuck onto the music'[94] should be understood as implying not the dominance of music over dance, but the interlacing of both within the 'musical-choreographic work' that Stravinsky spoke of. And the impact of the original production of *The Rite* seems to bear out what Nijinsky said. There was, to be sure, the usual disagreement between critics: while Cocteau thought that the dance stuck too close to the rhythm ('The fault lay in the parallelism of the music and the movements, in their lack of *play*, of counterpoint'), Vuillermoz complained that Nijinsky overemphasized the metre at the expense of rhythm.[95] But many observers seem to have shared the views of Colles, who said that it approached 'a real fusion of music and dancing. . . . The combination of the two elements of music and dancing does actually produce a new compound result, expressible in terms of rhythm—much as

[92] Interview published in *Hojas Musicales de la Publicidad*, Madrid, 26 June 1917; trans. in Stravinsky and Craft, *Stravinsky in Pictures and Documents*, 512.

[93] Jann Pasler, 'The Choreography for *The Rite of Spring*: Stravinsky's Visualization of Music', *Dance Magazine*, 55 (1981), 66–9: 68.

[94] 1917 interview (see n. 92), in Stravinsky and Craft, *Stravinsky in Pictures and Documents*, 512.

[95] Lederman (ed.), *Stravinsky and the Theatre*, 18, 22.

the combination of oxygen and hydrogen produces a totally different compound, water.'[96]

If the mention of 'fusion' already suggests an overall relationship of conformance between the media in the staged version of *The Rite*, the impression becomes even stronger in the 'Fantasia' sequence, where the visuals are again incorporated within the structural hierarchy of the music. Much of this is implicit in what I have already said about 'Fantasia': at the bottom of the hierarchy, the visual motions of stars, seas, and volcanic eruptions are appropriated by the audible rhythms of the score, as for instance when the eighth-note pulse of the music animates the volcanic explosions after **21**—an effect which, as I said, evaporates if the film is watched without the music. Further up the hierarchy, at intermediate levels, cutting rhythms act in much the same way as the 'contrapuntal' choreography of Stravinsky's annotations, aligning themselves with metrical or hypermetrical patterns or, on occasion, playing against them. (The cutting does not, incidentally, play against the powers-of-two phrasing after **95**, as Stravinsky's choreography did; instead, it underlines the very regularity of the music, which is aligned with tranquil scenes of dinosaurs feeding and their babies playing.) But the visuals of 'Fantasia' also do something that the choreography of *The Rite* does not, and that is to extend the hierarchy upwards beyond the highest level present in the music; I am referring, of course, to the constant motion of 'camera' or diegesis that runs through the opening three sequences of the film (space, volcanic eruptions, and lava flow), binding the music of the Introduction to Part I to that of 'The Augurs', and spilling over into 'Ritual of Abduction'. The result of all this is that music and visualization stack up into a single hierarchy whose highest level is visual. And in this way, what might be called the background model of the *Rite* sequence from 'Fantasia' is an unambiguous conformance.

That both the Stravinsky/Nijinsky *Rite* and Disney's visualization of it should approach an ideal of conformance is not really surprising. The first emerged out of the 'cultural synaesthesia', as I called it,[97] of turn-of-the-century Russia; while the second achieved its greatest success

---

[96] *The Times*, 12 July 1913; repr. in Lesure, *Igor Stravinsky*, 63–4. The tone of this review is strikingly different from that of 26 July (see above, p. 192), which reported that 'the incidents on the stage had been roughly fitted together and made to synchronize with the music because they happened to illustrate ideas conceived in a similar mood'; as neither review is signed, one suspects that one, at least, of Lesure's attributions may be incorrect. Colles—if it was Colles—went on to say that 'even the colours of the dresses are to some extent reflected in the orchestration—as, for instance, in the first scene, when a group of maidens in vivid scarlet huddled together to the accompaniment of closely-written chords on the trumpets'. Messiaen would have shared this synaesthetic perception, but not Rimbaud, Kandinsky, or Schoenberg.

[97] See Ch. 1, p. 49.

during the days of flower power, when ideas of cosmic harmony and synaesthetic fusion (in the form of the ubiquitous light show) enjoyed a brief revival. But if the argument of the previous chapters is correct, the principle of differential elaboration between media means that conformance can never be more than partial; that is what I meant by referring to it as a 'background' model. Within the overall framework of a single, stacked hierarchy, then, we can detect elements of contest as well as complementation in both the original *Rite* and the 'Fantasia' version. In the case of the Stravinsky/Nijinsky *Rite*, the contest largely takes the form of a collision between stage action and historically sedimented expectations, and follows as a direct consequence from Stravinsky's and Nijinsky's attempt to organize music and dance according to the same principles. Classical ballet has its own hierarchy based on a lexicon of established 'positions' and more or less codified rules for their combination; it is predicated on a relationship of complementation between music and dance, with each medium elaborating according to its own principles a shared kinetic content that is normally located at a middleground level. But Stravinsky's and Nijinsky's attempt to force music and dance into a direct, multi-level relationship meant totally disrupting the traditional hierarchy of ballet; in Millicent Hodson's words, it meant 'finding a new idiom for each dance rather than rearranging academic steps'.[98] (No wonder, then, that the dancers 'hated all this . . . why [they asked] were they trained as artists of the Imperial Ballet and graduates of the Academy? For this?'[99]) Of contemporary commentators, it was Jacques Rivière who perhaps expressed this most succinctly: 'by breaking up this movement,' he says (he is drawing a comparison with the 'liquid and continuous movement' of Fokine's choreography), 'by leading it back to the simple gesture, Nijinsky restored expression to the dance.' Less generous critics simply did not recognize Nijinsky's choreography as dance; for Alfred Kalisch it consisted of gestures that were 'stiff and angular and have been rejected by previous authorities because of their lack of charm and expressiveness', while according to Colles the general impression was that of children at play.[100]

---

[98] Hodson, 'Nijinsky's Choreographic Method', 9.

[99] Marie Rambert, paraphrased in a letter from Lincoln Kirstein to Robert Craft, 21 Oct. 1973, in Stravinsky and Craft, *Stravinsky in Pictures and Documents*, 513.

[100] Alfred Kalisch, *The World*, 25 July 1913, and Henry Cope Colles (but see n. 96 above), *The Times*, 26 July 1913; repr. in Lesure, *Igor Stravinsky*, 66, 67. Effects of contest also left their trace in both the vocabulary and the contradictory assertions of critics about the relative primacy of dance and music: for Christopher St-John, 'Nijinsky's choreographic innovations forced [the music] into the background' (*Time and Tide*, 17 June 1921; repr. in Lesure, *Igor Stravinsky*, 68), whereas according to Emile Vuillermoz, 'Stravinsky's work will always dominate any choreography. . . . You will try in vain to flee from the tyranny of this rhythm. It will bend you under its iron will' (in Lederman (ed.), *Stravinsky in the Theatre*, 31).

In 'Fantasia', by contrast, the issue of contest revolves around the distinction between the near-abstract representations of outer space, volcanic eruptions, and tidal waves on the one hand—some of which bear the marks of their own painterly status in perceptible brush strokes or blobs of paint—and, on the other, the conventional cartoon-style representations of animal life and of some of the geological sequences (particularly the earthquakes during the first part of the 'Dance of the Earth'). In each case image and music are co-ordinated by the same means; the rhythm created by a cartoon dinosaur's neck as it scoops water is no different from that of a semi-abstract plume of spray. And yet the perceptual effect is distinctly different. I referred to the visual motions of the stars and other semi-abstract images being appropriated by the audible rhythms of the score, but I could equally well have put it the other way round; if the images take on the rhythmic properties of the sounds, then equally the sounds take on the connotations of the images. (Disney presents the Introduction to Part I as a kind of updated, creaking music of the spheres that carries with it a sense of cosmic emptiness—which gives it a quite different quality from the imagery of Nature in terms of which Stravinsky described this passage.) One might borrow Lawrence Marks's term once more and say that image and music sop up one another's qualities; there is a reciprocal transfer of attributes between them. But this is not the case—or at any rate it is much less the case—with the dinosaur scenes. There the dinosaurs sop up the kinetic and affective qualities of the music—the panic of the 'orchestral haemorrhage' at **103**, the horror of the eleven fortissimo chords that follow—but there is much less in the way of reciprocation. To hear the 'Glorification' as dinosaur music is to hear it as background music, and one has the impression that the primeval terror of the fight was already there, and just as explicitly, in the music even before Walt Disney made it visible.

Technically we might say that the diegesis is so complete in the cartoon-style sections that the visual hierarchy becomes virtually impregnable; the two media retain their distinct identities, and so relate to one another only as elements co-ordinated within a common, high-level compositional framework. (My analysis of the fight sequence illustrated this, revolving as it did around the varying juxtaposition of two essentially separate hierarchies, that of the pictures and that of the music.) But to say no more than this is to miss a crucial point. To hear the 'Glorification' as background music is to hear it as dominated by the diegesis, and to hear it as dominated by the diegesis is incompatible with hearing *The Rite* as one of the key works of the modernist canon. There is, in other words, another, historically based collision: between a style of graphic representation that, in 70 years, has become so familiar as to appear transparent and the cultural values that channel, if indeed they do not determine, our responses. And for this reason it is hard not to sympathize with Horace English after all when, for a moment, he puts aside his essentializing objections to the animation of absolute music and says that 'most of the satisfying moments in *Fantasia* were those wherein representative visual form gave way to unstructured movement of color or abstract design'.[101] To be sure, the visualization of *The Rite* as dinosaur music has not provoked the almost universal disgust occasioned by the 'My Little Pony' interpretation of the 'Pastoral' Symphony, which Ernest Lindgren described as 'so destructive of my feelings about this music that that for a long time I feared I should never be able to efface Disney's images from my mind, and my enjoyment of it would be permanently marred'.[102] Lindgren continues by saying that 'The use of classical music for sound films is entirely to be deplored'. But this seems to me the wrong conclusion. The success of a multimedia complex depends on all the media involved, not just one; the problem with Disney's 'Pastoral' sequence surely lies in the pictures, not in the music.

But even if one can end up having a certain sympathy with English's feelings about dinosaurs and centaurettes, his diagnosis is still wrong. He begins his analysis, as I said, by distinguishing between programme music and absolute music, and saying that animation may be justifiable for the first but certainly not for the second. But it should by now be obvious that the line between *The Sorcerer's Apprentice* and *The Rite of Spring* is not so easy to draw as it might once have appeared (except in that Dukas did not subsequently attempt to argue that *The Sorcerer's Apprentice* was absolute music after all). In fact, the situation is hardly more straightforward in the case of the 'Pastoral' Symphony; scholars have been arguing for the last century, and will perhaps continue to do so for the next millennium, as to what Beethoven might have meant when he described it as 'an expression of feeling rather than a description'.[103] All this, however, begs the question of how relevant the composer's intentions are in any case. And here it is useful to draw a comparison with Chopin's First Ballade, Op. 23, which Karol Berger has

[101] English, ' "Fantasia" ', 30. At this point English adds an acid footnote: 'And it is interesting to note that many of these were removed when the film was cut for second-run theaters' (he is talking about the 82-minute version mentioned in n. 13 above).

[102] Ernest Lindgren, *The Art of the Film* (London, 1948), 140. In view of the international success of Mattel's 'My Little Pony' during the 1980s, there is prescience in Robert Herring's observation that 'the foals, both in drawing and conception, belong to . . . the world of the stuffed-toy department' ('Four Films', *Life and Letters Today*, 31/52 (Dec. 1941), 211–18: 214). By contrast, 'When Disney saw the final version of what his animators had done to the "Pastoral" Symphony, he was impressed. "Gee, this'll *make* Beethoven," he said' (Friedrich, *City of Nets*, 35).

[103] Letter of 28 Mar. 1809 to Breitkopf und Härtel, Leipzig; no. 204 in Emily Anderson (ed. and trans.), *The Letters of Beethoven* (London, 1961), i. 220.

interpreted in the light of the contemporary intellectual history. As Berger puts it, 'The narrative that provided the community Chopin identified with most closely, the Polish emigration in Paris in the 1830s and 40s, with their sense of who they were was the story of "Exodus", its fundamental structure of past enslavement, present exile and future rebirth.'[104] More specifically, they looked forward to the coming European conflagration in which, they believed, Poland would regain its unity. And Berger sees this narrative structure as homologous with that of the music: 'both', he says, 'are future- or end-orientated, and in both the envisaged ending is fiery and tragic.'[105] Of course, it is relevant to this interpretation to know that Chopin shared such hopes, and Berger duly provides evidence of this. But he adds that it 'should not be taken as a "private programme" which Chopin actually had in mind while composing but subsequently chose to suppress'.[106] On the contrary, the meaning Berger is talking about is a public one, and it is rooted in the expressive potential of the music.

At this point Berger quotes a passage from George Sand that purportedly expresses Chopin's views on musical meaning:

[M]usic is a human expression and human manifestation. . . . It is man in the presence of the emotions he experiences, translating them by the feeling he has of them, without trying to reproduce their causes by the sound. Music would not know how to represent these causes; it should not attempt to do it. . . . When Beethoven unchains the storm, he does not strive to paint the pallid glimmer of lightning and to make us hear the crash of thunder. He renders the shiver, the feeling of wonder, the terror of nature of which man is aware and which he shares in experiencing it. The symphonies of Mozart are masterpieces of feeling which every moved mind interprets as it pleases without risking losing its way in a formal opposition with the nature of the subject.[107]

And Berger adds his own gloss on this passage:

The intentional objects (or 'causes', as Sand calls them) of the expressive gestures enacted in instrumental music may, and should, remain unspecified by the composer. The gestures have sufficient generality to allow for a number of such objects or causes, though the range of possible causes is never unlimited. The listeners or critics, in so far as they want the music to be more than a purely formal game and want to make a connection between the music's significance and their own deep concerns, will propose appropriate causes, that is, the intentional objects that fall within the range of the possible ones. . . . But they will remember that the causes or objects they propose, even if plausible, are no more than exemplifications chosen from a number of possibilities.[108]

---

[104] Karol Berger, 'Chopin's Ballade Op. 23 and the Revolution of the Intellectuals', in John Rink and Jim Samson (eds.), *Chopin Studies 2* (Cambridge, 1994), 72–83: 76–7.

[105] Ibid. 77.   [106] Ibid. 80.   [107] Ibid. 78.   [108] Ibid. 80.

What is being proposed here is, of course, a version of the approach to musical meaning in terms of 'affordance' that I set out in Chapter 2; Berger's talk of 'exemplification' might have come straight out of Cone.[109] And this, as I see it, provides the definitive answer to English's critique. It is not a question of the meaning the composer intended, but the meaning the music will afford. And if the kind of meanings that can be articulated by words or pictures are 'no more than exemplifications chosen from a number of possibilities', then *of course* (to repeat English's words) 'There cannot be . . . any universally "right" visual pattern for one of Bach's fugues' or for any other piece of music. The obvious response becomes: whoever said there was?

English puts this forward as an objection to 'Fantasia' because he sees it as Disney's purpose to determine listeners' perceptions to music through channelling their responses; he sees the film as supplying specific intentional objects, and so precluding the aesthetic participation of those who watch it (that is what he means by saying that it makes them 'less musical'[110]). In other words, he sees 'Fantasia' as providing a ready-made, pre-digested interpretation. And as such he sees it as open to the charges of prescriptiveness and authoritarianism that can be levelled against all manifestations of institutionalized music appreciation. Though English does not cite them, this interpretation might gain credibility from the introductory remarks that Deems Taylor makes at the beginning of 'Fantasia', which say (specifically with reference to the Bach sequence) that it provides 'a picture of the various abstract images that might pass through your mind if you sat in a concert-hall listening to this music'—a position that can slip all too easily into a specification of the images that *should* pass through your mind. This kind of slippage probably seemed particularly threatening at the time when English was writing, for it ties in with the more general tendencies that commentators have noted in the Disney productions of the period. In the cartoons of the mid- to late 1930s, says Robert Sklar, such as 'The Band Concert', the fantasy that had once been a Disney trait disappeared; 'there is one right way to imagine (as elsewhere there is one right way to behave). The borders to fantasy are closed now. The time has come to lay aside one's own imagination, and together all shall dream Disney's dream.'[111]

[109] See above, p. 96. Berger compares what he calls the 'Chopin/Sand theory' with Hanslick, but the resonances with Schopenhauer are at least as strong (see pp. 90, 92).

[110] See above, p. 198.

[111] Robert Sklar, 'The Making of Cultural Myths—Walt Disney', in Peary and Peary (eds.), *American Animated Cartoon*, 65. One might perhaps relate this to the odd change in register in Deems Taylor's voice-over at the beginning of the *Rite* sequence, when the description of the representation of the growth of life as 'coldly accurate' is immediately followed by the instruction: 'Now imagine yourself out in space. . . .' The combination of fact and fantasy, of course, creates yet another connection with the original scenario for *The Rite*.

Yet there is something fundamentally wrong-headed about this kind of critique of 'Fantasia', involving as it does a false identification of the images on the screen and the experience of those who watch them. 'Fantasia', in short, is not a pre-digested interpretation of anything; it is a film. The problem is that, for English, film is a medium in which visual image inevitably dominates sound; and so he counterposes this with a demand that music should dominate image—a demand which, predictably, is transformed by stages into the effective demand that there be no images at all. What is lacking from his discussion is any conception of a genre which begins with music, but in which the relationships between sound and image are not fixed and immutable but variable and contextual, and in which dominance is only one of a range of possibilities. This genre has never acquired a name of its own, but the analogy with music video suggests that we might call it 'music film'. And if we see 'Fantasia' as possessing such a generic identity, then we shall be less likely to think of it as an arbitrary, and probably misguided, exercise in music appreciation, and more likely to think of it as I have suggested we see all multimedia: not as the projection through ancillary media of an originary meaning, but as the construction of a fundamentally new experience, one whose limits are set not by Stravinsky nor even by Disney (and certainly not by English), but by anybody who watches—and listens to—'Fantasia'.

6

Reading Film and Rereading Opera: From *Armide* to 'Aria'

T HE *ARMIDE* SEQUENCE from 'Aria' is based on the opera of that name by Jean-Baptiste Lully, first staged in 1686, and it is located at the intersection of two dimensions of intertextuality. What might be called the horizontal dimension concerns the collaborative nature of 'Aria'.[1] All films are collaborations between directors, actors, technicians, and producers (the list could be extended indefinitely); but 'Aria' is something more, for it consists of ten loosely linked sequences by ten different directors. Apart from Jean-Luc Godard, who directed the sequence based on *Armide*, the list includes Robert Altman, Derek Jarman, and Ken Russell. Each sequence is based on a different opera—sometimes just one number, sometimes excerpts from several—and in addition to Lully the composers include Rameau, Wagner, Verdi (no less than three sequences are based on Verdi operas), and Korngold. Each sequence is more or less self-contained, however, and in this chapter I shall be concerned exclusively with Godard's visualization of *Armide*. The more relevant dimension of intertextuality, then, is the vertical one, extending back in time from Godard to Lully and his librettist, Philippe Quinault. Indeed, it extends further back still, to the sixteenth-century Italian writer Torquato Tasso, whose epic poem *Gerusalemme liberata* appeared in 1581. This story of the Saracen sorceress Armida ('Armide' in French) who fell in love with her enemy, the Christian knight Rinaldo (Renaud), has formed the basis of almost a hundred dramatic compositions, beginning with a cantata by Monteverdi (which was written in 1626 but has not survived) and continuing into the present century with Dvořák's opera *Armida* (1904).[2]

Underlying the variations and elaborations introduced by each version is the same basic story, which is set at the time of the First Crusade. Armida/Armide captures the valiant Rinaldo/Renaud, attempts to kill him but instead finds herself falling in love with him, and takes him to

---

[1] 'Aria' is available on Vision Video VVD 546 (PAL), Lightyear Entertainment/Virgin Vision 54058-3 (NTSC).

[2] Tim Carter, 'Armida', in Stanley Sadie (ed.), *The New Grove Dictionary of Opera* (London, 1992), i. 196–7.

an enchanted palace from which he is eventually rescued by two of his fellow knights. It is when he glimpses his reflection in a diamond-studded shield that Rinaldo/Renaud realizes that he has been spell-bound and, realizing it, is so no longer. Tasso's poem goes on to tell of a further encounter between Armida and Rinaldo in Egypt (which con-tains a hint, at least, of a happy ending), but Quinault's adaptation stops with Renaud's departure from the enchanted palace. Although Quinault wrote his libretto expressly for Lully, apparently at the per-sonal suggestion of Louis XIV,[3] later composers also set it—most famously Gluck, whose own *Armide* appeared in 1777. Jeremy Hayes says of Gluck's version that 'Armide . . . dominates the opera, a Kundry-like combination of sorceress and temptress';[4] but the focus on Armide (and the consequent reduction of Renaud to the stature of Parsifal in Act II of Wagner's *Bühnenweihfestspiel*) is really built into Quinault's libretto, so Armide dominates Lully's opera as she does Gluck's. And what dominates Quinault's portrayal of Armide is the conflict between love and hate, or between reason and passion, as she finds herself unable to kill Renaud and tries to come to terms with her unruly feel-ings. In fact, Quinault heightened and prolonged the psychological drama by adding a scene of which there is no trace in Tasso, in which Armide summons up Hate and his attendant demons from the under-world, and charges them with driving love away from her—and then begs them to stop, for she cannot bear to be bereft of her love for Renaud.

It was on the grounds of its inspired portrayal of Armide's changing and conflicting passions that Lully's opera, and specifically the mono-logue 'Enfin, il est en ma puissance', came to be seen as a supreme model of dramatic composition in the decades around 1700. ('When Armida works herself up to stab Rinaldo in the last scene of the second act,' wrote Jean Laurent le Cerf de La Viéville in 1705, 'I have twenty times seen everybody seized by terror, holding his breath, motionless, all the soul in the ears and eyes, until the air of the violin which ends the scene gave leave to breathe, then at that point breathing again with a murmur of delight and admiration.'[5]) For this reason, 'Enfin, il est en ma puissance' became one of the bones of contention in the 'Querelle des Bouffons', the controversy which raged during the mid–1750s over the relative merits of French and Italian music. Rousseau, who was one of the principal protagonists of the 'Querelle', wrote a scathing critique of Lully's monologue, while his principal opponent, Rameau, wrote an

---

[3] Lois Rosow, 'Armide (i)', in Sadie (ed.), *New Grove Dictionary of Opera*, i. 200–2: 201.

[4] Jeremy Hayes, 'Armide (ii)', in Sadie (ed.), *New Grove Dictionary of Opera*, i. 202–4: 204.

[5] Jean Laurent le Cerf de La Viéville, Seigneur de Freneuse, *Comparison de la musique italienne et de la musique française*, trans. in Oliver Strunk (ed.), *Source Readings in Music History: The Baroque Era* (New York, 1965), 139. By 'the air of the violin' le Cerf de La Viéville means the instrumental pas-sage before 'Venez, venez seconder mes désirs'.

equally spirited defence of it. (I shall come back to Rousseau's and Rameau's commentaries when I discuss Godard's visualization of 'Enfin, il est en ma puissance'.) In spite of—or because of—its controversial status, *Armide* remained continuously in the repertory of the Paris Opéra until 1766, although it was subject to increasingly drastic updatings, most of which centred on the fourth act, which was seen as at the same time insufficiently developed and inadequately integrated into the overall action.[6] It is perhaps not surprising then—and at this point I am jumping more than two centuries—that when the first recording of Lully's opera appeared, in 1983,[7] the fourth act was omitted; in addition, as Lois Rosow has noted, 'numerous small, arbitrary cuts distort the remaining acts'.[8] This is the recording on which Godard based his sequence for 'Aria', which was released four years later.

Figure 6.1 lists the music which Godard selected, in the order in which it first appears in his film.[9] One possible criterion of selection is not evident in Figure 6.1: all the music comes from Side 3 of the recording. But there are more substantive criteria as well. Godard's film is dominated by Armide, and specifically by her two monologues 'Ah! Si la liberté me doit être ravie' (with which Lully opens his third act and Godard his film) and the already-mentioned 'Enfin, il est en ma puissance', which closes both Act II of Lully's opera and Godard's film as a whole. Between them, these two monologues account for almost nine of the ten-and-a-half minutes of Godard's film, and as a result the remaining brief selections (which feature Armide, Hate, and choruses of demons) have an essentially ancillary role. And this makes sense, because it is in the monologues that Armide's inner struggle and her efforts to come to terms with her feelings are set out. In other words, just as Quinault selected from Tasso's poem in such a way as to focus

[6] On these updatings see Lois Rosow, 'How Eighteenth-Century Parisians Heard Lully's Operas: The Case of *Armide*'s Fourth Act', in John Hajdu Heyer (ed.), *Jean-Baptiste Lully and the Music of the French Baroque: Essays in Honor of James R. Anthony* (Cambridge, 1989), 213–37.

[7] Jean-Baptiste Lully, *Armide*, soloists and Ensemble Vocal et Instrumental de la Chapelle Royale, conducted by Philippe Herreweghe, Erato STU 715302 (note that this is not the same recording as Harmonia Mundi HMC90 1456/7 [CD], also by Herreweghe); the part of Armide is sung (beautifully) by Rachel Yakar. Apart from the cuts mentioned below, this recording follows the 1713 edition of *Armide* (Jean-Baptiste Lully, *Armide: Tragédie mise en musique* (Paris, 1713; facs. repr., Béziers, n.d.)). Owing to the multiplicity of C clefs in the 1713 edition, readers may find it more convenient to refer to the edition prepared for the 1957 Bordeaux Festival by Henri Busser (*Armide: Tragédie lyrique en cinq actes et un prologue. Poème de Quinault. Musique de Jean-Baptiste Lully* (Paris, n.d.)), which, however, is significantly different from the 1983 recording; it incorporates material from the 1764 revival, as well as written-out ornaments and rather symphonic continuo realizations that sometimes make it hard to figure out what Lully actually wrote.

[8] Rosow, 'How Eighteenth-Century Parisians Heard Lully's Operas', 213 n. 1.

[9] Timings are taken from the beginning of the music (which comes during the link shot into the *Armide* sequence proper). Where there are textual discrepancies between the text of the 1713 edn. and that used in the Herreweghe recording (e.g. the 1713 edn. has 'connoît' instead of 'connaît' in the chorus of Act III, sc. iv), I have followed the Herreweghe version, since that is what was available to Godard.

0'00"–2'30"	'Ah! Si la liberté me doit être ravie' (Armide, Act III, sc. i)
3'00"–4'03"	'Ah! quelle Erreur! quelle folie!' (Chorus of (female) demons, Act II, sc. iv)
3'30"–3'44", 10'15"–10'30"	'Plus on connaît l'Amour' (Chorus of (male) demons, Act III, sc. iv)
4'12"–6'22", 7'31"–10'30"	'Enfin, il est en ma puissance' (Armide, Act II, sc. v)
6'24"–7'12", 9'25"–10'00"	'Je réponds à tes vœux' (Hate, Act III, sc. iv)
6'40"–7'02"	'Venez, venez, Haine implacable' (Armide, Act III, sc. iii)

Fig. 6.1 The music of Godard's 'Armide'

on Armide, so Godard selects from Quinault's and Lully's opera in such a way as to focus upon Armide's conflicting passions. He omits the narrative context with which much of the opera is concerned, and presents only the psychological drama. This explains the elimination of the ensemble numbers, of which the largest part of the opera consists; and above all it explains the elimination of Renaud, who simply does not appear in Godard's film.

But then one might say that none of Quinault's characters appear in Godard's film, which is set in a Paris gym (it was entirely shot on location). It features an indeterminate number of body-builders—the credits at the end of 'Aria' tell us that there are fifteen—and two 'young girls' (*jeunes filles*), as the credits describe them, who are seen in a variety of activities, ranging from the most realistic (wiping tables and floors, washing up) to the most unrealistic: posing nude in postures redolent of classical or classicizing art, or holding a dagger to the back of one of the weight-lifters. The latter, of course, relates directly to the stage action of 'Enfin, il est en ma puissance' (and the stabbing sequence first comes at the appropriate point of that monologue). Godard, then, has transposed elements of the original staging into his incongruous, anachronistic setting. But most of the action of his film bears no literal resemblance to the original, and this applies especially to the scenes in which the women mop, caress, or embrace the body-builders, who, however, remain entirely detached throughout, wholly absorbed in their own activities. 'Two young women try desperately to seduce the men,' writes Yosefa Loshitzky. 'They caress the developed muscles of the men and advance upon them with clear sexual intentions, but nothing seems to work.'[10] What Loshitzky says is certainly correct at one level, but her commentary might lead one to wonder whether she knows what Lully's opera is about (she does not actually mention that 'Aria' has anything to do with opera). For it could hardly be more obvious that the two women represent an externalization of Armide's inner struggle: their joint identification with Armide is made explicit at the point where the words of 'Enfin, il est en ma puissance' are lip-synched first by one and then by the other; but it is hardly less clear when one passes the dagger to the other, or later restrains her from using it. The women are not represented as characters in their own right, then, but as elements in a psychological depiction.[11] As for the men, they are entirely anonymous; they are represented as in some sense objects of passion, but certainly not as subjects.

Some of the directors featured in 'Aria' use only a single operatic number, and have it playing continuously throughout the sequence (this applies, for instance, to Bruce Beresford, Franc Roddam, and Charles Sturridge). Others (including Nicolas Roeg, Julien Temple, and Robert Altman) use excerpts from several numbers. None of them, however, does violence to the music in the way that Godard does. He does not just select and recombine his music; he fragments it, fading it in and out or interpolating silences into it, and sometimes he even superimposes one number on another. This constitutes an essential difference not only between Godard's sequence and those of the other directors in 'Aria', but between it and the examples of multimedia I have discussed in the two previous chapters. In what follows I shall argue that 'Armide'—by which I mean the Godard sequence from 'Aria'—can be understood in terms of an underlying level at which there are tight, and generally conventional, associations between media. At this level Godard's visualization can be seen as conforming to classical operatic principles of inter-media alignment. This underlying structure, however, is elaborated, fragmented, and subverted in such a way as to give rise to the multiply fissured, decentred surface that is characteristic of Godard's films in general. As I suggested by speaking of Godard 'doing violence' to the music, the ultimate relationship between the media of 'Armide' is one of unresolved contest. I shall present this argument by working at the same time from the underlying level to the surface and from the opera to the film, beginning with the two monologues that

[10] Yosefa Loshitzky, *The Radical Faces of Godard and Bertolucci* (Detroit, 1995), 158.

[11] An obvious precedent in terms of the visualization of opera is Hans Jürgen Syderberg's film of *Parsifal*, in which the eponymous protagonist is jointly represented by Michael Kutter and Karin Krick; for a discussion see Jeremy Tambling, *Opera, Ideology, and Film* (Manchester, 1987), 203. More generally, a comparison might be made with the nineteenth-century literary trope of the *Doppelgänger*, which generally represents the split between desire and knowledge (Andrew Webber, *The Doppelgänger: Double Visions in German Literature* (Oxford, 1996)).

dominate 'Armide' just as—indeed, even more than—they dominate *Armide*.

A summary shot list of 'Armide' may be found at the end of the chapter (Appendix 6.1), together with a translation of those sections of the libretto that Godard incorporated in his film (Appendix 6.2).

'Ah! Si la liberté me doit être ravie'

Unlike 'Enfin, il est en ma puissance', the monologue with which Godard begins his film, 'Ah! Si la liberté me doit être ravie', has a clear autonomous structure in musical terms: AABA, with the first 'A' being an instrumental prelude. Although not notated as such, it is in effect a miniature da capo aria, with a final section that exactly repeats the words as well as the music of the first vocal section. Maybe this autonomous structure and high level of internal repetition explains why Godard chose to begin his film with this number; it certainly means that, right from the start, the music is foregrounded within the film.

The da capo aria was a feature of Baroque opera that incurred heavy criticism after the rise of the Classical style, on the grounds that it represented a kind of formalist intrusion into the drama—not, to be sure, that writers of the late eighteenth and nineteenth centuries put it this way; they complained, rather, that the da capo repeat fragmented the development of the narrative. But then, 'Ah! Si la liberté me doit être ravie' quite explicitly represents a moment of reflection and introspection: Armide is trying, as I put it, to come to terms with her love. And so the first (which is also to say the last) four lines are addressed explicitly to the absent Renaud. They are set in the present tense, and they embody Armide's acceptance of the situation in which she finds herself, with the second line of each couplet posing a question ('Est-ce à toi d'être mon vainqueur?' 'Faut-il que malgré moi tu règnes dans ma cœur?') which the preceding line qualifies. The middle five lines, by contrast, are set predominantly in the past tense, and counterpose statements with questions, of which the last drops the I/thou address in favour of the third person: 'Se peut-il que Renaud tienne Armide asservie?' Unlike the first and last sections, the middle section has an ongoing, processive quality. It begins by opposing Armide's past hate ('Le désir de ta mort fut ma plus chère envie') to her present love, and links the transition from past to present with that from first- and second-person subjectivity to third-person objectivity; overall, then, this middle section can be seen as embodying a process of confirmation. At the same time the return to the present tense, and indeed the posing of the central question 'Se peut-il que Renaud tienne Armide asservie?', prepares for the repetition of the opening four lines.

The two central sections of Lully's setting of the monologue are shown in Example 6.1.[12] How do they relate to the textual exegesis I have just given? Obviously the da capo form represents a conformance of textual and musical structure. But we can go further than that. The

Ex. 6.1 'Ah! Si la liberté me doit être ravie', bars 8–24

---

[12] Transcribed from the 1713 edn. The first section is to all intents and purposes identical to the second one, with the instruments taking the vocal line, while the last section is an exact repetition of the second.

A section is in D minor throughout, although it is elaborated by a variety of chromatic inflections. The B section (bars 15–24) is quite different, however; as the linear-harmonic sketch in Example 6.2 shows, it has an open tonal structure, moving away from the D minor of the preceding section through cadences on V of A minor (bar 19) and, in turn,

Ex. 6.2 Sketch of 'Ah! Si la liberté me doit être ravie', bars 15–24

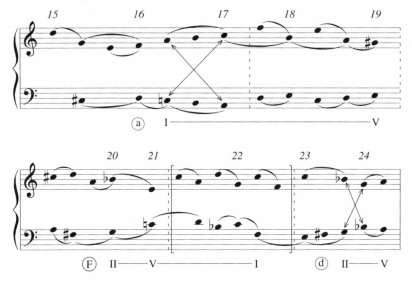

V and I of F major (bars 21 and 22:3 respectively). But even the perfect cadence in F is not a stopping-point. Its stability is weakened by virtue of its being in first inversion, and although it reaches root position on the following beat the downward motion of the bass continues on to the E of bar 23. This initiates the final phrase of the section (in terms of the text, the fifth and last line), which serves as an imperfect cadence in D minor, leading to the da capo. And the first three beats of bar 23 also do something else: they closely resemble the second bar of the A section, with its apparent inflection towards the tonic major in the bass (as V of IV), as well as its falling melodic contour, and so create a destabilizing anticipation of the formal repeat. The result of all this is to keep the music constantly on the move—or, to put it another way, to give it a processive quality that parallels that of the text.[13]

There is, then, a conformance between text and music based on the dynamic qualities of what I have referred to as acceptance and

[13] A parallel argument can be made as regards rhythmic structure, which I am consigning to this footnote on the grounds that it is more intricate than essential. The A section can be seen as having a regular though complex construction, consisting of four phrases 2, 1½, 2, and 1½ bars long respectively; the third phrase begins with the return to f¹ at bar 11:3, so the notated metre is deceptive, while the final beat of the last phrase is elided with the first beat of the following section, giving rise to the 3/4 cadential bar (this is most obvious at the transition from the introduction to the first A, bars 7–8). But there is no such regularity in the B section, whose five phrases could be read as consisting of either 1½ or 2 bars—but only by assuming the interpolation of additional beats at various points. It would be more reasonable to conclude that there is a perceptible periodic pattern underlying the A section, even though it lies some way under the surface, but that there is no such pattern in the B section. In other words, in the always problematic balance between music and words, it is music that has the upper hand in the A section, and words in the B section.

confirmation. To say this is in essence to say no more than that 'Ah! Si la liberté me doit être ravie' conforms with the aesthetic presuppositions of the time at which it was written, which understood all music (or at any rate all music worthy of serious consideration) to consist of the representation of the passions. But a more technical formulation may allow us to draw conclusions that were not made explicit by the aestheticians and theorists of the Baroque style. Text and music in 'Ah! Si la liberté me doit être ravie' elaborate a common modal content in the manner appropriate to each medium. (Throughout this chapter I use the word 'modal' to relate to mood, rather than in its music-technical sense.) And the principle of differential elaboration means that, as higher—more 'surface'—levels are reached, so disparities between the media are increasingly to be found. Lully generally ensures that the points of greatest registral or structural emphasis are aligned with appropriately resonant words, such as '*Ah!*' and 'fun*este*' on the high Fs at bars 8 and 11:3, while the setting of 'lan*gueur*' to the cadence on V of A at bar 19 (whose expressive appoggiatura, as in the Herreweghe recording, is more or less obligatory) could almost be called word-painting. But the perhaps even more expressive appoggiatura on B♮ at bar 9:3 coincides with 'être', which has no such resonance, while the contrast between the reassuring subdominant minor at bar 12:1 and the sharply affective chromaticisms at the equivalent point in the first phrase corresponds to nothing in the text. And such examples could easily be multiplied. Later criticisms that Lully's text-setting was wooden and inexpressive, of which more below, can thus be seen as reflecting a change in the level at which parallelism was sought between music and text—a migration towards the surface, which is entirely compatible with the changing performance practice of the period, and with the consequent revisions of *Armide* that were made on the occasions of its revival.[14]

How is Godard's visualization of 'Ah! Si la liberté me doit être ravie' adapted to this close association between music and text? In the first place, Godard provides a direct visual equivalent of the da capo structure, not, to be sure, by literally showing the same pictures twice, but by providing two parallel representations of the same scene. And before that he even provides a visual equivalent of the instrumental introduction. The music begins a few seconds before the first shot of the 'Armide' sequence proper, overlapping with a link shot of the interior of an empty opera-house; the camera pans upwards to the lights and

---

[14] This, at any rate, is my interpretation of the revisions for the 1746 revival as described by Rosow (see esp. p. 224 of 'How Eighteenth-Century Parisians Heard Lully's Operas').

zooms slowly in on them.[15] And then, on the second beat of bar 3, there is a cut to the first shot of Godard's sequence (**1** in Appendix 6.1), which shows two of the body-builders with one of the young women behind them, grouped in a strongly classicizing composition; the formal, almost statuesque effect is enhanced by the low camera angle, like that of the previous shot. A brief text screen ('I yield to / This victor / By pity / I'm won'—words taken from near the end of the monologue 'Enfin, il est en ma puissance'[16]) is followed by another posed group, this time incorporating the other young woman and a further two body-builders, one of whom flexes his muscles in the classic body-builder's pose. Towards the end of the shot the young woman, who rests her hand on the body-builder's forearm, drums her fingers and looks around her, and these small movements have the effect of underlining the artificiality of the otherwise motionless group composition—as does the background noise, of which more later. Finally there is a second text screen (this time the words come from 'Ah! Si la liberté me doit être ravie'). Shortly after it appears, the instrumental introduction ends, and the monologue proper begins.

Several features combine to give these opening shots their introductory quality. One is their intrinsic character; because of their static nature, the posed shots are reminiscent of the backdrops for credit sequences, while text screens are themselves a very traditional way of beginning a film. Then there is the symmetrical, self-contained construction of the sequence, with the two posed shots and the two text screens matching one another. And finally, these shots are quite distinct from anything that occurs elsewhere in 'Armide'; there could hardly be a more telling contrast between them and shot **5**, which starts shortly after the monologue proper begins and which, at nearly 40 seconds, is one of the longest shots in the film. It shows one of the young women wiping a table and then sitting down; I shall call her 'W1', since she generally appears before the other young woman (W2), as was the case in the opening poses.[17] And here the parallelism between Godard's visualization and the da capo structure begins, for shot **5** lasts for the whole of the A section of 'Ah! Si la liberté me doit être ravie'. The B section coincides with shots **6** and **7**, which show the women attending to the body-builders as they work out (more on these shots shortly), while the repeat of the A section corresponds to another

---

[15] The various individually directed sequences in 'Aria' are linked by a continuously unfolding series of shots, of which this is one. At the end of Godard's sequence the camera zooms back from the opera theatre lights, in a reversal of the introductory link shot.

[16] Godard has used the translation provided in the booklet of the Herreweghe recording (from which Appendix 6.2 is taken).

[17] The young women are played by (or perhaps I should say they *are*) Marion Peterson and Valerie Allain.

extended table-wiping shot (**8**, this time W2), now seen from a low camera position that makes the shot a little less domestic and a little more formal than shot **5**.

But Godard has made the parallelism of shots **5** and **8** much more elaborate than this might suggest, for both W1 and W2 go through the same sequence of gestures, and each gesture is co-ordinated with the same point in the music. Each wipes the table vigorously until bar 9:1 (bar 26:1 in the repeat), shakes her head at bar 9:3 (26:3), looks sideways and up at bar 10:3 (27:3), turns back at bar 11:3 (28:3), and touches her heart at bar 15:1 (32:1). The association of these gestures with the first and third beats of the bar says something about their choreographic nature, but there are also specific links with the text. One is that W1 looks sideways and up with the word 'toi'—the point at which Armide explicitly addresses her monologue to Renaud. The most obvious, however, is that she touches her heart at the word 'cœur', which also coincides with the final cadence of the A section. These gestures, then, correspond in a general way to the kind of action one might expect of the singer playing Armide in a staged performance of Lully's opera, except that in Godard's incongruous setting the gestures become alienated from their context and so take on a formal, ritualistic quality. But the delicately contrived repetition of the choreography between shots **5** and **8**, combined with sufficient alterations in action and camera angle to avoid an intrusive symmetry, goes beyond anything one might normally expect to see in the opera-house.

Godard's visualization of the A sections also, of course, parallels the introspective quality of the text: the downward tilt of each woman's head, her evident abstraction as she works (and indeed stops working), and the sequence of gestures all suggest some inner train of thought, without in any way conveying what it might be. His visualization of the B section is quite different, however, for here we see the women interacting—or, rather, not interacting—with the body-builders. As might be expected, shot **6** shows W1, and shot **7** W2. In shot **6**, a body-builder is using a machine consisting of a long hinged spoke that passes through a wheel, with the whole contraption rising and falling rhythmically in approximate time with the music (one cycle per half-note; there is also a clanging noise—it is not clear whether or not it is this machine that produces it—with a particularly resonant clang falling exactly on the cadence at bar 19). W1 approaches with a cloth, mops the body-builder's back (bar 15:3), kneels and puts a hand on the end of the spoke as it rises and falls (bar 17:1), drops her cloth (bar 18:1), and lets her hand fall from the spoke at bar 19:1, on the word 'langueur'. Nor is this the only example of a kind of oblique word-painting; W1's mopping of the body-builder's back—an action which in itself seems to constitute him as a kind of object, following as it does on her wiping of the table—coincides with the word 'désir' ('Le désir de ta mort fut ma plus chère envie', the text that appeared in translation in shot **4**), and the nature of this desire is none too subtly hinted at by the almost ludicrously penile quality of the body-building machine. I shall not describe shot **7** in the same kind of detail, but its main features are similar. This time the body-builder—another body-builder—is using a wall rail, raising and lowering himself once a bar (more or less on the downbeats of bars 21, 23, and 24); W2 mops him, circles round him, and embraces him momentarily before running off, but the body-builder continues his exercises without any apparent awareness of her presence.

Perhaps Loshitzky is adopting too realist a viewpoint when she speaks of the men remaining 'indifferent, completely detached—fully absorbed in their male narcissism'.[18] Perhaps the lack of interaction is meant to indicate that there is nobody *to* interact, and that the whole sequence consists of nothing but a fantasy—that it represents a mono-logue, in other words. And there is something else that contributes to the sense of introspection and abstraction: the silences that Godard cre-ates in the music. There are two ways in which he does this. During shot **5**, shortly after W1 sits down, the music is faded out; some sec-onds later it is faded back in, continuing from the same point where it stopped (bar 14:3), and the same happens on two further occasions. Such interpolations of silence have the effect of freezing the musical action, in rather the same way that da capo arias freeze the dramatic action of Baroque opera. As for the second way in which Godard cre-ates silences in the music, this first occurs during shot **7** when the music is faded at bar 21:2, reappearing after a few seconds. But this time it does not continue from where it left off. Instead, it continues from where it *would* have been had it not been faded (bar 23:1); Godard has simply left the record playing, fading it out and back in.[19] But he has chosen his fading points carefully, for, as can be seen from the brackets in Example 6.2, there is a logical continuity between the last music before the fade-out and the first music after the fade-in, so that the listener/viewer might reasonably think that no music had been omitted at all.[20] The next cut of this kind, from bar 28:3 to bar 30:2, is equally effective but in a different way: this is the third time that the

---

[18] Loshitzky, *Radical Faces*, 158.

[19] Godard used exactly the same technique in 'Pierrot le fou' (see Brown, *Overtones and Undertones*, 206).

[20] It is not just that the music stops and starts on a C major triad; one could understand it in terms of a voice exchange between the Cs and the Es at bars 21:1 and 23:1. What is more, the omis-sion of bars 21:2 to 22:4 reduces the B section to a normative four-phrase plan, matching the A sec-tion; Godard could hardly have done more to render this cut effectively imperceptible, perhaps forming a transition to the more perceptible cuts that follow. The majority of them consist of whole phrases, however, and a surprising number are between phrases which are fairly continuous with

A section has been heard, and its memorable nature means that the viewer/listener can hardly help imagining the music during the gap. And this is the method by which Godard introduces silences in the music throughout the remainder of the film, although it would sometimes take a listener who knew the opera by heart to be aware of what is happening.

But to refer to 'silences' is not quite accurate, for the disappearance of the music exposes ambient sounds that were previously covered up.[21] As the music fades out in shot **5**, there is a whistling that becomes a rumble and turns out to be a passing train, while the cessation of the music during shot **8** reveals the clunking of the unseen body-building machines. The effect is to create a kind of oscillation between different worlds of experience, between the inner world of the music and the outer world of the gym and the trains, and this further enhances the introspective character of the sequence. Godard does not allow ambient sounds to look after themselves, as might perhaps have been expected in a film shot entirely on location. This is obvious not only from the way in which background noise levels vary—Godard cuts them in and out, like the music, although not as obviously—but also from the way in which the train noises overlap shots **5** and **6**, and in particular the way in which diegetic gym noises (corresponding to what we see on the screen) overlap shots **6** and **7**. In such cases cross-fades have presumably been used, and it is impossible to hear the editing points. Here then—and in contrast to his characteristic practice[22]— Godard is using techniques generally associated with the transparency of the narrative cinema, in order to lend an illusory depth to a visualization that subordinates narrative diegesis to formal repetitions and symmetrical patterns whose source is musical. In the same way (and I am now talking in general terms rather than with specific reference to 'Ah! Si la liberté me doit être ravie'), Godard's cutting rhythms create an impression of transparency; they do not intrude upon the viewer's experience as independent structural elements, as is perhaps the case in 'Material Girl' and certainly in some parts of 'Fantasia'. It is as if Godard has retained the hierarchies of the narrative cinema in order the more effectively to fragment and disrupt them, and this is a point that I shall develop towards the end of this chapter.

one another in linear-harmonic terms (e.g. Act II, sc. v, bars 6–8, 56–8, and 101–7). It is interesting in view of all this to note that 'According to Legrand and other Godard composers, the director knows nothing about the technical end of music' (ibid. 189).

[21] I would like to acknowledge the influence here of Edward Latham, who made a presentation on 'Armide' (to be published in 'Indiana Theory Review', 18) as part of the postgraduate seminar I gave at Yale in 1994. Ted also corrected a number of mistakes in a draft version of this chapter.

[22] See the discussion of Godard's sound-editing in Chion, *Audio-Vision*, esp. 42–4.

'Enfin, il est en ma puissance'

Armide's famous monologue at the end of Act II, the one which most encapsulates the content of the opera as a whole, is much more open-ended in both modal and structural terms than 'Ah! Si la liberté me doit être ravie'. It consists mainly of a heightened recitative—something between the extremes of recitative and aria in Italianate opera—in which melody and harmony evolve in tandem with the progression of Armide's emotions. But there are still elements of autonomous structure. It begins with a self-contained instrumental prelude, in E minor, and continues in the same key when the singer enters. There are then a number of intermediary cadences (the strongest are perhaps those at bars 28, 42, 51, and 60, in E minor, G major, D major, and G major respectively), with a return to the tonic marked by the cadence at bar 71. The monologue—and the act, and of course the film—concludes with a final 'petit air', a miniature aria with its own instrumental prelude. Godard treats the 'petit air' as in effect a separate section, interpolating a break of about 40 seconds between the first and last bars of the prelude (bars 72 and 89).[23] But he also interpolates an even longer break after the first G major cadence of the monologue, at bar 42. In this way he breaks 'Enfin, il est en ma puissance' into three distinct sections, and I shall organize my discussion in the same way.

I

Following the prelude, the first section of the monologue (Ex. 6.3) begins with Armide's murderous rage, which gives way first to a surge of pity (bar 32) and then a period of confusion in which she wavers between the two emotions (bar 36). This was one of the passages which Rousseau attacked most scathingly in his *Lettre sur le musique françoise*, published in 1753.[24] His basic criticism was that Lully's setting was insensitive, and he complained particularly about Lully's failure to bring out the succession of Armide's passions by means of harmonic contrast. The tonic cadence on the words 'Je vais percer son invincible cœur', says Rousseau, is 'ridiculous . . . in the middle of a violent emotion'. Again, at the very point where Armide is first touched by pity (bar

[23] Users of the Busser edition (see n. 7 above) should note that the prelude given there is not the same as the one in the 1713 edition and the 1983 Herreweghe recording, which is based on the vocal melody of the 'petit air'. The singer enters at bar 90.

[24] Jean-Jacques Rousseau, *Lettre sur la musique françoise* (Paris, 1753); facs. edn. in Denise Launay (ed.), *La Querelle des Bouffons: texte des pamphlets avec introduction, commentaires et index* (3 vols., Geneva, 1973), i. 669–764; the passage dealing with 'Enfin, il est en ma puissance' begins on p. 753. The following discussion is partly based on Cynthia Verba, *Music and the French Enlightenment: Reconstruction of a Dialogue 1750–1764* (Oxford, 1993), esp. 20–9; the quotations from Rousseau and Rameau in this and the next paragraph are given in Verba's translation.

32), Lully stays on a D major chord, simply adding a seventh to turn it into a dominant of G. 'Heavens!', exclaims Rousseau, 'It is only a question of tonic and dominant at a moment where all harmonic ties should be broken.' And in the passage of confusion as Armide's contradictory emotions alternate with one another ('Achevons . . . je frémis! Vengeons-nous . . . je soupire!'), the passage that can be seen as the core of the monologue, and hence of the opera, Lully's music remains sedately in G major: 'Who would believe', Rousseau asks in

Ex. 6.3 'Enfin, il est en ma puissance', bars 20–42

exasperation, 'that the musician has left all this agitation in the same key, without the least intellectual transition, without the least harmonic departure, in such an insipid manner . . .?'

One way to respond to these criticisms might be to question Rousseau's underlying assumptions about the nature of musical expression, or at least to ask how far they coincided with Lully's. But in his rebuttal of Rousseau's critique, which appeared in the following year,

Rameau took a quite different tack.[25] Lully *does* bring out the succession of Armide's emotions, he says: 'Not only is all this agitation not in the same key' (he is referring specifically to the confused passage from bar 36), 'but there are chromatic changes every half-measure.' The problem is simply that Rousseau has not been able to see them—but then, Rameau adds nastily, 'It is necessary to have more than eyes . . . to judge an art where the cause resides as much in what is implied as in what is expressed.' For present purposes it is not necessary to go into the details of Rameau's explanation (he is basically arguing that each reinterpretation of a chord as a dominant should be understood as implying a chromatic alteration); the important point is that Rameau stresses the extent of conformance between the text and the musical surface. But he also emphasizes the need to understand individual chords in their larger context. The cadence on E minor at bar 28 is an expressive device, not a formalist intrusion, he says (though not, again, in so many words), for 'The key . . . which reigns in the whole monologue, which alone predominates, and which is desired more strongly than ever after all the different keys . . . returns and suddenly strikes on the tonic, exactly to express the decisive word.' And on the basis of all this, Rameau concludes that harmony—not melody, not even words—is the central source of operatic meaning: 'It is principally on the basis of harmony', he says, 'that the singer receives the feeling that he must paint: the words only serve . . . as an indication.' One has the impression that Rameau is here groping towards what Karol Berger calls the 'Chopin/Sand' theory of musical meaning.[26]

Cynthia Verba writes of this controversy that what separates Rousseau and Rameau is not just their opposed philosophical and ideological assumptions but something more basic: each, as she phrases it, puts forward 'a different reading of the music'.[27] And a reading informed by more recent linear-harmonic approaches can bring out the ebb and flow of passion of the music at a middleground level—a level, that is to say, which falls between, and links, Rameau's observations of the musical surface and his account of the role of the overall tonic. Example 6.4 provides such a reading of the passage, and what it shows is a series of foreground motions—often very emphatic ones in terms of register and textual declamation—that lack structural support. We can begin by observing that, as may be seen from Appendix 6.2, the first six lines of the scene fall into couplets, and that Lully sets them in such a way that each couplet ends with a climactic ascent. The first of these

[25] Jean-Philippe Rameau, *Observations sur notre instinct pour la musique* (Paris, 1754); facs. edn. in Erwin R. Jacobi (ed.), *Jean-Philippe Rameau: Complete Theoretical Writings* (6 vols., Rome, 1967–72), iii. 257–330.

[26] See above, p. 212.   [27] Verba, *Music and the French Enlightenment*, 25.

Ex. 6.4 Sketch of 'Enfin, il est en ma puissance', bars 20–42

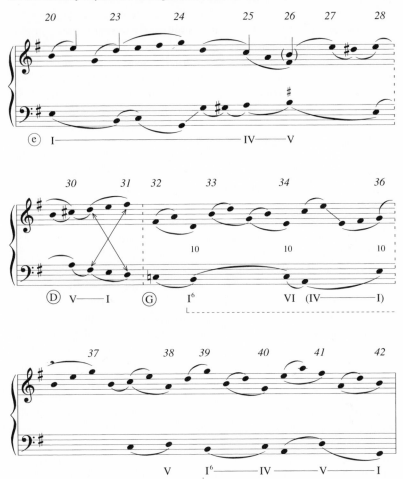

is in bars 23–4, to the words 'ce superbe vainqueur'; the phrase gains a climactic quality from the ascent to g², but without any voice-leading function it comes across as a mere frill. (If the effect is to undermine the description of Renaud as a 'victor', then the irony is Armide's.) The voice-leading, by contrast, continues down from the opening e² through d² and c² to an implied b¹ (bars 24–6); this is the passage in which Armide gloats over the subterfuge which has delivered Renaud into her hands, and the chromatic inflection from G to G♯ in the bass at bar 24 contributes to the effect of stealth that the words describe.

Then there follows the emphatic tonic cadence, on the words 'Je vais percer son invincible cœur' (bars 26–8), which is approached through another ascent to g². For Rousseau, as I said, this cadence represented an intrusive element of closure; for Rameau, on the other hand, it represented the climax of a process of intensification that begins with the subdominant, A minor, at bar 25 (Rameau stresses the significance of the minor mode), and continues through the dominant (bars 26–7) to the tonic.[28] But it also creates an effect that neither writer described, for it has a curiously vacuous, unconvincing quality. It is as if the louder Armide asserts her thirst for vengeance, the less she believes in what she is saying. To be sure, she is again being ironical; what else can it be to proclaim that she will pierce Renaud's 'invincible' heart? But this time the lack of middleground support for the cadence figure creates the effect of a deeper irony, as if the music—the repository, so to speak, of the operatic subconscious—was saying something quite different from what Armide is saying. There are two possible ways of explaining this effect in technical terms. One might say that there is a middleground continuity from the implied b¹ of bar 26, through the b¹ of bar 29, to the c♯² of bar 30, in relation to which the cadence is another extraneous frill. Alternatively, one might regard the e² at bar 28 as a resumption of the opening e²—in other words, as structural note after all—but in that case the emphatic ascent from b¹ to e² on the words 'Je vais percer' becomes a mere illusion of the foreground, to use Schenker's striking term, since there is no structural connection between these notes. Either way we have an emphatic foreground element that lacks middleground support.

If the music tells us that Armide's underlying feelings no longer support her words—which is in essence what I am suggesting—then the next line represents a resort to argumentation in order to bring about the passion that she expected to feel naturally. When she says 'Par lui, tous mes captifs sont sortis d'esclavage', she is setting out the reason why she *ought* to hate him.[29] (This is the passage which best merits le Cerf de La Viéville's description of Armide working herself up to kill Renaud—or perhaps 'winding' herself up would have been an even better term.) As one might expect, these words coincide with an apparent surge of harmonic directedness, with the E minor of the cadence being reinterpreted as the first chord in a II–V–I progression in D major, while the words 'toute ma rage'—the conclusion of the argument, so to speak—coincide with another climactic ascent, this time to f♯². And this is the point where Armide tries to stab Renaud, and cannot. For Rousseau, as we saw, there was no harmonic reflection of the transi-

---

[28] Verba, *Music and the French Enlightenment*, 26.

[29] This line refers to the Christian warriors whom Armide had captured before the action of the opera begins, who have been set free by Renaud.

tion to the following passage (bars 32–6), in which Armide is assailed by feelings of pity (although it is to be hoped that he at least noticed the fall in register from the f♯² of bar 31 to the f♯¹ of bar 32[30]). For Rameau the transition is marked by what he sees as a change of key from D major to G major, articulated by means of the c♮ in the bass at bar 32. But what Example 6.4 most strikingly reveals is the lack of middleground continuity between these two sections: if the middleground melodic motion of bars 28–31 is e²–d², then bars 32–6 do not follow on at all. Indeed they cannot, for there is no clearly discernible middleground motion in these bars, which instead consist of the same triadic motion stated three times in different transpositions (f♯¹–a¹–d¹, b¹–d²–g¹, g¹–b¹–e¹), leading to a very weak plagal cadence in E minor. The music, in a word, noodles.

What does Godard do with all this? The beginning of the instrumental introduction to the monologue overlaps briefly with a shot of W1 on her hands and knees with a bucket of water, wiping underneath a table (**14**); almost immediately, however, there is a cut to successive shots of body-builders at work. First there is a close-up of a man's arm as he pulls and releases a cable; the rhythm of his exercise is loosely coordinated with the music, which, however, soon fades, leaving the prominent rasping sound of the machine. Then, as the music fades back in, there is a cut to a man standing and preparing himself to start weight-lifting. Again the music fades, returning with the next shot (**17**)—a body-builder reclining on his back, rhythmically raising and lowering a dumb-bell. His motions are synchronized with the music; the dumb-bell rises and falls with every half-note, and the stately nature of the music lends an air of rather ludicrous portentousness to the proceedings. Then, with the final cadence of the introduction, W1 appears and kneels down behind him; she is wearing an overall, but it is open at the front. She puts her hand on the dumb-bell, and as the monologue proper begins, the weight-lifter stops exercising and sits up. It is at this point that the real action of the scene begins.

During the first couplet, W1 gazes at the weight-lifter (he has his back to her). With the third line—'Le charme du sommeil', the passage that I earlier described as stealthy—W2 appears; she kneels down next to W1 and rather insinuatingly proffers the knife to her. W1 grasps the knife, gets up, and positions herself directly behind the weight-lifter, while W2 looks on. And with the word 'cœur' ('Je vais percer son invincible cœur'), W1 matches word to deed and holds up the knife against the weight-lifter's back. In the gap before the next phrase of the music,

---

[30] If he did, however, he suppressed any mention of it. 'Quel trouble me saisit?', he says, begins on the same note, even on the same chord; 'there is not a single alteration to indicate the massive change in Armide's feelings and words' (Launay (ed.), *La Querelle*, i. 756).

however, W2 puts her hand on W1's arm in a gesture of restraint, and takes the knife from her; in this way Godard presents Armide's inner conflict before it has reached the level of her words (and by implication her consciousness), in precisely the same way as Lully's unsupported cadence did. A new shot (**18**) begins with the next phrase, showing the same scene but from a different angle. W2 still has the knife; W1 stares fixedly at the weight-lifter's back, briefly opening her overall to expose her breasts and then closing it again. With the word 'rage' (bar 31) she quickly takes the knife back from W2, and holds it up again to the weight-lifter's back. But as Armide succumbs to feelings of pity ('Quel trouble me saisit, qui me fait hésiter?'), the knife wavers; meanwhile W2 runs her fingers through her hair, feels her heart, and crosses her hands. These distracted actions, like the wavering of the knife, correspond to the noodling motions of the music to which I referred, with its equally distracted series of triadic motifs.

In the following section of explicit confusion, with its alternation of conflicting statements, Godard abandons his scenario. For the only time in 'Armide' he adopts the classic music video cliché and has his actresses lip-synch with the singing; we see their heads side by side, and the camera focuses on the one who is lip-synching. (This creates a visual disjuncture with the previous shot, in which the women were some distance apart.) But Godard undermines the identification with the music that lip-synching normally prompts through adding a high level of ambient sound; in this way the environment intrudes upon subjective experience. And, given that he has two actresses at his disposal, it is notable that he goes out of his way to avoid distributing the contradictory phrases in the obvious way, by having one mime the expressions of vengeance (which, incidentally, are consistently in the first person plural: 'Frappons . . . Achevons . . . Vengeons-nous'), and the other those of pity. (The first person singular of the latter dissociates Armide from the Saracen cause, so throwing her individual emotions into sharper relief.) To distribute the words in this way would, presumably, prompt too direct an association of W1 and W2 with Armide's contradictory emotions; it would transform the representation into a kind of allegory, turning W1 and W2 into dramatic subjects in their own right (in the manner of Quinault's personification of such emotions as Hate, Cruelty, and Rage). Accordingly, Godard has W1 lip-synch to the first three expressions ('Frappons . . . Ciel! qui peut m'arrêter? Achevons'), while W2 mimes the remainder. One might say that instead of representing Armide's divided emotions in a literal manner, Godard allocates her words to his actresses in such a way as to represent the *idea* of division.

Maybe Godard's strategy at this point should be understood as a statement that the inner drama is already all in the music. Whereas Rousseau complained that this passage was all in one key and Rameau retorted that, on the contrary, there were chromatic shifts twice a bar, Example 6.4 shows a kind of fission between foreground and background. At the underlying level, the passage is easy to read and links to the subsequent section expressing pity: the B in the bass at bars 32–3 supports a I^6 in G major that persists until bar 39, where it initiates the structural motion through IV, V, and I with which the section ends. But at surface level the music is disjointed and inarticulate. This is not just because it is made up of little motifs (the previous triadic motif at 'je frémis', and a variant at 'Vengeons-nous' and 'je soupire!'). It is also registrally dissociated, particularly between 'je frémis!' and 'Vengeons-nous', and melodically ungainly: the successive rising fourths from a^1 to d^2 to g^2 are decidedly unidiomatic. And the reason for this dissociated, distracted quality is the lack of any coherent connection between the surface and the underlying structure. The middleground has dropped out, leaving nothing in its place. What has happened to Armide's mind has happened to the music, and vice versa. It looks as if Godard was right.

II

As I have already said, Godard breaks 'Enfin, il est en ma puissance' at this point, separating its initial representation of Armide's rage, pity, and resulting confusion from the emotions that follow—which I shall summarize as, in sequence, the recognition of her own feelings (bars 43–60) and a provisional resolution of them (bars 61–71) that leads to the final outcome of the monologue (bars 72–112, the 'petit air'). In what follows I shall take the relationship of music and words as read, and concentrate on Godard's visualization.

In the first part of her monologue, Armide's vengeful purpose was subverted by the feelings of pity that welled up in her unbidden. Quinault has Armide express the resulting dissociation graphically in the second part of the monologue, when she says, 'Mon bras tremblant se refuse à ma haine'. (It is as if she only knew she could not hate him because she saw that she could not kill him.) By dubbing this section 'recognition' I mean to say that, in it, Armide accepts ownership of her feelings. In place of the see-sawing turmoil of the previous section, then, bars 43–60 can be called emotionally coherent: questions, statements, and exclamations follow one another in sequence, ending with two lines that unambiguously reflect the victory, for the time being at least, of pity over rage: 'A ce jeune héros tout cède sur la terre. . . . Il semble être fait pour l'Amour.' (The intervening line, 'Qui croirait qu'il fût né seulement pour la guerre?', is cut by Godard.) It makes sense, then, that Godard's visualization—which consists of a series of repetitions of the scene with the knife, interspersed with close-ups of one of the body-builders—can be more convincingly linked with Quinault's and Lully's scene in global terms than on the basis of surface links.

This is not to say that no such links can be found. In the repetitions of the scene with the knife, W2 turns and throws it away; the first time this happens is on the word 'dois' of 'je dois me venger' (bar 44)— where, of course, it controverts what is being said. But the next time she throws away the knife is at the words 'ma vengeance est vaine', so that the action becomes an illustration of the words. In the same way, in bar 46 W2 draws close to the body-builder with the words 'j'approche', while in the final and longest shot of the repetition sequence the words 'tout cède' coincide with her leaning against the body-builder's chest (in these shots W2 and the body-builder are facing one another). More interesting, perhaps, if more speculative, are two higher-level links between the music and the pictures. One is at bars 46–9, where a harmonic sequence is concealed behind the music's var-iegated surface (V^7–I of B minor, followed by V^7–I of A major); inten-tionally or otherwise, Godard mirrors this rhyme in the pictures, in each case cutting from the body-builder to the knife scene. The other possible higher-level link involves the concealed repetitions that popu-late the music between bar 50 and bar 55, for the figure at bar 50 is unmistakably similar to that of bars 29–30, the melodic motion from d^2 to $f\sharp^2$ at bar 51 and the subsequent fall of the d^2 to $c\natural^2$ echo bar 32, and the b^1–c^2–e^2–a^1 motif at bars 54–5 answers that of bars 37–8.[31] And it is noticeable that these repetitions, if that is what they are, occur in the original order. The effect is that bars 50–5 serve as a kind of sum-mary of what has gone before, contributing to the reflective and con-clusive nature of the text at this point, and Godard provides a visual equivalent to this by encompassing this passage within shot **34**, the final and longest shot of the repetition sequence, which for the first and only time pieces together the fragmentary contents of the earlier shots into a continuous whole.[32]

More secure, however—if less analytically intriguing—are the global links between music and pictures to which I referred earlier. To recog-nize an unwelcome emotional event—in this sense, to come to terms with it—is an intrinsically repetitive activity: you rehearse it again and

[31] At the risk of sophistry one might also point out that the figure at bars 37–8 is answered by the one at bars 54–5 in a more literal sense: 'Qui peut m'arrêter?', asks the first, while the second answers 'ce jeune héros'.

[32] It should be noted, however, that shot **34** begins on the I chord of D major at bar 51, whereas the first figure I have referred to (at bar 50) is part of the IV–V cadential progression that leads to it. This might reasonably be considered special pleading.

again in your mind. And this is, of course, the level at which Godard represents the psychological content of this section of Armide's monologue. But although the basic repetitive plan of Godard's visualization is easy enough to see, there are some subtleties of its realization that are worth pointing out. For one thing the repetitions are not, in fact, literal repetitions. Figure 6.2 shows the basic plan of the shots with the knife: as I said, shot **34**, the final shot, shows the entire sequence, beginning with W1 pulling off W2's overall and ending with W2 leaning on the body-builder's breast. The other shots, by comparison, show only part of the sequence, in a permutated order (shot **26** shows what happens *after* shot **28**, while shots **30** and **32** are included within shot **26**).

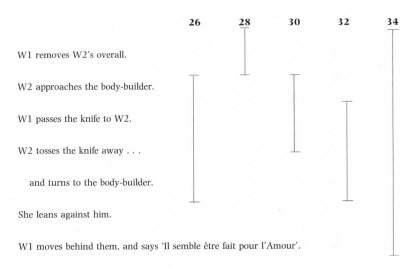

Fig. 6.2

The permutation invites you to piece together the shots into the single scenario shown in shot **34**; they lead you to assume that only one scene was filmed, and that the entire sequence was the product of the cutting room. But the details show that this is not the case. Most tellingly, each time we see W1 throwing away the knife, she does it more emphatically; in shot **26** her motion is perfunctory, while in shot **34** she turns right round before throwing it, and we hear a loud clunk as it lands somewhere off screen. And there is a further element of composition in this sequence which might not be apparent at first sight, but undoubtedly contributes to its effect. As I mentioned, the shots with the knife alternate with close-ups of one of the body-builders, a contrast which is heightened by the synchronization of loud ambient sounds

W1, W2		Body-builder		Total
26	7"	**27**	1"	8"
28	4"	**29**	2"	6"
30	4"	**31**	3"	7"
32	6"	**33**	6"	12"
34	28"			

Fig. 6.3 Durations of shots 26–34

with the latter. (This time the sound effect track is edited cleanly with the pictures.) The total duration of each knife/body-builder pair is fairly constant up to shots **32/3**, this last pair being longer; but the pattern is structured around a steady increase in the length of the interpolated body-builder shots (Fig. 6.3). The result is to heighten the disjointed quality, the obsessive repetitiousness, of this sequence; it is perhaps the only time in 'Armide' that cutting rhythm contributes as an independent parameter to the overall experience of the film.

Figure 6.2 includes one feature that I have not so far mentioned: towards the end of shot **34**, W1 walks behind W2 and the body-builder (W2 is still leaning on his chest) to the right of the screen, and says, 'Il semble être fait pour l'Amour.' This is of course the text of bars 59–60 of 'Enfin, il est en ma puissance', and in Godard's film the spoken words occur just before the corresponding point in the monologue; the music has been faded out, but it now returns just as these words are sung, and the effect is as if the singer were repeating what W1 has just said. Although this takes place during the section of Armide's monologue that I have described as revolving around recognition (and precedes Lully's structural cadence at bar 60), it can be seen as representing a transition to the following section in which Armide reaches a provisional resolution of her predicament. She does this in two senses. One relates to Quinault's text: the resolution is based on Armide's perhaps confused or dishonest idea (dishonest, that is, with herself) that she can punish Renaud with love as well as she could with death, so that in this sense 'Il semble être fait pour l'Amour' is the key to what follows. The other relates to Godard's visualization: the most striking feature of the following section of 'Armide', one that appears nowhere else in the film and as a result paradoxically comes across as an anomaly, is that the actresses speak.[33]

In shot **36** we see W1 crouching against W2, who strokes her hair; at the beginning of the shot, and again at the end of it, she says 'Il n'a pu trouver mes yeux assez charmants'. (The first time she says this is

---

[33] I distinguish such speaking from the screaming at the end, of which more below; the speaking is naturalistic, the screaming is the opposite.

directly on the cadence at bar 60, where Herreweghe's recording includes a massive rallentando, and in this way Godard counters the effect of segmentation that the recording creates.) These words, too, come from the text (bars 65–6), and in fact the second time W1 says them they would coincide with the music if it were not faded out just before; here, then, spoken words substitute for sung ones. One might think of this as a means of underlining the significance of the text, as in the case of 'Il semble être fait pour l'Amour', except that Godard's selective isolation of the words subtly alters their meaning: what is in the original a conditional clause leading to a scheming consequent becomes a stereotypical lover's complaint (and perhaps Godard is implying that that is what it really is, if Armide were being honest with herself). As for shot **37**, it forms a kind of symmetrical reversal of shot **36**; this time it is W2 who is crouching against W1 (who again strokes her hair), and W2 who says 'Ah ce que je voudrais vous détester'. These words do not appear in the text at all, but they converge in meaning with what is sung at this point ('s'il se peut, je le haïsse'),[34] with the second-person address—as opposed to the third person of Quinault's text—lending an air of diegetic immediacy to Godard's visualization. Godard has made no attempt to underline Lully's disguised repetition at bars 68–71, which echoes the cadential phrase in E minor at bars 25–7; there would have been no need, since the purpose of the repetition is to contribute to a sense of closure before the 'petit air' that follows, and the long break which Godard interpolates at this point creates closure in a different, and more straightforward, manner. But he does fade bars 65:3 to 66:1 in such a way as to emphasize the $c\sharp^2$–$d\sharp^2$–e^2–$d\sharp^2$ figure that follows, and so highlight its link with the identical figure in the 'petit air', at bar 92.

III

The final section of 'Enfin, il est en ma puissance'—the 'petit air' in which Armide bids her demons transform themselves into zephyrs and carry her and Renaud away to the ends of the world—need not detain us long, for Godard effectively treats it as a single shot. I say 'effectively' because we hear the last bar of the instrumental introduction and the first vocal phrase (bars 96–7)[35] during the previous shot, a close-up of

[34] The use of the word 'détester' may also be intended to link with the words of Hate and the demons' chorus in Act III, sc. iv: 'Plus on connaît l'Amour, et plus on le déteste'.

[35] I have already mentioned that the Herreweghe recording uses a different instrumental introduction from the one in the Busser edition, so that the vocal part begins at bar 90. The Busser edition also omits the repetition of the first vocal phrase, indicated by repeat marks in the 1713 score. I am numbering the bars as follows: 90, 91–7, 91bis–97bis (97bis is the second-time bar); the word 'cède', then, falls on the downbeat of bar 98. It should also be noted that the cadences in bars 108 and 111 are the same in the 1713 edition (i.e., they are both as Busser has bar 108).

W1 and W2 posing, but these materials are superimposed over music from Act III, scene iv (more on this shortly), and the result is very confused. The music from Act III, scene iv fades out at the same time as the first phrase of the 'petit air' ends (bar 97), and so the repetition of the phrase creates the effect of a new beginning—and this coincides, more or less, with the beginning of shot **41**.

Quinault's and Lully's 'petit air' is not a psychological representation in the manner of the rest of the monologue. Instead, it represents the outcome of Armide's reflections, and its closed formal structure contributes to this effect. It begins, then, with a call to action: 'Venez, venez, secondez mes désirs',[36] a formulation that neatly side-steps the issue of what Armide's real desires are, and whether indeed she herself knows what they are. The brief middle section (bars 98–106) summarizes Armide's recognition of what has happened ('Je cède à ce vainqueur, la pitié me surmonte'—the line translated in the first text screen, shot **2**). And then the final line ('Volez, volez, conduisez-nous au bout de l'Univers') reiterates the call to action, with the rhyming of 'Venez, venez' and 'Volez, volez' being echoed in the music, where the rhythm of 'Volez, volez' and the $c\sharp^2$–$d\sharp^2$–e^2–$d\sharp^2$ figure represent a compressed paraphrase of the opening of the 'petit air'; the repetition of this final phrase adds to the formal effect of closure. (It is perhaps worth pointing out that it is with this line that Armide, for the first time, conjoins Renaud with herself under the pronoun 'nous'.) Godard does not pick up on any of these textual or musical details, except in the sense that he fades the music during bars 101–8 (the lines that speak, perhaps irrelevantly from Godard's point of view, of Armide hiding her shame, together with the first occurrence of 'Volez, volez, conduisez-nous au bout de l'Univers'). What he *does* provide is a visual parallel to the formality of Quinault's and Lully's treatment.

The shot of W1 and W2's faces side by side has nothing to do with the environment of the gym (the effect of detachment is increased by the fact that no ambient sound can be heard), nor with Godard's epigrammatic staging of Armide's monologue; if it links with anything, it is with the posed shots that recur throughout the film and so punctuate it. At first W1's face is tilted up while W2's face is tilted down. W1 screams 'Non!' (this is at bar 96, but there is no obvious significance in the juxtaposition). W2 looks up and screams 'Oui!'. Then the content of the shot is repeated, with W1 again screaming 'Non!' and W2 screaming 'Oui!', and with the same tilting motions as before.[37] The last

[36] The 1713 edn. reads 'Venez, venez seconder mes désirs'.

[37] Without an authoritative shot list, it is hard to be sure whether or not there is a new shot at 10'22", between the two pairs of screams; a man passes briefly in front of W1 and W2, and when we see them again, they have already tilted their faces into new positions. If there is a new shot, it is not a strongly articulated one.

'Oui!' follows on the final cadence of Armide's monologue. These naked juxtapositions of negation and assertion reduce the content of the monologue—which is again to say of Quinault's and Lully's opera, and of Godard's film—to a purely formal opposition. Perhaps it is not going too far to say that they suggest the ultimate impossibility of synthesis, of the creative reconciliation of opposites. At any rate, they undermine the sense of resolution and the consequent call to action with which Armide's monologue ends. But then that sense of resolution was never very convincing in the first place.

Rereading Godard

For all its apparently enigmatic quality, Godard's 'Armide' can be seen as embodying a rather rational construction. The setting may be incongruous and the staging of the action may be selective and epigrammatic, but the basic way in which Godard links his visualization to Quinault's text and Lully's music is straightforward, and indeed traditional. Lully's music is structured not around Quinault's words as such, but around their meaning, and more specifically around the series of passions which they represent; and the same applies to Godard's visualization. In this sense one might almost think of Godard's film as stepping into the shoes of a late seventeenth-century staging of the opera. But of course this underlying structure based on modal conformance is confused and controverted by the way in which Godard fractures and redistributes his material, most obviously in his recomposition, if that is the right word, of the music.[38]

Even here, however, a rational plan can be discerned behind the paradoxical elaboration. Godard structures his film around 'Ah! Si la liberté me doit être ravie' and 'Enfin, il est en ma puissance', and, as I said, his selection of these two numbers makes sense, because they embody the heart of Armide's inner struggle. So does his inversion of their original order: the introspective nature of 'Ah! Si la liberté me doit être ravie' sets up 'Enfin, il est en ma puissance' as a process of reflection, rather than as a representation of external action. All this fits with Godard's psychological and symbolic, rather than dramatic, conception of the film. And if we see 'Armide' as organized around these two numbers and their internal divisions—which, it must be remembered, are

[38] In this context it is worth pointing out that in other films, too, it has been Godard's practice to recompose the music. In both 'Vivre sa vie' (1962) and 'Pierrot le fou' (1965), Godard commissioned autonomous scores rather than series of cues, and then edited them into the film; Royal Brown (who offers readings of both films) comments of 'Pierrot le fou' that 'One can almost sense a frustrated composer in some of the ways that Godard modified parts of Duhamel's score via music-editing technologies. . . . Working from his mixing board, Godard in essence has created his own theme . . . out of the raw material supplied by Duhamel' (*Overtones and Undertones*, 201, 205).

III.i	Introduction	**1–3**	Women and body-builders posing, text screens.
	A	**4–5**	W1 introspects.
	B	**6–7**	W1 and W2 attend to the body-builders.
	A	**8**	W2 introspects.
		*	
II.v	I	**15–16**	Introductory sequence of body-builders, leading to

17–18	Knife scene.
19	W1 and W2 lip-synch.

*

II	**26–35**	Knife scene, alternating with body-builders.
	36–7	W1 and W2 speak.

*

III	**41**	W1 and W2 scream 'Non!', 'Oui!'

Fig. 6.4 Basic formal scheme of 'Armide'

as much modal as musical—then we get the formal scheme shown in Figure 6.4. (The boxes point out a formal recurrence that links together the two main scenes with the knife, based on the parallel between shot **19**, in which W1 and W2 lip-synch, and shots **36–7**, where they speak.) As we have seen, Godard divides 'Enfin, il est en ma puissance' into three independent sections, separated by long, unmeasured gaps in the music; together with 'Ah! Si la liberté me doit être ravie' (which he treats as a single entity) we therefore have four musical units. The asterisks in Figure 6.4 represent the interstices between these units, and it is here that Godard interposes the additional musical and visual materials that give rise to the richly variegated, and indeed confusing, form of his film. It would be redundant to describe these additional materials in laborious detail—I hope that the general principles underlying Godard's alignment of pictures with music have by now become reasonably clear—and so I shall restrict myself to their most salient features. But two general points should be made at the outset. First, the interpolated materials are all associated in one way or another with Hate, or with demons in various guises. Second, in all three cases the interpolated materials involve the superimposition of music drawn from different points in the opera, which interact as different musical materials always do when superimposed: by erasing one another.

The musical materials interpolated between the end of 'Ah! Si la liberté me doit être ravie' and 'Enfin, il est en ma puissance' both consist of demons' choruses, but in other respects they are as different as could be. The first is 'Ah! quelle Erreur! quelle folie!', from Act II, scene iv, sung by what the 1713 score calls a 'Chœur de Bergers, et de Bergères Heroïques' (the shepherds, however, appear to be countertenors, and in the Herreweghe recording sound like a women's chorus). Despite appearances, the shepherds and shepherdesses are demons, and they have been charged by Armide to lull Renaud into an enchanted sleep; this is how he falls into her hands. In 'Ah! quelle Erreur! quelle folie!', then, they sing in praise of love: 'C'est aux jeux, c'est aux Amours / Qu'il faut donner les beaux jours.' The second demons' chorus, 'Plus on connaît l'Amour' (from Act III, sc. iv) represents the exact opposite. For one thing it is a chorus of men,[39] and for another they are in their own shapes, having accompanied Hate on his excursion from Hell. But, more important, their chorus is a vilification of love: 'Plus on connaît l'Amour,' they sing, 'et plus on le déteste, / Détruisons son pouvoir funeste.'

Godard, then, has chosen two excerpts with diametrically opposed characteristics and meanings, and during shots **12** and **13** he cross-fades rapidly between them. And this oscillation between the praise and vilification of love forms the basis of the entire interpolated sequence from shots **9** to **14**. The images overlaid upon it include body-builders working out, and a pair of shots of W1 and W2 posing like statues, but the only one that relates in any very obvious way to the words and music is shot **10**. This begins with W1 attending to a reclining weight-lifter, but as we hear 'Ah! quelle Erreur! quelle folie!', W2 appears in the background, whirling herself round with the music (her overall is open, and it is at this point that we become aware that the women are wearing nothing underneath their overalls). She taps W1 twice on the shoulder, as if to ask why she doesn't join in, but W1 does not respond, and walks stolidly to the other side of the body-builder while W2 dances. Indeed, we see W1 wiping the floor under the table as the chorus ends on the words 'les beaux jours' (shot **14**, which overlaps with the instrumental introduction to 'Enfin, il est en ma puissance'); a more glaring contradiction between text and picture could hardly be imagined.

Between the first two sections of 'Enfin, il est en ma puissance' (that is, between bars 60 and 61) Godard interpolates snatches of two numbers that are adjacent in the opera: Armide's invocation of Hate in Act III, scene iii ('Venez, venez, Haine implacable'—there is an obvious textual link with the 'petit air' at the end of Act II) and Hate's appearance

---

[39] This is another case where the Busser edition deviates significantly from the 1713 score and the Herreweghe recording. I have to say that I have never in my life heard such neat, well-scrubbed demons as Herreweghe's.

in the following scene ('Je réponds à tes voeux').[40] The original keys are D major and D minor, but both have been transposed down a semitone for reasons that will shortly become clearer.[41] Again the interpolated music has a consistent signification: the setting of Hate against love (apart from the opening, the one phrase of Armide's invocation that we hear clearly is 'Rendez-moi mon courroux, rallumez ma fureur'). And once more Godard adds an overlay of pictures that do not relate in any very overt way to the words or music, but rather relate to other shots in the film. There are alternating shots of a body-builder, and of the women wiping a table (**20–3**); during shot **23** we hear the two instrumental preludes on top of one another, and the sound is further confused by the regular clunk of the exercise equipment, whose rhythm is quite unrelated to either piece of music. And at the end of the interpolation there is an extended shot of W1's head (**25**). She is washing up (we cannot see this, but we can hear it); every now and then she looks up, or shakes her hair out of her eyes. The shot begins and ends in silence, but two phrases of music are spliced in: 'Rendez-moi mon courroux, rallumez ma fureur', to which I have just referred, and bars 10:3–13:2 of 'Je réponds à tes voeux'. The effect of the long silences and brief musical excerpts—the opposite balance to what is generally found in this film—is once again to underline the impression of introspection of which I have repeatedly spoken.

That leaves just one shot, **24**, which is in some respects anomalous: W2 is facing us, grasping the knife, while W1 holds her other arm in a gesture of restraint. (W1 is naked, while W2's overall is almost falling off, linking with the repetition sequence from shot **26** to shot **34**.) The camera, in other words, is more or less in the position of the body-builder against whom the knife is poised; we can just see him at the side of the picture. It might be argued that this isolated knife scene, quite different from the others in its composition, confuses the overall design of the film, if clarity of design is a relevant consideration; but it certainly illustrates the text in a straightforward enough manner, for the shot begins almost simultaneously with the beginning of Armide's invocation of Hate. And in terms of the opera's unfolding, this is a significant moment, because it represents Armide's explicit recognition that instead of her possessing Renaud, she is possessed by love; it marks, in other words, the abandoning of her never persuasive scheme of punishing Renaud through love instead of death. There is no doubt,

[40] In the Herreweghe recording, Hate is sung by a baritone (Ulrich Studer), not a mezzo-soprano as specified in the Busser edition.

[41] The Herreweghe recording is at so-called authentic pitch: that is to say, one semitone lower than today's standard. Therefore the notated D major of 'Venez, venez, Haine implacable', for instance, sounds like D♭ major in the recording, and Godard's transposition brings it down to C major.

then, regarding the effectiveness of Godard's illustration and consequent emphasis of this point in the dramatic process. What one might
question is whether the illustration of drama is a strategy consistent
with the psychological and symbolic, and in that sense anti-dramatic,
nature of Godard's visualization of 'Armide' as a whole.

The third and last interpolation, before the 'petit air' at the end of
'Enfin, il est en ma puissance', involves only one piece of music: the second part of Act III, scene iv, where Hate sings the words later echoed
by the demons ('Plus on connaît l'Amour, et plus on le déteste'). This
part of the scene is introduced by its own instrumental prelude, an upbeat march which, in the Herreweghe recording, is enlivened by the
addition of percussion instruments. Godard exploits the possibilities of
satire at this point by cutting, as the march begins, to shot **39**, where
we see W1 and W2 posing while the men leave the gym in a procession (for the first time the men, like the women, are undressed). The
men march from left to right in front of the women during the
antecedent phrase (bars 21–3), and from right to left behind them during the consequent (bars 24–6), and the effect is to make the men look
ridiculous in much the same way as with the synchronization of the
weight-lifting to the portentous music at the beginning of shot **17**. Shot
39 also links, through the posing women, with shot **11**, a connection
that becomes unmistakable with the following shot—a close-up of the
women posing, just like shot **12**. This pairing can be seen as the central node of an entire network of formal symmetries. First, the link
between shots **11–12** and **39–40** creates an element of symmetry
between the first and third interpolated passages. Second, it links
through the idea of posing, on the one hand, and the involvement of
the men in an activity other than exercising, on the other, with the
opening shots **1** and **3**. The effect is that if the latter represent the formal opening of the film, then shots **39–40** represent its formal close.
(That turns shot **41**, with its bare repetitions of 'Oui!' and 'Non!', into
a kind of summarizing coda.) And finally, it links with the other shots
of W1 and W2 that involve some kind of pairing or symmetry, in particular the lip-synching (shot **19**), the sequence where they speak and
stroke one another's hair (shots **36–7**), and of course the final shot
itself. At such moments dramatic or narrative considerations are completely subordinated to abstract form.

Since this final interpolated passage involves only one additional
musical excerpt, it cannot in itself result in superimposition. But during
shot **40** Godard repeats the opening two bars of Hate's second air ('Plus
on connaît l'Amour, et plus on le déteste'), a procedure that is anomalous in that there is no such repetition in the original recording, and
this overlaps with the beginning of 'Venez, venez, secondez mes désirs',

the 'petit air' from Armide's monologue. Here, then, we have a sustained superimposition of two quite separate pieces of music, one of which proclaims Armide's desire for love while the other pronounces it detestable, and Godard has gone to some trouble to ensure that the two pieces merge and blend in such a way that they cannot easily be disentangled. He has achieved this by the simple expedient of transposing the recording of Act III, scene iv, down a semitone (in other words he has played it back a little too slowly), so that instead of being in F major it comes out in F♭ major—and in consequence is heard as sharing the same tonic with the 'petit air' (which is in E minor). This, presumably, explains the downward transposition in the second interpolated passage, which I mentioned earlier, and the clearest indication that it represents a deliberate strategy rather than some technical accident comes during shot **41**, when we hear another anomalous repetition of the words 'Plus on connaît l'Amour, et plus on le déteste'. But this time the words come from the demons' chorus, which was in F major when it previously appeared during the first interpolated passage, but is now also in F♭. It is obvious that with these occurrences of unmotivated repetition, so to speak, and with the superimposition of additional music over that of Armide's monologue, the basic structural pattern which I have been describing is beginning to break up. If it is true that, as Philippe Beaussaut's note to the Herreweghe recording says, in the final act of the opera 'Little by little, the formal structure falls apart, and Armide's musical language grows broken and panting,'[42] then something similar seems to happen to Godard's film as it draws to a close.

We can see the three interpolated passages, then, as articulating both what might traditionally be called the expressive content of 'Armide' and its formal structure. In the first place, the association of the interpolated music with Hate, and the superimpositions that result, encapsulate the opposition between love and hate around which the whole of 'Armide' (and *Armide*) revolves. The progression from the cross-fades of the first interpolation to the sustained superimposition of the last conveys the irreconcilability of opposites, or at any rate the impossibility of deciding between them, that is epitomized in the alternations of 'Oui!' and 'Non!' with which Godard's film ends. At the same time these interpolated passages are associated with shots that recur throughout 'Armide'—images of the women involved in a range of menial tasks, carefully grouped posing shots—and these have both what I have termed an expressive and a formal significance: shots like **5** and **8** convey the effect that the entire film embodies an act of introspection or reflection, while the posed groups articulate the film's closure through

---

[42] Philippe Beaussaut, note in the booklet to Erato STU 715302, p. 9.

linking the opening 'stills', if one can call them that, with the concluding shots of the body-builders leaving. (As I said, that leaves shot **41**
hanging, as a kind of coda.) And finally the interpolations articulate the
underlying formal organization of the film: their immediately recognizable characteristics—in particular the superimpositions—point up the
points of elaboration that transform the basic structural scheme shown
in Figure 6.4 into the richly variegated and confusing surface, as I
called it, of the film we see and hear.

But it must be obvious that the conventional distinction between
expressive content and formal structure, and the distinction between
phenomenological experience and analytical clarification that it supports, is thoroughly suspect in this context (as, perhaps, in any other).
We might say, for instance, that 'Armide' is comprehensively structured around the idea of duality: most literally in terms of the duality
of men and women, but equally in terms of the dual representation of
W1 and W2, which is itself a means of representing the duality of love
and hate, or of reason and emotion (or conscious and unconscious). But
then duality is equally a formal principle, seen for instance in the symmetry of shots **36** and **37**, or in the binary oppositions of the final knife
sequence (shots **26–34**). Conversely, what I have been treating as the
most purely formal elements of the film—the classically composed
group shots that articulate its closure—contribute to the expressive
effect by virtue of their categorical separation from everything else.
They intrude upon the film, that is to say, and this intrusion constructs
duality at yet another level: that of the positioning of the viewer. (The
result is to distance the film from the viewer, so contributing to a certain remote, hieratic quality that parallels the classicizing tendencies
and courtly associations of Quinault's and Lully's opera.) The idea that
formal and expressive structure might be equally fundamental—that
they might operate at the same level, that they might indeed be the
same structures seen from another perspective—creates what looks like
a problem if one is trying, as I have been in this chapter and in the book
overall, to bring approaches derived from music theory to bear upon
the analysis of multimedia. Analysis has historically sought to demonstrate that the expressive content of music is to be understood as a consequence of its formal structure, meaning that analytical clarification
consists of the reduction of phenomenological experience to formal
structure. Indeed, from the analytical point of view one might say that
it is the possibility of reduction that *defines* expression, as illustrated by
the traditional Schenkerian usage according to which foreground
events 'express' underlying structural formations. Expression, in short,
is something to be explained away.

This is not the place for a sustained engagement with issues of analytical epistemology.[43] What I want to address are the more specific criticisms that the essentially music-based reading of 'Armide' which I have offered might easily give rise to, especially in readers who come from outside music theory: doesn't reducing Godard's film to a basic structural scheme like Figure 6.4 substitute an arid formalism for the richly and confusingly variegated experience of 'Armide'? Equally, why is it necessary to place so much emphasis on what may be termed the film's poiesis, and in particular its origins in Quinault's and Lully's opera (not to mention the extended family of works deriving in one way or another from *Gerusalemme liberata*)? Why not stay firmly within the domain of the esthesic, and analyse what is actually *there* in Godard's film?

We can explore what such objections might amount to by reference to Yosefa Loshitzky's reading of 'Armide', to which I have already referred, which is based entirely on its overt content, on what is actually there to be seen on the screen (she makes no reference to what is there to be heard on the sound-track). Accordingly, she characterizes it as 'an unsuccessful seduction scene . . . impinged upon by images drawn from stereotypical soft pornography, such as naked women costumed in the furs of wild beasts and so on'.[44] (I am not clear what the reference to the furs of wild beasts relates to, and classical or classicizing art seems as relevant a source for the imagery of 'Armide' as soft pornography—not that the two are mutually exclusive, of course.) Loshitzky concludes: 'Men are so absorbed in cultivating their masculinity (their muscles) that they cannot even see the Other, let alone desire it.'[45]

It would in fact be possible to add a historical dimension to such an interpretation, though Loshitzky does not herself do so. Quinault's representation of Armide can itself be understood not only vertically, in terms of other representations of Armide from Tasso to Godard, but also horizontally: in terms of the representation of women in his other libretti. According to Patricia Howard, Quinault habitually represented women in a way that can be directly related to the social and political context of operatic production in the late seventeenth century. A comparison of his libretti with their sources shows how he consistently adapted them in such a way as to depict women as 'creatures at the mercy of their emotions, exploited by masculine ambition, usually unhappy, and almost always powerless'.[46] *Armide* is an exception in

[43] A range of approaches to these issues may be found in Nicholas Cook and Mark Everist (eds.), *Rethinking Music* (Oxford, 1997).

[44] Loshitzky, *Radical Faces*, 158.   [45] Ibid. 159.

[46] Patricia Howard, 'The Positioning of Woman in Quinault's World Picture', in J. de la Gorce and H. Schneider (eds.), *Jean-Baptiste Lully* (Laaber, 1990), 193–9: 194; see also her chapter "Quinault Lully, and the *Précieuses*: Images of Women in Seventeenth-century France', in Susan C. Cook and Judy Tsou (eds.), '*Cecilia Reclaimed*': *Feminist Perspectives on Gender and Music* (Urbana, 1994), 70–89.

that, although Renaud conforms to Howard's stereotype of masculine heroism, he plays no active or voluntary role in this process of subordination; rather, Armide subordinates *herself* to Renaud as passion overcomes reason. And Godard provides updated images of women's powerlessness: we see them engaged in menial or domestic tasks such as wiping tables and washing up—work in which the men take no part. Gazing at the men, mopping their backs or furtively embracing them, Godard's women efface themselves at the same time as they reduce the men to objects of admiration or, perhaps, desire. For Godard's self-absorbed men have no more power than the women, and in this way Quinault's images of male hegemony are transformed into Godard's images of alienation. The historical perspective, then, sharpens Godard's deflationary interpretation of masculine heroism, which he reduces to an onanistic cultivation of musculature. Howard also emphasizes the extent to which Quinault's and Lully's operas were 'directed towards a specific audience of one',[47] namely Louis XIV, and the extent to which their heroines accordingly 'behave as those selected for the position of royal mistresses should behave' (they should be constant, free from jealousy, expect to be passed over, and so forth).[48] This, of course, provides a context for the scopophilic undercurrent of Godard's film; you might almost think that Godard was making a film of Howard's article rather than of the opera.

Loshitzky puts forward her reading of 'Armide' in the context of portrayals of gender and sexuality in Godard's other films, and it would be silly to deny that this kind of reading could have any application. At the same time, I would argue that her reading embodies a kind of generic error; it not only omits important dimensions of meaning which have to be understood from a poietic as well as an esthesic perspective, but also fails to address the issue of the genre to which 'Armide' belongs. In essence, Loshitzky is treating 'Armide' as a story: action is attempted (the women try to seduce the men), resulting in an outcome which might have been successful, but, in the event, is not. Of course she does not read 'Armide' as an example of narrative cinema in the Hollywood sense. Nevertheless, her conception of the film's content is such as to position it in relation to the established codes of the narrative cinema: which is to say, in terms of certain assumptions regarding the connectedness of one shot or sequence to another (the idea of success, for instance, implies a relationship of before and after), and also—perhaps even more to the point—in terms of certain assumptions regarding the representation of individuals engaged in social transac-

---

[47] Ibid. 198, quoting Patrick J. Smith, *The Tenth Muse: A Historical Study of the Opera Libretto* (London, 1971), 50.

[48] Howard, 'Positioning of Woman', 198.

tions. And this is where a production-oriented approach—one based on the relationship between 'Armide' and *Armide*, and on the underlying structures which Godard's film elaborates—comes in, as a means of reading against the grain, so to speak, of established cinematic convention (which is also to say, the established practices of film criticism).

Comparing 'Armide' with its operatic predecessor shows how Godard has turned drama into monodrama (which is to say, not drama at all), and how Loshitzky's young women are not really young women, but representations of a divided mind. Equally the comparison shows how Godard has fragmented and reconstructed *Armide*, crumpling up its linear unfolding so that words and musical materials that were originally distant from one another end up juxtaposed or superimposed. At the same time, he has elaborated the formal scheme shown in Figure 6.4 in such a way that the film obfuscates as much as articulates it. In each case the result is not simply to depict Armide's inner struggle, in the way that Quinault and Lully do. Rather, Godard *enacts* inner struggle, and the inner struggle is not Armide's, nor the young women's, but inner struggle *per se*. In a word, 'Armide' is not a representation of inner struggle, like *Armide*, but a presentation of it. And to say this is, at least, to hint at an answer to the issues of analytical epistemology that I raised a few pages back. If 'Armide' enacts inner struggle, then obviously this meaning is not contained 'in' a formal scheme like Figure 6.4 in the sense that clothes are contained in a suitcase. (This is like saying that a Schenkerian background has no meaning in itself.) But neither is meaning contained 'in' the phenomenal experience of the film; in itself, such experience is mute. Meaning emerges rather from the act of relating foreground to background, esthesic to poietic, 'Armide' to *Armide*. It is generated, in short, by means of the kind of critical oscillation that I have tried to exemplify in my commentary on 'Armide'. This is as much as to say that meaning is not something which we simply discover in multimedia, but something that we create through the very attempt at discovery; critical commentary, too, is as much a matter of presentation as representation. I shall return to this in the Conclusion.

If Loshitzky reads 'Armide' against the background of the narrative cinema, then equally I have been reading it against the background of French Baroque opera. And to put it this way is to stress the deconstructive—which is to say, negative—aspect of the process of interpretation; to read 'Armide' this way is to say what it is *not*. But there is also an important positive aspect to a music-based reading. Godard's primary strategy in deconstructing operatic or cinematic diegesis is to subordinate referential content to repetition, alternation, permutation, symmetry, and other purely relational structures. This is what we mean when we talk about 'musical' construction in films, and in 'Armide' it refers to two things: the direct co-ordination of picture structure and music (as in 'Ah! Si la liberté me doit être ravie'), and the use of commensurable principles of organization in different media. (The autonomous duration structure in the repetition sequence between shots **26** and **34** is a concise example of this.) These are, of course, the principles that I invoked in discussing the visualization of music in 'Material Girl' and 'Fantasia'; so it is natural enough that I have repeatedly used the terms 'visualize' and 'visualization' in discussing 'Armide'. Yet I have constantly felt (and resisted) the impulse to enclose these words in scare quotes when discussing 'Armide'—an impulse that I never felt in the case of 'Fantasia'. The reason, as I see it, is the flip side of what it is about 'Armide' that invites narrative or dramatic readings of the kind that Loshitzky offers. And I think I can explain it in technical terms.

As we saw in Chapters 4 and 5, it is characteristic of music videos and music films that they establish direct links between individual parameters within musical and narrative hierarchies, and so tend to fragment—or at least to restructure—those hierarchies. That is, in essence, what it *means* to call something a music video or a music film, if the terms are being used in a theoretically informed sense rather than a simply descriptive one. Another way of putting this is that music films and music videos involve horizontal segmentation (the connections between levels are severed). But in 'Armide' the hierarchies of musical drama and narrative film remain substantially intact. As we saw, the basic principle underlying Godard's visualization of 'Ah! Si la liberté me doit être ravie' and 'Enfin, il est en ma puissance' is very much that of late seventeenth-century French opera: namely, the congruence of different media at the level of mood. And I mentioned that, in 'Armide', cutting rhythms and ambient sounds are generally subsumed within the film hierarchy, rather than functioning as independent parameters; the same might be said of camera and diegetic rhythm. What 'Armide' lacks in horizontal segmentation, however, it makes up in vertical segmentation. The repetition sequence between shots **26** and **34** illustrates this in miniature: a linear narrative is chopped up and reconfigured on the basis of autonomous durational principles. One might say that a 'musical' logic is being brought to bear upon the continuities and certainties of narrative representation. But of course there is a difference. You *can* put together the dispersed fragments of the repetition sequence in order to arrive at a single narrative; that is what shot **36** does, thereby satisfying the interpretive desire created by the previous, fragmented shots. But you cannot do the same with 'Armide' as a whole. There is the same interpretive desire; that is what motivates

Loshitzky's attempt to discover a totalizing, ideological meaning in the film. But there is no single master narrative just waiting to be found. It is not hard to grasp the essentials of what 'Armide' is about, at least if you approach it from the perspective of Quinault and Lully. But there is much in it which is contingent, the meaning of which is emergent, and hence incapable of generalized explanation or totalizing interpretation.

'Armide' is not in any useful sense a narrative film, and the role played in it by Lully's music is certainly not that of 'film music'. But neither can it adequately be thought of as a 'music film', in the manner of 'Fantasia'. Despite the elements of conformance in its alignments of text, music, and pictures, 'Armide' is in the last resort an instance of irreducible contest between media. If the film does violence to the music, as I said near the beginning of this chapter, then equally the music does violence to the film. Or, to put it another way, music and film intrude upon one another, and they do so centrally, not peripherally. To be sure, there is nothing unique about this; in Chapter 3 I quoted Peter Conrad's observation that 'Words and music are united by antagonism. Opera is the continuation of their warfare by other means.'[49] However intrinsically conflicted opera may be, though, it has at least the spurious stability of tradition. 'Armide' does not; it wavers uneasily between genres. But then, maybe that is just the point. The ultimate artistic expression of a divided mind, after all, is a work that does not even know what genre it belongs to.

Appendix 6.1: Shot List of Godard's 'Armide'

0'09"	11"	1	Woman 1 and two men, posing (seen from below).
0'20"	4"	2	Text: 'I yield to / This victor / By pity / I'm won'.
0'24"	9"	3	Woman 2 and two men, posing (seen from below).
0'33"	3"	4	Text: 'My greatest wish /Was / That thou mightst lie / Dead'.
0'36"	39"	5	W1 wiping a table; she sits down and touches her heart.
1'15"	22"	6	Body-builders. W1 mops one and kneels before him.
1'37"	22"	7	Body-builder on a wall rail. W2 mops him, embraces him quickly, and runs off.
1'59"	35"	8	W2 wiping a table, seen from below. She moves in front of the table and touches her heart.
2'34"	23"	9	Body-builders exercising; women pass through them.

[49] See above, p. 000.

2'57"	32"	**10**	A weight-lifter, reclining; W1 attends to him. W2, in the background, whirls around and touches W1 on the shoulder; W1 moves to the other side of the man. W2 again touches her on the shoulder and whirls around.
3'29"	5"	**11**	W1 and W2 naked; W1 moves forward to pose.
3'34"	5"	**12**	Close-up of W1 and W2 posing.
3'39"	12"	**13**	Close-up of three body-builders exercising.
3'51"	26"	**14**	W1 on hands and knees, wiping under a table.
4'17"	9"	**15**	Close-up of a body-builder's arm.
4'26"	15"	**16**	Close-up of a weight-lifter (first his midriff, then his head).
4'41"	43"	**17**	Another weight-lifter, reclining. W1 joins him, and the weight-lifter sits up. W2 approaches, passes a knife to W1, who holds it up to the weight-lifter's back. W2 takes the knife.
5'24"	30"	**18**	W1 bares and covers her breasts, then takes the knife and holds it to the weight-lifter's back.
5'54"	31"	**19**	Close-up of W1 and then W2, each lip-synching with the music.
6'25"	1"	**20**	Body-builder lifting weights, one in each hand.
6'26"	5"	**21**	W2 wiping a table, with W1 behind.
6'31"	16"	**22**	As **20**.
6'47"	5"	**23**	As **21** but with W1, W2 reversed.
6'52"	4"	**24**	W1 and W2 naked, facing a body-builder; W2 holds up a knife, W1 holds her other arm.
6'56"	35"	**25**	Close-up of W1's head; she is washing up.
7'31"	7"	**26**	W2, naked, approaches a body-builder; W1 passes the knife; W2 throws it away and turns to the body-builder.
7'38"	1"	**27**	Another body-builder's face, looking at the camera.
7'39"	4"	**28**	As **26**, but W2 wears her overall round her waist; W1 pulls it off.
7'43"	2"	**29**	As **27**, with the body-builder's head moving sideways, to and fro.
7'45"	4"	**30**	As **26**; W1 passes the knife; W2 throws it away.
7'49"	3"	**31**	As **29**.
7'52"	6"	**32**	As **26**; W1 passes the knife; W2 throws it away and turns to the body-builder.
7'58"	6"	**33**	As **29**.
8'04"	28"	**34**	As **26**; W1 pulls off W2's overall and passes the knife; W2 throws it away and turns to the body-builder, and then leans on his chest. W1 moves behind them to the right and says 'Il semble être fait pour l'Amour'.
8'32"	5"	**35**	A different body-builder's face, looking at the camera.
8'37"	21"	**36**	W1 crouches against W2 and says 'Il n'a pu trouver mes yeux assez charmants'; W2 strokes her hair; W1 repeats 'Il n'a pu trouver mes yeux assez charmants'.

8'58"	11"	**37**	W2 crouches against W1, who strokes her hair. W2 says 'Ah ce que je voudrais vous détester'.
9'09"	17"	**38**	W1 and W2, in overalls, sitting on the floor.
9'26"	17"	**39**	W1 and W2 naked, posing; the body-builders pass in front and then behind.
9'43"	17"	**40**	Close-up of W1 and W2, posing.
10'00"	35"	**41**	Close-up of W1 and W2; men pass in front. W1 shouts 'Non!', W2 'Oui!'; again W1 shouts 'Non!', and W2 'Oui!'.

Times are measured from the beginning of the music.

Appendix 6.2: Extracts from *Armide* used by Godard

ACT II, SCENE iv

LES CHŒURS
Ah! quelle Erreur! quelle folie!
De ne pas jouir de la vie!
C'est aux jeux, c'est aux Amours
Qu'il faut donner les beaux jours.

ACT II, SCENE v

ARMIDE, RENAUD, *endormis.*
ARMIDE [*tenant un dard à la main*].
Enfin, il est en ma puissance,
Ce fatal ennemi, ce superbe vainqueur.
Le charme du sommeil le livre à ma vengeance.
Je vais percer son invincible cœur.
Par lui, tous mes captifs sont sortis d'esclavage,
Qu'il éprouve toute ma rage . . .
[*Armide va pour frapper Renaud, et ne peut exécuter le dessein qu'elle a de lui ôter la vie.*]
Quel trouble me saisit, qui me fait hésiter!
Qu'est-ce qu'en sa faveur la pitié me veut dire?
Frappons . . . Ciel! qui peut m'arrêter?
Achevons . . . je frémis! Vengeons-nous . . . je soupire!
Est-ce ainsi que je dois me venger aujourd'hui!
Ma colère s'éteint quand j'approche de lui.
Plus je le vois, plus me vengeance est vaine.
Mon bras tremblant se refuse à ma haine.
Ah! Quelle cruauté de lui ravir le jour!
A ce jeune héros tout cède sur la terre.
Qui croirait qu'il fût né seulement pour la guerre?
Il semble être fait pour l'Amour.
Ne puis-je me venger à moins qu'il ne périsse?

Ah! Error 'tis and pure folly
Life's Pleasures to neglect!
To sports it is, and to our Loves
That we must give our fairest days.

ARMIDA, RINALDO, *asleep.*
ARMIDA [*a dart in her hand*].
At last, he's in my power,
This fatal foe, this proud victor.
Sleep's charm delivers him to my revenge.
I'll pierce his heart, invincible.
'Twas he who freed my captive slaves,
Now may he feel my rage . . .
[*Armida goes to strike Rinaldo, and cannot pursue her design of taking his life.*]
What motion seizes me and makes me stay?
What is't that Pity'd say to me for him?
Come, strike! Ye gods, what holds me back?
Now to it . . . I tremble! Revenge . . . I sigh!
Is it thus that today I'm avenged?
My anger dissolves whene'er I approach.
The more I behold him, the vainer my rage.
My trembling arm refuses me my hate.
Ah! what cruelty 'twould be to take his life!
To this young Hero everything gives way.
Who'd think that he was born for War alone?
He seems made but for Love.
Is't only by his death I'd be avenged?

Hé! ne suffit-il pas que l'Amour le punisse?
Puisqu'il n'a pu trouver mes yeux assez charmants,
Qu'il m'aime au moins par mes enchantements,
Que s'il se peut, je le haïsse.
Venez, venez, secondez mes désirs,
Démons, transformez-vous en d'aimables Zéphirs.
Je cède à ce vainqueur, la pitié me surmonte;
Cachez ma faiblesse et ma honte
Dans les plus reculés Déserts:
Volez, volez, conduisez-nous au bout de l'Univers.
[*Les Démons, transformés en Zéphirs, enlèvent Renaud et Armide.*]

ACT III, SCENE i

ARMIDE, *seule.*
Ah! si la liberté me doit être ravie,
Est-ce à toi d'être mon vainqueur?
Trop funeste ennemi du bonheur de ma vie,
Faut-il que malgré moi tu règnes dans mon cœur?
Le désir de ta mort fut ma plus chère envie,
Comment as-tu changé ma colère en langueur?
En vain, de mille amants je me voyais suivie,
Aucun n'a fléchi ma rigueur.
Se peut-il que Renaud tienne Armide asservie?
Ah! si la liberté me doit être ravie,
Est-ce à toi d'être mon vainqueur?
Trop funeste ennemi du bonheur de ma vie,
Faut-il que malgré moi tu règnes dans mon cœur?

ACT III, SCENE iii

ARMIDE, *seule.*
Venez, venez, Haine implacable,
Sortez du gouffre épouvantable
Où vous faites régner une éternelle horreur.
Sauvez-moi de l'Amour, rien n'est si redoutable.
Contre un ennemi trop aimable
Rendez-moi mon courroux, rallumez ma fureur.
Venez, venez, Haine implacable,
Sortez du gouffre épouvantable
Où vous faites régner une éternelle horreur.
[*La Haine sort des Enfers accompagnée des Furies, de la Cruauté, de la Vengeance, de la Rage et des Passions qui dépendent de la Haine.*]

ACT III, SCENE iv

ARMIDE, LA HAINE, SUITE DE LA HAINE
LA HAINE
Je réponds à tes vœux, ta voix s'est fait entendre
Jusque dans le fond des Enfers.
Pour toi, contre l'Amour je vais tout entreprendre,

Ah! Would Love's punishments not be enough?
Since in mine eyes he found not charms enough,
Then by my spells at least I'll make him dote,
That I may hate him if I can.
Come, second my desires,
Ye Demons, take the shapes of Zephyrs sweet.
I yield to this Victor, by Pity I'm won;
My weakness and my shame come hide
In Deserts far removed: now bend
Your course, lead us to the world's end.
[*The Demons, changed to Zephyrs, carry Rinaldo and Armida off.*]

ARMIDA, *alone.*
Ah! If of Liberty I am bereft,
Is't thou must be my conqueror?
Too fatal foe of my life's happiness.
Must thou, despite me, rule within my heart?
My greatest wish was that thou mightst lie dead,
How hast thou changed my anger to these sighs?
In vain I saw a thousand suitors follow me,
None gave my rigour pause.
And can Rinaldo hold Armida in thrall?
Ah! If of Liberty I am bereft,
Is't thou must be my conqueror?
Too fatal foe of my life's happiness,
Must thou, despite me, rule within my heart?

ARMIDA, *alone.*
Come, come, implacable Hate,
From out the fearsome gulf emerge.
Where in eternal horror you do reign.
Save me from Love, nought's so redoubtable.
Against too amiable a foe
Restore my ire, rekindle now my rage.
Come, come, implacable Hate,
From out the fearsome gulf emerge,
Where in eternal horror you do reign.
[*Hate emerges from Hell, accompanied by Furies, Cruelty, Vengeance and Rage, and the Passions attendant upon Hate.*]

ARMIDA, HATE, FOLLOWERS OF HATE
HATE
Thy bidding I obey, thy voice was heard
Down to the depths of Hell.
For thee, 'gainst Love, all will I undertake,

Et quand on veut bien s'en défendre,
On peut se garantir de ses indignes fers.

LA HAINE ET SA SUITE

Plus on connaît l'Amour, et plus on le
    déteste,
Détruisons son pouvoir funeste,
Rompons ses nœuds, déchirons son ban-
    deau,
Brûlons ses traits, éteignons son flambeau.

[*Le chœur répète ces quatre derniers vers. La
suite de la Haine s'empresse à briser et à
brûler les armes dont l'Amour se sert.*

*La suite de la Haine commence l'enchantement
qui doit détruire le pouvoir de l'Amour.*]

And 'tis enough to wish it heartily,
To be set free from Love's unworthy chains.

HATE AND HIS FOLLOWERS

As Love familiar grows, so he grows loath-
    some too.
We must destroy his fatal power.
Break off his bonds, his blindfold tear.
His arrows burn, and douse his flaming
    torch.

[*The Chorus repeats these last four lines. The
Followers of Hate eagerly break and burn
Love's weapons.*

*Hate's followers then begin casting the spell
that is to destroy the power of Love.*]

Conclusion: The Lonely Muse

I cannot postpone any longer the question that I have been assiduously avoiding throughout this book: just what is a medium?

This is a case where traditional, common-language usage seems decidedly unhelpful. When one speaks of the medium of print, or the medium of the string quartet, one is implicitly assuming something that becomes explicit in one of the word's other applications: to the medium who is possessed by a spirit and speaks with a voice that is not his or her own. The basic idea of a medium, in other words, is that it is *just* a medium, a channel of communication, and as such transparent. To speak of the string quartet as a medium, then, is to imply that it is a means of communicating something independent of it, some kind of abstract music thought, as Schoenberg claimed when he said that 'Music need not be performed any more than books need to be read aloud, for its logic is perfectly represented on the printed page'.[1] Schoenberg's claim is astonishing in its baldness, and to take seriously the idea that the string quartet is just a medium—in the sense in which the word is ordinarily used—would be equally so. But the idea that anything can be *just* a medium has, of course, looked precarious ever since the days of Marshall McLuhan. We are nowadays inclined to think of 'the media' as determining, rather than reflecting, public opinion. And in the same way, my argument in this book is predicated on the assumption that media such as music, texts, and moving pictures do not just communicate meaning, but participate actively in its construction. They *mediate* it, in other words.

One person who has tried to define what 'medium' means in the context of what he calls 'hybrid art forms' is Jerrold Levinson. He begins by explicitly denying that the term 'medium' is 'equivalent to *material* or *physical dimensions*'[2]—what we might term the material traces of an art. 'Rather,' he continues, 'by a *medium* I mean a developed way of using given materials or dimensions, with certain entrenched properties, practices, and possibilities.' In other words, he sees the concept of medium as an intrinsically historical one. And this is understandable, for his purpose is to establish the category of hybrid art-forms, of which (he says) a necessary condition is that 'they must be understood in terms of and in light of these components',[3] and his argument is that such an understanding is itself historically based: it depends on the constituent media having their own historical identity. But that is exactly

---

[1] Dika Newlin, *Schoenberg Remembered: Diaries and Recollections (1938–76)* (New York, 1980), 164.
[2] Levinson, 'Hybrid Art Forms', 7; emphases original.   [3] Ibid. 6.

how hybrid art-forms differ from what is generally understood by 'multimedia', at least if this term is to include such things as the narrative cinema, one of whose characteristics is the effacement of its individual components (and in particular music). So Levinson's definition really only applies to those contexts where the concept of 'medium' converges to the point of inextricability with that of 'art'—as Levinson himself recognizes when he adds that ' "Medium" in this sense is closer to "art form" than to "kind of stuff".'[4]

This erases a distinction that Lawrence Kramer insists should be maintained. '[H]ow do music and poetry compare as forms of expression?', he asks, immediately adding that 'It is important to emphasize that this question is aimed at the *arts*, not at their media—sound and words.'[5] Kramer's formulation suggests that media might be understood as, in effect, arts minus history—just the opposite of what Levinson maintains. But it is not obvious how this equation is to be solved. If 'medium' is, after all, to be understood in terms of material traces, then sound and words reduce to ink on paper or its electronic equivalent, or alternatively they reduce to vibrating particles; in either case they become a single medium. Alternatively, we might think of the sensory impression of sounds and words (we would now be dealing with mental rather than material traces), but again the result is that the two collapse into a single medium: namely, the auditory. Perhaps, then, media should be defined in terms of not just the sensory mode by which they are apprehended, but the cognitive processing to which they give rise? Such an approach smacks, however, of psychological reductionism, and has a number of unwelcome consequences. Even if we are content to distinguish speech from other sounds in terms of psycholinguistic models of cognitive processing (and that in itself may be controversial), we have to assume that there are distinct cognitive processes corresponding to music (all music? Western music? which Western music?), and indeed to any other of the components of multimedia. In the case of Wagnerian music drama, for instance, we would have to assume that there were distinct mental operations or psychophysiological receptors corresponding to lighting and staging—or else, if this seemed untenable, we would have to conclude that lighting and staging are not in fact media at all, but something else. All this seems highly unpromising.

Kramer's formulation, then, leaves the idea of a medium in an uneasy limbo between material trace, sensory mode, and cognitive process. And I have no doubt that all these factors do indeed impinge upon our use of the term; they contribute to what we mean by

---

[4] Levinson, 'Hybrid Art Forms', 7.   [5] Kramer, *Music and Poetry*, 4.

'medium'. But I think that the kind of slippage which we have seen can only be controlled by means of a structural definition based on the idea of variance. When we speak of the ballet combining the distinct 'media' of music and dance, we do not simply mean that music and dance are art-forms with their own history (after all, ballet has its own history, too). Nor are we making statements about the material traces, sensory modes, or cognitive processes associated with music and dance (though, again, this is not to say that such things may not impinge upon their identity as media). What we *are* saying is that in ballet there is a degree of autonomy as between music and dance; they constitute independent 'dimensions' of variance (to borrow Levinson's term), and the aesthetic effect of ballet emerges from the interaction between the two. That is why it is perfectly appropriate to call ballet a form of multimedia. By contrast, it would be odd to call, say, classical guitar performance an instance of multimedia, despite the fact that it consists of the same two components: musical sound and physical gesture. The reason is that the physical gesture is massively determined by the sound. In order to produce a given chord, you *have* to place your fingers on given frets and pluck the corresponding strings.

There is some room for variation, of course; different players adopt slightly different hand positions, just as some players echo the rhythms of the music through torso or head movements while others keep their bodies rigid. But this is not enough to constitute gesture as a significantly independent dimension of variance; nor do guitarists intend it that way. At the same time, there are guitarists—and now I am thinking of rock rather than classical guitarists—who *do* use their bodies in a genuine counterpoint with the music. Jimi Hendrix is an obvious example; his stage performances were as much dance as music, in that while his physical motions were inevitably linked to the music (just as is the case in ballet), they went far beyond it. They became an independent dimension of variance in what can perfectly appropriately be called instances of multimedia. There was, in other words, a significant interaction between sound and body movement, and this interaction was a source of meaning. And it is precisely such interaction that, in Chapter 1, I maintained to be one of the definitional properties of multimedia. (It might, of course, be objected that what I have just offered is not the confirmation of my original premiss, but the completion of a circular argument. If so, I would merely maintain that the circle encompasses a significant field of human activity, and hope that the argument is justified by the explanatory richness of the results.)

If we see media as independent dimensions of variance, we can see a possible reason for the kind of slippage between media and arts to which Kramer objects. This is rooted in the identification of aesthetic value with structural unity, which, for well over a century, has formed the basis of much aesthetic writing and practically all musical analysis. If, like Rudolph Réti, you maintain that a musical master-work is characterized by relationships of strict determination (or 'inevitability', to use one of Réti's favourite words) between all compositional elements, then you are in effect saying that there is no room for variance within it. Schenkerian analysis, too, asserts strict relationships of entailment between different structural levels; in effect, it says that the structural hierarchy *is* the music, so that a comprehensive analysis will leave no remainder of contingency (provided of course that you are dealing with a *real* master-work, as Hans Andersen might have put it). In other words, the postulate of unity eliminates variance from art, and this means that there ceases to be any distinction between art and medium. Kramer objects to this identification because, like other post-modernist or deconstructively minded critics, he sees the postulate of unity as an ideologically motivated one, and ultimately a fiction, or even a lie. And to tell the truth, *any* analyst must surely admit that unified analytical interpretations, when they are available at all, are victories snatched from the jaws of irreducible diversity—or, to put it less figuratively, the relationships between the different elements of an analysis are not all conformant, but range from conformance to implacable contest. And this is as much as to say that there *are* independent dimensions of variance, after all. Under such circumstances, 'art' becomes an inclusive term, encompassing, and therefore distinct from, the individual relationships of variance that constitute 'media'.

But now we have another problem. If 'medium' means 'dimension of variance', then how are we to distinguish media, so defined, from those more general dimensions of variance that we commonly call 'parameters', such as pitch (or melody and harmony), duration (or rhythm and metre), dynamics, timbre, and texture? After all, the term 'parameter' has very similar attributes to those I have ascribed to 'medium': it has implications, often vaguely defined, regarding material trace, sensory mode, and cognitive process (pitch and duration tend towards the former, while melody, harmony, rhythm, and metre tend towards the latter), while relationships between parameters again range from conformance to contest. Perhaps there are additional features which distinguish what we generally call media from parameters, but the point I wish to make is that similar principles operate *within* music as *between* it and words, moving pictures, and so on. One consequence of this, of course, is that the concepts of conformance, complementation, and contest should be useful in the analysis of 'pure' or absolute music, Kivy's 'music alone'—music in which words, images, or other extra-musical contents play no overt part.[6] (I hope to pursue that line of argument elsewhere.) The second consequence, however, is to undermine the distinction that I have just invoked between absolute and other music, and indeed to challenge the very coherence of the concept of absolute music—a concept in which music aestheticians and analysts have a major investment, for it both underwrites and is underwritten by the postulate of unity. At this point, then, I want to pick up a suggestion I made in Chapter 2: that outside the imagination of aestheticians and analysts, music never *is* alone.

The idea of music alone (though not the phrase) developed in the first half of the nineteenth century, in tandem with the idea of the autonomous musical work.[7] It also coincided with the rise of public concerts, and the creation of purpose-built spaces for them, designed to accentuate the division between the outer world of society and the inner world of the auditorium.[8] Concert-halls and the social practices that accompanied them also enforced a rigid separation between the musicians and the audience, with the role of the musicians as intermediaries rather than as social participants being expressed through their dress: the dress of those who were in the midst of nineteenth-century bourgeois society, but who did not belong to it and were therefore in a sense invisible, namely servants. (Why else do waiters and orchestral musicians wear the same kind of clothes?) But this withdrawal of music from society has not excluded the role of senses other than the auditory in the experiencing of music. It is hard to overemphasize the role of the visual in the concert-hall (despite the mythology of closed eyes and furrowed brows, most concert-goers keep their eyes open most of the time), not only in the case of pianists—the seats on the left of the auditorium always fill up before the ones on the right—but even more in the case of conductors. I do not think it is cynical to suggest that the success of many conductors depends as much on how they *look* when they conduct as on how they make the music sound. And the reason why I do not think this is cynical is that I see it as an essential part of the conductor's role to interpret the rhythmic motion and morphology of music by means of a kind of choreography that often goes far beyond

---

[6] A precedent for this may be cited in the work of James Webster ('The Analysis of Mozart's Arias', 141), who extends his concept of 'multivalency' (relationships of congruence or non-congruence between text, music, etc.) to corresponding relationships between musical parameters; he refers to this as 'multifunctionality'.

[7] I am here touching lightly on a massive topic and an extensive literature. Key texts include Carl Dahlhaus, *The Idea of Absolute Music*, trans. R. Lustig (Chicago, 1989), and Lydia Goehr, *The Imaginary Museum of Musical Works: An Essay in the Philosophy of Music* (Oxford, 1992).

[8] For a convenient overview of concert-hall design, see Michael Forsyth, *Buildings for Music: The Architect, the Musician, and the Listener from the Seventeenth Century to the Present Day* (Cambridge, 1985). On the social practices of the concert-hall, see Marcia Herndon and Norma McLeod, *Music as Culture* (Darby, 1982).

the strict requirements of orchestral co-ordination. If it is true, as Roger Scruton has said, that 'the aesthetic response to music [is] a truncated dance',[9] then the conductor goes a long way towards reinstating what listeners lose through being immobilized in their seats.[10]

If the public concert began what might be called the narrowing of the doors of musical perception, the process has been completed by mechanical reproduction: the technology of radio, long-playing records, and CDs filters out everything from music except the sound. Social practice, however, has worked overtime to put back what technology has taken out; record sleeves and CD covers, in particular, have become the site of what—to hijack Goodwin's phrase once more—we might dub a musicology of the image.[11] (More recently, of course, video technology has transformed such images into moving pictures, resulting in a multimedia genre that has begun to spread from popular music to the classics.[12]) But, as I suggested in Chapter 2, it is the word that has become the most irrepressible partner of music, whether in the form of record-sleeve essays, radio talks, or the now ubiquitous news-stand music magazines. And this perpetuates a tradition that goes back to the earliest days of absolute music. For the establishment of the symphony as the flagship genre of the concert-hall did not involve the elimination of text from music, as the history books state; it involved, rather, its displacement. True enough, words were no longer to be found *in* the music. But they were to be found everywhere around it—most obviously in analytical programme notes (themselves an invention of the absolute music movement), but also in the rise of the music appreciation literature and, perhaps, in the kind of pretentious interval bar chatter that Schumann frequently satirized.[13] Absolute music, then, did not suppress words, but rather *re*pressed them from the cultural centre to the margins.

In some ways the story is a supremely paradoxical one. It is not just the fact that the rise of music alone—'music no longer in need of words', to repeat Scott Burnham's phrase[14]—was accompanied by a surge of verbiage about music. It is the way in which the integrity of

---

[9] Scruton, 'Notes on the Meaning of Music', 201.

[10] It is hard to say anything new; in *Philosophy in a New Key*, Suzanne Langer cites a statement made in 1910 by Jean d'Udine that 'All the expressive gesticulations of the conductor . . . is [sic] really a dance. . . . [A]ll music is dancing' (p. 226). For some suggestive remarks on what might be called the 'singer's dance' (in the context of the art song), see Sara K. Schneider, *Concert Song as Seen: Kinesthetic Aspects of Musical Interpretation* (Stuyvesant, NY, 1994).

[11] For Goodwin's phrase see above, p. 150; for an account of the way in which record sleeves function as critical discourse, see Cook, 'Domestic *Gesamtkunstwerk*'.

[12] Conspicuous examples are the video of Brahms's Violin Concerto featuring Nigel Kennedy with the London Philharmonic Orchestra, conducted by Klaus Tennstedt (PMI VHS 2100 (PAL), A5VD—91291 NTSC)), and the classical music videos of Zbig Rybczynski.

[13] See e.g., his merciless caricature of the babbling Beethovenites in Robert Schumann, *On Music and Musicians*, ed. Konrad Wolf, trans. Paul Rosenfeld (New York, 1969), 100–1.

[14] See above, p. 92.

music alone has been underpinned by formalist analysis, which consists precisely in bringing words and other graphic symbols to bear upon the music that supposedly no longer needs them. And it is the way in which those aspects of music that lend themselves most readily to cross-media representation—discrete intervallic classes, for instance, or rational duration relationships—have been treated as 'intrinsically musical', as the core of music alone, at the expense of those aspects of music that are genuinely ineffable: most obviously, nuance.[15] But then, there is nothing like the ineffable to provoke talk, and Hegel's argument that music 'demands a text which alone gives a content to the subjective life's outpouring in the notes',[16] which he intended as an argument against instrumental music, can be read just as well as an argument for the need to accompany such music with textual exegesis and critical commentary. (The same, indeed, might be said of Wagner's frankly sexual conception of music's craving for union with the word, which I cited in Chapter 2.[17]) Modern writers, too, insist on the way in which music demands words, the way in which it creates a kind of determinate verbal absence; the listener, says Jean-Jacques Nattiez, is 'seized by a desire to complete, in words, what music does not say, because music is incapable of saying it'.[18] And David Lewin broadens music's appetite for other media when he observes that 'The urge to supply a program for an instrumental piece . . . might fruitfully be viewed as an urge to supply a theatrical dimension for the music.'[19]

Underlying much writing on the appreciation of music is a premiss I have never seen specifically addressed in print: that as listeners we are somehow impelled to duplicate the music within ourselves, representing it to ourselves as we hear it and thus not only internalizing it but stabilizing our impressions of what, as sound, is wholly evanescent.[20] Such representation may equally well consist of the kind of anecdotal association that Marion Guck has described[21] or take the more institutionally approved form of technical analysis, and in either case the effect is to supply intentional objects to the music's affordances, so turning an experience into a story. We have an urge to share our experiences of music with others and even (if it makes sense to say so) with

---

[15] In referring thus to ineffability, I am again skirting a major area of controversy; the interested reader is referred to the discussion of nuance offered by Diana Raffman in *Language, Music, and Mind* (Cambridge, Mass., 1993), esp. ch. 5.

[16] G. W. F. Hegel, *Aesthetics: Lectures on Fine Art*, trans. T. M. Knox (Oxford, 1975), ii. 960; quoted in Kivy, *Fine Art of Repetition*, 368.

[17] See above, p. 92.   [18] Nattiez, *Music and Discourse*, 128.

[19] Lewin, 'Musical Analysis as Stage Direction', 176.

[20] An essay that skirts this issue, but never homes in on it, is Mark DeBellis, 'Theoretically Informed Listening', in Krausz (ed.), *Interpretation of Music*, 271–81.

[21] Marion A. Guck, 'Rehabilitating the Incorrigible', in Anthony Pople (ed.), *Theory, Analysis, and Meaning in Music* (Cambridge, 1994), 57–73.

ourselves; the urge is so strong that it is almost not an urge at all but a compulsion, like the compulsion to tell a secret. But there is one respect in which to talk of telling a story or telling a secret is misleading; for when we talk about music, we often do not tell it how it is, but rather how it is *not*. After all, Nattiez's point is that we are drawn to say *what the music does not say*; that is why we are drawn to say it. And indeed, the general assumption that critical, analytical discourse reflects people's experience of music can very easily be stood on its head.

The discourse of analytical unity emerged just as the apparently effortless unity of Classical music slipped out of composers' grasp; the more their music became audibly heterogeneous, the more obsessively nineteenth- and early twentieth-century composers talked about unity. Even more strikingly, the height of deterministic thinking about music coincided, in the Darmstadt community of the 1950s and early 1960s, with the production of compositions that struck most people who listened to them (though not many did) as unprecedentedly chaotic. There are good grounds, then, for saying that the role of talk is frequently—I can imagine a case for saying 'always'—not to reflect music, but to do the opposite: to contradict or compensate for it. And this, I hope, is enough to suggest that the principles of conformance, complementation, and contest may also apply to the dynamic encounter between music and word that is accurately reflected in the etymology of the word 'musico-logy'. If we do not think of musicology as multimedia, in other words, this is perhaps not because the relationship between its constituent media is fundamentally different, but because we choose to reserve the term 'multimedia' for artistic genres rather than commentaries on them—a distinction, of course, which postmodern thought has shown to be decidedly fragile.

But if the development of music alone was accompanied by a babble of controversy and justification, there is an even more basic way in which the alignment of different media is inscribed within the practice of absolute music: notation. No notation is a transparent representation of music; or, to put it the other way round, all notations are a blend of conformance, complementation, and contest. Just as musical cultures differ, so their notations (assuming they have them) embody and thus emphasize certain types of information while ignoring or suppressing others. Western staff notation specifies in exhaustive detail what might be termed the digital aspects of pitch and rhythm, resulting in representations of formal patterning that sometimes have a clarity not apparent in the sound of the music. On the other hand, it underdetermines timbre and, in effect, suppresses tonal and rhythmic nuance (as critics of the more fundamentalist sects of the authenticity movement have often pointed out). Early neumatic notation, by contrast, is highly conformant with the experienced qualities of melodic gesture, while massively underspecifying musically salient relationships of pitch and rhythm (this was of course no disadvantage to the extent that, unlike modern staff notation, it functioned primarily as an *aide-mémoire*). Tablatures are, by definition, more or less conformant with physical gesture, but have only an indirect relationship with experienced sound. Even here, though, there is much room for variation: Western lute tablature, for example, can be resolved into essentially the same specifications as staff notation, whereas the tablature used for the Chinese long zither (*gu-ch'in*) provides exhaustive timbral specifications at the expense of rhythm. The only notation that fully specifies sound is the digital recording, and for this very reason to call it a 'notation' is to strain against the limits of received linguistic usage.[22]

All musical notations in the normal sense, then, are conformant with musical sound at some level, but pull away from it at others; that is only what the principle of differential elaboration should lead one to expect. The most conspicuous example of such tension between sound and notation is probably the music of the post-war avant-garde, in which, as I said, extraordinary determinacies of notation coincided with sonorous effects that were largely indeterminate. But the point is a much more general one; even the Classical sonata, I would maintain, is animated by a tension between the imperatives of sound and those of notation. (Classical development sections, in particular, sometimes sound like laborious attempts to write novels in sound. Stravinsky's notorious quip that Mozart's symphonies would be much better without their developments may or may not be deplorable, but is certainly comprehensible.[23]) And underlying this is the very basic fact that, at least until the development of multi-tracking and computer-based sound technologies, composers have never put together (com-posed) sounds; what are put together are *representations* of sounds in other media. In this way, the specific pattern of divergence between sounds and the manner in which a given musical culture represents them is, as I have argued elsewhere,[24] a defining trait of that culture.

Language, however, predisposes us to overlook this. The vocabulary we commonly use for music might easily suggest that it is in essence a graphic art: composers 'write' music, and performers as well as critics offer 'readings' of it. Even the word 'composition' is associated in other

---

[22] I am building here upon issues I have described in more detail in *Music, Imagination, and Culture* (Oxford, 1990), 219–22; 'Music Theory and the Postmodern Muse: An Afterword', in Elizabeth West Marvin and Richard Hermann (eds.), *Concert Music, Rock, and Jazz since 1945: Essays and Analytical Studies* (Rochester, 1995), 422–39: 435; and 'Music Minus One'. Information on *gu-ch'in* tablature may be found in e.g. Walter Kaufmann, *Musical Notations of the Orient* (Bloomington, Ind., 1967).

[23] According to George Antheil, Stravinsky once said, 'If I had my way I would cut all the development sections out of Mozart's symphonies. They would be fine then!' (quoted in White, *Stravinsky*, 309).   [24] Cook, *Music, Imagination, and Culture*, 223.

arts with spatial arrangement—with relationships between enduring, physical traces, rather than evanescent experiences—and, of course, performers don't just perform; they give performances 'of' works. And what defines works is a tradition of writing. Particularly revealing in this regard is the complaint one sometimes hears that today's performers learn pieces from recordings instead of going back to the original written sources and developing their own interpretations—their own readings, that is to say.[25] What this complaint does is to locate the source of musical authenticity in writing; sound is implicitly demoted to a kind of supplementary role, as if there were no such thing as a purely sonorous tradition. And indeed musical sound is, in itself, both structurally inchoate and semantically vacuous. As I said in Chapter 3, music does not so much have meaning as potential for meaning, and the realization of this potential is a function of the context within which the music is received: a context which may involve the overt alignment of sound with other media (as in songs, operas, music videos and films, television commercials), or which may involve other media in ways that are less conspicuous but no less efficacious, such as verbally mediated traditions of interpretation.

Meaning lies not in musical sound, then, nor in the media with which it is aligned, but in the encounter between them. And for this reason it would in truth be just as crass a mistake to maintain that music is a purely graphic tradition—or a purely verbal one, or for that matter a purely kinesthetic one—as to maintain that it is a purely aural one. Musical cultures are not simply cultures of sounds, nor simply cultures of representations of sounds, but cultures of the relationship between sound and representation. The cohabitation and confrontation of different media are inscribed within the practice of Western classical music (and perhaps of all music), in the relationship of sound and notation, and in the relationship between music and verbal discourse. It is in this sense that music, even 'music alone', should properly be seen as a form of multimedia in which all the components except one have been forced to run underground, sublimated or otherwise marginalized. And whether one is dealing with music that expresses words (as in song) or with words that express music (as in musicology), the semiotic process is the same. If the argument of previous chapters is correct, then it follows that what applies to all multimedia applies to critical and analytical discourse about music: words do not transparently represent meanings that already exist in the music, but instead contribute to the emergence of meaning.

[25] I have, for instance, heard the pianist Susan Bradshaw say this (at the Colston Symposium on 'The Intention, Reception, and Understanding of Musical Composition', held at the University of Bristol in 1994).

It is like the history of *Armide* from Tasso to Godard, where instead of there being an originary meaning expressed variously by Tasso's epic poem, Quinault's and Lully's opera, and Godard's film, each expression of the story of Armide creates new meaning (which is, of course, why the word 'expression' is misleading in this context). In the same way, when Donald Tovey described the 'catastrophic return' of the first subject in the recapitulation of the first movement from Beethoven's Ninth Symphony, he no doubt believed that he was simply describing, in unusually vivid language,[26] what was already there in the music. But more than 50 years later it is easy to see that he was in fact creating a new interpretation, one which did much to mould the responses of a generation of British listeners and critics. Maybe in another generation people will be saying the same about Susan McClary's interpretation of the same passage.[27] The examples of Tovey and, McClary, then, are representative of the interaction between words and musical sound that constitutes all musicology. They illustrate how the interpreting subject contributes to the construction of the object of study. And an awareness of this relationship of mutual implication (to revert to Claudia Gorbman's phrase, which I invoked near the beginning of this book[28]) is the best definition I know of a musicology that is genuinely critical, because it is *self*-critical.[29]

And yet, and yet . . . the account I have offered of the emergence of meaning seems so abstract and laborious when you put it alongside the letter in which Schoenberg tried to tell Alma Mahler what he meant when he wrote *Die glückliche Hand*—or rather *not* what he meant, and certainly not what his *Gesamtkunstwerk* meant, but what kind of meanings he hoped that it might give rise to. 'It is not meant symbolically,' he said,

but only envisioned and felt. Not thought at all. Colors, noises, lights, sounds, movements, looks, gestures—in short, the media which make up the ingredients of the stage—are to be linked to one another in a varied way. Nothing more than that. It meant something to my emotions as I wrote it down. If the component parts, when they are put together, result in a similar image, that is all right with me. If not, it suits me even better. Because I don't want to be understood; I want to express myself—but I hope that I will be misunderstood. It would be terrible to me if I were transparent to people. Therefore I prefer to say

---

[26] '[W]e see the heavens on fire,' he wrote. 'There is something very terrible about this triumphant major tonic' (Donald Tovey, 'Ninth Symphony in D Minor, Op. 125: Its Place in Musical Art', in *Essays in Musical Analysis* (Oxford, 1935–9), ii. 83–127: 100). I have described Tovey's reception of this passage, and later critics' reception of Tovey, in Cook, *Beethoven: Symphony No. 9*, 65–7.

[27] McClary, *Feminine Endings*, 128–30.   [28] See above, p. 21.

[29] I have discussed the performativity of musicology, as I call it, at greater length in 'Analysing Performance, and Performing Analysis', in Nicholas Cook and Mark Everist (eds.), *Rethinking Music*, 243–65.

technical, aesthetic, or philosophical things about my works. Or this: certainly no symbolism is intended. It is all direct intuition. How I mean that you will understand best is if I tell you I would most prefer to write for a magic theatre. If tones, when they occur in any sort of order can arouse feelings, then colors, gestures, and movements, must also be able to do this. Even when they otherwise have no meaning recognizable to the mind. Music also doesn't have this meaning! What I mean is: this is music![30]

And of course, what *I* mean is: this is multimedia.

---

[30] Letter of 17 Oct. 1910 to Alma Mahler, quoted in Crawford, '*Die glucklicke Hand*: Further Notes', 73.

Index

Abbate, Carolyn 101–2, 120 n., 121 n., 122, 123, 124, 127, 129 n., 145
Adamson, Joe 178 n.
Adorno, Theodor 57 n., 64–5, 81, 86 n., 117 n., 126
affordance 23 n., 96–7, 213, 267
Agawu, Kofi 136 n.
Allain, Valerie 225 n.
Allanbrook, Wye 79 n.
Altman, Robert 215, 219
ambient sounds 228, 253
amplification (defined) 112
anchorage 93
Andersen, Hans 264
Antheil, George 269 n.
Appia, Adolph 43
Aquinas, St Thomas 33
'Aria' (collaborative film) 215, 218, 219
    see also Godard, Jean-Luc
Aristotle 117
Ashmore, Jerome 46 n., 50
Auner, Joseph 42 n., 43 n., 48, 51 n.

Babbitt, Art 175 n.
Babbitt, Milton 52
Bach, Johann Sebastian 198, 213
Bahr, Hermann 51 n.
Baker, James 38 n.
Balász, Béla 114
Baron-Cohen, Simon 25 n.
Barthes, Roland 84 n., 93, 119–20
Baudelaire, Charles 25, 47 n.
Beatles 175
Beaumont, Cyril 204 n.
Beaussaut, Philippe 248
Beethoven, Ludwig van 88 n., 124, 128, 145, 146
    7th Symphony 197 n., 211, 212
    9th Symphony 43 n., 93–4, 271
Bellini, Vincenzo 128
Beresford, Bruce 219
Berg, Alban 112
Berger, Arthur 192–3
Berger, Karol 211–13, 232
Bergeron, Katherine 122
Berio, Luciano 124
Bernard, Jonathan 28, 30–2
Bernstein, Elmer 117
Bernstein, Leonard 141
Bie, Oskar 43
Bjornberg, Alf 150 n.
blaue Reiter, Der 45

Bliss, Arthur 149 n.
BMW commercials 20
Bolivar, Valerie 67 n., 76 n.
Boulez, Pierre 184 n., 187
Bourgeois, Jacques 108 n.
Bowers, Faubion 28 n.
Bradley, Scott 177
Bradshaw, Susan 270 n.
Brahms, Johannes 92 n., 124
    Violin Concerto 266 n.
Brecht, Bertolt 86, 126
Breitkopf und Härtel 211 n.
Brown, Royal 58 n., 60, 123 n., 227 n., 243 n.
Brown, Peter 151 n.
Burnham, Scott 92, 266
Burt, George 114
Busser, Henri 217 n., 229 n., 241 n., 245 n., 246 n.

Cage, John 53
Carradine, Keith 147–8
Carter, Tim 215 n.
Chandos Records 71
Charlton, David 25 n.
Chion, Michel 115 n., 118 n., 134 n., 135 n., 159, 228 n.
Chopin, Frédéric 211–12, 232
Christgau, Robert 149 n.
Citroen commercial 4–8, 11, 18–19, 20, 22, 81–2, 103, 105
Clarke, Eric 69 n.
Cocteau, Jean 207
Cognitive blending 70 n.
Cohen, Annabel 67–9, 71, 76 n., 82, 84, 135
Cohen, Gustav 87 n.
coherence (defined) 98
Colles, Henry Hope 192, 207, 208 n., 209
complementation (defined) 103
Cone, Edward 95–6, 102 n., 109, 118, 123, 134, 159 n., 186 n., 213
conformance (defined) 100
    dyadic, triadic, unitary (defined) 101
Connelly, Christopher 171
connotation (defined) 118–19
Conrad, Peter 122, 145, 254
consistency (defined) 99
contest (defined) 103
contradiction (defined) 102–3
contrariety (defined) 102
Copland, Aaron 117
counterpoint 114–15, 206–7

Crawford, John 42 n., 44 n., 47 n., 48 n., 51, 121, 272 n.
Cunningham, Merce 53
cutting rhythm 143–5, 163–6, 189–91, 208, 240, 253
Cyr, Louis 176 n.
Cytowic, Richard E. 25 n.

Da capo aria 220, 227
Dahl, Ingolf 178 n.
Dahlhaus, Carl 265 n.
David, Jacques-Louis 71
Davies, Stephen 79 n., 86 n., 87–91, 93, 97
DeBellis, Mark 267 n.
Debussy, Claude-Achille 110–11, 112, 118
denotation (defined) 118–19
Derrida, Jacques 21
Deutsch, Stephen 141
Diaghilev 196 n.
Diderot, Denis 50 n.
difference test 102
Disney, Walt:
    'Fantasia' 76, 78, 79, 82, 105, 142, 164 n., 174–214, 228, 253
    'Pinocchio' 177
    'Snow White and the Seven Dwarfs' 177, 178 n.
    'The Band Concert' 178, 213
    'The Flying Mouse' 194
    'The Skeleton Dance' 178
distributional analysis (defined) 142
double address 148
Downes, Olin 198
Dukas, Paul 175, 176, 178, 197, 211
Dunsby, Jonathan 142 n.
Dvořák, Antonin 215

Eco, Umberto 124 n.
Eisenstein, Sergei 27 n., 49–65, 66, 67, 78, 80–1, 82–3, 84 n., 85 n., 86, 97, 113, 121 n., 125 n.
    'Alexander Nevsky' 57–65, 80, 84, 85–6, 100
    'Ivan the Terrible' 85
Eisler, Hanns 54 n., 57–65, 67, 81, 84 n., 86, 97, 113, 117, 123 n., 126, 2 06 n.
    Fourteen Ways of Describing Rain 63–5, 81–2, 86 n.
Elgar, Edward 91, 93
Ellis, Havelock 52 n.
emergence 82–6, 96, 115, 254, 270–1
enabling similarity (defined) 70
English, Horace 197–8, 211, 213–14
'expression theory' 86, 115, 149

Fauconnier, Gilles 70 n.
feminism 147, 148–9, 172
Fentress, John 67 n., 76 n.

Ferneyhough, Brian 114
Fischinger, Oskar 178–9
Fiske, John 119, 152 n., 163 n., 170 n., 171 n.
Fissinger, Laura 173 n.
Fokine, Michel 209
Ford, John 179 n., 183 n.
Forsyth, Michael 265 n.
Friedrich, Otto 174 n., 176n., 178 n., 183n., 211 n.
Frith, Simon 148, 164, 165 , 173 n.
Fröhlich, Franz 93–4

Galilei, Vincenzo 107, 125
gender 92–3, 104, 117–18, 121, 250–1
    see also feminism
Georges-Michel, Michel 196 n.
Gerstl, Richard 41–2
Gibson, J. J. 96
Gilleré, René 53
Glass, Frank 92, 93 n., 118, 120, 121 n.
Gleich, Clemens-Christoph von 38 n.
Gluck, Christoph Willibald von 107, 108
    Armide 216
    Orfeo ed Euridice 94
Godard, Jean-Luc:
    'Armide' 103, 142–3, 215–59, 271
    'Pierrot le fou' 227 n., 243 n.
    'Vivre sa vie' 243 n.
Goehr, Lydia 265 n.
Goethe, Johann von 46, 101–2, 107
golden section 166
Goodwin, Andrew vi, 76, 112 n., 128 n., 134, 148, 150, 170 n., 171–2, 266
Gorbman, Claudia 20–1, 22, 64, 86, 117, 144, 167, 271
Greimas, A. J. 102
Grigorovich, Yury 201 n.
Groos, Arthur 120 n.
gu-ch'in 269
Guck, Marion 267
Guido d'Arezzo 107

Hahl-Koch, Jelena 43 n., 48, 51
Hanslick, Eduard 79, 87–9, 92, 93, 94–5, 122, 127–8, 144, 213 n.
Harrison, John 25 n.
Hartley, John 119
Hartmann, Thomas von 45 n., 101
Hatten, Robert 102 n.
Haydn, Joseph 174
Hayes, Jeremy 216
Hegel, Georg Wilhelm Friedrich 267
Heider, F. 67 n.
Heine, Heinrich 105, 136, 139
Helmholtz, Hermann von 117
Hendrix, Jimi 263
Hermann, Bernard 66, 86, 104, 123
    see also Hitchcock, Alfred
Herndon, Marcia 265 n.

Herreweghe, Philippe 217 n., 224, 229 n.,
    241, 245, 246, 248
Herring, Robert 211 n.
Hertzka, Emil 43 n., 51 n.
Hicks, Jimmie 178 n., 183 n.
Hill, Geoffrey 123
Hitchcock, Alfred 144
    'Psycho' vi, 66, 68, 80, 81, 112
Hodge, Joanna 116, 120
Hodson, Millicent 202 n., 204 n., 209
Hoellering, Franz 197 n.
Hoffman, E. T. A. 25, 26, 28
Holloway, Robin 123
Howard, Patricia 250-1
Hubley, John 179 n., 183 n.
Hull, A. Eaglefield 33 n., 34 n., 35 n., 39,
    40 n.
Huntley, John 144 n., 150 n., 178 n.
Huron, David 17 n.
Huxley, Julian 183 n.
Huysmans, Joris-Karl 27
Hyde, Martha 47 n.

Imbrie, Andrew 187, 189
implication-realization analysis 142-3
inversion (definition) 135-41
Iser, Wolfgang 105 n.
Ivens, Joris 63

Jarman, Derek 215
Johnson, Robert Sherlaw 29 n., 31 n.
Johnson, Mark 70, 83, 98-100
Jones, Chuck 75 n., 174 n.
Judas Iscariot 52

Kalinak, Kathryn 114-15, 117, 119 n.,
    125 n., 149
Kalisch, Alfred 209
Kandinsky, Wassily 43 n., 45-56, 57, 65,
    77 n., 80, 100-1, 121, 127, 140-1,
    208 n.
    Der gelbe Klang 45, 49-50, 55, 100-1, 102
Kaplan, Ann 148, 167, 170 n.
Karajan, Herbert von 176
Kaufmann, Walter 269 n.
Kelsey, Dick 179 n., 192 n.
Kennedy, Nigel 266 n.
Kerman, Joseph 109-12, 118-19, 129
Kershaw, David 26, 117-18, 126-7
Kinderman, William 121-2
Kirstein, Lincoln 209 n.
Kivy, Peter vii, 23, 22 n., 79, 87-95, 97,
    109-12, 118 n., 264, 267 n.
Klempe, Hroar 82 n.
Koestler, Arthur 84 n.
Köhler, Wolfgang 75
Kokoschka, Oskar 43 n.
Korngold, Erich Wolfgang 215
Koussevitsky, Serge 35 n.

Kramer, Lawrence 3, 21 n., 104, 119, 123-4,
    127, 145, 262, 263, 264
Krasovskaya, Vera 201 n.
Krebs, Harald 48 n.
Kretzschmar, Hermann 3
Krick, Karin 219 n.
Krumhansl, Carol 67 n.
Kubrick, Stanley 205
Kutter, Michael 219 n.

Lakoff, George 70, 83, 98-100
Lambert, Mary 147, 163 n., 166, 195
    see also 'Material Girl'
Langer, Suzanne 79, 266 n.
Latham, Edward 228 n.
Lauper, Cyndi 76 n.
Layton, Lynne 172 n.
Legal, Ernst 51 n.
Leonard, Pat 156 n.
Lessem, Alan 41, 43, 44 n., 47 n., 48 n., 50,
    51 n., 52, 54
Lesure, François 192 n., 196 n., 204 n.,
    205 n., 208 n., 209 n.
Lévi-Strauss, Claude 142
Levinson, Jerrold 106, 261-2, 263
Levy, David 93 n.
Lewin, David 136, 140, 267
Lewis, Lisa 156 n., 162 n., 170 n., 172,
    173 n.
'Lighting Crescendo' (Die glückliche Hand)
    43-5, 47-8, 53, 54-5, 77, 101, 125
Lindgren, Ernest 104, 105, 128, 133,
    211
Liszt, Franz 35, 108, 110
Lockspeiser, Edward 26
Loshitzky, Yosefa 218-19, 227, 250-4
Louis XIV 216, 251
Lully, Jean-Baptiste 103, 215-59
Luria, Alexander 26, 27 n., 28

MacCabe, Colin 134 n.
McCay, Winsor:
    'Gertie the Dinosaur' 182 n.
McClary, Susan 148-9, 151 n., 172 n., 271
Macdonald, Hugh 34 n., 39 n., 40 n.
McLaughlin, Thomas 82 n., 83, 116, 120
McLeod, Norma 265 n.
McLuhan, Marshall 116, 261
madness, operatic depictions of 126
Madonna (Louise Veronica Ciccone) 195
    'Express Yourself' 172 n.
    'Like a Prayer' 149, 166
    'Material Girl' 103, 125, 142, 144-5,
        147-73, 228, 253
Maeterlinck, Maurice 110-11, 112, 118 n.
Mahler, Alma 271
Mahler, Gustav 42, 91, 93
Maltin, Leonard 174 n., 175, 177 n., 178 n.,
    179 n., 182 n., 192 n., 193

Man, Paul de 21
Manvell, Roger 144 n., 150 n., 178 n.
Marc, Franz 45
Margolis, Joseph 87
markedness theory 102 n.
Marks, Martin 64 n.
Marks, Lawrence 27, 28–9, 69–70, 75, 78,
    83, 96, 210
Marshall, Sandra 67–9, 71, 76 n., 82, 84,
    135
Marvell, Andrew 123
Massine, Leonid 196, 200–1
Mathias-Baker, Ian 17 n.
Méliès, George 78
Messiaen, Olivier 29–33, 37, 39, 40, 53 n.,
    208 n.
    Catalogue des oiseaux 31
    Chronochromie 31
    Couleurs de la Cité céleste 29, 31
    Sept Haikai 32
metaphor (defined) 69–70
Meyer, Leonard 3
Mickey Mouse 176, 178
mickey-mousing 179
Middleton, Richard 119, 120 n., 128 n., 159
Millet, Jules 25 n.
modes of limited transposition 30
Mokin, S. A. 71–3, 76
Momigny, J.-J. de 107 n., 122
Monelle, Raymond 102 n., 142 n.
Monroe, Marilyn 147
montage theory 84
Monteux, Pierre 196
Monteverdi, Claudio 107, 126, 215
Moravcsik, Julius 90
Morgan, Robert P. vi n.
motivic web 145–6
Mozart, Wolfgang Amadeus 95, 128, 212,
    269
    Così fan tutte 109–10, 111, 112, 129
    Don Giovanni 92 n.
    The Marriage of Figaro 4–5, 22, 81–2, 105,
        109, 136, 139, 141
Mozer, Alexander 39
Murch, Walter 118 n., 122 n.
'music film' 214, 254
Myers, Charles 34, 35 n., 36 n.

Narmour, Eugene 3
Nattiez, Jean-Jacques 32, 79, 96 n., 106,
    142 n., 267, 268
Newcomb, Anthony 90–1, 93
Newlin, Dika 261 n.
Newton, Isaac 26, 37 n.
Nijinsky, Vaslav 188, 196, 200–2, 204,
    207–9
Norris, Christopher 21 n.
Noske, Frits 129
Nouvel, Walter 200 n.

Offenbach, Jacques 62
Osgood, Charles 68 n.

Paglia, Camille 148 n.
paradigm classes (defined) 142
parallelism 114–15
Parker, Roger v, 107 n., 114, 120, 122 n.,
    128 n., 129 n., 133, 139, 144
Pasler, Jann 47n., 202 n., 204 n., 207
Pavlenko, Piotr 62 n.
Payzant, Geoffrey 87 n.
Peacock, Kenneth 28 n., 35 n., 38
Penn, William 66 n., 78, 107 n.
Peopli, Count Carlo 128 n.
Peterson, Marion 225 n.
Picasso, Pablo 73–4
Plato 107–8, 116, 117, 133
Poizat, Michel 107 n., 108, 113, 119, 124 n.
Ponte, Lorenzo Da 109–10
Prendergast, Roy 58 n., 177 n.
projection (defined) 112
Prokoviev, Serge 58, 63, 82–3, 84, 85
Prudential commercial 12–16, 18–19, 80–1,
    103, 125, 168 n.
Pudovkin, Vsevolod 84
Putnam, Daniel 22
Pythagoras 46

quasi-synaesthesia 28, 33, 75, 81
Queen:
    'Bohemian Rhapsody' 165 n.
Querelle des Bouffons 108, 216
Quinault, Philippe 215–16, 250–1
    see also Lully, Jean-Baptiste: Armide

Raffman, Diana 267 n.
Rambert, Marie 209 n.
Rameau, Jean Philippe 215, 216–17, 232–4,
    235, 237
Rans, Robert 151 n.
Rap 159, 186 n.
Razin, Stepan (Stenka) 71
reader-response criticism 105
reading for gaps (defined) 141–2
Réti, Rudolph 264
Rilke, Rainer Maria 128
Rimbaud, Arthur 25–8, 208 n.
Rimington, A. Wallace 32–3
Rimsky-Korsakov, Nicholas 34–5
Rivière, Jacques 204 n., 209
Roberts, Bill 179 n.
Robinson, Paul 112–13
Roddam, Franc 219
Roeg, Nicolas 219
Roerich, Nikolai 196, 199, 204–5
Roller, Alfred 42–3, 50, 121, 194
Rolling Stones viii–ix
Rosand, Ellen 126
Rosar, William 79 n.

Rosow, Lois 216 n., 217, 224 n.
Rossini, Gioacchino 178
Rössler, Almut 33 n.
Rosza, Miklos 107 n.
Rousseau, Jean-Jacques 216–17, 229–34, 237
Russell, Ken 215
Ruwet, Nicolas 142 n.
Rybczynski, Zbig 266 n.

Sabaneev, Leonid 34–8, 40, 45, 53
Sacrati, Francesco 126
Sams, Eric 136, 140
Samuel, Claude 30 n.
Sand, George 212, 232
Sante, Luc 171 n., 172 n.
Saslaw, Janna 70 n.
Satterfield, Paul 179 n.
Schafer, R. Murray 26 n.
Schenck, Diane Lynn 67 n.
Schenker, Heinrich 79, 128, 139–40, 142, 234, 249, 252, 264
Scher, Steven Paul 136 n.
Schneider, Sara 266 n.
Schoenberg, Arnold 37, 105, 125, 127, 150, 194, 208 n., 261, 271
    Die glückliche Hand 41–56, 101, 121, 125, 150 n. 271
    Erwartung 41
    'Herzgewachse' 45
    Moses und Aron 42
    Pierrot Lunaire 63
    The Book of the Hanging Gardens 124
    see also 'Lighting Crescendo'
Schoenberg, Mathilde 41
Scholes, Percy 26, 32, 33 n., 37 n., 38, 39, 46 n.
Schopenhauer, Arthur 90, 92, 108, 110, 118, 120, 213 n.
Schröter, Corona 101
Schruers, Fred 156 n.
Schubert, Franz 101, 124
Schumann, Robert 266
    'Wenn ich in deine Augen seh'' 136–41, 142
Scott, Cyril 26
Scruton, Roger 33, 79, 266
semantic differential technique 68, 167
semiotic analysis 142
serialism 37, 52
Sert, Misia 201
Sessions, Roger 85 n.
set-theoretical analysis 31, 142
Shapiro, Michael 102 n.
Shepherd, John 118
similarity test 98
Simmel, M. 67 n.
Sirius, George 69 n.
Sklar, Robert 213
Skriabin, Alexander 121 n.

Prometheus 34–41, 42, 45, 53, 55, 100, 101
    7th Sonata 37
Smith, David 178 n.
Smith, Patrick 251 n.
Solomon, Maynard 128 n.
spheres, music of the 46, 53, 210
Springer, Craig M. 17 n.
St-John, Christopher 209 n.
Stacey, Peter 107–8, 125
Stanger, Claudia 106 n.
Starkie, Enid 25, 27 n.
Steblin, Rita 35–6
Steinberg, Maximilian 200
Steiner, Ena 41 n., 42 n., 43 n.
Stewart, Maclaren 179 n.
Stock, Chester 183 n.
Stokowski, Leopold 174, 176, 179, 181, 193
Stravinsky, Igor 86, 159 n., 269
    Pulcinella Suite 73–4
    Rite of Spring 159 n., 174–214
Stuckenschmidt, H. H. 51 n.
Studer, Ulrich 246 n.
Sturridge, Charles 219
sublime 44
Suci, George 68 n.
Sundberg, Johan 79
Surrealism 84 n.
Syderberg, Hans Jürgen:
    'Parsifal' 219 n.
synaesthesia 24–56, 75, 97, 100, 121, 208–9
    see also quasi-synaesthesia

Tambling, Jeremy 219 n.
Tannenbaum Percy 68 n.
Tarasti, Eero 102 n.
Tarkovsky, Andrey 143, 144 n.
Taruskin, Richard 198–200, 205 n.
Tasso, Torquato 215, 216, 217, 250, 271
Taylor, (Joseph) Deems 179, 213
Tchaikovsky, Peter Ilich:
    2nd Symphony 71–3, 76
Temple, Julien 219
Tennstedt, Klaus 266 n.
theosophy 39, 46
Thomas, Tony 66 n.
Toorn, Pieter van den vii, 176 n., 184 n., 187, 189, 191, 192, 197, 198, 202, 203
Tovey, Donald 271
transfer of attributes (defined) 70
Truman, Philip 42, 43, 44, 46
Turner, Mark 70 n.
Turner, W. J. 95–6

Undine, Jean d' 266 n.

Verba, Cynthia 229 n., 232, 234 n.
Verdi, Giuseppe 107 n., 215
Vershinina, Irina 202 n.

vertical montage 84–5
Viéville, Jean Laurent le Cerf de La 216, 234
Volvo commercial 17–20, 22, 76, 77–8, 83, 95, 103, 105, 142
Vuillermoz, Emile 196, 207

Wagner, Richard 41, 43, 79, 86, 92–3, 108, 117–18, 120–2, 126, 145, 215, 262, 267
 Die Meistersinger 42
 Götterdämmerung 121, 122
 Lohengrin 49
 Parsifal 77 n., 216
 Siegfried 121
 Tannhäuser 122
 Tristan und Isolde 42–3
Walkers crisps commercial 9–12, 18–19, 95, 96, 103, 105, 142
Wallace, Robert 93 n.
Ward, Tom 171–2

Warren, G. 159
Webber, Andrew 219 n.
Webster, James 134 n., 265 n.
White, Eric Walter 204 n., 269 n.
Whittall, Arnold 142 n.
Widgery, Claudia 49 n., 58 n., 60, 62 n., 64 n., 78–9, 80, 81 n., 84 n., 117, 119 n., 143–4, 174 n.
Wiley, John 104 n.
Wittgenstein, Ludwig 116, 121

Yakar, Rachel 217 n.
Yarilo 205
Youens, Susan 110, 118
Young, Stephen 149, 163 n., 166

Zarlino, Gioseffo 107
Zbikowski, Lawrence 70 n.
Zelter, Carl Friedrich 102
Zuckerkandl, Victor 86 n.